RIGHTEOUS
INDIGNATION

A JEWISH CALL FOR JUSTICE

RIGHTEOUS INDIGNATION

A JEWISH CALL FOR JUSTICE

Edited by
RABBI OR N. ROSE
JO ELLEN GREEN KAISER
MARGIE KLEIN

Foreword by Rabbi David Ellenson

For People of All Faiths, All Backgrounds
JEWISH LIGHTS Publishing
Woodstock, Vermont

Righteous Indignation:
A Jewish Call for Justice

2008 First Printing

Library of Congress Cataloging-in-Publication Data

Righteous indignation : a Jewish call for justice / edited by Or N. Rose, Jo Ellen Green Kaiser, Margie Klein ; foreword by David Ellenson.
   p. cm.
  Includes bibliographical references.
  ISBN-13: 978-1-58023-336-1 (hc)
  ISBN-10: 1-58023-336-8 (hc)
  1. Judaism and social problems. 2. Social justice—Religious aspects—Judaism. 3. Justice (Jewish theology) 4. Jewish ethics. 5. Human ecology—Religious aspects—Judaism. 6. Economics—Religious aspects—Judaism. I. Rose, Or N. II. Green Kaiser, Jo Ellen. III. Klein, Margie.
  HN40.J5R54 2007
  296.3'8—dc22

2007040127

10 9 8 7 6 5 4 3 2 1

Manufactured in the United States of America
❀ Printed on recycled paper
Jacket design: Joshua Meyer & Tim Holtz

For People of All Faiths, All Backgrounds
Published by Jewish Lights Publishing
A Division of Longhill Partners, Inc.
Sunset Farm Offices, Route 4, P.O. Box 237
Woodstock, VT 05091
Tel: (802) 457-4000   Fax: (802) 457-4004
www.jewishlights.com

CONTENTS

PART VII THE SEVENTY NATIONS: GLOBAL CONCERNS

FOREWORD

RABBI DAVID ELLENSON, PhD

Rabbi David Ellenson, PhD, is the president of Hebrew Union College–Jewish Institute of Religion, and the I.H. and Anna Grancell Professor of Jewish Religious Thought. He is also a fellow at the Shalom Hartman Institute of Jerusalem, and a fellow and lecturer at the Institute of Advanced Studies at Hebrew University in Jerusalem. Ellenson is the author of *Tradition in Transition: Orthodoxy, Halakhah and the Boundaries of Modern Jewish History*; *Rabbi Esriel Hildesheimer and the Creation of a Modern Jewish Orthodoxy*; and *After Emancipation: Jewish Religious Responses to Modernity*, winner of the National Jewish Book Award in Modern Jewish Thought and Experience.

We live at a time marked by both an increasing interest in individual spiritual growth and, within the American Jewish community, a legitimate and needed return to classical religious ritual behaviors that promote community and religious devotion. Some fear that the renewed interest in ritual life will lead to Jewish insularity, which could cause the American Jewish community to abandon its longstanding commitments to social concerns. *Righteous Indignation* is a clarion call from those who are determined that this not be so.

Indeed, this book reminds us of Rabbi Abraham Joshua Heschel's observation that individual spiritual devotion and social justice are partners. Writing about his personal participation in the famed 1965 civil rights march he made with Dr. Martin Luther King Jr., Rabbi Heschel wrote, "It is vital to learn how to stand before God. For many of us, the march from Selma to Montgomery was both protest and prayer. Legs are not lips, and walking is not kneeling. And yet our lips uttered songs. Even without words, our march was worship." Today, the question that flows from this observation—"What are the qualities that are required for us to stand before God?"—remains more compelling than ever, and this work is an attempt to provide answers to that question.

Engaging many of the finest minds in the progressive Jewish community, the essays contained in this volume cover a wide array of social justice topics. While the contributors express a diverse spectrum of postures on the various issues, they all reject the notion of Jewish communal isolation from the larger world and they all believe that Judaism must address the total human situation. These essays correctly teach that the command to work for social justice is a Jewish imperative.

After all, Jewish tradition requires Jews to apply the foundational Jewish values of righteousness and mercy to all humanity. Thus, in *Hilchot Melachim* (Laws of Kings) 10:12, Maimonides writes, "One ought to treat the resident stranger [non-Jew] with *derekh eretz* [civility and humanity] and *hesed* [mercy and kindness] just as one does a Jew." Indeed, he justifies his position by citing a passage from Psalm 145:9, "God is good to all and [God's] mercy is on all [God's] works." God is made holy as our community displays a concern for all those in need.

While I must confess that I do not agree with all the normative conclusions that every contributor advances in each essay, each article is provocative and thoughtful as well as passionate. Each essay will engender considerable discussion and, in many instances, promote action.

Rav Kook, the first Ashkenazic chief rabbi of the State of Israel and one of the great spiritual mentors of our time, summed up well the position that animates this book when he wrote, in his *Orot Hakodesh*, "The love for Israel [*ahavat Yisrael*] entails a love for all humankind [*kol ha'adam*]." In displaying the concerns it does, *Righteous Indignation* comports to the highest elements in Jewish tradition and seeks to help mend a fractured world.

ACKNOWLEDGMENTS

Assembling an anthology requires the work of many hands. We first want to thank those individuals and organizations who helped us understand the depth and breadth of the current movement for progressive Jewish social justice in the United States:

Jeffrey Dekro, Rabbi Mordechai Leibling, Mik Moore, and the Jewish Funds for Justice; Ruth Messinger, Aaron Dorfman, Jacob Feinspan, Merril Zack, and the American Jewish World Service; Rabbi Steve Gutow and the Jewish Council for Public Affairs; Jane Ramsey and the Jewish Council on Urban Affairs in Chicago; Rabbi Sid Schwarz and PANIM; Vic Rosenthal and Jewish Community Action in St. Paul; Daniel Sokatch, Rachel Biale, and the Progressive Jewish Alliance; Dara Silverman and Jews for Racial and Economic Justice in New York; Liore Milgrom-Elcott and the Coalition for Judaism and the Environment; Nancy Kaufman and Nommi Nadich and the Jewish Relations Council of Greater Boston; Rabbi David Rosenn, Rachel Chertok, and AVODAH; Rabbi Jennie Rosenn and the Nathan Cummings Foundation; the staff at the Jewish Coalition for Service; Lori Leibowitz and Jews United for Justice in DC; Rabbi Arthur Waskow, Phyllis Berman, and the Shalom Center; Dr. Dianne Balser and Brit Tzedek v'Shalom; Rabbi Michael Lerner, *Tikkun*, and the Network of Spiritual Progressives; Jennifer Butler and Faith in Public Life; Rich Kotchmar, Lindsay Moseley, and Orli Cotel at the Sierra Club; Joy Heine and Kim Bobo at Interfaith Worker Justice; Zach Teutch and the SEIU Community Strength Division; Michael Brown and the Jewish Organizing Initiative; Idit Klein and Keshet; and Mark Hanis and the Genocide Intervention Network.

We also could not have crafted this book without the inspiration and guidance of several teachers and mentors: Rabbi Arthur Green, Rabbi Zalman Schachter Shalomi, Rabbi Sharon Cohen Anisfeld, the Reverend William Sloane Coffin (of blessed memory), Rabbi David Gordis, Dr. Barry Mesch, Rabbi Elliot Dorff, Dr. Leonard Fein, Rabbi David Ellenson, Rabbi Harold Schulweis, Rabbi Toba Spitzer, Rabbi

Sheila Pelz Weinberg, Rabbi Edward Feld, the Reverend Dr. Gloria White Hammond, Judith Tumin, Shoshana Jedwab, Rabbi Dov Lerea, Rabbi Fred Dobb, Rabbi Shai Held, and Rabbi Ebn Leader.

We also want to thank all those who helped to make the book a physical reality: Thanks to Rabbi Sue Fendrick, Sarah Swartz, and Julia Appel for their fine editorial work. Thanks to Joshua Meyer for his creative design work, and Daniel Sieradski for website expertise. Special thanks to Emily Wichland, Jessica Swift, and the production team at Jewish Lights, who worked overtime to publish this book in a timely fashion; and to Stuart M. Matlins, founder and editor in chief of Jewish Lights Publishing, for his vision and determination.

Finally, each of us would like to thank the people who supported us most daily while we worked on this project.

Jo Ellen: Thanks to my colleagues at *Zeek* for their support for this project; to members of my shul, Congregation Sha'ar Zahav, and its SFOP project for showing me social justice in action; and most of all, thanks to my family, David and Zoe, for their love and support.

Margie: Thanks to my community at Moishe House Boston: Kavod Jewish Social Justice House, especially my housemates over the long summer of editing—Ari, Ben, Joe, and Sarah; to my friends at the Hebrew College Rabbinical School, especially Steven, Lisa, and Minna; to my interfaith partners-in-crime Rev. Manikka Bowman, Bilal Kaleem, and Najiba Akbar; to my family, to Shalom, and to my best friend, Diana, who gave me endless love, good ideas, and encouragement throughout this project; to my grandmother and activist hero Pauline Bograd, in whose memory I dedicate my work on this book.

Or: Thanks to the students, faculty, and staff of Hebrew College. One could not ask for a more compassionate community in which to work as an educator and activist. To my parents and siblings, Neal and Carol, Ari, Carnie, Kliel, and Adira Rose—thank you for the love you have shown me over these many years. I also wish to thank my wife's family, Stanley Rosenbaum, Paula Hyman, and Adina Rosenbaum, for their kindness, generosity, and respect. Finally, to my wife, Dr. Judith Rosenbaum—"This is my beloved, this is my friend." Thank you for inspiring me to enter the activist fray, and for challenging me to live my ideals at home and in the world. May our children, Ma'ayan and Aviv, be blessed to live in a world of greater justice and compassion.

INTRODUCTION

If you have opened this book, you have heard the call for justice. If, in the words of the Torah, you have "eyes that see," "ears that hear," and a "heart that perceives" (Deut. 29:4), you can bear witness to the sources of righteous indignation all around us. We live in a world in desperate need of repair. War and genocide continue despite our promises of "never again." Poverty, crime, and disease embitter the lives of countless numbers of people. Global warming, caused largely by our own failings, threatens life as we know it on the planet.

The creation of a just and sustainable world requires the cooperative efforts of people from all walks of life. We issue our call for action to two primary audiences:

- We call out to individuals active in the organized Jewish community—in synagogues, schools, and other communal institutions—with the message that to live as responsible Jews in this day and age requires us to dedicate more of our time and energy working for systemic change in the United States, Israel, and elsewhere in the world.
- We call out to Jewish activists who are uninvolved in or alienated from organized Jewish life, with the message that the religious teachings and practices of our tradition can be profound sources of inspiration, guidance, and support for the work of social justice.

We also encourage others who do not see themselves as part of either of these cohorts to explore the materials in this collection and to grapple with the issues raised by our contributors.

In assembling this anthology, we draw strength from past Jewish activists who sought to meet the justice needs of their times. The biblical prophets take as their primary task to teach people the need to create just communities. Isaiah tells us to "learn to do good, devote yourselves to justice, aid the wronged, uphold the rights of the orphan;

defend the cause of the widow" (Isa. 1:17). Jeremiah berates the people for not giving "a hearing to the plea of the needy" (Jer. 5:28). Amos famously cries, "Let justice roll down like waters, and righteousness like a mighty stream" (Amos 5:24).

Since the days of the ancient prophets, there have been many others in the Jewish tradition who have called on our community to rededicate itself to the cause of justice. One such modern figure, who serves as a source of inspiration to many of the contributors in this anthology, is the great theologian and activist Abraham Joshua Heschel, of blessed memory (1907–1972). Commenting on Amos, Heschel asserts that social justice is not "a mere tributary" of the Jewish tradition, but a major current of the religious life. As Michael Lerner writes in this volume, a Heschelian Judaism requires that "we respond to the Ineffable not only with prayer but with acts of kindness, love, and generosity."

In communities around the country, increasing numbers of Jews are following Heschel's lead. There is a growing movement of activists who view their justice work as integral to their identities as Jews, and who view the teachings of Judaism as foundational to their activist efforts. We are proud to highlight the work of many of the people and organizations shaping this movement in this anthology.

In approaching the ever-widening universe of Jewish social justice work (here we use this term broadly to include environmental activism), we choose to begin, in fine Jewish fashion, not with answers, but with questions.

Jewish: Why should American Jews turn to Judaism's religious teachings for help in addressing contemporary justice issues?

Social: Does Jewish social justice mean creating a just Jewish society, or pursuing a Jewish way of creating justice in the broader society in which we live?

Justice: Why do we talk about social justice and not about social action or direct service? What do we mean by *justice*?

Toward a *Jewish* Social Justice

While some people might think of Judaism—and religion in general— as a fundamentally conservative force, we believe that our religious heritage offers us important insight into the creation of a just and compassionate world. We turn to Judaism for the sacred framework it provides for our justice work, and for its many teachings on personal and communal ethics and the interconnection of all life. It is our experience that the religious practices of Judaism—prayer, observing Shabbat and holidays, life-cycle rituals—help us sustain ourselves in the face of the suffering and despair we encounter daily in our work.

Further, in a time when religious fundamentalism is on the rise throughout the world, and the Religious Right is successfully organizing around a conservative agenda in this country, it is critical that we religious progressives articulate our values publicly, offering alternative visions of religion and public life.

We recognize, however, that Judaism is a multi-vocal tradition, containing some ideas and practices that are in conflict with our contemporary values. Judaism has evolved over thousands of years in different geographical locations and within distinct cultural contexts. As a result, our sacred texts do *not* say any one thing about any issue of significance. While there are majority and minority opinions, more and less popular trends, Judaism is above all else an interpretive tradition. Rabbi Akiva, Maimonides, and the Ba'al Shem Tov all considered themselves a part of the Jewish tradition, but held very different views on matters large and small.

One of the central aims of this anthology is to provide readers with a set of intellectual and spiritual resources to encourage a sophisticated conversation about Judaism, social justice, and environmental responsibility. It is an attempt to help our community move beyond simplistic and clichéd conversation and to challenge us all to think more deeply about the role of Judaism in creating a just and sustainable world. While the contributors to this volume argue passionately for their particular views, they are all aware of the fact that there are many "Jewish" views on any substantive issue.

Though most of the contributors to this volume identify themselves politically as Democrats, liberals, or progressives, they do not agree on all of the issues discussed in this anthology (Israel-Palestine being one particularly contentious issue). What they do share in common is a passionate commitment to Judaism and to democratic values, and an understanding that we must engage in a rigorous critique of the religious and secular cultures in which we participate if we are to create a just and sustainable world.

Toward a Jewish *Social* Justice

One way to understand the phrase *Jewish social justice* is as a reference to the work Jewish activists do within Jewish communities. There are good reasons to focus our justice efforts inward. The Jewish community, like all other groups, is imperfect and requires us to carefully examine our treatment of our own community members, particularly those who are often marginalized in Jewish and American life. How do we treat gay, lesbian, bisexual, and transgendered Jews? What about Jews of color and those who experience physical or mental challenges? Are we willing to speak openly about domestic violence within the Jewish community?

As American Jews, we must also reflect upon our relationship to the State of Israel. Are we willing to celebrate its accomplishments and critique its shortcomings? Have we been sensitive enough to the suffering of the Palestinian people? Are we advocating for a peaceful and just solution to this tragic conflict? We must also be attentive to the continuing threat of anti-Semitism in the United States and abroad, and the choice of some in the progressive political world to ally themselves with anti-Semites.

Yet as a cursory glance at the essays assembled in this volume will demonstrate, we believe that our justice work must also be directed to the world at large. We go so far as to say that at this stage of our development as a people, we are required to address universal concerns, including issues of domestic and international poverty, global warming and ecological degradation, and genocide and war. However, there is a very real tension between the Jewish emphasis on particularism and universalism. As Aaron Dorfman and Ruth Messinger ask in their essay, what is the scope of our "universe of obligation"? In a world that is broken, do we begin by addressing Jewish issues, American issues, or global issues?

Without oversimplifying the matter, the answer our contributors offer in this book is that the American Jewish community has the creative, financial, and political resources to work on several fronts simultaneously. Sections in this volume move from the universal but self-sustaining obligations we have for the environment, our bodies, and for American culture (in parts two through four); to the particular obligations we have for the Jewish community and for Israel (parts five and six). In the final section of the book (part seven), we expand outward again, addressing our obligations to other peoples and cultures around the globe.

Toward a Jewish Social *Justice*

While it is clear that the world is in need of repair, how we "do justice" is not an easy question to answer. Volunteering in soup kitchens is certainly an act benefiting the social good, as is visiting the sick and the elderly. But direct service alone is simply not enough. Such action addresses only immediate needs and not root causes. Further, there are justice issues that cannot be addressed at all—foreign policy issues, for example—without political advocacy.

None of the essays in this book addresses direct service because we feel that the American Jewish community does this work very well. Virtually every synagogue we have entered has a "social action committee" and provides congregants with ways to serve the needy. Very few social action committees, however, actually empower congregants as political advocates. And without political action, there can be no deep and lasting change.

We hope this book assists those who are trying to reorient the Jewish justice agenda—and the national religious agenda as a whole. Along with essays that address specific areas of Jewish social justice work, we include essays that focus on how to transform theory into practice, ideas into advocacy. For example, David Saperstein writes in part one of the need to train rabbis to be more effective political agents. In part three, Jonah Dov Pesner shares with us the story of how congregation-based community organizing helped transform the health care system in Massachusetts. Arthur Waskow and Phyllis Berman show us in part seven the power of interfaith initiatives in the quest for peace.

The Possibility of Change

In his contribution to this volume—a provocative essay on homosexuality and Judaism—Jay Michaelson writes:

> I today know, as much as I know anything, that the loving God
> ... the God of Abraham, Isaac, and Jacob, could not possibly
> wish for Her creations to distort, repress, deny, and mutilate
> themselves.

Michaelson is speaking about embracing sexual difference, but he could be speaking about other aspects of human behavior as well. In too many ways we have distorted and mutilated the world in which we live, and denied and repressed the ability of our fellow human beings to live in it. Yet our tradition tells us that we can change our ways and transform our world. This is the essence of *teshuvah* (repentance). We have the power to repair our lives and life as a whole if only we are willing to do the work.

The essays in this anthology demonstrate how many people are already working to create a more just and sustainable world. We hope that this book will help strengthen those engaged in this sacred endeavor and inspire others to join them.

In the words of our Sages, "It is not incumbent upon you to complete the task, but neither are you free to desist from it" (*Pirkei Avot* 2:16).

Or N. Rose, Jo Ellen Green Kaiser, and Margie Klein

PART I
JUDAISM, JUSTICE, AND AMERICAN LIFE

Can Social Justice Save the American Jewish Soul?

RABBI SIDNEY SCHWARZ, PhD

Rabbi Sidney Schwarz, PhD, is the founder and president of PANIM: The Institute for Jewish Leadership and Values, which promotes Jewish activism and social responsibility. A winner of a Covenant Award for his social entrepreneurship in Jewish education, he is the author of *Finding a Spiritual Home: How a New Generation of Jews Can Transform the American Synagogue* and *Judaism and Justice: The Jewish Passion to Repair the World* (both from Jewish Lights).

For most of my professional life as a rabbi, a teacher, an author, and a community activist, I have tried to advance the idea that social justice needs to be more central to the program of the American Jewish community. The idea is so simple and, seemingly, so obvious that it is hard to understand why it cannot gain traction.

Isn't it obvious that social justice is the primary mandate of Judaism? Isn't it obvious that there is no attitude or behavior as universally shared by American Jews as their commitment to the ideals of tolerance, peace, and justice for all people? Isn't it obvious that if the Jewish community made social justice a core commitment in the way it spoke and acted in the world that it would attract tens of thousands of Jews who are otherwise turned off to Jewish affiliations and who spend their time and money on a host of causes and organizations that advance the common good in our society and in our world?

The answer to these questions lies in the origins of Judaism. As I outline in my book, *Judaism and Justice: The Jewish Passion to Repair the World* (Jewish Lights), we have a tribal obligation to each other as Jews and a convenantal obligation to the world as ethical human beings.

A Nation with a Mission

Based on my reading of Judaism, there are two compelling answers to the question "What is the purpose of Judaism?"

The first purpose is based on Genesis 18, when God expands on an initial charge to Abraham to go forth from his land to the land that God will show him. In 18:19, God adds a critical prerequisite that will enable Abraham to fulfill his destiny and become the father of a great nation. He is to obey God's commandments and "extend the boundaries of righteousness and justice in the world," *la'asot tzedakah umishpat*.

The second purpose of Judaism is based on God's revelation to Moses, which is recounted in Exodus 19:6. The Jewish people are told to be "a kingdom of priests and a holy nation," a *mamlechet kohanim* and *goy kadosh*. The Hebrew word for holiness—*kedusha*—comes from a root that means separate and apart.

Judaism is a religion based on a paradox: Jews are expected to maintain a holy apartness as God's chosen people and, *at the same time*, are expected to be totally engaged with the world around them. The observance of ritual laws must be combined with acting toward others with justice and compassion to be loyal to God's covenant with the Jewish people.

Each of these core mandates of Judaism—tribe and covenant—are rooted in the Torah, which has made them part and parcel of Jewish consciousness and identity. The Exodus from Egypt is a political act that liberates a people from slavery and gives them a sense of common history and destiny. The political consciousness it generates among a newly created Children of Israel (*b'nai Yisrael*) is supported by the teachings that Israel is an *am segulah*, a treasured and exceptional people (Deut. 14:2); a *goy kadosh*, a nation that is holy and apart (Exod. 19:6); and "a nation that will dwell alone," *am levado yishkon* (Num. 23:9). I call this Exodus consciousness.

If the Exodus created an ethnic/tribal consciousness among Jews, it was Sinai that invested in them an understanding of their mission in the world. Jewish existence was to be based on bringing *tzedek* and *mishpat*, righteousness and justice, to all God's children. The covenant forged at Sinai committed the Jewish people to a life of ethics and values. It was the spiritual/moral genesis of the Jewish people, and it was powerfully connected to the Jewish people's understanding of what God wants of them. The Torah's teachings about acting with compassion (*chesed*), protecting the stranger in one's midst (*ahavat ger*), and pursuing peace (*shalom*) and truth (*emet*) shaped the Jewish notion of how one should live in the world. Sinai consciousness is at the root of the Jewish understanding that to live true to the covenant that God established with the Jewish people at Sinai is to live a life of social responsibility.

Tribal Jewish Identity

Modernity and the experience of the American Jewish community have brought into bold relief the growing gap between covenantal and tribal Jewish identity.

Tribal Jewish identity in the twenty-first century is relatively easy to define. The State of Israel is the single largest tribal Jewish polity. You are either a citizen of the state or not. A Jew living in the Diaspora has the opportunity to express loyalty for the State of Israel by joining an organization that works to raise money or generate political support for the Jewish state. This, too, makes that Jew a member of the tribe.

Jews also can declare their tribal identity by making a financial contribution to their local Jewish federation, which supports a wide range of local and international Jewish needs. The same is true for memberships in synagogues and in Jewish cultural, philanthropic, public affairs, and/or educational organizations. Payment of these voluntary "taxes" also essentially makes one a member of the tribe.

This means of creating tribal identity has the useful side effect of allowing us to measure, quantitatively, the size of the Jewish world. What we discover is that, while the population of the State of Israel continues to grow, the affiliation numbers in the rest of the Jewish world show a steady decline, a phenomenon that leads those very organizations to have a heightened sense that the future of the Jewish people is at risk. Those committed to the perpetuation of the Jewish community will continually be challenged to find ways to capture a larger market share of the Jews who do not choose to belong to the tribe in any tangible way.

Covenantal Jewish Identity

To understand the decline of Jewish tribal affiliation, it is critical to understand what covenantal identity means to contemporary Jews. Throughout the generations, the Rabbis recognized that the covenantal spirit of Abraham's legacy was as important as the specific behavioral commandments that later made up the substance of Jewish life and observance. Rabbi Joseph Soloveitchik, perhaps the most respected Orthodox sage in the history of American Jewry, asserts that the *brit avot*, the covenant of Abraham and the patriarchs—a covenant with a universal thrust focused on the welfare of the entire world—was more important than the specific laws given in the Torah and in later rabbinic codes, laws intended to preserve Jewish particularity. The legacy of Abraham's response to God's call to righteousness and to justice shaped the values and consciousness of Jews for all time.[1]

In a similar vein, Rabbi Abraham Isaac Kook, who served as the first chief rabbi of Palestine from 1921 to 1935, believed that the early Zionists—who observed few, if any, of the ritual commandments of Judaism, and who wore their secularism proudly—were agents for a divine plan for the Jewish people in the world. Unlike Theodor Herzl, Kook did not see a Jewish homeland as primarily a place to provide safe refuge for persecuted Jews. Rather, he believed that the upbuilding of Israel was part of a divine plan to bring healing to the entire world.

This more universal (and potentially secularizing) understanding of Jewish faith and destiny is at the core of modern covenantal Jewish identity. Rabbi Kook challenged the normative rabbinic reading of the verse "thou shalt love thy neighbor as thyself" as referring only to other Jews. He believed that Jews must read the verse to refer to all humanity.[2]

It is not easy for the organized Jewish community to assess how Jews might be living out covenantal Jewish identity when it is stripped of all elements of tribal association. It is easier to identify a Jew who takes on the particular details of Jewish observance and faith than it is to identify a Jew who has no such practice yet lives in accordance with

Jewish ethical and moral principles. There are data that can tell you how many Jews belong to synagogues, how many contribute money to federations, and how many travel to Israel. One can also discover how many Jews keep kosher and how many light Hanukkah candles. What cannot be as accurately determined, however, is how many Jews feel Jewish, or how many Jews view Judaism and Jewish ethics as an important part of their identity.

Expanding the Tent

Many Jews define large parts of what drives their actions in the world through the context of the Judaic heritage, even when they have no Jewish affiliations or do not engage in any Jewish religious practice. They adhere to what I call Sinai consciousness, or what the sociologist Herbert Gans calls "symbolic ethnicity."[3]

Given the way that the Jewish community currently functions, such Jews are effectively defined as being outside of the tribe. It becomes a self-fulfilling prophecy. Jews who might otherwise be open to initiatives or programs of the Jewish community when such endeavors align with their values and ethics are driven away by an implicit attitude coming from communal institutions that they have "not paid their dues" to the tribe, not only financially but also by their lack of regular association with communal institutions.

The organized Jewish community is not very good at understanding and validating this kind of covenantal Jewish identity. The leadership of the American Jewish community often feels that the community is under siege and/or at risk. Any manifestation of anti-Semitism at home or abroad, and any threat to the security of the State of Israel, sends the community to its battle stations. When in this mode, the Jewish community has a tendency to circle the wagons and ostracize those Jews whose opinions stray too far from the party line, as evidenced by the experience of Breira in the 1970s and *Tikkun* magazine for much of its history.

During rare moments, like the mid-1990s, when Israel seemed to be on the road to peace and the Jewish community did not feel besieged by outside enemies, the demons became internal. Predicting "death by demography," communal leaders sounded alarm bells over the results of Jewish population studies that showed soaring rates of intermarriage and assimilation and declining affiliation patterns.

In either mode—under siege or at risk—the Jewish community tends to draw hard and fast lines on who belongs and who does not. And the harder the lines, the less likely that covenantal/Sinai Jews, whose identity is soft and ambivalent, will see themselves as part of the Jewish community.

It is here that the organized Jewish community has created for itself a catch-22 situation. In a social milieu in which fewer and fewer Jews deem ethnic affiliation a necessity, the Jewish community is nevertheless desperate to get marginally affiliated Jews to make overt commitments to communal institutions by joining Jewish organizations and contributing money to Jewish causes.

The target audience is large. When one extrapolates from membership statistics and patterns of observance from recent Jewish population studies, it could be argued that more than half of American Jews are "potentially" affiliated Jews.[4] These Jews may be open to deeper involvement in the Jewish community, but only on their terms. They don't feel that they need it. But if inspired and convinced that it will add meaning and purpose to their lives, they are "available." The form that their availability will take is very tentative. They are more likely to dabble in a Jewish event here, make a modest gift to a Jewish cause there, than they are to become flag-waving, highly affiliated Jews overnight.

For a Jewish organization that invests money in some kind of outreach strategy, this is an unsatisfactory, short-term return. So, instead of meeting covenantal Jews halfway and appealing to their sense of universal justice, the Jewish communal establishment continues to focus on rallying the highly committed. Yet the language used by these Jewish organizations—constantly sounding the warning bell of imminent extinction—is the language least likely to attract marginal Jews to the fold. Why would anyone join a sinking ship if they did not have to?

The divide between Exodus/tribal Jews and Sinai/covenantal Jews is wide and getting wider. The Holocaust and the birth of the State of Israel were formative events for Exodus/tribal Jews. It would be hard to invent a more compelling narrative for why Jews need to band together, whether in a nation-state or through diaspora Jewish organizations, to protect themselves and watch out for each other in a hostile world. Yet those dual experiences are becoming more remote with every passing year. They are not the life experience of Jews born after World War II. And while Exodus Jews still see Israel as the biblical David doing battle against an array of Goliath enemies in the world and thus worthy of unqualified support, to the majority of Jews, the narrative is much more morally complex. Israel is no longer the engine to Jewish identity or to Jewish philanthropy that it once was.

Why Jewish Particularism Is Okay

What, then, might draw marginal Jews closer to the Jewish community? I believe that social justice is one of the most compelling answers to that question.[5] It will not be a straight shot. There is much that stands in the way. But I will try to make the case.

It is critical to recognize how central social justice is to Jewish consciousness. The concern for the stranger, the pursuit of justice and peace, the empathy for the poor, and the commitment to truth and fairness is buried deep in the soul of every Jew. It transcends denominational boundaries, geographical contexts, and historical eras. It is acted out by Jews who wear *kippot* (head coverings) and by those who would not step foot in a synagogue. It is rooted in the sacred texts of the Jewish people, so it is familiar to the knowledgeable Jew. But in ways that serendipity or faith can only explain, it has become a large part of the identity of Jews who have never opened a single Jewish book. Despite the hand-wringing by those most committed to the continuity of the Jewish people, many Jews live the values of the Torah even though they have no formal affiliation with the Jewish community. It is what I have called Sinai consciousness.

The historical experience of the Jewish people has helped to acculturate Jews into the communal ethic of righteousness and justice. The admonition to "care for the stranger, for you were once strangers in the land of Egypt" (Exod. 22:21) was not only about Egypt, just as the Passover seder was not just about Egypt. It was about the persecution of Jews in every era and in almost every place they lived. It developed in Jews a commitment to come to the aid of fellow Jews when circumstances made it possible. It developed in Jews an instinctual sympathy for others who similarly came to experience persecution and oppression.

Sinai consciousness explains the terrible guilt that American Jews felt about their failure to help their European coreligionists during the Holocaust. It explains why so many Jews rallied to the cause of civil rights for American blacks. It explains the Soviet Jewry movement and the development of an Israel lobby. It explains the prominence of Jews in organizations that work for the underprivileged and the protection of human rights around the world. This culture of empathic compassion is what explains Jewish voting patterns and attitudes that defy the typical pattern that links rising socioeconomic status with growing political conservatism. Sinai consciousness, it turns out, is more tenacious than economic interests.

When Jewish communal organizations provided a context to work for the broader welfare of American society and the world, Jews pursued those goals with vigor. When, on the other hand, the organized Jewish community pursued its organizational mandates and missions largely focused on defense and survival—quite adeptly and appropriately, I might add—the Sinai consciousness of many Jews emerged elsewhere.

One of the most welcome developments of recent years is the evidence of an unselfconscious Jewish identity among younger Jews, who are eager to combine their passion for justice with their identification with the texts and values of the Jewish tradition. Michael Schwerner and Andy Goodman—two Jews who traveled to the South to help in the civil rights struggle of the 1960s and were killed by members of the Ku Klux Klan along with African-American James Chaney—clearly were motivated by a desire to advance social justice, but they had no connection to their respective Jewish identities. There are young Jews today who are not satisfied simply to ally with the most vulnerable members of our society. Increasing numbers of Jews are eager to root such behavior in the language of Jewish texts and to do the work under identifiable Jewish banners. This is cause for celebration, and it points to a healthy maturation of the American Jewish community.

What is unassailable is that social justice continues to be among the strongest factors that unite Jews. A 2000 study, conducted by Steven M. Cohen and Leonard Fein under the auspices of a short-lived organization called Amos: The National Jewish Partnership for Social Justice, asked the question, "Which of the following qualities do you consider most important to your Jewish identity?" Forty-seven percent of respondents cited "a commitment to social equality," 24 percent cited "religious observance," and 13 percent cited "support for Israel."[6]

Many will say that social justice is not enough. It certainly would fail the tribal loyalty test as defined in the minds of the stewards of the organized Jewish community. But take the hypothetical American Jew who is an active member of a human rights organization, an environmental organization, or a civil liberties organization, or who is active in local politics. Assume that this individual is not a member of any Jewish organization and gives no money to any Jewish causes. Engage this person in a conversation about what drives his or her volunteer and philanthropic activity, and in many cases we will find that it traces back to that person's Jewish roots, be it a grandparent role model, identification with one or more aspects of the Jewish historical narrative, or the reading of a book of Jewish fiction. Expose that person to a Jewish institution that speaks to his or her values, to a Jewish teacher who frames those values in the words of classical Jewish texts, to a social justice initiative sponsored by a Jewish organization, and there is a very good chance that such a person can be drawn closer to the Jewish community.

I know. I have been part of such education and outreach for three decades, and I can count hundreds of such Jews who "discovered" that there are Jewish institutions through which they can fulfill their personal passions. These Jews represent a gold mine of talent that is largely unrecognized and untapped by the organized Jewish community.

Is Social Justice Enough?

There are obstacles. The Amos study revealed a deep ambivalence on the part of those surveyed about whether they felt they needed to do their social justice work under Jewish auspices. Reflecting the same phenomenon uncovered by the 1990 and 2000 National Jewish Population Surveys, Jews are less and less likely to join Jewish organizations because they have so successfully integrated themselves into America. They don't need the communal support that was welcomed by their parents and grandparents when they first came to America, seeking a familiar context as an ethnic minority in a new milieu.

I would go one step further. I find that the younger the Jews, the more likely they are to manifest "post-tribal syndrome." Younger Jews tend to push away any and all elements of the Jewish heritage that smack of parochialism. The very elements of tribal connection that have kept the Jewish people united across the world for centuries are regarded with increasing disdain by younger Jews. Add to this bias a general suspicion of religious organizations that is supported by media revelations of unethical behavior by clergy and religious institutions and you begin to understand the deep aversion many younger Jews have to associating themselves in any way with the Jewish community.

Ironically, beneath these biases lie many noble and commendable values and aspirations. One young Jewish social activist who now works for the Greater Boston Interfaith Organization, building relationships between synagogues in the Boston area and local community-organizing efforts, recently reflected on his youth at a well-established Conservative synagogue in the suburbs of Washington, D.C. He was turned off by "empty ritual and an emphasis on couture over action." He contrasted his home congregation's $2 million capital campaign to make the synagogue more aesthetically pleasing to its upscale membership with a Lutheran church in Harvard Square, Cambridge, that launched a $1.5 million campaign to fix up its basement to better assist the homeless men and women served by the church's programs.[7] This is a harsh assessment, and not many religious institutions in America would pass this level of ethical scrutiny. Yet it is a good example of how Sinai consciousness can drive many Jews away from Jewish institutions.

The same people who dismiss religion, and Judaism along with it, believe in many of the core Jewish values that are behind Judaism's historic commitment to social justice. Many of them would like to contribute to efforts that help such values influence the conduct of society. Yet in a world that is increasingly polarized and partisan, religions and religious institutions stand suspect. There is evidence to support the indictment. The Jewish community must be able to articulate why particularism is okay, why religion can be a force for good, and why Judaism is a worthy and morally compelling life path.

The Jewish community desperately needs to attract these Sinai Jews. With each passing generation, they make up a larger and larger percentage of the American Jewish community. They will not resonate to the tribal appeals that worked for their parents or grandparents. They are, mostly, highly educated, affluent, and interested in things that might give their lives added meaning and purpose. They will not affiliate with the Jewish community unless a piece of the message resonates with them. The Jewish community must make the case.

Why Judaism?

All of this brings us back to the millennial tension in Judaism between Exodus and Sinai impulses. Every faith community is committed to the survival and perpetuation of its own. Judaism is not immune to these tendencies. Judaism has often fallen prey to the tendency, affecting all groups, to see itself in parochial terms, to believe that the interests of the group supersede all else. This is especially true in times of crisis. In modern times, this defensiveness extends to times when Israel is at risk, either from war, terrorism, or worldwide campaigns to discredit Zionism and the right of Jews to collective existence in their ancestral homeland.

Still, the Jewish tradition's universal teachings about responsibility toward all human beings and to the entire world continue to bring us back to the needed equilibrium between self-interest—the Exodus impulse—and the interests of humanity—the Sinai impulse. Even when, or perhaps especially when, the Jewish world tends toward the parochial, there are voices in our midst that call us back to our prophetic legacy to be agents for the repair of the entire world.

Rabbi Joseph Soloveitchik, the Orthodox leader cited earlier, spoke to the tension between Exodus and Sinai in the consciousness of the Jewish people in another way: In order to explain the difference between the people of fate and the nation of destiny, it is worth taking note of the antithesis between camp (*machaneh*) and congregation (*edah*). The camp is created as a result of the desire for self-defense and is nurtured by a sense of fear; the congregation is created as a result of the longing for the realization of an exalted ethical idea and is nurtured by the sentiment of love.[8]

The Jewish community cannot realize its fullest potential to become a people of the covenant, committed to the ethical principles of righteousness and justice, if it remains in its tribal camp, paralyzed by fear and consumed by its perceived need to defend itself from every threat, real and imagined. It is true that without the proper communal mechanisms and political advocacy to properly defend the Jewish people at risk, no Jew would have the luxury to pursue the more lofty Sinai agenda. At the same time, unless the Jewish community begins to give higher priority to an agenda of righteousness and justice—the agenda that started with the first Jew, Abraham—it will have confused the means and the ends.

That prophetic legacy is why the Jewish people were put on this earth.

What Does *Tikkun Olam* Actually Mean?

RABBI JANE KANAREK, PhD

Rabbi Jane Kanarek, PhD, is assistant professor of rabbinics at Hebrew College, where she teaches Talmud and Jewish law. She received rabbinic ordination from The Jewish Theological Seminary of America, and a doctorate from the University of Chicago. Rabbi Kanarek is an alumna of the Wexner Graduate Fellowship.

Today, the term *tikkun olam*—usually translated as "mending the world"—is used throughout the Jewish world to summarize the efforts of Jewish social justice movements. We view *tikkun olam* as our Jewish inheritance, a mandate to Jews to make the world in which we live a better place. But the term *tikkun olam* itself has become a cliché, used so often that it offers little real guidance for social justice efforts.

What if, though, we were to look more deeply within Jewish tradition at the roots of the phrase *tikkun olam* to see what guidance that perspective might provide us? What might this deeper look at the meaning of the words *tikkun olam* teach us about how we, today, can better mend our own worlds? What kinds of possibilities for change might our eyes become open to that we had not previously considered?[1]

"Because of *Tikkun Ha'olam*"

One of the first uses of the phrase *tikkun olam* can be traced to the Mishnah, one of the earliest sections of the Oral Law, composed sometime around 200 CE. The words *tikkun ha'olam* (a more grammatically correct version of the phrase, as it uses the definite article before the word *world*, *"olam"*) appear a total of fifteen times in the Mishnah and in the context of a number of different legal concerns, including divorce, marriage, slavery, captivity, sacred literature, debt, loans, land ownership, lost property, and relationships to non-Jews.[2] In each of these instances, a change in current legal practice is mandated and the reason given is simply, "because of *tikkun ha'olam*." The Mishnah does not provide us with further explanation of these words, but a close examination of two examples can clarify what the Mishnah may mean by using this language and how that can help us.

The first example comes from the realm of divorce law. According to the Mishnah, only the husband can initiate formal divorce proceedings. Divorce is carried out through the mechanism of a husband literally giving his wife a document of divorce, commonly known as a *get*, before witnesses. A husband can also empower an emissary, or representative, to deliver the *get* to his wife in his place. The Mishnah in question addresses the following situation: a man has sent a *get* to be delivered to his wife through an emissary. However, before the emissary reaches the woman, the husband changes his mind and decides to convene a court of law, a *beit din*, to cancel the *get*—without the knowledge of either the emissary or the woman. Can the husband do this?

> At first, he [the husband] would convene a court of law in another place and cancel it [the divorce document]. Rabban Gamliel the Elder decreed that they should not do this, because of *tikkun ha'olam*. (Mishnah, *Gittin* 4:2)

Rabban Gamliel sees an injustice in the legal order. If a man can cancel a *get* without the emissary or wife's knowledge, the emissary will deliver the *get* and the woman will incorrectly think herself divorced. While Rabban Gamliel's decree is an attempt to ensure there is no ambiguity in marital status (so that a woman will not remarry when she is in fact still married, something forbidden by Jewish law), it is also a decree that mandates a woman's full knowledge of her status. A husband cannot simply go behind his wife's back and cruelly cancel the divorce, putting her future status and that of any children she may have with a new husband in jeopardy. While Rabban Gamliel's decree may not go as far as we would like in correcting the systemic inequities between women and men in Jewish divorce law, his legal change is still an acknowledgment that the law as it currently stands is unjust. This law needs to be changed in order to create a more just, but not necessarily perfect, social order.

The second example concerns Jewish captives. Here the Mishnah says the following:

> One does not redeem captives for more than their worth because of *tikkun ha'olam*. One does not help captives to escape because of *tikkun ha'olam*. Rabban Shimon the son of Gamliel says: because of the decree of the captives. (Mishnah, *Gittin* 4:6)

This discussion is even more enigmatic than the previous one. Here the Mishnah informs us that we should not ransom captives for more than their worth or help captives escape—in both cases because of the principle of *tikkun ha'olam*. Rabban Shimon the son of Gamliel thinks that the reason we should not help captives escape is "because of the decree of the captives." In some ways, this Mishnah is counterintuitive—surely helping people achieve freedom is creating a better social order! So what does the Mishnah mean?

The Babylonian Talmud, our central book of the Oral Law, tries to clarify the meaning of the phrase "because of *tikkun ha'olam*" in the first line of the Mishnah ("one does not redeem captives for more than their worth").[3] The Talmud offers two possibilities: the first is the financial distress the community might find itself in if it must redeem captives regardless of the monetary cost. If there are no rules about the ransom price of captives, captors could continuously raise payment amounts, and eventually the community would become bankrupt.

The second meaning behind the ransom rule, according to the Babylonian Talmud, is the danger of giving an incentive to kidnappers. If kidnappers know that the community will ransom captives at any price, they will then be tempted to kidnap more people, or worse, to retake the captives that have just been ransomed and hold them for even more money. So *tikkun ha'olam* is related to communal distress— either financial or in the taking of further captives. *Tikkun ha'olam* requires an abstraction from the particular person imprisoned to a concern for the entire community's future, whether it is preventing a community from sinking into poverty or a fear for the community's very existence.

The Talmud now turns to addressing the next clause of the Mishnah—we are not permitted to help captives escape. It wants to know the practical issue that divides Rabban Shimon the son of Gamliel (we must not help captives escape "because of the decree of the captives") from the anonymous voice that precedes it (we must not help captives escape "because of *tikkun ha'olam*"). It gives us a very brief answer: what divides them is the case where there is only one captive. What does this mean?

Rashi (Rabbi Shlomo the son of Yitzhak, 1040–1105), one of our most important commentators on the Talmud and the Bible, gives us a very interesting answer. He says that the anonymous voice in our Mishnah is concerned with the state of the entire world. Our anonymous speaker is worried about the treatment of captives that will inevitably be taken prisoner in the future. If we help current prisoners escape, then future ones will be treated much more cruelly, placed in chains and trenches. So whether it is one person or a hundred in prison, we are forbidden to help anyone escape out of fear of the treatment of future captives.

Rabban Shimon the son of Gamliel, though, takes a more localized approach. He is not concerned with the fate of the world, current and future, but rather the immediate situation. If there are multiple prisoners, one prisoner alone should not be helped to escape. Doing so would result in cruel treatment for the remaining prisoners. However, if only one person is being held prisoner, that person can be helped to escape. As there are no other prisoners, there would be no further repercussions.

In Rashi's understanding, *tikkun ha'olam* becomes a vision of concern not only for the present, as for Rabban Shimon, but also for the future, as the anonymous voice suggests. Even more specifically, it becomes a vision for understanding that our present actions will affect our future worlds. What may seem positive in the short term may have profoundly damaging consequences for the long term.

In the *Mishneh Torah*, the twelfth-century law code written by Maimonides (1135–1204), Maimonides returns to the arguments in the Mishnah and the Talmud.

We do not redeem captives for more than their worth because of *tikkun ha'olam*, so that enemies should not chase after them to kidnap them. And we do not help captives escape because of *tikkun ha'olam* so that enemies should not make their [the captives'] yoke heavy and guard them zealously. (*Mishneh Torah*, Laws of Gifts to the Poor 8:12)

The issue is decided. We do not ransom captives lest kidnappers be tempted to imprison others, and we do not aid captives in escaping lest future captives be imprisoned even more cruelly. *Tikkun ha'olam* is a phrase that drives legal decisions. It reflects an understanding that part of the law's purpose is to create a more just society, rather than a perfect one.

In the world of the Talmud, we cannot totally prevent the taking of captives. However, that reality does not imply powerlessness. Rather, existent law must be recalibrated to aim at the formation of a better world. Looking at the examples of women divorced without their knowledge and captives in need of ransom, we see that we are dealing with a world of inequities—of men over women and captors over captives. But within this world, there is still an acknowledgment that there can be too much inequity, too much imbalance. *Tikkun ha'olam* may be translated and understood as a recalibration of the world, a recognition that the world is out of balance and that legal remedies are needed in order to readjust the world to a better balance. The focus is not so much on the power of an individual to effect change, but rather on the power of the law to correct systemic injustice.

Repairing the Shards of the World

Moving from the realm of law to that of mysticism, we now turn to Lurianic Kabbalah, the genesis of the modern revival of the idea of *tikkun* (repair). Isaac Luria (1534–1572), the founder of Lurianic Kabbalah, teaches that when God created the world, God contracted God's own glory to create something finite from the infinite. The pressure, however, was too much, and these finite vessels shattered, leaving holy sparks of the Divine mixed together with the vessels' earthly shells. The job of each individual is to try and redeem these holy sparks and to return them to their Divine source and so repair the shattered world. This mending takes place through a Jew's performance of mitzvot, study of Torah, worship of God, and righteous actions.

The focus of *tikkun olam* in this mystic view is not primarily on this world but rather on the audacious idea that human actions have the potential to affect and heal the Divine. As we mend our own inner lives through the performance of commandments, we also mend God. This idea of *tikkun ha'olam* as a healing of the cosmic realm is a far cry from that of the Talmud! What began as a concept of bettering the earthly world through law has become a concept of fixing the Divine through individual performances of commandments, prayer, and study.

Acts of Healing or Acts of Kindness?

Most people using the phrase *tikkun olam* today think neither of legal practice nor of mystical fulfillment but of an attitude both more everyday and more personal: an attitude expressed by the words *compassion*, *generosity*, and *lovingkindness*. Jewish tradition embraces such individual acts of kindness, but gives them another name: *chesed*.

Chesed is considered one of the most important of the Torah's values:

> Rabbi Simlai interpreted: The Torah begins with deeds of loving-kindness and ends with deeds of loving-kindness. It begins with deeds of loving-kindness, as it is written, "And the Lord God made for Adam and for his wife garments of skins and clothed them" (Gen. 3:21). It ends with deeds of loving-kindness, as it is written, "And God buried him [Moses] in the valley" (Deut. 34:6). (B. Sotah 14a)

In this passage, kindness forms the bookends of our tradition, and God is its model. God begins the Torah by acting kindly toward the first humans by giving them clothing, and God ends the Torah by showing kindness toward Moses by burying him. Acts of *chesed* are immediate responses to an individual in need. A person is cold: give her clothes. A man dies: bury him.

Acts of *chesed* are responses from one individual to another in a difficult or desperate time, a response to help that person get through the day. The person performing the act of *chesed* does not ask why a person has that need or attempt to plan for the future. God buries Moses, but does not create a burial society. God gives Adam and Eve clothes, but does not legislate that society must provide clothing for all its members. Each act is an individual act of grace.

Tikkun ha'olam is quite different from these immediate acts of *chesed*. In the Talmud, *tikkun ha'olam* is a response not to one person but to a perception of overarching injustice, a sense that existing law must be modified to create a more balanced society. In Lurianic Kabbalah, *tikkun olam* is an attempt to mend the Divine realm through the active performance of God's commandments. What distinguishes *tikkun ha'olam* from acts of lovingkindness is that *tikkun ha'olam* is geared to the future as much, or even more, than it is geared to the present.

Creating Systemic Change

The discussions of *tikkun ha'olam* in the Mishnah and Talmud teach us the importance of creating systemic change through law. In the Jewish tradition, law is an essential instrument for recalibrating the world to be a more just society.

As we pursue *tikkun olam* in the contemporary world, we follow the path of our ancestors when we reexamine our laws to make sure that they are helping to achieve the world we want. We should ask ourselves: Are our existing laws helping to end poverty? To provide universal health care? To tackle hunger? How are our laws fostering justice and equality in race, gender, and class? Does the law that I helped pass five years ago to reform the public school system serve the purpose that I thought it would, or do I need to rethink it—recalibrate it—for the current situation?

The Mishnah and Talmud help us ask the big structural questions, forcing us to focus on underlying causes of suffering and to address them—they also remind us that the goal of *tikkun olam* is not necessarily the world's perfection. As *Pirkei Avot* tells us, "It is not upon you to finish the task, nor are you free to desist from it" (*Pirkei Avot* 2:21).

From Lurianic Kabbalah, we can take the idea that the social justice work we do is also divine, spiritual, and particularly Jewish work. For the kabbalists, living Jewishly, performing commandments, and studying Torah are all part of the fabric of creating a better world. And mending the world is not just good on its own; it can also redeem some of the divine sparks, bring them back to God.

We do not live in isolation from God. Rather, our efforts to heal the world also heal a fractured God. This idea that God needs us to heal the world we live in can sustain us through the difficult work of *tikkun olam.*

Tikkun olam means Jewish social justice. It means having a large vision of the world as it ought to be, and working through and with the Jewish tradition to achieve that vision.

As we pursue this lofty goal, however, it is important to bring with us a reminder from the world of *chesed*. All too often, as we pursue our grand visions for the world, we can forget the people who are in the immediacy of suffering. *Chesed* is our reminder that as we ask why people suffer from hunger, we also remember to bring meals to the hungry and to contribute to organizations that provide food to the poor. *Chesed* is our reminder that as we work for universal health care, we do not forget to visit the sick in the hospital or to contribute to organizations that care for people with AIDS.

Chesed reminds us not to forget the people that make up our societies. *Tikkun olam* teaches us to try and change society itself.

Divine Limitation
and Human Responsibility

RABBI OR N. ROSE

Rabbi Or N. Rose is associate dean at the Rabbinical School of Hebrew College. He is the author of *Abraham Joshua Heschel: Man of Spirit, Man of Action*, and coeditor of *God in All Moments: Mystical & Practical Spiritual Wisdom from Hasidic Masters* (Jewish Lights). He is a contributing editor for *Tikkun* and is on the advisory board of *Sh'ma: A Journal of Jewish Responsibility*. Rose is currently completing a doctorate in Jewish thought at Brandeis University.

Exactly one week before Passover, I spoke at a suburban Boston synagogue about the genocide in Darfur (western Sudan). My task was to convey to the assembled group of adults and teens the basic facts of the crisis and some Jewish teachings that might motivate them to take action. I shared the podium that evening with an extraordinary young man named Panther Alier, who was part of a group known as "The Lost Boys of Sudan."

The Lost Boys were a group of child refugees who were orphaned or separated from their families in an earlier conflict in southern Sudan, in which government and paramilitary forces destroyed numerous villages in brutal counterinsurgency operations. The younger boys in these communities survived in large numbers because they were either away tending herd or were guided by elders into nearby jungles. Alone, with no family or financial support, the children banded together and made long and arduous journeys to international relief camps in Ethiopia and Kenya, battling starvation, disease, wild animals, and roving soldiers and bandits. Many of the Lost Boys later resettled in the United States and elsewhere in the West.[1]

Although I had heard Panther speak several times about his harrowing experiences as a refugee, the story he shared that evening shook me to the core. He described an incident when the Lost Boys, traveling through a jungle, were pursued by a group of militiamen allied with the Sudanese government. The militiamen screamed wildly and fired their guns as they chased the children through a densely wooded area. As the boys ran from the fighters, they entered a clearing with a large swamp before them; the waters were infested with alligators.

Facing imminent danger in front and in back of them, the children were terrified. Some leaped into the swamp, others climbed trees, and some, paralyzed by fear, stood still, unable to move. The outcome was disastrous: while a number of the boys managed to escape, others were eaten alive by the alligators or taken captive and shot to death by the soldiers.

As I listened to Panther speak, I immediately thought of the epic biblical tale of the parting of the Sea of Reeds (Exod. 14–15). But unlike that mythical story, God did not intervene supernaturally on behalf of Panther and his companions. The waters did not split, the refugees did not cross over to safety, and the fighters did not drown in the swamp. There was no singing, dancing, or jubilation among the surviving Lost Boys. In fact, Panther's reflection, though certainly not intended as such, made the Exodus narrative feel hollow.

I left the synagogue that evening dejected. Though I am not a literal believer in the Hebrew Bible, the symbolic power of Panther's story and the timing of the event in relation to Passover sent me into a theological tailspin.

Where was God in this story, and in the pursuit of justice? Could I, as a religious activist, develop a spiritual narrative that accounts for such instances of injustice? More importantly, could I help others— particularly those suffering from oppression and degradation—frame their experiences in meaningful theological terms?

A Turn to Tradition: Hasidic Inspiration

In attempting to respond to Panther's experience and regain something of my spiritual equilibrium, I turned to several Jewish sources (as rabbis tend to do) that have nurtured me over the years. One text that has been particularly important is a book called the *Kedushat Levi*. It is a collection of sermons on the weekly Torah portions and the Jewish holidays by the famed Hasidic master, Rabbi Levi Yitzhak of Berditchev (1740–1809).

What first attracted me to this text were the legends I had read about Levi Yitzhak in anthologies by Martin Buber and Elie Wiesel.[2] In story after story, the Berditchever (as he is affectionately called by Hasidim) is depicted as a person of great compassion, who supported and defended the poor and the downtrodden in his community. He seemed to embody a unique blend of mystical piety and righteous indignation. In exploring his sermons, I have found that this same spirit permeates his teachings.

The following is a translation of a brief homily from the *Kedushat Levi*[3] comparing and contrasting the revelatory experiences of the Israelites at the Sea of Reeds and at Mount Sinai. This sermon is not simply an explanation of these dramatic narratives, but a fascinating reflection on the roles God and humankind play in the creation of a just and compassionate society.

> "At the Sea of Reeds He appeared to them as a young man, and at Mount Sinai He appeared to them as an old man" (Pesikta Rabbati 21:5).
>
> Behold, the Holy Blessed One constricts [*metzamtzem*] Himself in the worlds. However, at the Sea of Reeds, where there was a change in nature, He was not garbed in the worlds, and the Children of Israel saw him unclothed. At Mount Sinai, however, the Holy Blessed One dressed Himself such that the worlds could maintain their natural existence.
>
> Now in the writings of Isaac Luria of blessed memory [1534–1572] clothing is associated with hair. That is why at the Sea of Reeds He appeared to them as a young man without facial hair—without any worldly garb—while when giving the Torah He revealed Himself to them as an old man with hair—dressed in the garb of the worlds. This is alluded to in the words of our sages of blessed memory: "At the Sea even the maidservant saw that which the prophet Ezekiel did not see"

(Mekhilta de Rabbi Ishmael, Shirata 3). For Ezekiel and the other prophets saw God clothed in the world, as it were, according to the measure of the worlds. But at the Sea, everyone saw God unclothed. However, at Sinai He had to garb Himself so that the Children of Israel would understand the Torah. That is why it is written [in the Rosh Hashanah liturgy], "You appeared in the cloud of Your glory"; that is to say, in clothing, by limiting His great light, for a cloud is a symbol of darkness... But does the liturgist explain why this was so? It is for this reason that he continues by saying, "... upon Your holy people to speak to them"; meaning, He needed to speak to them so that they would understand His holy words.

(Kedushat Levi, Yitro)

The Berditchever opens this imaginative text by stating that under ordinary circumstances, the Divine reveals the Divine Self to us subtly through the natural workings of the world. While God is present throughout the cosmos ("the worlds"), animating all of life, God is "garbed" or hidden within corporeality. However, at the Sea of Reeds, God revealed God's self to the Children of Israel in an extraordinary manner, by removing the worldly dress[4] and upsetting the rules of nature. Using the imagery from Pesikta Rabbati (an eighth- or ninth-century midrash for festivals and special sabbaths), Levi Yitzhak envisions God as a young warrior who, in Herculean fashion, boldly saved God's people and crushed their enemies, demonstrating God's supreme might to all.

The Berditchever then links this rabbinic image to a teaching from the kabbalist Isaac Luria about facial hair—another form of covering—explaining that at the Sea of Reeds God was beardless, unclothed, God's power uninhibited. So intense was God's presence at the Sea that even the maidservant—the simplest person among the Israelites—beheld a vision of God more brilliant than the apparitions of Ezekiel and all other Israelite prophets.

If the theophany at the Sea is a model of divine strength, then the theophany at the mountain is a model of divine restraint. Unlike the earlier revelation, God did not topple the natural order at Sinai. While God's descent upon the mountain caused it to smoke and quake (Exod. 19:18), the earth did not crumble under the weight of God's holy presence. Levi Yitzhak teaches that this revelation needed to be more deliberate than the previous one, because God's goal at Sinai was to communicate with the People of Israel (directly and through Moses), to share with them the sacred teachings of the Torah. Using the rabbinic and Lurianic texts to support his claim, Levi Yitzhak now envisions the Divine as a wise elder (with a long flowing beard) who understands the importance of self-limitation, *tsimtsum*,[5] in interacting with his youthful community. In symbolic terms, God was both "garbed" and "bearded" at Sinai, God's power bounded and measured.

In the concluding sentences of this sermon, the Berditchever turns to the Rosh Hashanah *mahzor* (prayer book) to further buttress his reading of the revelation at Sinai. Why did God appear to the Children of Israel in a dark cloud (Exod. 19:18)? The answer, states Levi Yitzhak, is found in the liturgical statement "to speak to them," meaning that the Divine "dressed" the Divine's self in the thickness of the cloud so that the Divine could communicate with the People of Israel without overwhelming them. While God's heroic actions at the Sea of Reeds may have been necessary to impress the Israelites and to astound any would-be foes, at Sinai God wished to provide God's people with the spiritual and ethical tools—Torah—to function as an increasingly independent community, no longer reliant on God's supernatural intervention in human affairs.

Reading Levi Yitzhak Today

Though Levi Yitzhak does not say so explicitly, there is an obvious theological question that motivates this sermon: if God performed great wonders for our ancient ancestors, why does God not do so today? The Berditchever's answer is that while the Divine acted supernaturally for Israel in its infancy, God intended this only as a short-term arrangement. It was God's plan from the outset of creation to slowly recede from the foreground of history and allow people to grow as independent actors, capable of fashioning their own lives without the aid of miracles. Just as God grew from being a young man at the Sea to an old man at Sinai, so Israel was to undergo an extensive maturation process.

This is, in fact, a central theme in the *Kedushat Levi*. It is no wonder that the only sermons this preacher published in his own lifetime were on the holidays of Hanukkah and Purim, the two festivals in which human heroes—Mattathius and his sons, and Queen Esther and Mordechai—take center stage, while God is seemingly absent.

I find much of Levi Yitzhak's presentation resonant with my own life experience.[6] While I do not believe that the Divine ever performed supernatural feats for Israel or anybody else, I do believe that God is both the Creator and Sustainer of all life. Experiencing such natural phenomena as sunsets, oceans, and snowfall, I sense the Divine at work in the world. Interacting with my children, I feel God's presence in our midst. One of my favorite prayers is the Yotzer blessing in which we say, "In [God's] goodness [God] renews daily, perpetually, the work of creation." Importantly, this liturgical statement affirms not only God's creative power, but also God's goodness. The Divine is not a mad scientist or a solipsistic artist, but a loving Spirit who enters into the creative process in order to share God's goodness with all of creation. It is no accident that the Yotzer blessing is followed by the prayer Ahavah Rabbah, which opens with the words, "With abounding love have You loved us YHWH our God," and continues by speaking of our desire to emulate the Divine by living as loving and responsible beings, guided by the teachings of the Torah.

Among the deepest expressions of God's love and respect for humankind is the gift of free will. With this gift, we are invited to participate with the Divine in the establishment of a caring and equitable world. However, in order for us to live as free beings, God must restrain God's self so that people can make independent choices—even when these choices harm others and ourselves.

The plight of the Lost Boys reminds me of a statement by Rabbi Abraham Joshua Heschel (a direct descendent of Levi Yitzhak of Berditchev) about the Holocaust: "The question about Auschwitz is not where was God, but where was man." Heschel, an Eastern European refugee who lost most of his family in the Holocaust, refused to blame the Divine for the barbaric actions of the Nazis and their collaborators, and for the inaction of all those throughout the world who stood idly by.

Translating this point back into the Berditchever's language, I would say that to live "after Sinai" means that we must recognize that God will not swoop in, like at the Sea of Reeds, and destroy the

Pharaoh-like forces that embitter our lives. The Divine may inspire, agitate, and comfort (from within a state of *tsimtsum*), but human beings must act to create a just and compassionate world, minimizing the pain and suffering of all God's creations.

Protest, Mystery, and Faith

While this Hasidic text was very helpful to me in responding to Panther's story and to other cases of human misconduct, I also recognize that it offers but a partial answer to the larger question of theodicy.[7] Rabbi David Wolpe articulates the issue clearly:

> For there are catastrophes we have not made and cannot stop, such as disease and natural disaster. Even were all human wickedness to be blamed upon us alone (and that too can be questioned, for we did not fashion human nature), there is still a large residue of suffering that is certainly not the fault of humanity.[8]

The matter was not lost on Levi Yitzhak of Berditchev. According to legend, one Yom Kippur eve, just before the *Kol Nidre* service, the great rabbi stood before the ark and spoke these words: "Master of the Universe, I come before You on behalf of my community, as I do every year, seeking forgiveness for the sins we have committed against You. But in the past year we have caused no deaths—we have brought no plagues, no earthquakes, and no floods upon the earth. God, You have done these things, not us. Perhaps You should ask us for forgiveness." After pausing for a moment to wipe the tears from his eyes, the Berditchever continued, "But since You are God and we are mere mortals, we have no choice but to pray." With that, the rabbi began the *Kol Nidre* service.[9]

Like Levi Yitzhak, I am often confounded by the ways of the Divine. I do not know why people are stricken with cancer or are swept away by tsunamis. Is God unwilling or unable to prevent these tragedies? Are they a part of an inscrutable divine plan? And yet, despite my feelings of confusion, anger, and disappointment, I continue to believe in a loving, ethical, and powerful God, clinging to the notion that, as Heschel put it, there is "a meaning beyond mystery."

What I do know is that we human beings cannot allow questions of theology to paralyze us. Even if we are uncertain about the nature of our Divine partner, we must still uphold our half of the partnership. Inspired by the teachings of the Torah and other great sources of wisdom, I continue my work as a religious activist, listening carefully for the still, small voice of the Divine urging me forth in my efforts to help mend the world.[10]

Preaching What I Practice
The Power of Jewish Organizing

MARGIE KLEIN

Margie Klein is a student at the Rabbinical School of Hebrew College and the founder and leader of Moishe House Boston: Kavod Jewish Social Justice House. A graduate of Yale University, she founded and directed Project Democracy, a youth voting project that mobilized 97,000 college students to vote in the 2004 election.

It takes a certain amount of chutzpah to believe that you are linked with the fate of all oppressed peoples of the world, when you have never personally experienced any similar hardship. But that is how I was educated at the Abraham Joshua Heschel School in New York City, where we learned about civil rights in social studies class, the fair distribution of wealth in math class, and business ethics in Talmud class, not to mention our lunchtime Jewish environmental club.

Upon graduating from the Heschel School in eighth grade, I expected the wider Jewish community's primary focus to be social justice. So it seemed strange to me that while we talked about ethics all the time at my synagogue, people were either uninvolved in social justice or their commitment was disconnected from their synagogue life. I started shopping around, attending synagogues and Jewish communal gatherings all over the city, and was surprised at how few offered social justice programs. I was able to make peanut butter and jelly sandwiches at the Jewish Community Center (JCC) or attend a park cleanup with a Reform congregation in Brooklyn, but these activities did not feel like the real deal.

Though I couldn't explain it then, what I was discovering was the difference between direct service and social justice. When I began volunteering regularly in soup kitchens, I couldn't help but notice that week after week, I served the same people bread and soup, without offering any path that might help them overcome their difficult circumstances. I was glad to serve, but I often felt discouraged that my volunteering was doing little to narrow the wide economic gap between our guests and me. I feared that my service did more to assuage my own liberal guilt than to create the kind of social change that would significantly impact our guests' lives. And though I learned a great deal from our guests, I had suspected that our efforts only heightened our experience of inequality, repeatedly reinforcing that they needed us, but not vice versa.

As I learned from a rabbinical student who worked at the soup kitchen with me, Maimonides tells us that the highest level of *tzedakah* is to help the poor become financially independent, so that they no longer must ask for or take charity (*Mishneh Torah*, Laws of Gifts to the Poor 10:7–14). That sounded good, but, I asked myself, how could we translate that lofty goal into more effective volunteer work? How could I move from direct service, with its focus on mitigating an individual's hardships, to social justice, which would address the source of those hardships? And what would social justice look like in a Jewish context?

From Direct Service to Grassroots Organizing

I first learned how to do grassroots organizing[1] from Ella Dunkins[2] when I was a leader with the Yale Hunger and Homelessness Action Project (YHHAP). Ella visited our weekly meeting in New Haven, Connecticut, to tell us about Mothers for Justice, a group of formerly homeless women who advocated on behalf of families and children. Speaking with the quiet power of someone who has been through more than she cares to describe, Ella explained that she had personally experienced hunger and homelessness, and believed that she and her peers should have a significant role in solving the problems that faced her community.

Ella told us that her group was working to pass the New Haven Child Poverty Referendum, a law that would compel the city to spend more money on affordable housing, food pantries, food stamps for women with children, and after-school programs. When she was finished explaining the details of the referendum, she said simply, "We need your help. People won't listen if it's only us. We need you to win."

Exhilarated to find a project that might profoundly better people's lives, the leaders of YHHAP and I pledged our support to Ella and Mothers for Justice. We spent the next two months coalition-building, calling on and canvassing every neighborhood of New Haven, and working closely with people the referendum would affect most. When Election Day arrived, the referendum won with over 90 percent of the vote. I could hardly believe it. We had seen a problem and helped to solve it in a way that might actually make a difference in people's lives. When I saw Ella the next week, I expected her to want to reflect on our victory. Instead, she was ready to talk about the next campaign, and I realized I was, too. It was as if, in experiencing our own power, Ella and I learned that winning was a possibility, and that gave us the ability to dream of even bigger victories.

The Child Poverty Referendum campaign gave me the strength to believe that I could influence the policies that affect my life and the lives of others. More powerful still was the recognition that by striving for a common goal, two disparate groups were able to form a community where everyone counted. Ella had articulated the problem as "We need your help." But we needed Ella's help, too. Ella allowed us to participate in creating the kind of city we wanted to live in, and to be part of a community that supported our values. By working together, we not only have strength in numbers but also strength in solidarity, strength in community.

Sanctifying Our Work

In college, my social justice work was disconnected from my Judaism. While my experience as a child at the Heschel School sparked my interest in social justice, I struggled to integrate Jewish learning and ritual observance into my life as an adult. Like most Jews, I knew Judaism was firmly grounded in a commitment to justice—Torah tells us, "Justice, justice, shall you pursue" (Deut. 16:20). But I didn't know which aspects of the Jewish tradition would add meaning and power to my work.

After graduating from college, I became a full-time environmental organizer. My work took me to the Midwest and the South, places without large Jewish communities, so I began hosting Shabbat dinners for my activist friends. Though most people at the dinners were not Jewish, we were all hungry for an ethical and/or spiritual framework on which to place our desire to improve the world, and for inspiration to keep us going when our work got tough.

One night, I decided to adapt a ritual I'd seen in college, asking people to go around and each share one moment from their week that made them say, "Wow." I explained that if Shabbat is like a foretaste of a redeemed world, then we can get in the proper mind-set for Shabbat by remembering those brief moments in our week that felt redemptive. After each person shared a personal moment, he or she would pour a little wine from his or her individual Kiddush cup into the communal cup, so that by the time the cup went all the way around the table, it was overflowing with sacred memories.

The ritual was powerful because it allowed us to understand our own lives in dialogue with generations of people longing for a better world. It also gave us a way to reflect on the week and talk about what was meaningful about our work. The ritual helped build community and made people feel that each of us mattered. We also began to understand that one of the functions of memory is to empower us to keep going—we learned to retell our stories in order to give ourselves strength when victories were few and far between.

Where once Shabbat had been the "Jewish part" of our week, the Kiddush ritual helped us integrate our political and Jewish lives, so that our workweek became "Jewish time" that built up to Shabbat. Conversely, Shabbat allowed us to remember the purpose of our work: the creation of a just and compassionate world, in which all people can celebrate life's bounty with friends and loved ones.

Religious and Progressive

As it turned out, my attempts to integrate my religious and political lives mirrored the actions of other activists around the country. Members of the Christian Right had been working on this project for years. Meanwhile, those of us on the Religious Left and in the Jewish world were just getting started.

The value of incorporating religious belief into political organizing became clear to me as I traveled the country on behalf of Project

Democracy, a national nonpartisan group I co-founded to mobilize college students to vote. In speaking to hundreds of students about their values and attitudes toward voting, I found that contrary to popular belief they were not apathetic. Rather, many students remained uninvolved in politics and justice work because they felt disempowered and confused about how they could make a difference.

In addition, many students saw a great deal of hypocrisy in politics and were not sure where to look for moral authority, and who to trust in deciding which candidates or issues to support. This was especially the case in the Midwest and the South, where the loudest moral voices were those of right-wing Christian clergy, who asserted that the key moral issues of the election lay in personal choices related to sex—specifically, abortion and gay marriage. Whether or not they felt strongly about these particular issues, many students, too, assumed that these were the key moral issues of the election and were not sure what weight to give their other concerns—such as poverty, global warming, war, and genocide.

In contrast to the Republicans and the Religious Right, the Democrats and progressive nonprofits generally ceded the morality debate and promoted their social justice and environmental policies from a practical and personal standpoint. For example, on economic justice issues, one heard messages such as, "Democrats will create policies that will ensure better wages for American workers. You want better wages, don't you? And, even if you are happy with your wages, poverty breeds violence! Our policies will make your streets safer!"

Whether it was the lack of a moral language or the fear of sounding uncritically religious, progressive leaders did not sufficiently articulate social justice issues as moral issues. They shied away from talking about the values at stake. For me, this seemed morally disingenuous and strategically ruinous. Why shouldn't we be upfront that our campaigning for a living wage is grounded in the belief that every person deserves to be treated with dignity? To paraphrase the Rev. Martin Luther King, Jr., I cannot be what I ought to be until you are what you ought to be. From a Christian perspective, King and other religious leaders of the civil rights movement taught that emulating Jesus meant caring for the poor and marginalized in society and working to change the systems that dehumanize them. In Jewish terms, if every person is created in the Divine image, then mistreating a worker is a desecration of God.

Stepping Up

I had high hopes that our efforts would turn the country around, so when Election Day came, I was devastated by the outcome. Although Project Democracy tripled our goal and mobilized 97,000 students to vote, any pride I might have felt at our group's success was overshadowed by my sense that our country was heading in the wrong direction.

On November 4, 2004, two days after the election, I wrote my application essay for rabbinical school. Although I had no real desire to leave politics, I felt that I couldn't face the many student leaders I had trained unless I did everything in my power to bring about long-term change. I had been complaining for months about how rarely I saw religious communities organizing around social justice and environmental issues. I kept waiting for someone else to speak up—but then I realized that, of all the political organizers I knew, I was the most religious. It's time, I thought, for me to step up and start preaching what I practice.

After two years of rabbinical school, I now more fully understand the kinship with marginalized people I sensed as a young girl. The Torah reminds us repeatedly to treat the stranger with dignity because we were once strangers in Egypt (Exod. 22:21). The Jewish experience of oppression and degradation over the centuries compels us to act on behalf of others who are unable to act for themselves, or with others who need our support. However, as Jethro advised an overwhelmed Moses, we must share the burden of our work and not try to shoulder it alone. Like the ancient Israelites, who each brought personalized donations to the *Mishkan* (Tabernacle), we must create communities of action in which every person is valued and given an opportunity to contribute meaningfully to the cause.

Finally, like the great prophets in our tradition, we must cultivate a vision of redemption. In the midst of the darkest times, we must likewise envision a better world and prepare to make it so, even though it seems irrational to believe in transformative change. When we cultivate a vision, share it with others, and use our collective power to compel decision-makers to make the right choices, we ennoble ourselves—and we really can win.

Organizing is a self-fulfilling prophesy, or, as I like to think of it, meeting God halfway in the work of creating a just world. Each day, each week on Shabbat, each year on Passover, we must remember that we are always in a moment of possibility, and together we can change the world.

The Legacy of Abraham Joshua Heschel

Jewish Spirituality and Political Transformation

RABBI MICHAEL LERNER, PhD

Rabbi Michael Lerner, PhD, is the editor of *Tikkun* (www.tikkun.org), rabbi of Beyt Tikkun synagogue in San Francisco and Berkeley, national chair of the interfaith Network of Spiritual Progressives (www.spiritualprogressives.org), and author of many books, including *Jewish Renewal* and most recently *The Left Hand of God: Healing America's Political and Spiritual Crisis*.

Abraham Joshua Heschel (1907–1972) was for many Jews in the West the most inspiring Jewish theologian of the twentieth century, revitalizing our understanding of Shabbat (in *The Sabbath*), our understanding of revelation (in *God in Search of Man*), and providing a powerful new reading of Jewish philosophy (in *The Prophets* and in *Who Is Man?*). Yet he was also an inspiring civil rights activist, marching in solidarity with Martin Luther King, Jr., and taking a lead in the anti-Vietnam War movement.

Heschel, like the ancient Hebrew prophets about whom he wrote so passionately, proposed a unique synthesis: a politics that was rooted in God and the spiritual wisdom of the ages, yet committed to the human rights vision that had been most clearly articulated in Western societies. Heschel was not moved merely by God's voice in the Bible to align himself with the social justice and peace movements; he was also insistent on bringing into those movements the voice and consciousness of a spiritual wisdom that roared through the words of the prophets. He understood that the political movements of Western societies, lacking a mooring in a transcendent vision of the universe and of the meaning of human life, were one-dimensional and hence unlikely to ultimately have the capacity to achieve the transformations of society that they justifiably sought.

For the Hebrew prophets and for Heschel, their articulator in contemporary terms, the problem was not only the denial of social justice or peace, but it was also the denial of the fundamental spiritual truth of the universe: that God, the Creator of heaven and earth, has a stake in human life; that the separation of politics from spirit is a distortion of Jewish teachings; and that the murder that we politely call "war" and the oppression we politely call "inequality" are violations of the spirit of God embodied in every single person, and a wild misunderstanding of the nature of reality.

Heschel's classic work, *The Prophets*, seeks to demonstrate that one of Judaism's central contributions to humanity was precisely its integration of spirituality and the struggle for equality and justice. Yet Heschel goes far beyond that, and his worldview and teachings are a challenge to secular liberals allergic to spiritual sensibilities as well as to political conservatives.

For many liberals, progressives, Democratic Party operatives, and elected officials, and for the people who fill the liberal and progressive think tanks and magazines, human beings are best conceptualized as individuals who are adorned with a set of rights, and the task of social movements is to ensure that those rights that have been systematically undermined by the capitalist marketplace or by the irrational acts of individuals or state institutions get reinstated through some combination of popular movements, government regulations, and new laws. This was the legacy of the New Deal.

In the 1960s and 1970s, that agenda was expanded to focus on those who had been left out of the wealth that Western societies had amassed at the expense of the Third World: women, African-Americans, gays and lesbians, and Western minority groups. The New Left demanded inclusion in the material well-being and political rights that had been achieved by many. This is important work, and of course I fully support it, as did Heschel.

In the 1980s and 1990s, however, most of the existing Jewish establishments abandoned these goals and began to redefine their primary interests around support for Israeli policy and resistance to the anti-Semitism (real or perceived) that those policies were generating in the world. In response, frustrated young Jews in the 1990s and early twenty-first century created new institutions or ethnically Jewish organizations that cite the works of Heschel and reclaim the commitment to "rights" and "inclusion" that was largely abandoned by the organized Jewish community (with the sparkling exception of the Religious Action Center of Reform Judaism).

Tikkun magazine, which began in the darkest days of the Reagan Administration in 1986, is proud to have been founded as a voice for Jewish liberals and progressives and for those who were turned off by the materialism, spiritual deadness, conformism, and blind loyalty to whatever policies were being supported by the Israeli government. It was the first major location in the Jewish world where Jewish feminists, GLBT, environmental, peace, social justice, and human rights activists and Israeli peaceniks could publicly discuss their joint concerns, both in the magazine and in frequent Tikkun Community conferences and weekend seminars. As we enter our twenty-second year in 2008, these activities continue. These projects are an important element in what *Tikkun* means when we talk about "healing and transforming the world." Although we've been critical of how the notion of *tikkun olam* has sometimes been appropriated by groups of Jewish liberals to mean little more than doing hands-on charity work to repair some of the worst damage caused by the competitive global market, but not really engaging in developing strategies for how to fundamentally change the larger social and economic systems of the planet that are the cause of the pains that then require so many bandages, we've never denied the importance and nobility of doing the "bandage work" that some of the new liberal or progressive Jewish groups embrace.

In my years as a student, then later as a friend and colleague of A. J. Heschel in the antiwar movement, we often talked about the importance of linking our specifically Jewish struggles with those of our Christian neighbors. Heschel became one of the national chairs of the interfaith Clergy and Laity Concerned about the War in Vietnam, recently resurrected as Clergy and Laity Concerned about the War in Iraq.

So it was natural for *Tikkun* magazine, which from the beginning saw itself as an inheritor of the Heschelian tradition, to see ourselves not only as a Jewish voice, but also, and increasingly in recent years, as an interfaith voice for *tikkun olam*. Heschel taught me to read God's word to Isaiah, "My house shall be called a House of Prayer for All Nations" (Isa. 56:1) as an injunction that Jewish ethical issues that concern the entire world should often be done in an interfaith context. If we wish an end to poverty, if we want environmental sanity, if we seek peace and social justice, we can do this as Jews, unashamedly bringing our Jewish vision into larger interfaith organizations.

Unfortunately, for many of the newly emerging Jewish liberal and progressive organizations, what makes them Jewish is just that they recruit Jews around a politics that is fundamentally indistinguishable in orientation from the non-Jewish organizations working on the same issues, and their only addition is to bring in some biblical or Talmudic quotations to bolster their commitment. When entering into larger coalitions, the primary thing they can offer are Jews, but not a specifically Jewish perspective, certainly nothing close to what Heschel and the prophets sought to encourage: a unity between a spiritual vision of a world that elicits awe and wonder and radical amazement and a universe to which we respond to the Ineffable not only by prayer but also by acts of kindness and love and generosity. Indeed, it is very hard to find a Jewish organization outside of *Tikkun* that talks about these spiritual issues in a public way that includes the Jewish demand not just for fairness (John Rawls's formulation of justice[1]), but also for love, for kindness, for generosity, and for awe and wonder at the grandeur of the universe. Too often Jewish organizations are merely cheerleaders for the same policies that the liberal world pursues, using the same language, and constrained by the same demand to be "realistic" and avoid utopian (which is to say, religious visionary) discourse, and little more.

But when we turned to the non-Jewish "religious Left" we found the same problem. Too often the most famous spokespeople for the mainstream (that is, Christian) Left function as cheerleaders for this same rights-and-inclusion-oriented liberal/progressive agenda, providing quotations from the Bible or other religious texts to show that the liberal agenda really squares with or even emanates from the texts of the tradition. Of course, right-wingers have their texts as well. I've argued in my book *Jewish Renewal* that both a hopeful and a fearful voice is predominant in all of us; the voice we respond to is not necessarily what is mandated by the texts, because in the texts both sensibilities can be found. So there is a built-in limit on the value of what the religious Left can offer the liberal/progressive movement.

Heschel had a much deeper agenda, because he understood that the fundamental alienation in our society is not only about the deprivation of material goods and political rights. Without for a moment abandoning the struggle for rights and inclusion, Heschel tried to focus our attention on the deeper spiritual crisis that comes from being alienated from the spiritual core of our being, an alienation that he rightly understood to be endemic in the money- and power-oriented societies constructed in the West. His sometimes romanticized accounts of Eastern European Jews were meant to supplement his more rigorous account of the "bottom line" of Western societies, the frenetic pursuit of power and wealth and domination that goes under the name of "progress" or "productivity" or "rationality" or "efficiency." Heschel tried to show that the West's bottom line of money and power was not the only possible reality, and that the world could be radically reconstructed in relationship to our rediscovered connection to the ultimate spiritual reality of the universe.

Although *Tikkun* magazine became famous first for our role as a voice for all those who believed that Israel's policies toward Palestinians were both immoral and self-destructive, our founding statement made clear that our goal was at least equally to change the liberal and progressive forces so that they could understand the way that spiritual needs were central to the American public. We have long argued that the failure to address those needs by the Left (Jewish, interfaith, and secular) has made it possible for the Right to become the major force articulating the hunger that many Americans have for a life connected to a higher meaning and for a world that makes it easier to build lasting, loving relationships. The Right's economic and political agenda has appropriated and distorted those needs, yet it has recognized, however, that these needs are not only legitimate but also an indispensable element for many Americans, whose primary source of pain is not the deprivation of money but the deprivation of meaning and deep love.

What *Tikkun* understood, and the Left (Jewish, interfaith, and secular alike) doesn't yet "get," is that lasting social change can only be won with building a politics that speaks not only to peace, environmental sanity, rights, and inclusion but also to the hunger for meaning. We want to be recognized as beings who are not here on this planet to be "used" for others' purposes, but who are intrinsically valuable and embodiments of the sacred. We long to be supported rather than undermined for our capacities to be loving and generous; we long for a world that is valued not only as a necessary "resource" for human survival but also as a sacred mystery, the understanding of which requires both science and song, awe and experimentation, joyful celebration and humility.

So *Tikkun*, moving in the spirit of Heschel, concluded that America needs a different kind of political movement today, a movement of spiritual progressives, a movement that can clearly articulate the deprivation of meaning, of our alienation from our own selves as created in the image of God and yearning for a reconnection to the God of the universe, a deprivation that is built into and reinforced by every aspect of the economic and political order in which we live. Heschel's warning to liberals became the founding notion of a new interfaith national organization, The Network of Spiritual Progressives, sponsored by *Tikkun*: "The most urgent task is to destroy the myth that accumulation of wealth and the achievement of comfort are the chief vocations of man. How can adjustment to society be an inspiration to our youth if that society persists in squandering the material resources of the world on luxuries in a world where more than a billion people go to bed hungry every night? How can we speak of reverence or the belief that all men are created equal without repenting for the way we promote the vulgarization of existence?"[2]

At *Tikkun* and The Network of Spiritual Progressives, we've turned Heschel's words into a spiritual progressive agenda through programs like our New Bottom Line and Global Marshall Plan. Much more visionary than any other plan currently under consideration by liberals or the Left, the Global Marshall Plan dedicates between 1 to 2 percent of the Gross Domestic Product of the United States and other advanced industrial countries every year for the next twenty years to once and for all end global poverty, homelessness, hunger, inadequate health care, and inadequate education, and to repair the global environment.[3] This vision, actually quite reformist in its first articulation, can only work with a spiritual transformation of the fundamental values that drive Western societies. It's also the best strategy for dealing with immigration (by creating a world in which there is plenty of economic prosperity so that people no longer feel that they must cross borders to get to the only place where they could make a decent living for their families). In my book *Healing Israel/Palestine*, I apply this same spiritual consciousness to provide a path for lasting peace between Israel and Palestine. Spiritual consciousness is the necessary foundation for any global environmental movement to succeed.

Honoring Heschel is not about taking a few selected quotations to bolster our own individual projects—it is about creating a spiritual politics that embodies not only the social justice and peace consciousness of our prophets, our mystics, and our poets, but also their vision of a world permeated with and part of the God of the Universe. I'd be happy to hear your responses to this vision and work with you to implement it: please contact me at RabbiLerner@tikkun.org.

Religious Leadership and Politics

RABBI DAVID SAPERSTEIN

Rabbi David Saperstein has served as the director of the Religious Action Center for Reform Judaism for over thirty years. He co-chairs the Coalition to Preserve Religious Liberty and serves on the boards of numerous national organizations, including the NAACP and People for the American Way. In 1999, Saperstein was elected as the first chair of the U.S. Commission on International Religious Freedom.

Social justice has been central to the ethos, culture, and program of American Jewish life, serving as the most common organizing principle of Jewish identity. Academics have probed the economic, cultural, political, and historical factors that drive this passion; pollsters have charted it; politicians have tapped into it. I want to focus, however, on an indispensable player in American Jewish engagement with social justice: the rabbi, particularly the congregational rabbi. In part because of the strong religious underpinning of the Jewish commitment to *tikkun olam* and in part because of the distinct role of the American congregational clergy in public affairs, rabbis have played, and will continue to play, a leading role in shaping, leading, and maintaining this dynamic.

Social Justice and the Religious Worldview

Over and above its sociological and economic sources, the American Jewish commitment to social justice owes much to the powerful intersection of three religious sources. The first is derived from the texts of traditional Judaism. From Torah text, we can cite the revolutionary social justice implications of Sinai and God's call to us to be a holy people (Leviticus 19). Judaism began as *ethical* monotheism.

These biblical injunctions led to the prophetic tradition, with its mix of particularistic and universal expressions of social justice. They led to the rabbinic Halachic creation, in Talmudic times, of one of the world's first social welfare societies. They animated 1,500 years of remarkable communal charitable undertakings in the self-governing Jewish community that, in some areas of the world, only finally ended in the Holocaust.[1]

Second, grafted onto the classic God-mandated call to justice and peace was the advent of the Age of Reason. Whatever the rationalists' views of God, almost all accepted and many taught that the most logical, hence most important, aspect of religion was its focus on ethics and justice. This emphasis on ethics enormously influenced many areas of Western thought, leading to both the social gospel tradition in Christianity and, in a very real sense, to the development of American democracy. America was the first nation born into the Age of Reason, based on principles its founders drew from their understanding of the Hebrew scriptures: the fundamental dignity, value, equality, and freedom of choice of all people. Their endorsement of free speech and publication, and the right to petition the government for redress of grievances, shaped a society that welcomed us in our historic task of speaking truth to power.

Within the Jewish tradition, the Age of Reason gave rise to Reform, Conservative, and Reconstructionist Judaism (and significantly influenced Orthodox Judaism as well). These denominations flourished in America, creating a distinctly American Judaism that drew—and draws—religious energy from its focus on social justice. In the synthesis of our Jewish and America identities, including our shared belief in the perfectibility of human society and our embrace of a central role of the public sector in creating a more just and compassionate society, our religious expressions of social justice found societal and cultural affirmation. As the twentieth-century liberal expansion of our fundamental rights led to a more open and accepting America, the commitment to be involved in shaping a better world was embraced by American Jewry.

JUDAISM, JUSTICE, AND AMERICAN LIFE

More recently, a third source of religious legitimacy strengthening the American Jewish community's engagement with social justice has come from a renewed interest in those manifestations of religion that bring existential fulfillment to our individual and communal lives. Here, the concern is less with God's commandments per se, less with pure logic or reason, and more with our "quest for meaning" as the lodestone of religious legitimacy. That quest for meaning finds answers from many sources, among them the impact of our societal and cultural values and priorities. One key impact of America's sharing of our Jewish social justice values and its welcoming of our self-perceived role of being a light to the nations was to existentially affirm, legitimize, and strengthen our individual and communal Jewish identity through the work of *tikkun olam*.

American Jewry is an amalgam of these God-oriented, rationalist-oriented, and existentially oriented religious worldviews—each with its distinctive embrace of *tikkun olam*, each reinforcing and validating the other's focus on social justice.

Relatedly, there is our recent history—and how we have come to understand it. In the sobering wake of the Holocaust, we came to understand and believe that good people must never stand idly by while others are oppressed, persecuted, and victimized. Together with our contemporary understanding of the rabbinic rubric of *mipnei darkhei shalom* (that to ensure the goal of shalom in our communities, the social benefits to which Jews are entitled must be shared equitably with non-Jews in our communities), this historical imperative translated into the widespread belief that we Jews will never be safe, never secure, as long as we live in a world or society in which any group can be the victim of persecution, oppression, discrimination, or deprivation. Social justice involvement thereby became a matter not only of Jewish morality and values but of Jewish self-interest as well, thus strengthening our communal commitment to social justice. Imbued by the lessons of our history and the convergence of these religious sources, it is no wonder, then, that studies for two generations have found that involvement in social justice is the leading expression of Jewish identity among American Jewry, outstripping even support for Israel and involvement in Jewish ritual and worship.

Rabbi as Social Justice Interpreter

In the twentieth century—and particularly in America—the rabbi emerged as the primary interpreter of these religious and historical social justice imperatives. This was a largely new development in Jewish history. In the past, while the rabbis set the Halachic norms of social justice, it was frequently the lay leaders who played key roles in what today we would call social justice activities. It was generally lay leaders who in freer societies became involved in politics, particularly politics outside the community (think of the Court Jew, of Hasdai Ibn Shaprut or Shmuel Hanagid in the Golden Age of Spain, or of the lay *va'adot*, who were so influential in self-governing Jewish communities for a thousand years). In twentieth-century Jewish life, this long tradition continued in the strong lay leadership involved in a broad array of social justice endeavors (for example, of the national defense organizations, women's organizations, and pro-Israel groups, and in the growth of the federation system and its remarkable social service networks; outside the structures of the community, it was similarly manifest in the disproportionate role played by Jews in every battle for social justice: labor, civil rights, women's rights, civil liberties, etc.). But now the rabbi emerged as an influential public player as well—not just as an arbiter of Jewish law on communal issues, but as a major communal spokesperson and, within our communal life, as a source of much of the energy behind this social justice passion.

For the Age of Reason had changed the role of the rabbi. As Jews entered the outside world, the model of the Christian clergy's communal leadership influenced the Jewish community as well. The rabbi became the interpreter of outside life to Jews and the spokesperson for the Jewish community to the Christian world and general community. The rabbi became the articulator of Jewish religion, values, and history as they applied to contemporary social justice concerns.[2] The social justice focus of towering rabbinic figures like Stephen S. Wise, Emil Hirsch, Arthur Hertzberg, Jacob Weinstein, Emanuel Rackman, Walter Wurzburger, Abraham Joshua Heschel, Roland Gittelsohn, Balfour Brickner, Maurice Eisendrath, Harold Schulweis, and Alexander Schindler set the rabbinic standard in the twentieth century.

In turn, the rabbi's role in communal leadership led rabbis to intensify the social justice aspects of Jewish ritual life and holiday celebration. Holiday observances now emphasized social justice themes. The seder became the template for battles for equality and civil rights in America and abroad. Hanukkah became the template for religious liberty and national liberation struggles. The Reform and Reconstructionist movements changed the High Holy Day Torah readings to emphasize social justice themes, along with expanding the already strong social justice themes of the traditional Shabbat and weekday liturgy.

The focus on social justice was also translated, by congregational rabbis, into direct service in their shuls. Beginning in the 1950s, social justice activity became a mainstay of synagogue youth groups, both capturing and intensifying the young's social idealism; in the same period, the emergence of the congregational social action committee became a well-accepted part of synagogue life. All this was led by the rabbis. Leonard Fein's MAZON was embraced by much of the rabbinate and made a part of Jewish celebratory life. "Mitzvah" (i.e., social justice) projects became a normative part of the bar/bat mitzvah experience.

Rabbinic Responsibilities

The rabbi's distinctive and indispensable role in keeping the flame of social justice burning brightly generation after generation comes with its own set of responsibilities. The rabbi is now expected to take on the responsibility for community relations leadership, representing the Jewish community and its values to the broader world; to shape effective social justice programming in our synagogues, including both direct service and broader society-wide organizing work; and to use the power of the pulpit to preach and teach about social justice challenges.

But with these responsibilities comes the need for effective skills training—both in rabbinic seminary education and in the continuing education that rabbis can experience while working in congregations, Hillels, and Jewish organizations. For decades, our rabbinic seminaries and organizations did little to provide this training, with the main exception being the Religious Action Center's rabbinic student and rabbinic training seminars (in which some eight hundred rabbis have participated since the 1960s). In the past decade, far more opportunities for train-ing have developed across the entire spectrum of our religious streams. There are more electives; some seminaries now have required courses in social justice and direct service; direct service opportunities are part of ongoing seminary life; partnerships with outside groups such as Jewish Funds for Justice (with its emphasis on community organizing skills), American Jewish World Service, PANIM, and local Jewish social justice organizations have enhanced training options. (The Religious Action Center is launching the Brickner Rabbinic Seminar and Fellowship Program to further strengthen such efforts to support rabbis in the field.)

Less common has been the full integration of social justice themes, study, and skills into the core curriculum of most of the semi-naries.[3] More needs to be and can be done. Consider the skills rabbis need in the three areas of responsibility mentioned above.

Community Relations Leadership Skills

Every rabbi who serves a congregation (and many who serve in organi-zational capacities) is considered a "Jewish leader" by the general com-munity and a "spokesperson" for the Jewish community. Indeed, in smaller communities, the synagogues are often the only Jewish institu-tion in town, and the rabbi is the figurehead of the Jewish community.

Rabbis need skills training to know how politicians and the public view rabbis, how they can be effective advocates, and what political- and electoral-related activities are permitted them, whether as congregational rabbis or as individuals. They need to know how to deal with the press and how to build coalitions with a variety of religious and ethnic groups, some raising special challenges. They need to know how to respond when the mayor asks for support on an issue or when faced with an anti-Semitic incident in their community, when they need to interpret events in Israel for their community, and how to deal with their own dif-ferences with Israeli government policy, should such differences exist.

Social Justice Programming

In most congregations, rabbis are the professionals most involved in social justice programming. How do they put together a strong pro-gram? How do they recruit people and sustain their interest? How do they deal with the phenomenon of members who play out their social justice involvement, professionally or as volunteers, outside the synagogue but are reluctant to do so within? How do they deal with political differences within the membership or board of the synagogue? What are the rabbi and the synagogue permitted to do politically without jeopardizing the synagogue's 501c(3) tax exemption? When, how, by what process, and in whose name should a rabbi or a social action committee speak out on controversial issues? How should a synagogue or a rabbi balance the five basic types of social justice programming (educating the synagogue or broader community on issues, providing social services, community organizing, legislative advocacy, and *tzedakah*)?

Social Justice Sermons and Teaching

Almost all rabbis give sermons or adult education programs (many fairly frequently) on social justice themes and on pressing public policy concerns facing their nation, Israel, their local communities, or the Jewish people. What kind of training do we give that is specifically geared to helping them use this as an opportunity for rooting these concerns in Jewish texts and values? Considering that sermons on social justice or political topics are far more likely than most to alienate or provoke synagogue members, are the particular demands of social justice sermons discussed and analyzed in homiletics classes?

And how firmly are these issues, and the values needed to address them, rooted in the classes of our rabbinical schools? Do students have the requirement or even the opportunity to take a course on Judaism and contemporary moral problems? (One example: HUC–JIR professor Dr. Eugene B. Borowitz gave an elective in this for a couple of years and produced a wonderful book as a result of the classes.) More broadly, do our rabbinic courses:

- Lift out the social justice themes in primary text study?
- Explore how Jewish communities historically addressed similar social and political concerns?
- Examine how Jewish philosophy addressed ethics and social justice themes?
- Study important strands of Jewish ethical literature?

- Promote educational techniques to incorporate the message of social justice into our religious schools, youth groups, and adult education curricula?

Just to state an obvious but important point, as cantors and educators become involved in social justice education and programming, the need for training in these matters becomes equally crucial for them.

A century ago, when the rabbi was often one of the most educated people in the synagogue, a primary source and interpreter of Jewish news, and the expositor of a broad communal consensus on the social justice themes of Judaism, the role of social justice leader and spokesperson came naturally. Today, when synagogue members have the same access to the news of the Jewish world as the rabbi, when many members have graduate degrees matching or exceeding those of the rabbi, and when the centrality of social justice has been balanced with the growth of other manifestations of Jewish life, a rabbi's authority will come only through the rabbi's skills and the rabbi's training in rooting these social justice ideals in Jewish values that flow from our tradition, philosophy, texts, and rituals. For rabbis of the twenty-first century to remain a goad to the conscience of the Jewish community and the larger American community, they will need seminaries and organizations committed to providing the training and skills that support them firmly in that leadership tradition.

As we look toward this new century, it should be clear that if the Judaism we offer our community and our young does not speak to the great moral issues of their lives, their country, and their world, it will fail to capture their imagination or loyalty—and will fail to capture the authentic meaning of Judaism for our lives. The American rabbinate has helped shape such a rich Judaism in this past century; if in the next, Judaism will indeed thrive as a light to the nations, it will be in large measure due to the creativity and inspiration emanating from a skilled and prepared rabbinate able to enhance the Jewish people's commitment to *tikkun olam*.

PART II
RENEWING CREATION: JUDAISM AND THE ENVIRONMENT

Rereading Genesis
Human Stewardship of the Earth

ELLEN BERNSTEIN

Ellen Bernstein founded Shomrei Adamah, Keepers of the Earth, in 1988, the first national Jewish environmental organization; she is author of *The Splendor of Creation* and serves as a consultant for the Society for the Protection of Nature in Israel. Bernstein also edited *Ecology & the Jewish Spirit: Where Nature & the Sacred Meet* (Jewish Lights). To find out more about her work, visit www.ellenbernstein.org.

And God blessed them and God said to them, "Be fruitful and multiply and replenish the earth and master it, and have dominion over the fish of the sea and the flyer of the heaven, and every live creature that creeps on the earth." (Gen. 1:28)

In 1967, historian Lynn White argued in a now famous essay in *Science* magazine that the Bible gave humanity a mandate to exploit nature when it empowered the *adam*/human to "master the earth," and "have dominion over" it.[1] Many environmentalists and theologians are still haggling over White's thesis even after hundreds of articles and books have tackled the topic over the last thirty years.[2]

In my environmental studies courses at University of California—Berkeley in the early 1970s, we read White's article and were taught that the theology of the Bible laid the ideological roots for the current environmental crisis. I naively accepted this idea, having no real knowledge of the Bible and no positive experience of religion. It was comforting to find a scapegoat to blame for society's problems, and religion has always been an easy target.

White's interpretation of Genesis had enormous ramifications on a whole generation of environmentalists and their students. I still encounter people who challenge my work, insisting that Judaism couldn't possibly have ecological integrity because "the Bible encourages people to control nature." They shun organized religion, claiming that it is the source of the environmental problem.

It is conceivable that people who have little experience reading the Bible could examine this verse and decide that the language of "dominion" and "mastery over nature" is anti-ecological. But a verse is not a collection of words, just like nature is not a collection of plants and animals. Extracting a word or verse out of its context is like removing a tree from its habitat, taking it from the soil, the weather, and all the creatures with which it lives in total interdependence. It would be impossible to really know the tree outside of its relationships. It's no different with the Bible. When you read the Bible, you have to consider the derivation of the words under consideration, the meaning of the neighboring words and verses, the message of the Bible as a whole, the context in which it was written, and how others have understood the verse throughout its 3,000-year history.[3]

The concept of "dominion" in this context is a blessing/*bracha*, a divine act of love. While God blessed the birds and fishes with fertility, God blessed humanity with both fertility *and* authority over nature. In more abstract terms, fish receive a blessing in a horizontal dimension, while the *adam* is blessed in both horizontal and vertical dimensions. Like the animals, the *adam* is called to multiply and spread over the earth, but unlike the animals, he stands upright as God's deputy, overseeing all the animals and the plants.[4]

Caring for Creation is an awesome responsibility. The psalmist captures the sense of undeserved honor that humanity holds:

What are human beings that You are mindful of them,
mortals that You care for them,
You have made them a little lower than God,
and crowned them with glory and honor.
You have given them dominion over the works of your hands,

You have put all things under their feet,

all sheep and oxen and also the beasts of the field the birds of
the air

and the fish of the sea, whatever passes along the paths of the
sea. (Ps. 8:5–9)

As a blessing, responsibility for Creation is a gift. According to anthropologist Lewis Hyde, the recipients of a gift become custodians of the gift. The Creation is a sacred trust and dominion is the most profound privilege.[5]

It is necessary to remember the context of the blessing as we examine the roots of the words in question: *kvs*, "master," and *rdh*, "have dominion over." It is also important to remember that Hebrew is a more symbolic, multilayered, and vague language than English is—any single word root can have multiple meanings, and often a word and its opposite will share the same word root. According to the Judaic scholar Norbert Samuelson, both *kvs*, "master," and *rdh*, "have dominion over," appear here in these particular grammatical forms, and nowhere else in the Bible. Translating them is not a cut-and-dried affair. The root of the Hebrew word for mastery, *kvs*, comes from the Aramaic "to tread down" or "make a path." In the book of Zechariah, the root *kvs* is interchangeable with the root *akl*, the word for "eat." Although *kvs* is often translated as "subdue" or "master," it appears to have agricultural implications.

The root of the Hebrew word for "have dominion over," *rdh*, generally refers to the "rule over subjects." In a play on the word *rdh*, Rashi, the foremost medieval rabbinic commentator, explains that if we consciously embody God's image and rule with wisdom and compassion, we will rise above the animals and preside over, *rdh*, them, ensuring a life of harmony on earth. However, if we are oblivious to our power and deny our responsibility to Creation, we will *yrd*, sink below the level of the animals and bring ruin to ourselves and the world.[6] If we twist the blessing to further our own ends, the blessing becomes a curse. The choice is ours.

As I was writing this essay, I had long discussions with environmentalists and feminists who urged me to substitute a less "offensive" word for the word "dominion," the traditional translation of *rdh*. They argued that "dominion" carries the negative connotations of control and domination. I considered what they said, and pondered the nuances of other words such as "govern" or "preside over," (one feminist suggested "have provenance over). I decided that while these words are less offensive, they are also less inspired; they do not carry the sense of dignity and nobility captured by "dominion"; they do not capture the sense of taking responsibility for something much larger than oneself.

Like the Hebrew *rdh*, "dominion" implies two sides: graciousness *and* domination. Dominion, like money, is not in itself bad; it all depends on how we exercise it. As Rashi said, we can recognize our responsibility to nature and rise to the occasion to create an extraordinary world, or we can deny our responsibility and sink to our basest instincts (dominating nature) and destroy the world. Such is the human condition. It is time that we understand our conflicting tendencies and deal with them, rather than deny their existence.[7]

Humanity's role is to tend the garden, not to possess it; to "guard it and keep it" (Genesis 2), not to exploit it; to pass it on as a sacred trust, as it was given. Even though we are given the authority to have dominion over the earth and its creatures, we are never allowed to own it, just like we can't own the waters or the air. "The land cannot be sold in perpetuity" (Lev. 25:23).

The land is the commons, and it belongs to everyone equally and jointly. In the biblical system, private property does not even exist because God owns the land and everything in it. (When the State of Israel was established, the Jewish National Fund took responsibility for the management of the land—with an original intention to ensure its perpetuity.)

The blessing of mastery over the earth calls us to exercise compassion and wisdom in our relationship with nature so that the Creation will keep on creating for future generations. We use nature every day in every thing we do; nature provides our food, shelter, clothing, energy, electricity, coal, gas. "Mastering" nature involves determining how much land to us, which animals should be designated for human use, how to manage the development of civilization, and what should remain untouched.

According to Saadia Gaon in the eleventh century, "mastery" of nature meant harnessing the energy of water and wind and fire; cultivating the soil for food, using plants for medicines, fashioning utensils for eating and writing, and developing tools for agricultural work, carpentry and weaving. It meant the beginning of art, science, agriculture, metallurgy, architecture, music, technology, animal husbandry, land use planning, and urban development.[8]

That the power is in humanity's hands is clearly a risk for all of Creation. Indeed, the Rabbis questioned why God created humanity with the capacity to do evil in the first place. Some of them figured that humanity would only destroy itself and the world. But our ability to choose between good and bad is what makes us human. Free choice is what distinguishes us from animals, who follow their instinct, and angels, who have no will of their own and act entirely on God's decrees. It is up to us to determine if we will make of ourselves a blessing or a curse. To rule nature with wisdom and compassion is our greatest challenge, our growth edge. It demands that we understand ourselves and guard against our own excesses and extremes; it demands a constant level of heightened awareness.

One of the pleasures of grappling with a biblical text is that we can always find new meanings in it. Over the years as I've turned this verse over and over, I've discovered a psycho-spiritual nuance. The complementary pair of blessings: "fertility" and "mastery," can be understood as blessings for "love" and "work." Fertility implies love, creativity, and being; mastery implies work, strength, and doing.

For most of us, love and work are the two dimensions that define our lives; for Freud, they set the criteria for a healthy life. The complementary pair of love and work take other forms such as being and doing, sex and power. God blesses us with the ability to experience both. Yet our contemporary worldview attributes more value to our dominating side, to work, than to our fertile side, to love. It's important to temper our dominating tendencies with our fertile, creative ones, and to remember that mastery over the earth is a sacred act, just like love is. They both invite the Divine in us.

Jewish Textual Practice and Sustainable Culture

Rabbi Natan Margalit, PhD

Rabbi Natan Margalit, PhD, is the director of the Oraita Institute for Continuing Rabbinic Education of Hebrew College, and assistant professor of rabbinics at Hebrew College. His writings on rabbinic literature and on Judaism and the environment have appeared in several academic and popular journals.

As my wife nurses our infant, I wonder about the reports that mother's milk may contain dangerous levels of pesticides—one small example, but perhaps no better symbol, of how the sacred circle of life that connects us all has been badly damaged. Largely due to human intervention, the earth is out of balance.

Judaism tells us that one of our primary responsibilities to our community and to our world is *tikkun olam*. Writing in this anthology, Jane Kanarek has reminded us that while the literal meaning of *tikkun ha'olam* is to repair the world, the Rabbis particularly understood that task to mean "restore balance." From a Jewish perspective, the world's ecological crisis requires us to ask, "How can Judaism contribute to the search for ways to restore the balance to our earth?"

With so many people writing and thinking about environmental change, why is the Jewish perspective important or useful? The answer, simply, is that we will need more than technical solutions to solve this crisis. Finding new sources of energy or some miracle crops is not enough. The market-based ideology that inspires product-based thinking is one of the main reasons we have come to this crisis. Instead of looking for solutions within our consumer culture, we need to transform the way millions of people think by offering an alternative to the reigning market-based corporate culture of domination and exploitation.

Because we are calling upon Judaism to change the way we see, hear, and interact with our world, we must do more than mine our tradition for specific statements about particular practices or behaviors. While preserving natural resources such as trees (*ba'al tashchit*) and preventing cruelty to animals (*tza'ar ba'alei hayyim*) are important elements in any effort to restore ecological balance, they can take us only so far. In order to make a deep impact, we need to locate an "eco-theology" based in Jewish sources.

The benefit of a Jewish eco-theology will be twofold. Through the development of an eco-theology, Judaism can inspire the kind of foundational thinking that the environmental movement needs. At the same time, such ecological thinking may well help uncover aspects of Judaism that we may not have noticed before, enriching Jewish thought and practice.

None of this is simply theoretical. Bringing about foundational changes in the way we think is an essential part of changing our actions. Religions such as Judaism are not simply thought systems, but organized communities, and these communities are powerful vehicles of social, economic, and political action. Organizing our communities for practical activism today is essential; we need to use our political power in the present moment to advocate for cleaner transportation, a better deal for sustainable farming, increased recycling, and many other important causes, yet such practical activism is not enough. I advocate searching for an eco-theology because I believe that only with a clear new paradigm of thinking will we be able to harness the full power for activism latent in our communities.

A String of Jewels

Jewish eco-theology could begin with a midrash about Rabbi Ben Azzai, which refers to verse ten from the first chapter of Song of Songs: "Your cheeks are comely with plaited wreaths, Your neck with strings of jewels."

> Ben Azzai was sitting and learning and there was fire all around him. The other students went to Rabbi Akiva and told him. He

came and said, "I hear that you were learning and fire was all around you." He answered, "Yes." He said, "Perhaps you were dealing with the Chambers of the Chariot?" He answered, "No, I was sitting and stringing together words of Torah, and from the Torah to the Prophets, and from the Prophets to the Writings, and the words were as joyous as on the day they were given on Sinai, and they were as sweet as when they were first given."

(Midrash Shir HaShirim Rabbah, Parsha 1)

Although it hardly mentions the natural world, and is, in fact, a meditation on the process of learning Torah, this midrash points us in the direction of some building blocks for an eco-theology. First, we observe that Ben Azzai's *understanding comes through connecting, and that this brings joy.* Ben Azzai reaches a mystical state, not because he "solved" the problem of the Torah, or got the "right answer," but by connecting words and creating new juxtapositions. His Torah was a living Torah because he creatively found new patterns.

Writing in a 1980 essay "Solving for Pattern," environmentalist Wendell Berry contrasts the distanced, one-dimensional "solutions" of agribusiness with the complex, satisfying web of relationships that constitute the health of a small farm. Whereas corporate agriculture may create high crop yields, in fact this "solution" brings with it more problems, such as a heavy dependence on oil, loss of soil quality, pollution of water systems, and social damage to farming communities. A good farmer, Berry suggests, has an intimate knowledge of the particulars of his farm and skillfully manages the relationships that keep the ecosystem healthy. The crops feed the animals, whose manure enriches the soil for the crops; the shade of trees keeps the animals happy and provides wood, a home for birds, and roots to hold the soil. All form a complex pattern of health for a working farm.

The principle of a healthy, balanced farm is never "the more, the better," as with industrial economies of scale, but "how much is enough." The aim of the small farmer is to maintain the dynamic balance of relationships within the natural world she tends. The monotony of corporate agriculture's endless fields of a single crop contrasts with the pastoral beauty of the small farmer's fences, woods, animals, gardens, and diverse fields, which are not only beautiful but also essential to the energy cycles and relationships of a small farm. An absentee landowner can't have this kind of knowledge.

Caring and quality go together in maintaining the health of the land and the people on it. Our most important work needs to be thought about and practiced with attention to pattern. Only then will the work of the world be done with love, with life-enhancing care, and with joy.

Language and Nature

Returning to Ben Azzai's "string of jewels," we also notice in this midrash that *"the words were joyous."* In our culture, words often are taken to be either illusions, covering the real truth, or the opposite, beckoning us to the spiritual reality behind the mundane illusions of ordinary life. Judaism, however, doesn't separate words and world, spirit and things, but connects them. The Hebrew for *word, davar,* also means "thing."

In our spiritual seeking, we try to see beyond the world to a unifying Source, but in the process, we still affirm this world in all its rough, uneven, stubborn materiality.

Arthur Green, author of *Ehyeh: A Kabbalah for Tomorrow* (Jewish Lights), and others have pointed out that our creation myth starts out with language: "God said ... and it was." Language is embedded not only in human culture; it is the basis of all creation, all nature. Nature, the world, and all that is in it, is, in essence, a kind of language, a weave, or a text. In Jewish mysticism, the world is created through the letters of the alphabet. Just as we can read the letters and words of the Torah in order to gain access to a deeper, inner Torah, and ultimately, to the One behind all the words, so too can we read the patterns in the world at large in order to get intimations of the divine essence of nature.

This "reading" of nature is often not intellectual, but intuitive and emotional, such as when we feel a spiritual uplift walking in a beautiful forest or sitting on a beach watching the sunset. Yet, if we want to bring our daily lives more in line with these moments of insight, we need to learn how to understand nature, and then bring our economic, agricultural, and social systems into harmony with this knowledge.

This linguistic view of nature is not simply mystical; it has been articulated scientifically by one of the great, creative thinkers of the twentieth century, anthropologist Gregory Bateson. Bateson said that all life is characterized by "the pattern which connects." He brilliantly connected nature to culture by showing that the perception of *difference* is the essential ingredient in all living systems, whether it be proteins reacting to differences encoded in a chain of DNA, a bird sensing a change in light or temperature and beginning a migration, or a Jew seeing three stars and knowing that it is time to start the new week. And, as in the notes of a melody or the composition of a painting, difference, and the relationships that differences create within a whole, is the essence of pattern.

In the modern world, we've broken that pattern of connection. We isolate, separate, and distance ourselves from one another, from the world, and even from our own being. The warnings of Jeremiah ring true for us, "They have forsaken Me, The Source of Life, and hewn themselves cisterns, broken cisterns which don't hold water ..." The inert, human-created stone of the cistern, which doesn't renew itself, is an apt symbol for our culture of technological arrogance, which has brought us many impressive gains but is now beginning to fail us. Will we return to the Living Source?

A Garden Ethic

One of the practical results of thinking in terms of patterns of nature and culture is that it gives us a way of understanding how we can act on and within our environment while still feeling a deeper sense of connection, a sense of belonging to a larger whole. A basic problem that still plagues environmental thinking today is the mental divide between Nature—pure, pristine, beautiful wilderness—and society—jobs, economy, prosperity, comfort, and growth. Unfortunately, in our culture, this dualism often gets unconsciously translated as "sentimental/ serious" or "pretty/useful," and, implicitly, "feminine/masculine." In the old story of Western culture, we know which one usually triumphs.

Michael Pollan, an important contemporary writer on issues of our relationship to nature, claims that environmental thinking in the United States is still enthralled with the romantic tradition of Thoreau, and holds to a "wilderness ethic." He suggests a more integrative alternative, what he calls a "gardener's ethic," because the gardener knows what it is to work with nature at the same time as she asserts human will upon nature, choosing tomatoes and carrots over weeds, and creating neat rows behind fences. Although Pollan makes no claim to connect his ideas to Judaism, I would like to suggest that his gardener's ethic dovetails with our Jewish eco-theology, starting in the Garden (of Eden). In the Jewish creation myth, humans in the Garden of Eden were told *l'ovda u'l'shomra*, "to work it and guard it." Our task is not to worship pristine wilderness, but to work the land with stewardship and caring. As we impose human order on the land, we also are commanded to listen to and respect nature's inherent patterns.

One of the ways Pollan characterizes the gardener's relationship with nature is as a running argument, one that the gardener doesn't expect to win. Abraham, Moses, and Job fit into this mold, arguing constantly with God; indeed, the Jewish predilection for such arguments is part of who we are.

One argues when one feels securely a part of a whole, belonging to something larger than oneself. The good gardener knows that to vanquish nature would be self-defeating, as he ultimately depends on nature's bounty for the fertility of his garden. The gardener, the garden, and nature are actually all parts of a larger whole. It might be tempting to spray pesticide to kill the insects that are eating your lettuce, but that "victory" would also kill off the good insects that are eating the harmful ones, leaving a residue that is harmful to humans, and weakening the garden plants' own defenses.

Similarly, I suggest that the Jewish tolerance for differences of opinion can be traced to a sense of belonging. A sense of peoplehood goes deeper than any particular idea or dogma. A covenant with God exists on a more profound level than any of either partner's actions. We are thus free to argue, complain, and protest, knowing that the deeper connection isn't so easily broken.

A Jewish eco-theology starts from this same sense of belonging to a larger whole. As Jews, we must realize today that our sense of belonging and connection is with all of creation, no less than with the Jewish people or with God. We can assert ourselves in nature, "argue" with it, even make changes and improvements, but with the awareness that we are ultimately a part of nature, part of a greater unity.

Loosening Our Grip on the World

"I was sitting and stringing together words ..." Ben Azzai wasn't looking for the answer to the puzzle of the text. He was enjoying a continuing process of interpreting it. If we understand nature as a living set of patterns, like a text, we will understand that we are never in a position to dominate it or control it completely. One of the most destructive habits of modern civilization is to try to achieve perfect control over our lives and our environment. We go to great lengths for the perfect lawn, or the perfect room temperature, not really thinking about the cost. A garden ethic, or "to work and to guard," includes manipulating the world but in an organic give-and-take with nature, not seeking ultimate domination.

Life is not smooth. Difference, separation, and division are, in fact, essential to pattern. But, as with music, where the difference in tone creates melody and harmony, so too, paradoxically, can difference and multiplicity lead us to the One Source, as long as we see the differences within a larger whole. In the realm of time, Judaism separates out one day, Shabbat, in order to teach us the holiness of all days. At its best, Judaism maintains this pattern-approach with regard to peoplehood, holding on to our particularity at the same time as we affirm the universal holiness of all peoples. We need to apply this ethos equally to every area of life.

Just as Ben Azzai was joyous in his continual discovery and creation of changing combinations and new juxtapositions, so too should we not look to find the answer to life, to escape the ups and the downs, but to *live* life. It is a spiritual practice to construct economic, agricultural, and social modes that work together in dynamic patterns. When we do this, the whole world will be as happy as a new creation and as sweet as new life.

Wonder and Restraint
A Rabbinical Call to Environmental Action

WRITTEN UNDER THE AUSPICES OF THE COALITION
ON THE ENVIRONMENT AND JEWISH LIFE (COEJL)

COEJL is the leading Jewish environmental organization in the United States, representing twenty-nine national Jewish organizations spanning the full spectrum of Jewish religious and communal life. COEJL is a program of the Jewish Council for Public Affairs (JCPA)

A t this very moment, our Earth is hurtling through space at 18.5 miles per second while the sun burns with an internal heat of 20 million degrees. Forests and vegetation sweep the planet's atmosphere of carbon dioxide and provide oxygen and food for countless creatures. A 40-ton humpback whale sings a symphonic cycle of songs in the depths of the sea; a tiny hummingbird flaps its wings 4,500 times per minute as it sips nectar from flowers. The million-year-old messages of our DNA repair and reproduce themselves and create a spectacular diversity of human beings on Earth.

These interwoven testaments to the God of Creation, unveiled by our senses and by the probings of science, have stirred millions of people to become mindful guardians of the biosphere.

Now our Jewish tradition must, and can, do likewise.

As rabbis of long experience, we are moved by psalms of praise and blessing—"You have gladdened me by Your deeds, O Lord; I shout for joy at Your handiwork ..." (Psalm 92). We have studied the texts of Mishnah and Gemara explicating the Halachic duties derived from the law of *lo tashchit*, "you shall not waste" (Deut. 20:19). We take to heart the curses of Deuteronomy 28, which chillingly resemble the environmental catastrophes now being predicted by an overwhelming majority of the scientific community— "The Lord will strike you ... with scorching heat and drought, with blight and mildew ..." We are inspired by the proclamations of the kabbalists and the Hasidic rebbes— "All that we see, sky, earth and its fullness, are God's outer garment" (Rebbe Shneor Zalman, *Tanya*).

Yet we worry that the same factors of abundance and alienation in modern life that have inured people to the pleading voices of nature could inure them, as well, to these voices of Torah.

We know that within Jewish texts, law, theology, philosophy, and ritual practice are spiritual resources that could profoundly transform our people and influence a human race estranged from the essences of life. Within the Jewish tradition reside rich teachings about the unity of creation, about boundaries and limits, about deeds and consequences, about poverty and wealth, and about individual and communal responsibility, which together form a comprehensive environmental vision and provide practical guidance for environmental balance and restoration.

Within Jewish history, moreover, the reality of annihilation, and the process by which it results from a society's worship of false gods, has been made terribly clear.

How, then, can we help the Jewish people hear the covenantal heartbeat of Judaism and feel it racing as a pulse through our bodies? How do we turn the notion of *tselem Elohim,* that human beings are made in the Divine image, into a living identity of stewardship and responsibility for God's Earth?

Beginning with Wonder

The awakening we seek begins with wonder: the wonder that turned Moses aside to regard the burning bush and realize that he was standing on "holy ground" (Exod. 3:3–5). That vision of light is what we all see every year in the buds of spring, the spawning of new generations, the migrations of birds, mammals, and fishes, the cleansing streams of atmosphere and oceans—in all of the miraculous processes by which life awakens from dormancy and recovers from stress, even from disaster, to re-create the world right before our eyes.

Traditionally, Jews express this sense of wonder by reciting some hundred blessings a day, at all the junctures of interaction with Creation that constitute our lives. But to paraphrase the words of the prophet Isaiah, are these the blessings that the Creator desires? To give thanks for the bounty of our meals while our industrial farming system despoils the waterways? To praise the splendor of a rainbow while driving a wasteful, polluting vehicle? To kiss the mezuzah on the doorpost of an oversized, energy-inefficient house that consumes enough electricity to power a shtetl? To give *tzedakah* while we invest our personal or institutional wealth without regard for which corporations are pouring pollutants into the soil, the water, the air?

No, says our Torah, *these* are the blessings required:

- that we unify our words and our deeds;
- that we sustain and expand our awe, not simply discharge it with a prayer;
- that we unveil revelation with all of our God-given capacities and respond, with humbled hearts, to the "signs and marvels" (Exod. 7:3) with which God animates our world;
- that we respond to God's summonings by declaring ourselves ready, as a people, to renew the covenant made at Mount Sinai. There, in the wilderness of life, amid "thunder and lightning, the blare of the horn and the mountain smoking" (Exod. 20:18), our ancestors, freed from enslavement in Egypt, awoke *en masse* to the responsibilities of their freedom. And had they not, the Midrash warns, the world would have been returned "to desolation and chaos" (Babylonian Talmud, *Shabbat* 88a).

Today, the "blare of the horn" is louder than ever. As the oil economy heats the atmosphere and disrupts the climate; as the ice shelves of Antarctica, frozen for eons, melt and break off into the sea; as fisheries around the globe collapse; as our world's ecosystems, and the systems of our own human bodies, are forced to absorb a plethora of artificial chemicals; as the Earth loses its animal songs and the ancient text of DNA gets trampled by human-propelled forces of extinction; as the entire planet groans in bondage to its human slave drivers—the horn that summons us to covenant is blaring in our ears.

Two Covenantal Responsibilities

Two covenantal responsibilities apply most directly to the environmental challenges of our time. The first demands inwardness, the second, outwardness. The first fulfills the traditional Jewish role as a "holy nation," the second, as a "light unto the nations."

The first, in a word, is *restraint:* to practice restraint in our individual and communal lives. Judaism encourages this sensibility in many of its most fundamental metaphors and mitzvot. There is the restraint embodied by Shabbat, our central holy day of wholeness and not-producing. There is the restraint expressed through kashrut, dietary consciousness, which gives us an appetite for sacredness instead of gluttony.

There is the restraint expressed as *ba'al tashchit*, the injunction against wanton destruction that is rooted in the Torah's responses to the environmental ravages of warfare, and as *tza'ar ba'alei chayyim*, pity for the suffering of living creatures, requiring us to treat our fellow creatures as sentient beings, not as objects for exploitation.

There is the restraint required to fulfill the demands of *kehillah*—the communal and intergenerational obligations that Judaism applies to our wealth, our private property, our decision making, and our salvation. In the tradition of Maimonides, modesty and open-handed generosity have long been hallmarks of Jewish life.

There is the restraint implied by *shmirat haguf*, protection of our own bodies, and by *pikuakh nefesh*, the commandment to protect life at nearly any cost. There is the restraint mandated by *s'yag l'Torah*, building a "fence around the Torah," which bids us to err on the side of caution when it comes to matters of life, limb, and spiritual integrity—all of which are surely endangered by the destruction of biological diversity and the degradation of the biosphere, most obviously by the catastrophes likely to be induced by global warming.

In the Jewish mystical tradition, it is God who sets the example of restraint by practicing *tsimtsum*, self-withdrawal, in order to permit the universe to emerge into being. The mystics, drawing upon the

Talmud (*Chagigah* 12a), linked this creation story to the appellation Shaddai, usually translated to mean "Almighty," but understood by mystics as the One who said to the infant universe, "*dai*," "enough," and thus gave form and boundary to the chaos.

Today, we who are made in the image of Shaddai must emulate this act of *tsimtsum* if we want our world to persist in health and abundance. Human activity is now as consequential to the Earth and its wealth of species as glaciers, volcanoes, winds, and tides—so we cannot persist in the illusion that the world is inexhaustible. Human activity has split the seas, brought down manna from heaven, cured pestilence, built vast tabernacles—so we cannot continue to quake and stammer at the prospect of assuming the responsibility given to us along with our power. Instead, we must transform ourselves from nature's children to nature's guardians by learning to say "*dai*," "enough," to ourselves.

But not only to ourselves: for the second covenantal obligation that our Earth and our faith require is that we speak out, and speak truth, to the world's leaders.

We are obliged to contrast our religious and ethical values with the values of self-indulgence, domination, warfare, and money worship that fuel the ravaging of the Earth.

We are obliged to support policies that ease poverty and spare the planet its ravages; that protect underdeveloped countries from serving as the world's environmental dumping grounds; that tie economic development to environmental stewardship; and that enable poor people to pursue sustainable economic lives.

We are obliged to dialogue with corporations that are motivated by the sole purpose of profit and petty self-interest, rather than acting symbiotically with the natural world, and that tamper with fundamentals of Creation without caution, without reverence, as well as to guide them in promoting more sustainable practices.

We are obliged to challenge the fever of consumption that drives unsustainable economic growth.

We are obliged to challenge public officials who deify property and wealth, reducing our living planet to a commodity.

We are obliged to seek peace and pursue it—to oppose easy recourse to military violence, not only for its destruction of human life and health, but also for its shattering impact on nature and natural resources.

It is precisely in taking these kinds of prophetic stances, lifting our voices to join protest to prayer, that we renew Judaism's capacity for stirring the *Rachamim*, the womb-love, of God and of the human race, thus keeping the gates open to a healthy future for our planet and its inhabitants.

Hopeful Realism

"Too much singing," warns a Yiddish folk saying, "and not enough noodles!" Before we conclude this letter, we want to be realistic and careful to leave no sense of hubris or overreaching that might disconnect our message from the world of the possible and the plausible.

We know, for example, that many of our people are unaware of, or indifferent to, the teachings of Judaism that we have been expounding.

We realize, moreover, that the Jewish people number barely 2 percent of America's population and only fractional percentages elsewhere—and that the environmental health of the planet will ultimately depend on decisions made in the developing world, with its vast populations, where Jews have virtually no presence.

We recognize that in Israel, the one land under Jewish dominion, despite the back-to-nature idealism of Zionism and the environmental guidance and vision of Judaism, even the sincere activism of Israeli environmentalists has been unable to protect the country's environment from the overwhelming pressures of nation-building, economy-building, and national defense.

Finally, we admit that Judaism, as filtered through our people's centuries of urbanization and ghettoization, has been estranged from much of the Creation-centered sensibility that saturated its early formation.

Nevertheless, we have every reason to hope that we can catalyze new levels of participation and leadership in environmental protection among the Jewish people today.

Our hope is rooted in the belief that our people, for all of their worldliness, are not so far removed from the Jewish values we seek to invoke—"for surely," as our Torah says, "this is a wise and discerning people" (Deut. 4:6), who show every evidence of retaining a covenantal sensibility even at a remove from the language and metaphors of Judaism. The environmental wisdom of our tradition does not require a conversionary experience, a renunciatory lifestyle, or a suspicious stance toward science and modernity. To the contrary, Judaism counts science, technology, and the human capacity for innovation as among our greatest blessings and our greatest tools for partnering in Creation.

We are hopeful, too, because, notwithstanding our small numbers, Jews of conscience and integrity have overcome obstacles of discrimination and oppression to gain positions of influence within economic, intellectual, and policy-making institutions throughout the developed world. This is especially so in the United States, the world's leading economic and military power—where great prosperity has been purchased at great cost to the biosphere. American Jews therefore have an indispensable role to play in political and civic institutions, corporate boardrooms, the courts, and academia, to help guide our country to lead and build alliances in response to global warming, deforestation, overfishing, and other environmental crises of our generation.

Finally, we are confident that the State of Israel will serve, in a time of peace, as a tremendous asset, scientifically and spiritually, to a world confronting the demands of development with limited natural resources. And we are grateful for the fact that the modern renaissance in Jewish life has embraced Jewish festivals that connect us with nature (such as Rosh Chodesh, Sukkot, and Tu B'Shevat) and explored a theology that identifies God most powerfully and most intimately with our perceptions of unity and interconnection.

Being realistic also means defining policies and benchmarks of progress that the Jewish community might use in strengthening its commitment to environmental protection. Happily, these have begun to be defined through the collective Jewish effort represented by the Coalition on the Environment and Jewish Life (COEJL, www.coejl.org), which is the organizing force behind this rabbinic letter and a founding member, with major Christian faith groups, of the National Religious Partnership for the Environment (www.nrpe.org). Among the policies deserving our most immediate commitment are:

- the pursuit of low environmental impact practices in our own households, workplaces, synagogues, and other Jewish institutions (e.g., reduce, reuse, recycle, conserve energy and water);
- the encouragement of sound and positive environmental business policies through our expenditures and our investments;
- the incorporation of environmental considerations, particularly the urgency of global warming and biodiversity loss, in the formulation of political, religious, and cultural Jewish communal policies, and a heightened emphasis on environmental justice and wholeness in our public policy statements and activities;
- the integration of nature-oriented activities and Creation concerns in our observances of holy days, our Jewish education for children and adults, our liturgies, and our life-cycle ceremonies.

In addition, we take special note that for individuals, families, and congregations, Shabbat presents a weekly opportunity to reawaken our sense of wonder and to practice restraint. On Shabbat, we can connect with the wonder of Creation through liturgy, outdoor experience, and reflection. We can practice restraint by removing ourselves from the consumption economy for one day each week and by focusing instead on the interactions with family, friends, and community that give our lives richness and meaning.

God willing, we will have time to pursue a transformation of our Jewish environmental consciousness and commitment while our Earth continues to journey through space and spin on its axis to bring evening and morning, morning and evening to innumerable creeping, crawling, climbing, swimming, walking, and flying creatures. God willing, elephants will continue to bury their dead and call to each other in subsonic voices that travel for miles across the savannah, and ants will continue to herd aphids and feed on their honeydew. God willing, new species and variations of flora and fauna will continue to evolve and fill the Earth, and the good garden of Creation will continue its renewal and rebirth.

Let us rejoice that we, as children of God, have been endowed with the intelligence, reverence, scientific capacity, and faith to serve as the caretakers for such an extraordinary world! And when God declares to us—"Look at My works! See how beautiful they are—how excellent! For your sake I created them all. See to it that you do not spoil and destroy My world, for if you do, there will be no one else to repair it" (*Ecclesiastes Rabbah* 7:13)—let us respond, with unified voice: "We will do and we will hearken" (Exod. 24:7).

Signed,

Lawrence Bush, editor, *Jewish Currents,* Accord, NY; head writer of the team consisting of:

Saul J. Berman, associate professor of Jewish Studies, Stern College of Yeshiva University; director of Continuing Rabbinic Education, Yeshivat Chovevei Torah, New York, NY

Sharon Bloome, founding chair, Coalition on the Environment and Jewish Life, Seattle, WA

Rabbi Nina Beth Cardin, director of Jewish Life, Jewish Community Center of Greater Baltimore, Baltimore, MD

Rabbi David Ellenson, president of Hebrew Union College–Jewish Institute of Religion, New York, NY

Rabbi Nancy Fuchs-Kreimer, director of Religious Studies Program and associate professor of Religious Studies, Reconstructionist Rabbinical College, Wyncote, PA

Rabbi Arthur Green, rector of Rabbinical School at Hebrew College, Newton Centre, MA

Susannah Heschel, PhD, Eli Black Associate Professor of Jewish Studies, Department of Religion, Dartmouth College, Hanover, NH

Rabbi Charles A. Kroloff, past president of Central Conference of American Rabbis, Westfield, NJ; vice president for Special Projects, Hebrew Union College–Jewish Institute of Religion

Elliott Norse, PhD, president of Marine Conservation Biology Institute, Redmond, WA

Rabbi David Saperstein, director of Religious Action Center of Reform Judaism, Washington, DC

Rabbi Ismar Schorsch, chancellor emeritus of The Jewish Theological Seminary of America, New York, NY

Mitchell Thomashow, EdD, president of Unity College, Unity, ME

Rabbi Lawrence Troster, former rabbinic fellow of Coalition on the Environment and Jewish Life; director of Fellowship Program, GreenFaith, New Brunswick, NJ

Toxic Waste and the Talmud

JEREMY BENSTEIN, PhD

Jeremy Benstein, PhD, is a founder and associate director of the Heschel Center for Environmental Learning and Leadership. He is the author of *The Way Into Judaism and the Environment* (Jewish Lights), and a regular contributor to the *Jerusalem Report*.

When my sister's Talmud teacher in our Midwestern day school began his class on damages with the example, "If an ox gores another ox, and he dies ..." she and her friends rolled their eyes at the irrelevancy of it all. Sensing their criticism, he tried to bring things up to date: "Okay, if while walking down Greenfield Avenue an ox gores another ox ..." Some things, it seems, just can't be updated.

Or can they? Many contemporary environmental problems are some of the newest things under the sun—what did the Rabbis know about global warming, or dioxins, or ozone?—but they nevertheless may be particularly amenable to the laws of damages outlined in *Parashat Mishpatim* (the weekly Torah portion literally called "rulings").

We don't usually think of Torah as having relevant insights into toxic waste disposal. Talk of Judaism and ecology usually centers on fostering feelings of awe toward Creation, celebrating nature in the Hebrew calendar, or examining lifestyle issues such as consumption. Legislation and policy are often disassociated from Jewish tradition for reasons including relegation of religion to the private sphere, fear of coercion, stigmatization of religious law as backward, and the claim that "secular" policy is a realm for politicians and experts, not rabbis.

So it's interesting to note that according to the Talmud (*Bava Kamma* 30a), one of the distinguishing characteristics of the truly pious (the *Hasidim rishonim*) was being especially concerned with the proper disposal of hazardous waste. This is one aspect of what Rav Yehudah meant when he said that the key to a truly spiritual life was scrupulous observance of the laws of damages (*nezikin*). These laws regulate not only injury or harm inflicted by a person or their livestock on another person or their property, but also misuse of the environment as a cause of damages to others. If I dig or uncover a pit in the public domain, I am liable for damages that may ensue. Similarly, if I place a jug or barrel (or thorns or broken glass) in a communal place, and someone is injured—again, I must make restitution. Even activities initiated on my property that spread and do damage elsewhere—a fire that gets out of control, an animal that gets away—are my complete responsibility. It is not a far cry from the menace of air pollution and leaky toxic dumps of our day.

The Mishnah enumerates different classes of damages (*avot nezikin*), but the underlying principle is the same: the liability rests on the individual. How far we are in our society from such simple common sense. Industries create hazardous waste all the time, harming people through polluted air and water, and the legal system often has difficulty reining in the perpetrators, or making them pay. Standard economic theory sees our environment as up for grabs, just so much unowned raw material or a place to dump industrial outputs. It belongs to no one, and so can be appropriated by anyone for essentially any purpose. Liberal philosophy, which underlies so much of our culture, sees the individual and his property as inviolable—a concept that has been extended to corporations with disastrous effect. Corporations are seen as persons before the law, with many of the rights that accrue to individuals, rather than as bodies serving the public good, with all the obligations that this entails.

Traditional societies, Judaism included, held to a different level of private responsibility for public welfare. Then came the modern economic notion of the "invisible hand," which claimed that through enlightened self-interest, people working hard for themselves benefit everyone. Biologist Garrett Hardin's famous 1968 analysis of the "tragedy of the commons" showed that in our world the opposite is the case, that unbridled accretion of private profit at public cost can lead to ruin for all.

Environmentalists who emphasize the need for strong personal commitment and clear legislation protecting public welfare—even at the expense of curtailing certain primitive free-market notions of commercial liberty—speak the same language of concern as the Torah. *Bava Kamma* also tells the story of a man who was removing stones from his field to a public thoroughfare. When one of the pious remonstrated with him, saying: "Fool, why are you removing the stones from property that isn't yours, to that which is?" he merely laughed. What could the pious man mean? Surely he was moving the stones from his property—his field—to the public thoroughfore, which, after all, did not belong to him. Later, he was forced to sell his field, and while walking along the thoroughfare, he tripped over his old stones. "That Hasid was right about removing stones from property that was not immutably mine to that which is," he commented.

Behind the simple parable is a body of legislation that enforces the profound value of the environment as being not nobody's, but everybody's. Economic activity that leads to a polluted stream or global warming should be as illegal as it is impious. Without a strong ethic of the public good, and legal responsibility for the effects on that which is all of ours, privatization and economic globalization are pure plunder.

Judaism, Oil, and Renewable Energy

SHANA STAROBIN

Shana Starobin trained as a grassroots organizer with Green Corps and has since worked on several environmental campaigns throughout the country. A graduate of Harvard University and the Dorot Fellowship Program in Israel, Starobin is currently a candidate for a joint master's degree in environmental management and public policy at Duke University.

According to Rabbinic legend, when the Maccabees defeated their enemies and rededicated the ancient Temple in Jerusalem, they discovered a jug with enough sacred oil to fuel the menorah for only one day; it would take eight days to produce more. Miraculously, the oil they found provided enough light for eight days, and the reconsecrated Temple did not go dark.

Beginning on the twenty-fifth of the month of Kislev each year, when we kindle the lights of the Hanukkah menorah, we remind ourselves that in a time of destruction and darkness, our ancestors found light.

Unfortunately, many of us live as if the miracle of Hanukkah is an ongoing reality. We act as though oil—a non-renewable resource—will continue to power our economy long after the time scientists tell us it will surely be used up. Unless we change our practices now—individually and communally—we will face a day when we try to light our modern-day *menorot* and the oil will have simply run out. No miracles will rescue us.

Our Heads in the Sand

Whether we know it or not, the oil crisis has already impacted other peoples, threatening their way of life and their very survival, as well as the health of the Earth. As nonrenewable energy sources dwindle, energy companies are being compelled to drill in more unpredictable and environmentally sensitive locations, subjecting to possible damage and contamination valuable ecosystems that people rely on for essential sustenance, and that are important for global ecological balance. In no place has the impact of such drilling on local people been clearer than in Colombia, where the U'wa people threatened mass suicide in 1995 if Occidental Petroleum went ahead with plans to drill for oil 550 yards from U'wa land.

While Occidental ultimately backed off, the U'wa continue to struggle for their land rights today. They argue that their lands contain a fragile and significant ecosystem that would be destroyed by the roads, equipment, and pollution drilling would bring, and it would be threatened by the danger of oil spills from broken pumps or truck accidents. According to a petition signed by fifty-seven NGOs (non-governmental organizations) in support of the U'wa in 2006, the lands contain "montane cloudforests that scientists consider to be one of the planet's most biologically diverse and most endangered ecosystems."[1]

The U'wa live off the land, depending, as the NGO petition continues, "on clean water, intact forests, and biodiversity of flora and fauna for their physical and spiritual survival." Their campaign is not just about protecting the beauty and diversity of their lands, but about protecting their lives. According to the same document, the nearby territory of Arauca, where drilling has proceeded, "has been marred by violence and poor environmental practices, resulting in devastating socio-economic impacts such as polluted local rivers and streams, soil, and ground water."

In addition, guerillas opposing the Colombian government have been regularly blowing up Occidental Petroleum's already existing Colombian oil pipelines. Drilling in U'wa land would enmesh the U'wa people in a dangerous civil war that they have so far managed to avoid.[2]

The same kinds of environmental and cultural stresses are felt elsewhere in the world where First World companies dig Third World oil. In the Niger Delta, for example, some of the poorest people on Earth (living on less than U.S. $1 per day)[3] reside atop one of the richest oil reserves in the world. However, the people of the Niger Delta reap little benefit from the vast amounts of oil that are extracted daily from their lands.[4] Rather, they continue to pay for others having pursued oil development in the Delta region—losing productive agricultural land, watching their rivers turn into polluted streams, and risking their communities' health as gas flares have burned interminably in their backyards for forty years.

Like the Maccabees, the U'wa and the residents of the Niger Delta are not only fighting for their communal integrity and way of life, but for their lives—on land that means more to them than the oil trapped beneath its surface, or any temporary payoff that oil might secure them.

Ba'al Tashchit

In the face of oil's unsustainability, as well as its devastating impact on local peoples and ecosystems where drilling occurs, it is unthinkable for Jews—steeped in a tradition that first instructs us in the Torah against wanton destruction—to hold back from speaking out and working for change. We should marshal our best intellectual and spiritual resources to strengthen the growing movement for the development of renewable energy sources and technologies.

The classical Jewish source on conservation is the passage in Deuteronomy that introduces the commandment *ba'al tashchit* (literally, "do not destroy"), forbidding needless waste and destruction:

> When in your war against a city, you have to besiege it a long time in order to capture it, you must not destroy its trees, wielding the ax against them. You may eat of them, but you must not cut them down. Are trees of the field human to withdraw before you into the besieged city? Only trees that you know do not yield fruit may be destroyed; you may cut them down for constructing siegeworks against the city that is waging war on you, until it has been reduced. (Deut. 20:19–20)

As Jeremy Benstein points out in *The Way Into Judaism and the Environment* (Woodstock, VT: Jewish Lights, pp. 93–101), the original prohibition was only against the destruction of fruit trees in wartime. According to this passage, fruit trees are innocent bystanders in a human conflict. In comparing fruit trees to humans, the Torah implies that trees (like human beings) have inherent value and are deserving of honor and respect. Further, cutting down fruit trees during battle means cutting off post-war sources of food and livelihood. We are given here a special obligation to preserve those things in nature with potential utility for humans in the future—both because of the trees' inherent value and because our obligations to others and to future generations are, in part, mediated through our relationship to nature.

In the Talmudic tractate *Shabbat* (67b), the ancient Rabbis extend the prohibition against the destruction of fruit trees to include times of peace as well as war and to forbid a broader range of acts of environmental degradation and misuse of natural resources. For example, Rav Zutra states, "One who covers an oil lamp, or uncovers a naphtha lamp, transgresses the prohibition of *ba'al tashchit*, since these acts cause the lamp to burn with unnecessary speed." To Rav Zutra, it was clear that we should not needlessly waste fuel, and that such a prohibition was, as it were, a natural extension of the biblical *ba'al tashchit*.

The thirteenth-century *Sefer Hachinuch* extends this further:

> To love that which is good and worthwhile and to cling to it, so that good becomes a part of us and that we will avoid that which is evil and destructive—this is the way of the righteous and those who improve society ... that nothing, not even a grain of mustard, should be lost ... if possible they will prevent any destruction that they can. Not so are the wicked, who rejoice in the destruction of the world, and they are destroying themselves. (#530)

As *Sefer Hachinuch* so beautifully teaches, our ability to conserve natural resources is connected to our ability to recognize our blessings, to strive to improve the world from a place of awareness and gratitude. Whether we emphasize energy conservation and the development of renewable energy for the sake of our own generation, future generations, or nature itself, the principle of *ba'al tashchit* affirms that our consciousness must be directed toward resources great and small, that the Earth and its gifts are not ours to destroy. Since Creation, humanity's intended relationship to the natural world has been *l'ovdah u-l'shomrah*—to use it responsibly, and to protect it carefully.

Lech L'cha to a Renewable Energy Future

Like Noah, who built an ark for his family and a saving remnant of the animal kingdom in anticipation of the flooding of the Earth, we may be tempted simply to do our best to purchase organic foods, recycle paper and plastic products, drive hybrid cars—and shut ourselves off from societal approaches and larger global issues. We may be overwhelmed by the magnitude of the environmental crisis, or live with the unconscious fantasy that we can shield ourselves from the problems of nonrenewable energy, environmental destruction, and global warming if we simply act with ecological sensitivity in our private lives. But we have no exemption from being affected by all of these issues, and the teachings of our tradition do not allow us to shirk our responsibilities as stewards of the Earth.

The Torah describes Noah as "a righteous man in his generation," but the ancient Rabbis saw this description as damnation with faint praise; being righteous in comparison to Noah's generation is perhaps no great compliment. The Rabbis were uncomfortable with Noah's inability or unwillingness to reach out and help others change their behavior. They compare him unfavorably to Abraham, whom they see as a great man for *all* times, who not only heeds God's word, but who also teaches others the insights of monotheism (*Genesis Rabbah* 30:10).

There will be no ark uniquely sheltering the Jewish people from the flood of rising seas, or protecting us from environmental catastrophes brought about by collective exploitation of natural resources. As denizens and citizens of the world, these are our problems, too.

At no time in history have Jews in North America had a greater combination of financial resources, communal security, and political power, and we have a sacred obligation to use them to turn the tide of history and sustain life on this planet. We have the power to make real change that will have an impact for generations. As Jews, we have a responsibility to take up the Abrahamic mantle and help move public policy and public discourse in a new direction, to bring the message of conservation and sustainability to the halls of government and to the streets.

Becoming a messenger in the political realm might seem somewhat outside the ways we typically imagine ourselves pursuing change in our Jewish life. Jewish tradition often leads us to think more about personal change or behavior modification in accordance with previously established laws. Some people may believe that shifting our society away from unsustainable sources of energy will only come when everyone changes their behavior. Though these tangible changes to our lives are certainly important and might additionally influence the behavior of others around us, behavioral change as a core solution to energy independence will not fundamentally alter the set of options available to us.

If we want to ensure a better, livable future—for ourselves and the rest of the world—we must raise our voices for change and embark with faith on a journey toward sustainability. Like Abraham, we must "*Lech l'cha ... mi-beit avichah*" ("Go from our father's house," Gen. 12:1) and leave behind our archaic notions of a fossil-fueled world, where the "haves" can only survive at the expense of the "have-nots." We may not know what this new world will look like, but, nevertheless, we must leave the old one behind. Only then can we hope to move as a people beyond Noah—to stop thinking only of the ark we believe we must construct for ourselves and to focus instead on working together to halt the floodwaters before they ever begin to rise. And if there is to be another ark, just in case, we must build this ark big enough to hold not only ourselves but also the entire planet.

PART III

THE TEMPLE OF THE SPIRIT: THE HUMAN BODY

Redemption for Radicals
Jewish Congregation-Based
Community Organizing

RABBI JONAH DOV PESNER

Rabbi Jonah Dov Pesner is the founding director of Just Congregations. As a congregational rabbi at Temple Israel in Boston, he developed the award-winning "Ohel Tzedek / Tent of Justice" social action initiative. He is a leader in the Greater Boston Interfaith Organization, and serves on the Task Force on Congregation-Based Community Organizing of the Jewish Funds for Justice.

In March 2006, Massachusetts passed historic health care reform, which, when fully effectuated, will mean that hundreds of thousands of people will for the first time receive quality, affordable health care. The bill was signed by a Republican governor and passed by a Democratic majority in the legislature. It was supported by business leaders, unions, and advocacy groups. It was a courageous bill that required political will. How could so much broad-based support be generated for such sweeping reform? Believe it or not, the bill resulted in large part from the efforts of the faith community of Greater Boston. How was this possible? The religious community got organized.

Over a period of eighteen months, thousands of people gathered in churches, synagogues, civic organizations, and homes throughout the state and told the stories of their struggles with health care. At my own synagogue, Temple Israel of Boston, Andy McAfee, an emergency room doctor, expressed his outrage that he was constantly seeing people with preventable illnesses who were suffering needlessly because they lacked insurance. We heard stories from our sister churches, like those of Peter Brook and Margarita DePina. Peter is single and diabetic. Making $20,000 as a construction worker for a small company that provides no benefits, he can't afford insurance so he takes the enormous risk of reusing his insulin needles. Margarita works full time as a hospital technician and her husband is a janitor. Even though he works double shifts, they were nearly bankrupted caring for their daughter with special needs.

Andy, Peter, Margarita, and thousands of others refused to suffer alone in righteous indignation. By telling their stories at their synagogues and churches, they were able to hear each other's call for justice—and they got organized. Priests, ministers, and rabbis met and studied our faith traditions and taught each other the mandates of health care in their religious texts. Five hundred clergy ratified a statement articulating the moral imperative of health care access.

Through hundreds of meetings, they engaged thousands of their neighbors in a coordinated effort to pass meaningful, ambitious health reform. They met repeatedly with their elected leaders in their own institutions, and at the State House. Together with allies in a statewide coalition of organizations and civic institutions, they collected more than 130,000 certified signatures of registered voters to force a referendum on their bill. The political and corporate leadership had no choice but to support the clear will of the people.

Though the story of the recent Massachusetts health reform is powerful, it is not unique. It is but one example of Jewish participation in the emerging movement called Congregation-Based Community Organizing (CBCO). Across the country, we are writing new stories of justice as Jews join with Christians, Muslims, and others who share a common vision. Together, we are acting as a potent force—the force of organized people—to hold our nation accountable to its articulated values of equality, dignity, and opportunity.

For Jews, this "call to justice" should mean no less than redemption. Redemption is the transformation of the world as it is to the world as it should be. "We were slaves in Egypt, and then we were redeemed ..." Redemption is about restructuring the very social order, the system that keeps some in bondage.

Too often in Jewish communal life, we confuse service-oriented work at soup kitchens, mitzvah days, and *b'nai mitzvah* projects with the work of redemptive social justice. While such good works can be useful in exposing people to injustice and providing short-term relief for the symptoms of injustice, they are only a beginning. At worst, these projects undermine our commitment to systemic change.

It is time for the Jewish community to begin living out the vision of Isaiah that we read at Yom Kippur each year. Instead of spending one or two days "donning sackcloth," we must become the "repairers of the breach" (Isa. 58:12) of our social fabric. Doing so requires that we become organized in both senses of the term: to work on social issues in a systematic and sustained way, and to get organized in the way that community organizers talk about—to strengthen community relationships, set communal goals, and mobilize to achieve these goals. Synagogues need to become places where we can tell each other the stories of our lives. They need to be institutions that foster strong relational networks among congregants, and then create more powerful networks by joining together with churches, mosques, and other civic institutions. In these networks lies the power for redemption.

It is time for us to write new stories of redemption.

Hearing Our Common Cry

For people of faith, the first step toward justice is when we cry out. The story of our redemption is a story of cries that were heard. Pharaoh's daughter hears the cry of the baby Moses. Moses hears the cry of his kinsman being beaten by an Egyptian and acts to save him. When the people of Israel, groaning under their bondage, cry out to God, "God heard their cries, and remembered the covenant with Abraham, Isaac, and Jacob" (Exod. 2:23–24).

Like the ancient Hebrews, the real people of Massachusetts who suffered from a broken health care system needed to learn to cry out. Peter Brook, Margarita DePina and Andy McAfee had to become aware that their suffering was not their own private problem, but a communal problem—to learn and to teach each other, together with others, to cry out together.

These cries could be heard in part because listeners were in place to hear them. The real work of the health care campaign had actually begun many years before under the aegis of the Greater Boston Interfaith Organization (GBIO), a broad-based community of religious congregations and civic institutions, itself an affiliate of the Industrial Areas Foundation (IAF), founded by Saul Alinsky in the 1940s. In his seminal book, *Reveille for Radicals*, Alinksy wrote:

> What is the American radical? The radical is that unique person to whom the common good is the greatest personal value. He is that person who genuinely and completely believes in mankind. The radical is so completely identified with mankind that he personally shares the pain, the injustices, and the sufferings of all his fellow men.[5]

Alinsky advocated a paradigm in which radicals would work with others and train leaders to organize their communities to build power for real change. The current incarnation of the IAF (along with three other major CBCO networks across the country) trains leaders to create a strong network of folks inside their congregations, and then join together with congregations in their area to become a force for the common good.

Members of the GBIO organizing staff trained Temple Israel leaders to conduct a "congregational development campaign," one of several such campaigns that took place throughout the more than seventy institutions that are GBIO. The campaigns had two goals: first, to identify the deeply and broadly felt concerns that bind the members of a congregation; and second, to create a relational network in which people feel connected to each other's personal narratives.

A leadership team was trained. They then set the vision for and implemented a campaign in which members of the congregation talked to each other. Over three months, having set as a target 500 individual conversations between members, they actually carried out 807 meetings. In each, members told each other their stories. They explained why they belonged to the congregation. They discussed the role of Judaism in their lives. And finally, they told each other stories of what they really struggled with. They asked each other, "What keeps you up at night?"

All that talking taught us that we are not alone. Our stories of frustration are not isolated. We found ourselves connected to a community of souls who could do more than study and pray together; we could be honest about our lives, and begin to find comfort in common concern. We also learned that the things that are broken around us are not our private challenges. They are public, collective problems.

Our Ancient Story:
The Potential for Redemption Is in Our Relationships

The Exodus from Egypt, the master story of our tradition, told and retold from generation to generation, is a template for all redemption. First and foremost, it teaches that in every time and place, redemption is possible. It begins with a cry, as those who suffer become aware of their suffering. It continues with rage at the injustice, and a willingness to act. It requires leadership and relationships. As the circle of leadership and participation widens, the community gains power. The people must begin to articulate their story—both the story of their outrage and the story of the just society that they can imagine for themselves and each other. In the Exodus story, God answers the people's cry by giving the Torah, a retelling of the past and a series of laws to provide a standard of justice for the future. The encounter with God, the Ultimate Other, serves as a model for encountering any Other.

Assembled at the mountain, the Israelites respond with one voice to God, *"na'aseh v'nishma*—all this we shall do and we shall hear!"* (Exod. 24:7). With these words, they enter a dialogue with God, not just crying out with their own painful story but expressing a willingness to listen to the common story of humanity and to act upon it. Redemption culminates as the people stand in relationship together, bound by a new, shared story.

The Power for Redemption Outside of Ourselves

In the globalized twenty-first century, justice transcends categories of race, class, and faith. Today, standing together for redemption means discovering our shared suffering and being challenged by each other's divergent traditions. If our work inside of GBIO taught us that we are not alone as individuals, most of all it taught us that we are not alone as Jews. As an example, consider the story of the GBIO nursing care campaign.

Many of the congregants in the GBIO listening campaign told stories of struggling to care for their aging parents. Some were stretched to the limits by caring for dependent parents at home; others agonized over the poor conditions of the nursing homes to which they had entrusted their beloved parents.

As it happened, nine Haitian churches were participating in that particular campaign, and they told an agonizing story about nursing care—from the other side. We discovered that 90 percent of all certified nursing assistants in Boston are Haitian immigrants. In their meetings, members of the Haitian community described how they were overworked, mistreated, and disrespected. They told stories of their own suffering—and how their elderly charges suffered as a result.

GBIO gave a context for people to know each other's stories across boundaries not usually crossed: racial, religious, and, especially, class. Not only did we begin to hear each other's stories, but we also discovered how profoundly connected we were. The result of this dialogue about nursing care was a nursing care and worker bill of rights. Teams met with nursing home directors and challenged them to sign the bill, and many did. The campaign culminated with a meeting at one of the Haitian congregations at which the State Attorney General was asked to listen to our stories and issue a public advisory to the nursing care industry clarifying the law.

The State Attorney General arrived at this meeting, packed with hundreds of people from all faiths and ethnic backgrounds, ready to refuse our request. After hearing our testimonials and standing with us in prayer, he rose to speak. Departing from his prepared text, he described the pain of watching his own immigrant mother suffer as a poorly treated domestic worker. In an incredible public shift, surprising to his own staff, he committed himself to issue the advisory.

It was clear as we continued meeting in the months after the successful campaign, how much real change took place. Workers were treated better. Residents received better care. People felt less powerless to care for their aging parents. Such a victory could only happen with the power of organized people.

Conclusion: Redemption Is for Everyone

Year after year, we hear Isaiah's call anew. But in our isolation, we are powerless. Hearing his words as we stand alone, they are a rebuke. In the midst of our prayer and fasting we are ashamed: the world as it is is parched with oppression. But we are *not* alone. Isaiah's ancient words echo across the centuries, calling us to wake up and become the people of redemption. Together. His radical call addresses not the single "you," but the communal you.

The power for systemic change emanates from the Divine, but it comes only from authentic relationships both inside the Jewish family and beyond, with other communities who share a vision of a world redeemed. We can harness the power of our relationships and engage together in bold, public action, across lines of faith, class, and race, and address the structural sources of economic and social injustice.

Isaiah, the ultimate radical, calls to us: redemption is possible. Let us write a new narrative, in which we teach each other how to tell each other the real stories of our lives. Let the synagogue be a place where personal suffering becomes understood as a public problem. Let our congregations become strong social networks that can act together to become a force for change. Let us build power with our sisters and brothers of faith, with all our neighbors who would join us and discover the awesome power of our relationships.

Let us become real "repairers of the breach." Let us bring on the redemption of a world that is "like a watered garden; like a spring whose waters never fail."

Redemption isn't just for radicals. Redemption is for everyone.

The Blood of Our Neighbors
American Health Care Reform

SANDRA M. FOX, LCSW AND MARTIN I. SELTMAN, MD

Sandra M. Fox, LCSW, is a licensed clinical social worker in private practice. She also serves as chair of the Western Pennsylvania Coalition for Single-Payer Healthcare, is the organizer of Healthcare-NOW, and chair of the Single-Payer Health Care Task Force of the Pittsburgh Interfaith Impact Network.

Martin I. Seltman, MD, is Family Practice department chair at the Western Pennsylvania Hospital, residency director at the Forbes Family Practice, and a member of Physicians for Social Responsibility, Physicians for a National Health Program, and the Western Pennsylvania Coalition for Single-Payer Healthcare.

According to the 2005 U.S. Census, 15.9 percent of the population, or 46.6 million people, are without health insurance.[1] This represents an increase of 4 million from 1999 Census figures.[2] The numbers continue to grow, with fewer employers offering insurance, and increases in medical expenses far outpacing the rate of inflation and wage increases.

The number of *under*insured people is even higher, as more employers and consumers are switching to high-deductible plans in an effort to curb monthly premiums. Unfortunately, this leaves many people unprotected from anything short of catastrophic illness. Out-of-pocket costs inhibit the use of primary and preventive services, especially for middle-income families who don't qualify for Medical Assistance and can't afford tax-free Health Savings Accounts. Stripped-down versions of coverage lack essential ingredients of care, such as prescription drug coverage, mental health benefits, and drug and alcohol treatment. Whether under the Blue Cross/Blue Shield's so-called "Complete Care" or through state programs like Pennsylvania's Adult Basic for low-income adults (which has a waiting list of more than 70,000 people), substandard coverage is disappointingly common.

According to a February 2007 *New York Times*/CBS News poll, "Access to affordable health care is at the top of the public's domestic agenda."[3] A recent survey by Jewish Funds for Justice revealed that health care reform is the number one voting issue for Jews.[4] But is there a "Jewish position" on health care reform? Most of us can recite in our sleep the biblical commandment, "You shall not stand idly by the blood of your neighbor" (Lev. 19:16). What about our neighbor who is sick, but not yet bleeding? What about when the bleeding person is not a neighbor, but someone in a different town or state, of a different race or class background?

The Torah teaches that if a dead body is found abandoned in a field, the elders of the nearest town must prepare and bury the body, make a sacrifice, and pronounce a formula absolving them of any guilt: "Our hands did not shed this blood, nor did our eyes see it done."[5] The Rabbis of the Mishnah rightly ask: Why must the elders make such a declaration, when no one would have suspected them of committing the crime in the first place? The Rabbis explain that the elders need not proclaim that they are innocent of murder, but rather that they are innocent of ignoring a person at risk and in need. "He came not into our hands that we should have dismissed him without sustenance, and we did not see him and leave him without escort!"[6] The town elders must swear that there was nothing they could have done to prevent this death. The implication is that if the elders had known about the danger, they would have been obligated to step in and prevent harm. The dead person could be a local or a foreigner, Jewish or non-Jewish, but unless we intervene, we are guilty.

While some Americans continue to take pride in the U.S. health care system, believing it to be among the best in the world, we are doing abysmally by Jewish standards, which implore us at every turn to prevent harm to others and to take care of those in need—the poor, the widow, and the orphan among them.

We also have a shameful record by international standards. In addition to having a shocking number of people without adequate health coverage or any health insurance at all, the United States is ranked by the World Health Organization thirty-seventh in the world for overall health system performance. According to the Institute of Medicine, an estimated 18,000 people die prematurely every year in this country for lack of health insurance. Longevity is greater and infant mortality lower in countries with national health insurance, including our Canadian neighbor. Yet the United States spends a much greater proportion of its Gross Domestic Product (16 percent) on health care than any other country.

So, where is all this money going? According to the *New England Journal of Medicine*, 33 cents on the health care dollar goes to administrative costs, marketing, and the salaries of executives.[7] Costs of pharmaceuticals are notoriously higher in the United States than in countries that are able to negotiate lower drug prices. The insurance industry is largely unregulated, and consequently many of the neediest people are unable to secure quality (or any) coverage, due to prohibitive costs or rejection due to preexisting conditions.

Who are the faces of the broken U.S. health care system? Sarah, a grade school teacher in her mid-thirties, has asthma that has been very well controlled with medications.[8] She's never been hospitalized and has rarely needed to go to an emergency room. After leaving her full-time job, Sarah attempted to purchase health insurance as an individual. Her application was denied because of her "preexisting condition." Even after her physician wrote a letter explaining that Sarah's asthma was well under control, the insurance company maintained its denial. Sarah's health care was deemed too expensive to be covered. In the current health care marketplace, insurance companies have an incentive to provide coverage only to those who need it the least, because they know that fully healthy people are the least likely to collect on their premiums.

Jack is a nurse in his late twenties. He is HIV-positive, but feels fully healthy and has never had any complications from his disease. He recently chose one of the lower-cost insurance policies offered by his work. Despite the fact that he has been feeling well and still passionately wants to serve others in his job, his lab reports indicated that it was time to start anti-retroviral medications (which, since the 1990s, have been increasingly effective in controlling the infection and preventing the dreaded complications of AIDS). Jack's new medication, only one pill per day, costs $1,300 per month. After two months, Jack learned that he had reached the limit of his drug coverage and would have to pay for his medication out of pocket for the rest of the year—on a salary of $30,000 per year. And his modest salary makes him ineligible for indigent care from the pharmaceutical company (which would entitle him to free medication). Though Jack spends his time caring for the sick, he cannot afford to take care of himself. He is not counted among the uninsured, but his insurance coverage is inadequate to meet his health care needs.

In contrast, the insurance and pharmaceutical industries are doing very well. In Pittsburgh, Highmark Blue Cross/Blue Shield (a "nonprofit" that pays no taxes) had a surplus announced in 2006 of $2.8 billion. Its CEO made $3.2 million in 2006; the combined pay of its top ten executives increased 41 percent last year, from $8 million to $11.3 million, while premiums went up. The world's thirteen largest drug companies recorded $62 billion in profits in 2004.[9]

Why are we supporting the huge profits of the insurance and pharmaceutical industries at the expense of our neighbors' health, and our own? And, how can we justify the fact that people cannot get decent health care because they cannot obtain adequate insurance coverage that meets their needs? As Jews, we cannot.

Maimonides anticipated contemporary concerns centuries ago, when he wrote in his oath:

> The eternal providence has appointed me to watch over the life and health of Thy creatures. May the love for my art actuate me at all times; may neither avarice nor miserliness, nor thirst for glory or for a great reputation engage my mind; for the enemies of truth and philanthropy could easily deceive me and make me forgetful of my lofty aim of doing good to Thy children.[10]

While Maimonides was expressing the moral aim of a single physician, the values in this passage are easily translatable to the public policy level. Patients are not to be seen as sources of profit, but as God's children, all equally deserving of good medical care. Elsewhere,

Maimonides lists provision of health care as the most important service a community needs to offer its residents.[11]

So, how can we "watch over the life and health" of *all* Americans without putting us all in financial jeopardy? How can we create a system that can afford to insure people with significant medical needs, regardless of their ability to pay?

The solution is single-payer universal health care. A single government body would collect the revenue and pay private providers; patients would have free choice in choosing doctors—without restrictive networks, monthly premiums, co-pays, or deductibles. Office visits, hospitalizations, emergency care, prescription drugs, durable medical equipment, long-term care, mental health services, drug and alcohol treatment, dental treatment, vision, hearing aids, and chiropractic care would be covered.

The barriers to passage of single-payer universal health care are daunting, given the threat to the financial interests of health insurance and pharmaceutical companies. They will understandably use their political clout to fight the move toward a single-payer system. According to OpenSecrets.org, the industry that spent the most money on lobbying from 1998 to 2005 was "Pharmaceuticals/Health Products"—$900,792,455. The second-highest industry during the same period was the insurance industry, at $760,469,198. Add to this the millions spent on campaign contributions and marketing (all of which we are ultimately paying for in our premiums and drug costs), and we have powerful political and financial interests working against affordable, quality health care. But history has shown us that powerful political change *can* happen when citizens mobilize and build power. Today, creating an equitable system of affordable, quality health care is a struggle for human dignity and life.

National surveys repeatedly indicate that a majority of people in the United States believe the federal government should provide quality health care for all its citizens.[12] As Jews, we also remember the story of the dead body in the field, and the commandment to the elders in the nearest town to absolve themselves of guilt. If the community, or the body politic, has the power to prevent life-threatening illness, or to treat that illness, and does not, it stands liable. The Torah also more generally reminds us—thirty-six times, according to Rabbinic tradition—"Remember the stranger!, for you were once strangers in the land of Egypt." Our tradition simply will not let us rest while illness threatens the lives of the most vulnerable among us.

What can individuals do? A growing grassroots movement includes physicians (Physicians for a National Health Program), nurses (e.g., California Nurses Association), labor groups, faith groups, and many others. The national grassroots organization Healthcare—NOW! (www.healthcare-now.org), led by Marilyn Clement (who at one time worked with the Rev. Martin Luther King, Jr.), is leading the way to inspire, educate, develop, and implement strategies that build this movement from the ground up and effectively push for change through a broad-based coalition, including members of the Jewish community.

Efforts to advocate for single-payer universal health care in this country began under President Truman. In the Jewish community, the Union for Reform Judaism (URJ), which serves Reform congregations in North America, adopted a resolution at its biennial conference in 1993 calling for "Reform of the Health Care System." This document states:

> Our resolutions on "social insurance" for adequate health care date back to 1948, and on a single-payer approach to national health care, to 1975.... We seek a national health care plan which grants universal access to health care benefits, including access to primary and acute health care, immunization services, early diagnostic and treatment programs, provider and consumer education, programs of extended care and rehabilitation, mental health, and health and wellness promotion.... An effective plan will provide for cost containment, equitable financing, and assure quality of services.

The 1993 resolution advocates for "a single-payer system as the most likely means of fulfilling the principles articulated in past UAHC and CCAR resolutions on health care reform" and encourages "congregations to continue their educational effort on the issue of health care, with a special focus on promoting advocacy by our congregations, their members, and UAHC [now URJ] affiliates."

Less than one week after the November 2006 elections, the health insurance industry's main lobbyist group—America's Health Insurance Plans (AHIP)—declared its support for universal coverage. Why this turn of events? We believe it is because insurance companies have taken seriously the public's dissatisfaction with the current health care system. These companies surely read the 2005 Pew Research Survey, reporting that a 65 percent majority "favor a government guarantee of health insurance for all Americans, even if it means raising taxes."

While the insurance industry realizes that public opinion has turned against it, it has not forgotten about its own bottom line. The industry is putting forward a universal plan that—unlike the single-payer model—keeps the insurance industry at the center of health care. Instead of the government standing in for the insurance companies, reducing administrative costs and executive salaries, and negotiating lower prices from pharmaceutical companies, the industry proposes that the government would subsidize purchase of their own insurance packages.

In this scenario, taxpayers would still be paying the same high price to insurance companies for their exorbitant administrative costs, CEO salaries, and profits. Without more government regulation of the pharmaceutical industry, taxpayers would also pay more to cover drug costs for those who need them. Jack would still be underinsured, unable to pay for anti-retroviral drugs for his HIV. Taxpayers would continue to pay more when Jack and others land in the emergency room as a last resort. Personal bankruptcies would continue for those with insurance, due to inadequate coverage and soaring out-of-pocket costs. And American businesses will remain at a competitive disadvantage globally, as they struggle to stay alive and pay inflated health care premiums. A real solution to our nation's health care crisis must go further in reducing costs and providing quality care for all.

In the book of Genesis, Joseph is thrown by his brothers into a pit, and then, transported to Egypt, he gets thrown into prison. There, Joseph transforms himself from self-centered adolescent to morally responsible adult. He *notices* and *asks* two of the prisoners why they appear sad (Gen. 40:6, 7), signs that his own suffering has taught him empathy and compassion. He learns to listen to the dreams of others, not just his own. His compassion and wisdom save his life, when he is able to interpret Pharaoh's dreams. Ultimately, his careful listening, diagnosis, and responsible planning save the lives of countless Egyptians and his own estranged Israelite family during a grave famine.

We are all at risk of great suffering; some of us are already in pain. We need to hear the cries. Our country is bleeding, and we are standing idly by, unable to proclaim our innocence; our hands may not shed blood, but our eyes are seeing it done. No ritual can absolve us of our responsibility—to work toward a transformation of the U.S. health care system, so that it can truly serve the health of all, leaving no one behind.

The Global AIDS Crisis

Caring for the Sick by Standing with the Activists

JACOB FEINSPAN AND JULIA GREENBERG

Jacob Feinspan is a senior policy associate at the American Jewish World Service (AJWS) and directs AJWS's advocacy programs on global HIV/AIDS, international debt cancellation, and Darfur in Washington, DC. In addition to representing AJWS on Capitol Hill, he coordinates the grassroots advocacy of thousands of AJWS supporters around the country.

Julia Greenberg is the director of grants at the American Jewish World Service. A graduate of Wesleyan University, she spearheaded the AJWS HIV/AIDS program in Africa.

At one point in my life AIDS was beating me, leaving me bedridden for more than a year. I didn't have a plan for the future except waiting for my death and thinking about the virus, crying every day. With the availability of free anti-retroviral treatment [ART] … I was able to get well again. But in order to maintain my health through effective ART use, I needed to earn money to support myself and my family. This motivated me to be a member of this group. Now, I don't have the time to think about the virus. I'm busy every day and surrounded by others in the same situation as me. As I am living with the community, community members are changing their attitudes towards people living with the virus.

—Yalemzewd, 35 years old, mother of two, a client of Mekdim ("Pioneer"), Ethiopia's first association of people living with HIV/AIDS

In 2005, 4.3 million people were newly infected with the HIV virus, bringing the total number of people living with HIV close to 40 million. In the same year, nearly 3 million died from the virus, bringing to 25 million the number of people who have died since the AIDS crisis began.1

Why, in this essay, do we choose to focus on HIV/AIDS when the leading causes of death in most poor countries are still common diseases such as diarrhea and pulmonary failure, usually associated with maternal and infant health and childbirth?[2] We chose this focus because the global AIDS activist movement is a model for modern struggles to secure economic, social, and cultural rights around the world. If the Jewish community is going to broaden its role supporting global social justice struggles, and it should, then a close examination of this movement is necessary, not only for lessons learned, but also for inspiration.

The AIDS activist movement began in the United States when the Reagan Administration dismissed AIDS as a gay disease not only to be ignored, but to be used to inflame hatred and homophobia. In response, the people most affected by HIV organized (most famously and effectively in the group named ACT UP), taking to the streets with slogans like "Silence Equals Death" and wearing pink triangles (the symbol Nazis used to label homosexuals in the concentration camps) to claim their human right to health.

The global treatment access movement has since spread from the streets of New York and San Francisco to the streets of Lagos and Delhi and the dusty roads of rural Uganda and Cambodia. Everywhere that HIV/AIDS is impacting people, community-based organizations are being created by those affected to make social change. One organization that supports such community groups is the American Jewish World Service, where the authors of this essay are staff. We believe that supporting people who are claiming the tools and resources that are rightfully theirs to care for one another represents the ultimate Jewish response to this pandemic. After all, the most powerful words in the story of the Exodus, the foundational story of the Jewish people, are "Let *my* people go." The true power of the Exodus is not simply that the Israelites moved from bondage to freedom, but rather that they exercised their own power in doing so.

This does not mean that Jews can or should stand on the sidelines as spectators. When given the opportunity to save a life, we must do so. But we also must recognize that more lives will be saved when we stand in solidarity with those demanding their own liberation. We can't demand it for them.

The Fight for Treatment

In the 1990s, while AIDS was spreading throughout Africa, public health institutions and governments publicly pronounced that it would be prohibitively expensive to treat the millions of people living with AIDS or to strengthen the health care infrastructure necessary to support the rollout of AIDS treatments. Focusing what efforts they made on prevention, these institutions effectively wrote off the lives of millions.

That inaction was met by a global demand from people infected and affected by HIV/AIDS for access to life-saving AIDS treatment. Though this movement is called the treatment access movement, the activists involved recognize that pitting prevention against treatment is a false debate. What treatment activists bring to the table is the understanding that treatment, prevention, and community-based care must go hand in hand.

When parents have the treatment that prolongs their lives, their children do not become orphans. When treatment brings viral loads down to undetectable levels, it is less likely that the virus will be passed on. When women can access drugs that prevent mother-to-child transmission of HIV, there are fewer infected children. When people understand that AIDS is not a death sentence, they get tested, and knowledge of their HIV status helps them make the right decisions about prevention and care.

The AIDS treatment access movement has successfully challenged government inaction and corporate greed and profiteering. The AIDS crisis has had the effect of placing systemic poverty in poor countries under a magnifying glass and exposing some of the factors that perpetuate it—most significantly racism, gender inequality, and violence.

Early in the crisis, ACT UP shamed governments and pharmaceutical companies into naming the crisis and investing in research for treatment and vaccines. At the 1996 AIDS conference in Vancouver, scientists unveiled evidence showing that a combination of therapies, known as anti-retrovirals (ARVs), could suppress the virus in the body to undetectable levels, and significantly prolong lives. Almost immediately, HIV-positive people's lives were transformed with drugs costing approximately $14,000 a year.

Between 1997 and 2000, a global activist movement began to take root, fueled by the glaring disparity in access to treatment between Western people living with AIDS and their counterparts in developing countries. For example, $14,000 represented nineteen times the annual income of the average African affected by AIDS. This fact was a wakeup call for Western doctors, scientists, and activists, many of whom were confronting the realities of poverty in the developing world for the first time.

In 2000, South African activists took to the streets of Durban to demand treatment during the first international AIDS conference held in a developing country with a high HIV prevalence rate. They were joined by activists from around the world wearing the now famous "HIV POSITIVE" T-shirts created by the South African Treatment Action Campaign (TAC). TAC's leader, Zackie Achmat, an HIV-positive man with access to treatment, refused to begin therapy until the South African government made it available to all those who needed it.

Emboldened by the solidarity demonstrated at Durban, TAC and its allies around the world shamed the world's largest pharmaceutical companies (many represented by PhRMA, the Pharmaceutical Research and Manufacturers of America) into dropping their plans to sue the South African government to prevent it from importing cheaper generic medicines to treat AIDS. In 2001, when the U.N. convened its first special session on AIDS, civil society showed up in force demanding the "three Ds": dollars (for the recently established Global Fund to Fight Tuberculosis, AIDS, and Malaria), drugs, and drop the debt.

In 2002, the Thai Network of People Living with HIV/AIDS won a precedent-setting case against drug giant Bristol-Myers Squibb in which the court declared the company's patent application in Thailand illegal—a ruling that made it possible for Thailand to produce a generic form of an ARV. Finally, in 2003, TAC won a case against the South African government in its Constitutional Court that compelled the reluctant ministry of health to provide a simple course of therapy to prevent mothers from passing on HIV to their children during childbirth. In 2004, after a TAC civil disobedience campaign, the cabinet agreed to roll out a national plan to provide anti-retroviral therapy to all people living with AIDS who needed it. Zackie Achmat began taking his drugs and continues to lead TAC today.

These victories for people over profits actualized what Jewish thinkers have also taught for generations—saving life trumps nearly everything. Almost 1,500 years ago, the Babylonian Talmud (*Yoma* 82a) recorded, "There is nothing that can stand before [the duty of] saving life, with the exception of idolatry, incest, and bloodshed [which are prohibited in all situations]." In large part due to the work of these activists, this value is now being codified in international law. The World Trade Organization recently agreed that countries can break patents to produce or purchase generic medications to respond to public health emergencies.

The Future of the Fight

Today, international policy makers and governments are acting on their historic commitments to fight AIDS. In 2002, the Global Fund to Fight Tuberculosis, AIDS, and Malaria, an independent funding mechanism called for by activists, began its work, and it has now committed U.S. $7.1 billion in 136 countries. In 2003, President Bush announced the President's Emergency Plan for AIDS Relief (PEPFAR), committing $15 billion to fight the disease. UNAIDS and the World Health Organization have announced a global goal of providing universal access to treatment by 2010. Private foundations are also joining the fight. Between massive commitments by the Bill and Melinda Gates Foundation and successful efforts by the William J. Clinton Foundation to bring down the price of ARVs in the developing world, we see a world that has changed significantly as a result of the voices of grassroots communities affected by AIDS who fought to be heard.

In *Pirkei Avot* (1:14), Hillel teaches, "If I am not for myself, who will be for me? And if I am only for myself, what am I?" Some argue that before we can begin to concern ourselves with poverty and disease around the world, we must first put our own house in order. Others insist that we cannot wait to address the global crisis any longer—the cost is simply too high. Hillel's teaching highlights the tension between one's inner circle and the greater community. But it is also predicated on the assumption that we are less connected to those physically further from us.

People living with AIDS around the world asked themselves, "If I am not for myself, who will be for me?" They began to speak publicly about living with AIDS in the face of intense stigma and discrimination. And activists from wealthy countries, having fought and won access to life-saving drugs, responded by saying, "If I am only for myself, what am I?" They joined in with their brothers' and sisters' struggle halfway around the world.

What is our obligation as Jews to join in the continuing struggle to address the impact of the global AIDS crisis when we still fight poverty and disease in America, and even within the Jewish community?

There is still plenty to do at home. Today, black women living in the United States are thirteen times more likely to die of AIDS than white women. Despite massive public education campaigns, the number of new HIV infections has not decreased for more than a decade and recent analyses suggest a potential rise among some populations. And in our nation's capital, one in twenty adults is HIV-positive.

But what happens at home doesn't just impact those affected by HIV/AIDS here in the United States. Because of the dangerous infiltration of right-wing ideology into U.S. government-funded prevention efforts, the critically important Emergency Plan for AIDS Relief (PEPFAR) under President Bush mandated that one-third of all HIV prevention funding must support abstinence-until-marriage-only programs. This ideological change from funding condoms to funding abstinence has had a measurable impact in Uganda, where HIV prevalence rates, which fell from as high as 15 percent to 5 percent in 2001 under the impact of a comprehensive prevention program that stressed condom use, began to rise again under a new abstinence-only policy. [3]

The medieval Jewish philosopher Maimonides wrote that not only are we permitted to break other commandments to save a life, but that if we fail to act, than we have ourselves transgressed.[4] Maimonides's writings suggest that the nature of the threat, its imminence, or even what is required to intervene are irrelevant; we are equally guilty of transgression if we fail to act to save a life, no matter the circumstances. And we *can* act to fight AIDS:

- As philanthropists, we can advocate among faith-based organizations that orphanages are not the answer to the orphan crisis and that resources must be committed to bolster the strained extended family systems of Africa.
- As a faith-based community, we can advocate that the U.S. government refrain from attaching conditions to AIDS funding that are informed by religious ideologies rather than good science, for example, by ending the abstinence-only earmark and increasing funding for general reproductive health and rights work.
- As people standing in solidarity with the oppressed, we can support emerging lesbian, gay, and transgender movements that have become visible and active in part because of globally funded prevention efforts. These communities can't protect themselves from HIV if they continue to face insurmountable levels of discrimination and violence.
- As advocates, we can demand that the U.S. and European governments end their practice of poaching health care workers from developing countries, and instead invest in training, support, and salaries, both domestically and internationally, so that we can all receive the high-quality medical care we deserve.

Today, people living with AIDS in poor countries and communities are fighting for their lives. Only sustained pressure by activists will ensure that the international community lives up to its commitments. A recent report by the International Treatment Preparedness Coalition titled "Missing the Target" showed that only a quarter of people who need treatment are accessing it.[5]

But we shouldn't forget that only four years ago it was fair to say that practically no one in the developing world was on ARVs. The global treatment access movement can claim credit for saving the lives of the 2 million people who are taking these life-saving drugs daily.

Certainly, as Jews we understand the imperative of the fight for community survival. Indeed, it is an unsettling fact that there are three times as many HIV-positive people in the world as there are Jews. By raising up their collective voices to say "Let our people live," the HIV-positive community is leading a new Exodus. And by demanding that our government redouble its efforts to fight the global AIDS pandemic by providing our fair share of the global resources needed to reverse the tide of this disease, we stand in solidarity with those demanding their own liberation and truly fulfill our annual obligation to retell the story of our own.

A Jewish View of Embryonic Stem Cell Research

RABBI ELLIOT N. DORFF, PhD

Rabbi Elliot N. Dorff, PhD, is the rector and Distinguished Professor of Philosophy at the American Jewish University. Dorff is vice-chair of the Conservative Movement's Committee on Jewish Law and Standards. His many publications include: *Matters of Life and Death: A Jewish Approach to Modern Medical Ethics*; *To Do the Right and the Good: A Jewish Approach to Modern Social Ethics*, winner of the National Jewish Book Award in Contemporary Jewish Life; and *The Way Into* Tikkun Olam *(Repairing the World)* (Jewish Lights), a finalist for the National Jewish Book Award.

In the Jewish tradition, our bodies belong to God; we have them on loan during our lease on life.[1] God, as owner of our bodies, can and does impose conditions on how we use them. Among these conditions is the requirement that we seek to preserve human life and health (*pikuakh nefesh*). As a corollary to this, we have a duty to seek to develop new cures for human diseases.

In the case of most diseases, the process of finding a cure does not present ethical problems. Growing penicillin (a mold) in a petri dish, discovering that willow bark makes a useful pain reliever and blood thinner (aspirin), or using sutures to help the body knit itself back together are natural means of overcoming illness, of the kind the human species has used for centuries. More modern inventions, such as heart-lung machines, do raise ethical questions (e.g., when does life end?) but do not raise questions about the legitimacy of the cure itself.

The Jewish tradition accepts both natural and artificial means to overcome illness. Physicians are the agents and partners of God in the ongoing act of healing. Thus, the mere fact that human beings create a specific therapy rather than finding it in nature does not impugn its legitimacy. On the contrary, we have a duty to God to develop and use any therapies that can aid us in taking care of our bodies, which ultimately belong to God.

Stem cell research, however, does raise moral questions. All human beings, regardless of their levels of ability and disability, are created in the image of God.[2] Embryonic stem cell research raises the question of whether such cells, given that they have the potential to become human beings, must be treated with the same level of value with which we treat any other human being.

A second objection to embryonic stem cell research that some have raised is that when we manipulate such cells, we are "playing God." Clearly, we are not omniscient as God is, and so we must take whatever precautions we can to ensure that our actions do not harm ourselves or our world in the very effort to improve them. A certain epistemological humility, in other words, must pervade whatever we do, especially when we are pushing the scientific envelope, as we are in stem cell research. We are, as Genesis says, supposed to work the world *and* preserve it; it is that *balance* that is our divine duty.

To answer these questions raised by embryonic stem cell research, we must first understand what they are to see whether they meet the criteria of being a human being created in the image of God. To meet the second objection, we must learn why scientists are interested in doing research on them, and how they are obtained, to make sure we balance the potential for cure with any harm to people or the world that the cure could cause.

The Current State of the Science of Stem Cells

For an accurate description of stem cells, we turn to a document issued in May 2000 by the director of the National Institutes of Health (NIH) titled "Stem Cells: A Primer."[3]

> Stem cells are best described in the context of normal human development. Human development begins when a sperm fertilizes an egg and creates a single cell that has the potential to form

an entire organism. This fertilized egg is *totipotent*, meaning that its potential is total. In the first hours after fertilization, this cell divides into identical totipotent cells. This means that either one of these cells, if placed into a woman's uterus, has the potential to develop into a fetus. In fact, identical twins develop when two totipotent cells separate and develop into two individual, genetically identical human beings. Approximately four days after fertilization and after several cycles of cell division, these totipotent cells begin to specialize, forming a hollow sphere of cells, called a blastocyst. The blastocyst has an outer layer of cells, and inside the hollow sphere there is a cluster of cells called the inner cell mass.

The outer layer of cells will go on to form the placenta and other supporting tissues needed for fetal development in the uterus. The inner cell mass cells will go on to form virtually all of the tissues of the human body. Although the inner cell mass cells can form virtually every type of cell found in the human body, they cannot form an organism because they are unable to give rise to the placenta and supporting tissues necessary for development in the human uterus. These inner mass cells are *pluripotent*—they can give rise to many types of cells but not all types of cells necessary for fetal development. Because their potential is not total, they are not totipotent and they are not embryos. In fact, if an inner cell mass cell were placed into a woman's uterus, it would not develop into a fetus.

The pluripotent stem cells undergo further specialization into stem cells that are committed to give rise to cells that have a particular function. Examples of this include blood stem cells, which give rise to red blood cells, white blood cells, and platelets; and skin stem cells, which give rise to the various types of skin cells. These more specialized stem cells are called *multipotent*.

The ethical questions raised by embryonic stem cells do not apply to the use of multipotent cells or to the use of adult stem cells in blood, skin, and other parts of the body. This is because such cells have been differentiated to the point where they can only produce other cells like themselves (they are only "multipotent"). Embryonic stem cells, however, can and do transform themselves into all of the tissues of the body (they are "pluripotent").

Why do scientists want to use pluripotent embryonic stem cells rather than restrict themselves to multipotent stem cells? According to the NIH document referenced above, scientists hope to learn or do at least the following three things:

1. *Learn about the process of cell specialization.* How do stem cells decide which tissues to become and how many to make of each type of tissue? We know that turning genes on and off is central to the process of human development, but we do not know much about how these decisions are made in the process of human development or how stem cells are turned on or off. Some of our most serious medical conditions, such as cancer and birth defects, are due to abnormal cell specialization and cell division. A better understanding of normal cell development is necessary for scientists to learn what goes wrong with cells when cancer or birth defects occur so that hopefully some day such abnormal developments can be arrested and reversed.
2. *Test drugs more safely and efficiently.* Research on pluripotent human stem cells could also dramatically change the way we develop drugs and test them for safety. Only the drugs proven to be safe and effective in cell line testing would graduate to further testing in laboratory animals and ultimately in human subjects.
3. *Develop cell therapies.* Each year thousands of people die for want of a suitable organ for transplant. Pluripotent stem cell research has the potential to resolve our problem of organ shortage. Once we know how to direct such cells to create specific kinds of cells and how to turn them on and off, we have the potential to use them to create whatever organs are needed.

Furthermore, stem cell therapies may cure conditions that organ transplantation has not yet been able to cure. Specifically, scientists hope to use cell therapies to cure Parkinson's and Alzheimer's diseases, spinal cord injuries, strokes, burns, heart diseases, diabetes, osteoarthritis, and rheumatoid arthritis. Preliminary work in mice and other animals has already demonstrated that healthy heart muscle cells transplanted into a diseased heart successfully repopulate the heart tissue and work together with the host cells to repair diseased heart muscle; it is therefore not simply a "pipe dream" to imagine that the same kind of therapy might work in humans.

The source of embryonic stem cells raises its own set of ethical issues. Embryonic stem cells may be derived from any of the following sources:

1. *Aborted fetuses.* This method, of course, immediately raises the issue of the conditions under which abortion is permitted, if ever. In the context of America's "abortion wars," researchers do not plan on using this source of stem cells.

2. *Frozen embryos destined to be discarded.* Couples having difficulty conceiving a child may use in vitro fertilization (IVF)—that is, fertilization in a glass dish—in that effort. When the couple has had as many children as they plan to have, or give up trying, they commonly ask that their remaining frozen embryos be destroyed so that they no longer have to pay for the frozen storage. But with the informed consent of such couples, the embryos may be used instead for medical research. It is this method that most scientists interested in carrying out embryonic stem cell research plan on using.

3. *Stem cell "farms."* Very few couples, though, agree to have their frozen embryos used for medical research, probably because producing them in the first place was so expensive and emotionally draining for the infertile couple. Moreover, researchers worry about the quality of frozen embryos from couples who had difficulty conceiving: was the problem they encountered in the delivery system of the couple (the testicular tubes in the man or the fallopian tubes or vaginal mucous membranes in the woman) or in the embryos they produced themselves? For such reasons, in 2001 the Jones Institute for Reproductive Medicine of Eastern Virginia Medical School revealed that it had procured sperm and eggs from donors who had expressly agreed that their gametes would be used not to overcome infertility but

for medical research. This raised a storm of protest. Now, however, scientists have perfected the methods for freezing eggs as well as sperm and embryos, and that means that young and healthy men and women can donate gametes for research, regardless of their marital status. This has raised this possible source of embryonic stem cells anew.

In addition, scientists are experimenting with several other methods to produce stem cells: somatic cell nuclear transfer (SCNT), the same technique that has been used for cloning plants and animals; extracting a cell from an embryo; and even electronically and chemically prompting the egg cell alone to produce stem cells.

Jewish Views of Genetic Materials

During the first forty days of gestation, the fetus, according to the Talmud, is "as if it were simply water," and from the forty-first day until birth it is "like the thigh of its mother."[4] Neither men nor women may amputate their thigh at will because that would be injuring their bodies, which belong to God. Thus according to Jewish law, abortion is generally prohibited, not as an act of murder (the Catholic position), but as an act of self-injury. On the other hand, if the thigh turns gangrenous, then both men and women have the positive duty to have their thigh amputated in order to save their lives. Similarly, if the woman's life or health is at stake, an abortion *must* be performed to save the life or the physical or mental health of the woman, for she is without question a full-fledged human being with all the protections of Jewish law, while the fetus is still only part of the woman's body.

When there is an elevated risk to the woman beyond that of normal pregnancy but not so much as to constitute a clear threat to her life or health, abortion is permitted but not required; that is an assessment that the woman should make in consultation with the father of the fetus, other members of her family, her physician, her rabbi, and anyone else who can help her grapple with the many issues involved in her particular case. Some recent authorities, including the Conservative Movement's Committee on Jewish Law and Standards, would also permit abortions in cases where testing indicates that the fetus is "severely defective," suffering from serious malformations or terminal diseases like Tay-Sachs.[5]

The upshot of the Jewish stance on abortion, then, is that *if* a fetus had been aborted for legitimate reasons under Jewish law, then the aborted fetus may be used to advance our efforts to preserve the life and health of others. If we may and even should use the bodies of human beings to enable others to live through organ transplantation, then how much the more so may we use a part of a body—in this case, the fetus—for that purpose? Using aborted fetuses to do *research* is not as directly and clearly permitted as using them for the cures themselves once they have been developed; however, since aborted fetuses would otherwise just be discarded or buried, we may and should extend the permission to use them for research that holds out the hope for curing diseases and saving lives.

Stem cells for research purposes, though, can also be procured from donated sperm and eggs mixed together in a petri dish and cultured there. Since genetic materials outside the uterus have no chance of developing into a human being, they have even less legal status in Jewish law than zygotes and embryos in the first stages of gestation, when the Talmud classifies them "as simply water." Abortion is still prohibited during that time except for therapeutic purposes, for in the uterus such gametes have the potential of growing into a human being, but outside the womb, at least as of now, they have no such potential.

In our own day, when we understand that the fertilized egg cell has all the DNA that will ultimately produce a human being, we must clearly have respect for human embryos and even for human gametes alone (sperm and eggs), for they are the building blocks of human procreation. That is, given modern scientific knowledge, we cannot simply say that since the sources of Jewish law never talk about embryos outside the womb, no law exists on the subject, and we may rule however we wish. Rather, we must take modern science into account in our decisions. For that matter, even the ancient Rabbis who proclaimed the embryo in the first forty days to be "simply water" were certainly announcing an analogy and not an equivalence, for they clearly knew that from that water a child might develop, unlike any glass of drinking water!

Still, while we should have respect for gametes and embryos, they may be discarded if they are not going to be used for some good purpose. On the other hand, it would be much better if they were used for good purposes. One such purpose would be to implant the embryo in a surrogate mother to gestate the child so that the couple can have a child of their own. Another would be to donate the embryo to a couple where the woman can gestate a child but one or both of the members of the couple cannot produce viable gametes, thus enabling that couple to have a child. Another good purpose, though, is to produce stem cells for medical research. Indeed, couples should be encouraged to donate their extra embryos for such efforts.

What about creating embryos specifically for the purpose of doing medical research? That lacks the justification of using materials that would just be discarded anyway, but creating embryos specifically for research is nevertheless permissible under one condition.

Unlike the Catholic view, the problem in doing this for the Jewish tradition is *not* that it would amount to murder to destroy an embryo outside the uterus, for in that state an embryo has even lesser status than an embryo in its first forty days in utero, where it is "simply water"; it is not even a thigh, much less a person. Further, procuring the sperm for "farmed" embryos through masturbation would not constitute "wasting seed," for here the purpose of masturbating would be specifically to use the man's sperm for the consecrated purpose of finding ways to heal illnesses.

Procuring eggs from a woman for this purpose, however, does pose a problem. It is not so much that this requires subjecting her to an invasive medical procedure, for now eggs can be procured without surgery and with minimal risk or pain, through laparoscopy. To produce the eggs, though, the woman must be exposed to drugs that hyperovulate her—that is, cause her to produce more than the usual one egg per menstrual cycle—and there is some evidence that repeated use of such drugs increases a woman's risk of ovarian cancer.[6] While such risks may be undertaken to overcome a woman's own infertility or even, I have held, to donate eggs once or twice to infertile couples, assuming such risks for medical research is less warranted, especially since embryos can also be obtained from frozen stores that couples plan on discarding and possibly from some of the other new methods that researchers are now developing.[7] Thus while obtaining embryonic stem cells from frozen embryos that would otherwise be discarded is best, embryos may also be specifically created for purposes of medical research on the condition that the woman providing the eggs for such efforts do so only once or twice.

Other Factors in This Decision

Given that the materials for stem cell research can be procured in permissible ways, the technology itself is morally neutral. It gains its moral valence on the basis of what we do with it.

The question, then, reduces to a risk-benefit analysis of stem cell research. The articles in two issues of the *Hastings Report* raise some questions to be considered in such an analysis, and I will not review them here.[8] I want to note only two things about them from a Jewish perspective.

First, the Jewish tradition sees the provision of health care as a communal responsibility, and so justice arguments have a special resonance for Jews. Especially since much of the basic science in this area was funded by the government, the government has the right to require private companies to provide their applications of that science to those who cannot afford them at reduced rates or, if necessary, even for free. At the same time, the Jewish tradition does not demand socialism, and for many good reasons, we, in the United States, have adopted a modified, capitalistic system of economics. The trick, then, will be to balance access to applications of the new technology with the legitimate right of a private company to make a profit on its efforts to develop and market applications of stem cell research.[9]

Second, as difficult as it may be, we must draw a clear line between uses of this or any other technology for cure, which are to be applauded, as against uses of technology for enhancement, which must be approached with extreme caution. Jews have borne the brunt of campaigns of eugenics in both the United States and Nazi Germany,[10] and so we are especially sensitive to creating a model human being that is to be replicated through some of the technologies that have evolved in our time and in times to come. Moreover, when Jews see a disabled human being, we are not to recoil from the disability or count our blessings for not being disabled in that way; we are rather commanded to recite a blessing thanking God for making people different.[11]

We probably want to argue that we should value disabled human beings already born while still striving to cure disabilities. We might even want to argue that some enhancements would be good. Defining exactly where the category of disability ends and where the category of enhancement begins is itself a hard problem. Although these issues are raised far more by genetic engineering than by stem cell research per se, it is important to underscore that in what I have said above I have addressed stem cell research used only for purposes of medical cures; a discussion of the use of this or any other technology for purposes of enhancement requires much more thought.

Conclusion

When used in research to cure diseases, embryonic stem cell research is definitely permitted. Rabbi Mark Washofsky, writing for the Reform movement, Rabbi Moshe Tendler, writing for the Orthodox community, and my own *teshuvah* for the Conservative Movement's Committee on Jewish Law and Standards all endorse such research, so if you ever want to know whether Jews agree about anything, yes, we agree about stem cell research!

Moreover, in light of the strong mandate of the Jewish tradition to seek to heal and the impressive prospects that this line of research has for curing devastating and even lethal diseases, all three of us believe that we should not only proceed with such research, but we should do so aggressively. This is especially true because experiments with animals indicate that this is not theoretical or, worse, a pipe dream; such experiments indicate that this mode of research holds out the most promise to cure diseases since the discovery of antibiotics. We obviously must also pursue other promising lines of research for medical cures; this should not take over the entire research agenda in medicine. Furthermore, we must balance this important effort with other social needs, including health care, infrastructure, education, social welfare, etc. In some ways, giving the homeless food, clothing, and shelter and providing basic health care for everyone in the world are more important goals to pursue. But to the extent that we devote money to medical research—and we definitely should—both adult and embryonic stem cell research should be high on our list of priorities.

The Brownsville Legacy
Judaism and Reproductive Rights

JUDITH ROSENBAUM, PHD

Judith Rosenbaum, PhD, is director of education at the Jewish Women's Archive and co-curator of the online exhibit *Jewish Women and the Feminist Revolution*. Rosenbaum earned a BA summa cum laude in history from Yale University and a PhD in American civilization, with a specialty in women's history, from Brown University.

For nearly a week I waited for the call to action. It came one afternoon when five women with babies in their arms called on me. They came from Brownsville."[1] In this account of the first birth control clinic in America, opened in October 1916, Margaret Sanger identifies the Jewish immigrant mothers of Brownsville, Brooklyn, as her "call to action," the inspiration behind her initial clinic. The Jewish women of Brownsville did not awaken Sanger to the birth control issue; her experience working as an obstetric nurse with Lillian Wald's Visiting Nurses' Association on the Lower East Side of New York City in the 1910s had taught her about the need for birth control in the teeming immigrant neighborhoods.[2] But Brownsville's Jewish mothers were not only the clientele of Sanger's first clinic. More important, they helped articulate the connection between contraception and issues such as poverty and hunger, defining the economic context that made legal birth control a political imperative.

Sanger recalls that the Brownsville women who came to her door "told of the ravages of infantile paralysis in their district, of the low wages of the men, of the high cost of food. They told how their neighbors talked of the clinic, what a blessing, a godsend, it would be over there."[3] These women were not alone in their support of Sanger; the neighborhood in general—men and women—provided a receptive atmosphere for the first clinic. The Jewish landlord of the space Sanger rented for the clinic even offered her a rent reduction when he heard her intentions.[4]

Hundreds of women responded to the clinic's advertisement notices, printed in English, Yiddish, and Italian.[5] Before the clinic doors opened on the morning of October 16, 1916, there were already more than 150 women standing in line, many carrying babies and pushing carriages. When the police raided and closed the clinic nine days later, it had recorded 464 clients, and those still waiting in line followed the police wagon, trailing it all the way to the station and standing outside for hours.

The Jewish community remained supportive of Sanger throughout the trial that followed, and before Sanger had even finished serving out her thirty-day sentence, the Brownsville women had extended their activism around birth control to address the high food prices in New York City. Throughout February and March 1917, food riots led by Jewish immigrant women swept through the Lower East Side, Brownsville, and Williamsburg. As one Brownsville woman, Sarah Goldstein, wrote to the *Birth Control Review*, "We women here want to find out what the president, the mayor, and the judges, and everybody is trying to do. First they put Margaret Sanger in jail for telling us women how not to have any more children, and then they get busy for the starve [sic] of the ones we've got."[6]

Reproductive Rights Are Human Rights: The Contemporary Picture

Jews have long played a significant role as advocates for reproductive rights, from those early days as Sanger's "call to action" to recent opposition to the Bush Administration's attacks on abortion and contraception. Along the way, Jews—as individuals and as a community—have continually been prominent voices in support of women's right to an abortion, to safe birth control, and to health care. In each political battle, Jews have understood that reproductive rights form a central nexus of economic power, medical power, and women's self-determination. Our social position in America has shifted remarkably in the course of the past century, from that of poor immigrants to affluent and influential players in contemporary politics. For most of us today, reproductive rights no longer determine our economic survival. However, our history and our current influence demand that we speak out about and take a stand on the still-central power struggle around reproductive rights.

Though many have come to take reproductive rights for granted in the past thirty-four years of abortion's legality and thirty-five years of contraception's availability to unmarried people, during this time these rights have been precarious and elusive, especially for the poor. The framing of reproductive rights in terms of "choice" in the modern abortion rights movement obscures the fact that without public aid to pay for abortion or mandated medical coverage of contraception, these rights lie out of reach for many Americans—those for whom they are often most crucial. Women's "choice" to terminate a pregnancy dwindles year by year, as the number of abortion providers declines precipitously. The "choice" discourse has further obscured the key political issues at the core of reproductive rights, lending the issue an air of frivolity rather than stressing the foundational role of these rights in any discussion of poverty, health, and self-determination.

The current moment is particularly dire, as the Bush Administration tries to roll back the clock on reproductive rights. The April 2007 Supreme Court ruling upholding the federal Partial-Birth Abortion Ban significantly undermines the 1973 *Roe v. Wade* decision that legalized abortion. Though the ban only prohibits one rare type of abortion procedure (provocatively labeled "partial birth" by anti-abortion activists), it redefines the abortion landscape by including no exception for the woman's health and intervening in doctor/patient care; any doctor who violates the ban would face criminal penalties of up to two years in prison, even if the doctor were acting to protect the health of the woman (the patient). Furthermore, Justice Kennedy's majority opinion in this case presents an archaic and paternalistic attitude toward women, claiming to protect them from undergoing a procedure they do not fully understand and would later regret. Finally, and terrifyingly, this decision swings wide open the door to further challenges to *Roe*.

This is only the latest step in a larger program of circumscribing reproductive rights, from a policy of only funding abstinence-only sex education, to the obstacles placed in the way of FDA approval of emergency contraception, to allowing pharmacists to refuse to fill prescriptions for birth control pills due to their personal religious beliefs.

And this is just in the United States. Globally, reproductive rights are an even larger issue, given the dire statistics on maternal health. Here are just a few shocking examples: every minute, a woman dies in childbirth (mostly in sub-Saharan Africa), amounting to 529,000 preventable deaths each year.[7] Pregnancy is the leading cause of death for girls ages 15 to 19 worldwide.[8] In Sudan, women are more likely to die during pregnancy or childbirth than to finish primary school.[9] When we add the risks of sexually transmitted diseases such as HIV to the mix of reproductive rights issues, the global picture further darkens, with 14,000 people newly infected with HIV each day.[10]

Under the Bush Administration, the United States has only exacerbated these sobering global conditions, with policies such as the global gag rule, which denies funding to foreign NGOs (non-governmental organizations) that offer, fund, advocate for, or even mention abortion, and recent cuts in funding to organizations such as UNFPA: United Nations Population Fund, which works for reproductive health and gender equality in the developing world.

These statistics highlight the fact that reproductive rights are a fundamental component of human rights, despite our tendency in the United States to subsume them within the category of women's rights, which is (incorrectly, given the fact that women are the majority of the population) deemed a secondary, niche issue. Without the ability to control reproduction and without access to safe reproductive health care, a woman's life, and by extension, that of her family, is severely circumscribed. Without reproductive rights, women are less likely to get an education. Their health may be compromised by limited access to reproductive medical options or information. These factors only exacerbate the obstacles they face in attaining economic success for themselves or their families. As the Brownsville mothers articulated, the absence of birth control and abortion is inextricably linked to family poverty, which further impedes family health. Reproductive rights are crucial to the health and development of society overall.

Judaism and Reproductive Rights

Why should we, as Jews, be particularly committed to the issue of reproductive rights? Beyond the historical legacy we bear, we are also in the unique position of being able to advocate for reproductive rights from a religious standpoint. In the United States, debate over reproductive rights has often aligned along religious/secular lines, with the opponents cloaking themselves in religious language about the "sanctity of life." Judaism, however, unlike Christian traditions, provides us with religious frameworks for supporting reproductive rights.

Procreation is a central value in traditional Judaism, as reflected in the biblical commandment of *pru ur'vu*, "be fruitful and multiply," but the plural voices of Rabbinic law have allowed for multiple interpretations of this dictum. The assertion by some Rabbis that the commandment to procreate is fulfilled through the birth of one son and one daughter, for example, has been used to support contraception. The Talmud even discusses the permissibility of birth control in the case of a nursing mother, who might risk the life of her child by early weaning due to another pregnancy.[11] Additionally, women are not considered directly commanded to procreate and only indirectly obligated to fulfill their husband's commandment, thus making women's use of contraceptive devices theoretically acceptable.

Significant in light of contemporary debates over abortion, Rabbinic law generally treats the fetus not as a full person but as part of the mother (*ubar yerekh immo*) and prioritizes the health and survival of the mother over that of the fetus (*tza'ara d'gufah kadim*).[12] In fact, because Jewish law does not consider a fetus a full person but only a potential life, a mother is forbidden from choosing to die in order to save her fetus—Mishnah *Ohalot* 7:6 specifically requires abortion in a case where the mother's life is at risk.[13] These concepts allow for at least therapeutic abortion,[14] and, just as importantly, reorient the religious reverence for life toward the life of the mother—a vital corrective in light of the "pro-life" claims of the anti-abortion movement, which singularly values the life of the fetus while disregarding the needs of the mother.

Though traditional Judaism's approach to sex is certainly conservative by contemporary standards—limiting sexual contact to those within the context of marriage, for example—it is ultimately "sex positive," asserting the potential for sex to be a holy act, the centrality of sexual intimacy to healthy marriages, and even women's right to sexual pleasure! Today, many Orthodox communities are increasingly restrictive and rigid in their application of Jewish law to issues of reproductive rights and sexuality, but the sex-positive values within traditional Judaism remain an important basis for progressive Jewish perspectives on these issues.

Conclusion: Carrying the Legacy Forward

Given our historical legacy as pioneering activists for reproductive rights, and our unique position as Jews to support these rights from a religious standpoint, the Jewish community should prioritize reproductive rights among the human rights we actively and vociferously promote. Jewish women's groups such as the National Council of Jewish Women have, admirably, been doing so for years. It is high time, however, that we move reproductive rights out of the category of "women's concerns" and acknowledge them as essential building blocks of a just society. The Jews of Brownsville did so; when Margaret Sanger received the American Women's Association medal in 1931, fifteen years after the Brownsville clinic, the Brownsville mothers who attended the honorary dinner presented her with flowers along with the weighty declaration, "You are our Abraham Lincoln."[15]

Just as Jews carried on Lincoln's work in our prominent involvement in the civil rights movement, so, too, should we commit ourselves to the legacy of the Brownsville women and place reproductive rights at the center of our social justice agenda.

Looking Inward
Domestic Violence within the Jewish Community

NAOMI TUCKER

Naomi Tucker is the co-founder and executive director of Shalom Bayit (Bay Area Jewish Women Working to End Domestic Violence). She is past chair of the Jewish Women's Caucus of the National Coalition Against Domestic Violence and currently serves as a national consultant on faith-based approaches to ending violence in the home.

I met my former husband at a synagogue youth camp when I was fifteen. I was smitten. Somehow, I felt destined to be with this man. Years later, I married him. He was a public figure, a macher *in Jewish circles with active involvement in his synagogue and on various boards serving the Jewish community. As a wife of a public figure, I was very effective at presenting a cheerful, positive picture to the Jewish community and to my circle of friends, as well. At home, I was terrorized.*

—Judy

Social justice movements seek to end inequalities and systematic oppression of one group by another. Looking around us, we can readily identify power imbalances in the world that we seek to rectify. But how often do we look inward, at the misuses and abuses of power that take place in our very own community? How can we seek to restore justice to the world, if we do not teach and live and experience justice within the bounds of our own lives?

One of the most pervasive, pernicious, and yet silenced injustices is violence against women.[1] More than 25 percent of all women will experience some form of sexual assault or intimate partner violence in their lifetimes.[2] Domestic violence is the leading cause of homelessness among women in the United States.[3] With a woman (physically) battered every nine seconds in this country, with 1,200 women murdered each year in the United States at the hands of an intimate partner, and with domestic violence named as the single major precursor to child abuse–related deaths,[4] that puts domestic violence as one of the greatest daily dangers to half the human population.

Despite rabbinic responsae dating back hundreds of years that clearly document that domestic abuse has always existed within the Jewish community and been debated among Jewish religious leaders,[5] the Jewish community over time has managed to convince itself that this problem only happens to other people, not us. Being terrorized at home, however, is just as great a risk to Jewish women as to anyone else. In 1979, researcher Ellen Goldsmith surveyed Jewish women seeking emergency room care in Los Angeles and found that a shocking 20 percent were arriving at the hospital for injuries related to domestic violence.

If we as a Jewish community want to talk about equality for women, or the pursuit of justice in the world at large, we must address the number one danger that impedes the safety and well-being of nearly one-quarter of adult Jewish women today. Even with our historical memory of enslavement in Egypt and communal commitment to end all forms of modern slavery, many Jews are still unaware of how many women—Jewish or not—are literally enslaved today in their own homes, trapped and tortured by the ones who professed to love them.

A Societal Problem

Jewish women have always resisted violence. Historically, our role model has been Queen Vashti, who refused to dance naked for the public pleasure of her husband. Today, hundreds of Israeli *agunot* (literally, "chained women") protest because religious courts will not grant them a divorce without their husband's permission.

In the 1980s, a movement began to address intimate partner abuse within Jewish households. Today many large Jewish communities have some form of domestic violence program (there are nearly sixty such programs throughout the U.S. and Canada), though most remain underfunded and underrecognized within the mainstream Jewish community.[6] As a result of these programs, and of national leadership and awareness-raising by major Jewish organizations such as Jewish Women International, the National Council of Jewish Women, and Hadassah (notably all women-led organizations), domestic violence is finally on the radar screen. Slowly, as these groups break the shame and silence surrounding Jewish domestic violence, women have begun to come forward and admit, "It happened to me too."

Due to my involvement with one such program, Shalom Bayit in the San Francisco Bay Area, I can attest that the programs we and other services offer are powerful and transformative for survivors. Yet, it is not enough to provide counseling or refuge to those who have been abused—we must work to create a community that does not tolerate abuse in the first place, as well as steer our communal institutions to embrace a more just response when it does occur. That is why domestic violence programs are rooted in a purpose much larger than providing a social service—and include prevention, advocacy, and a comprehensive array of ideas to transform the community's response to abuse.

Domestic violence continues because there is no widespread societal outcry against intimate partner abuse. Even in this day and age, male dominance and access to power remain socially sanctioned. When battered women break the silence and seek an escape from abuse, they often find themselves blamed, revictimized, and unprotected by courts, police, rabbis, and other institutions that should protect them. Abusers, on the other hand, often face little or no consequence for terrorizing their partners or children at home. The Jewish and American ethic of "innocent until proven guilty" translates into unequivocal support of abusers, leaving the burden of proof on the victim.

Domestic violence cannot be solved if it is understood as an individual problem, anomaly, or psychopathology. It is a societal problem requiring a societal response. Solutions that only address the individual fail to solve the larger problem of domestic violence and do not result in lasting behavior change for perpetrators. This includes anger management and couples counseling (both dangerous and ineffective strategies that do not address the power and control dynamics inherent in perpetrators' tactics), and even therapeutic responses that focus solely on the individual. One need only ask batterer intervention programs about their admittedly low success rates to underscore the systematic failure of individual-focused interventions.

For survivors, programs must promise safe housing, money, food, a job, childcare, legal protection, and counseling or other crisis support. Rabbinic support, spiritual direction and other spiritually-based forms of healing can be a lifeline for abuse survivors overcoming seemingly insurmountable obstacles. But all attempts at healing risk being ineffectual if there is no sense of safety and justice for the woman who was abused.

Similarly, to end the cycle of abuse itself, domestic violence programs must include prevention, advocacy, community and peer accountability, and addressing the underlying beliefs that allow people to feel entitled to control their partners. The community must take responsibility and be willing, when asked to make the choice between abuser and victim, to choose the victim.

If a congregant has a restraining order and her abuser violates that order by showing up to Shabbat services or the Lag B'Omer community picnic, will the rabbi or congregation enforce the restraining order? Will they call for police protection? In my experience, a more typical response is to declare "he has a right to be here too" despite the legal order of protection—or to refuse involvement on the grounds of not wanting to "call attention" to the matter, "cause a stir," or "take sides."

What happens when an abuser has a public position in our community? Do we as a community distinguish between private and public ethical behavior? How can we honor with integrity someone's social justice work feeding the homeless or reducing global warming, or their contributions of time and money to the congregation, when they are privately committing acts of terror? What does it mean to call people to bless the Torah, to etch their names prominently on a donor wall, to honor them as upstanding members of the community, if they believe it's acceptable to slam their partner's head into the wall for not cooking the fish properly? And what sense of justice will the victim of that abuse feel when the community says "It's just a private matter," or worse, believes she is "just exaggerating" or "clearly making it up" because they can't imagine their friend to be capable of such acts?

This lack of social and communal consequences for abusers is what allows abusers to continue their behavior unchecked. If we don't interrupt the behavior, call it out, ensure that the perpetrator can't "get away" with it, then we are condoning the abuse. The battered woman learns that her community will ultimately not stand behind her. And the community suffers too, as it leaves the abuser free to commit the abuse again—to her, or to someone else.

Safety Requires Justice

Maimonides taught that the commandment to justice in Deuteronomy 16:20, *Tzedek, tzedek, tirdoff* (Justice, justice, shall you pursue), referred to two types of justice. He stated that the first *tzedek* refers to the pursuit of justice in the courts, but the second repetition refers to the pursuit of justice in our own lives. Most abused women in the Jewish community feel they have been doubly wronged: once, by the person who professed to love them but caused harm instead; and again, by a community that believed or supported the abusers over the victims. Justice, then, must incorporate both a public validation of the victim's experience and a restoration of dignity.

The Jewish community has an opportunity to create such justice by providing alternative, community-based solutions to domestic violence within a Jewish framework. These solutions include advocacy and social justice approaches to domestic violence that are not found in secular violence prevention programs, such as:

- *Rabbinic and congregational advocacy:* Domestic violence staff/volunteers can provide not only counseling and resources, but an advocate to help the survivor seek safety and justice within the community. This might include helping a mother establish safe custody and visitation arrangements; insuring that the religious school director knows which parent is legally allowed to pick up the children at what times and to whom information is to be released; enforcing protective orders (such as restraining orders); arranging safety plans so that the person who was abused does not have to sit in shul with the person who harmed her; or simply finding a supportive rabbi who will listen and provide spiritual guidance to support the abused person toward safety. It might also include clear consequences for the perpetrator.

- *Authentic teshuvah (healing and repentance)* processes should hold abusers accountable for their actions, and provide opportunities for lasting behavior change. Such accountability is often the missing link for batterer intervention programs, for if there is no peer or community incentive to change one's behavior, re-education programs are unlikely to succeed in promoting behavior change. Teshuvah should include a community-monitored process of restitution, behavior change, and accountability to the person who was abused so that she is not further harmed, and the community is not further manipulated or endangered.

- *Premarital counseling* with thorough screening for abuse can provide early intervention to help couples (or individuals) make healthy choices about their relationship before it is too late. Clergy have a unique role in preventing abuse in that they may see couples and/or hear about their relationship challenges long before other helping professionals are called for help—and thus may be the first to identify warning signs.

- *Healthy relationships education built into religious school programs* can prevent abuse from happening in the first place, by providing a foundation of skills and values necessary to build healthy families as well as by identifying successful interventions for teens in unhealthy or abusive relationships.[7]

- *Congregational policies and procedures* for handling domestic violence, sexual assault, sexual harassment, elder/dependent adult abuse, child abuse, and clergy misconduct help community leaders understand how to respond when complex situations arise, and then base decisions on ethics and standards rather than on personal relationships.

Domestic violence can and should be viewed as an immediate-priority social justice issue for our community. How can we work to end oppression, remember our people's enslavement at our Passover seders, or fight to end human rights abuses when we know people are being mistreated here in their very own homes? How can we say we have created gender equality when teenage girls and women are still subjugated in intimate relationships? How can we justify venerating community leaders who cannot model ethical treatment of others in their own family or workplace?

Our children learn a great deal from what they see in their own home: much of how they make friends, resolve conflict, create intimacy, and interact in the world will be based on what they learn in their own family. So it is critical for the very health, vitality, and continuity of the Jewish community that we give children a head start on healthy relationships—and that we build homes and families that are peaceful, loving, and violence-free. World peace begins at home—and there is no time like the present.

Grateful acknowledgment to Paul Kivel for contributing ideas for this article.

PART IV
THE YOKE OF OPPRESSION: SOCIAL AND ECONOMIC JUSTICE

Hearing the Voice of the Poor

ARYEH COHEN, PhD

Aryeh Cohen, PhD, is associate professor of rabbinic literature at the American Jewish University in Los Angeles. He has taught at Hebrew Union College–Jewish Institute of Religion, the Reconstructionist Rabbinical College, and Brandeis University. Cohen is the author of *Rereading Talmud: Gender, Law and the Poetics of Sugyot*, and coeditor of *Beginning/Again: Towards a Hermeneutics of Jewish Texts*. He is a founding member of Jews Against the War.

I live in one of the larger Jewish neighborhoods in Los Angeles. It is called Pico-Robertson by those of us who live here (the romantic moniker designates the intersection at the heart of the neighborhood). It is called "Beverly Hills adjacent" by the real estate brokers, and SoRo or South Robertson by the city. Usually when friends come to visit and they want to see the city I take them north and then east to Hollywood and the studios or west to the rich peoples' houses and the beach. However, if we traveled further south, we would see a completely different Los Angeles. Two rival street gangs are competing for control of the neighborhood that begins two blocks south of my house. This has resulted in three teenagers being killed in drive-by shootings in the past few weeks. For the gangs, controlling the neighborhood means being able to spray paint your gang's name on the local walls and fences—and controlling the drug trade. This is why high school kids are being killed.

If we continued south and east we would get to the area around Los Angeles International Airport, or LAX. This area is known as the Century Corridor—named for Century Boulevard, which runs from the airport and through the neighborhoods of Hawthorne, Lennox, and Inglewood. Just as industrial towns in the past grew up around mines and railroads, Century Corridor grew up around the tourist industry. Most of the residents of these neighborhoods work at LAX or one of the thirteen hotels along Century Boulevard. Once, the three thousand-plus jobs that the hotels provided were well-paying union jobs that allowed workers to live a middle-class life. But 9/11 changed everything. The drop in tourism allowed the hotels to lay off many workers, and then some hotels were sold to owners who did not renew union contracts; others closed for "renovations," at the end of which they did not rehire union workers.

The vestiges of a middle-class lifestyle are visible in the "house and garden" blocks of the neighborhoods. The facades of these homes, however, hide the fact that behind most houses is an illegal or "unrecognized" addition that houses many more people and gives these neighborhoods a population density eight times higher than in the rest of Los Angeles County. In this community, one in four families lives below the federal poverty line, half the families living in poverty have at least one family member employed full time, more than 40 percent of children here come from poor households, and the median household income is 25 percent lower than in Los Angeles County as a whole. Lennox, which is an unincorporated city, did not have regular trash removal until 2005.

The distance between the impoverishment of a community and the withering of the social fabric is not great. The murder rate in Lennox is seven times higher than that of Los Angeles County as a whole. The violent crime rate overall is five times higher.

Usually, though, I don't take my friends that far south unless they are going to the airport.

First Story

On an otherwise unremarkable March evening in Los Angeles, I find myself in Koreatown, in a second-story office above a store on a usually bustling street. I am sitting in a room with seventeen Latino workers, two Korean-American labor organizers, and three other members of the Progressive Jewish Alliance (PJA), on whose board I sit. This motley, multiethnic, classically Angeleno crew was brought together by the employment of the Latino workers in a kosher market in my overwhelmingly Jewish neighborhood. We learn during the course of the evening about wage and hour problems and physical and verbal abuse of the workers by their Iranian Jewish employers.

The Latino workers came to the Korean labor association because the latter specializes in representing workers at small markets. The labor association came to the PJA looking for a Jewish community group to support the workers' struggle. The Asian Pacific American Legal Center pointed the Korean Immigrant Workers Association in our direction based on sweatshop work we had done together.

The four of us from PJA leave deeply moved by the difficulties facing the workers and by their gratitude that members of the Jewish community are reaching out to help them. Over the next year we are forced to confront our own limitations as an organization whose membership is almost wholly Ashkenazi while we attempt to reach out to the Persian-Jewish community, and as an organization whose membership is largely secular while we reach out to the religious community— Orthodox, Conservative, and Reform. We are far more successful at the latter than at the former.

Second Story

The emergency meeting of our neighborhood association was held at the Robertson Rec Center. About sixty people sat on folding chairs on the parquet floor of the basketball court (which also serves as a theater) listening to representatives of the Los Angeles Police Department gang unit and representatives of various elected officials talk about how they were responding to the recent drive-by shooting. Luckily, no one had been hurt in the incident, but the whole neighborhood heard the shooting as a wakeup call.

Sitting among my neighbors, I was impressed at the care residents, police, and elected officials expressed for the neighborhood. The lead officer seemed to know everyone in the neighborhood, and he was keeping an eye out for those who would threaten the peace. We were living, unfortunately, in a neighborhood that was the disputed territory of two different gangs. The gang unit explained the dynamics and history that led to the shooting and what they were doing to confront it and head off future shootings.

During the discussion period the questions of the residents started to move away from ways to deal with gang members to ways to deal with an R.V. that was parked in front of the local park. The R.V. had been there for a few weeks, obviously inhabited by a person who had no other home. The questions were becoming increasingly belligerent in demanding that the police find a way to remove this person (whom nobody knew and who had not apparently done anything wrong). Various statutes and strategies were discussed, and nightmare scenarios were proffered as if based in fact. ("I heard that sometimes people who kidnap children hide out in R.V.s.") I was becoming increasingly uncomfortable as the meeting drew to a close.

After the meeting I approached one of the officers to clarify that I was all for aggressive policing to identify the people who shot up the apartment, and to prevent those types of incidents in the future. I was not, however, interested in him spending his time rousting homeless folks. Drive-by shooting are dangerous crimes. Homelessness is neither dangerous nor a crime.[1]

Principles for Urban Justice

Many of us live in megalopolises—urban areas so large that they almost boggle the imagination. Can we articulate principles by which we can live so as to promote justice in our urban areas? I think we can. One of the first, and perhaps the first, question we need to ask is: how can we think about the way our urban areas are planned so that the planning itself promotes justice?

In thinking through these questions—something I have been doing for some years now—I turn to rabbinic texts, the touchstones for any traditional discourse on justice grounded in Jewish principles.

A short digression on *traditional* is demanded here.

By *traditional* I mean relating to the textual tradition of Judaism as a vocabulary and a horizon of philosophical and theological possibilities (to go Heideggerian for a minute). In other words, rather than arguing for first principles (what is "the good"? what is "justice"?) I will be thinking through and with texts that have come through many

THE YOKE OF OPPRESSION: SOCIAL AND ECONOMIC JUSTICE

centuries of study. I will not give them a veto (to switch to a Kaplanian metaphor) over other possibilities, but will rather start with a subtle and nuanced reading of certain texts in order to draw from them a conceptual vocabulary that I can employ to understand the issues we are discussing.

This drawing out will not be a claim for a literalist reading of texts or an insinuation of (the discourse of) commandedness into the political and ethical vocabulary of justice. It will rather be a display of the textured use of the vocabulary that the Jewish legal/textual tradition presents. This is itself a goal, since the larger exercise (of which this essay is a part) is staking a claim to a Judaism that privileges justice, and in which justice is the warp and woof of its texture.

Building a Gatehouse

We start with a Mishnah from the first chapter of tractate *Bava Batra*—the tractate that deals with contractual relations between people of various types. The first chapter is focused on the laws governing relations between neighbors.

> They may coerce him to [participate in the] building of a gatehouse and a gate for the [joint] courtyard. (Mishnah, *Bava Batra* 1:5)

> Rabban Shimon ben Gamliel says, "Not all courtyards need a gatehouse." (Babylonian Talmud, *Bava Batra* 7b)

This Mishnah describes the laws of living in a cooperative courtyard (something like a condominium but with joined houses surrounding a central court). To understand this Mishnah we have to draw out some of the implications that are not explicit. For example, from the fact that "they may coerce him" we can infer that the ruling here is not put forward as a suggestion (something one could do) but as actionable and backed up—somewhere along the line—with a court and a police force. While the "they" (in the first line) is probably the other folks who live in the courtyard, the source of the coercion is almost definitely institutional.[2]

The debate between the anonymous first opinion in the Mishnah and Rabban Shimon ben Gamliel is most likely a debate about public policy. Is a gate and/or a gatehouse an obvious good such that every set of courtyard residents might coerce their confrères to participate in building one? The first opinion thinks that it is, and Rabban Shimon ben Gamliel disagrees. So far this is pretty straightforward. Yet, with the Talmudic commentary comes a strange twist. Let us then jump forward some four or five centuries.[3]

The discussion in the Babylonian Talmud (*Bava Kamma* 7b) comments on this law and then introduces a short story of Elijah and a Hasid, a righteous person.

> This implies that the building of a gate house is a laudable thing. However, there is [the story of] that righteous person whom Elijah spoke with [regularly]. He built a gatehouse for his house, and Elijah no longer spoke with him.

In opening this section, the anonymous editorial voice of the Talmud (referred to as the *stam*, or "anonymous") draws a seemingly unproblematic inference from the Mishnaic law. If the Mishnah mandates coercive action to compel one to contribute to the building of the gatehouse, it would obviously be because the Sages thought that a gatehouse was a good thing. One would hope that one was only coerced to follow public policy that led to a positive result.

One who is fluent in Talmudic rhetoric would already know that the formula "this implies that *x*" is not an innocent turn of phrase. It is, rather, a setup. The *stam* wishes to point out a contradiction between the black-letter law of the Mishnah and another more authoritative source at his disposal. Here, then, is the rub. Here, though, the source that the *stam* introduces is a story of the prophet Elijah. While later on in Jewish textual history, especially in the mystical tradition, a revelation from Elijah assumes a certain authority, this is not true for the Sages. The Sages are very wary of oracular, prophetic, or supernatural authority of any kind. Why, then, is *this* story of Elijah brought to contradict our Mishnah?

In order to answer this question we will first have to embark on a tangential journey to inquire as to Elijah's role in the Babylonian

Talmud. We then will have to inquire after the Hasid. What does it mean to be righteous?

Finally, in order to complete our interrogation of this little story, we need to glance at the marginal commentary of Rabbenu Shlomo Yitzchaki, universally known as Rashi.[4] Commenting on the line in the story "and Elijah no longer spoke with him," Rashi writes, "For it gates off the poor people who are shouting [tzo'akim] [for money or assistance] and their voices are not heard."

Rashi understands that Elijah no longer appeared to the righteous person because the gatehouse—which that person built—served as a barrier to the voices of the poor, with the result that the people living inside could no longer hear their shouts. Rashi repeats this comment in the continuation of the discussion (which I will not reproduce here) three times. Each time Rashi uses the same language. Their shouting could not be heard. Each time some form of the Hebrew word tza'akah is used. This raises the questions: Why does Rashi say this? How does Rashi know this? There does not seem to be any particular reason to interpret the Talmudic text in this way. Yet Rashi, and the commentary tradition in general (both preceding and succeeding Rashi), interpret this story in this way. Why?

Elijah

I will investigate these questions in order. Elijah appears in numerous stories in the Babylonian Talmud. The story that seems to most closely resemble ours is from the tractate *Ketubot* (106a). It is told there that a certain man brought a present to Rabbi Anan, a Sage.[5] When the latter asked the man for the reason for this display of generosity, he replied that he wished Rabbi Anan to adjudicate a dispute he was involved in. Rabbi Anan immediately refused the gift and refused to serve as judge in the dispute, lest his judgment be tainted in any way. Rabbi Anan referred the man to another Sage, Rabbi Nachman. Upon seeing that the fellow was recommended by Rabbi Anan, Rabbi Nachman stopped hearing the case that was in front of him and brought this case forward. When the fellow's opponent in the case saw the honor that Rabbi Nachman accorded the man referred by Rabbi Anan, the opponent withdrew his complaint, feeling that he had no chance to prevail.

As a result of this affair, Elijah, who had previously been a regular study partner of Rabbi Anan's, stopped appearing to Rabbi Anan. (The latter fasted and repented, and Elijah returned to teach him.)

Why would Elijah stop seeing Rabbi Anan? It would seem that Rabbi Anan had done exactly the right thing. He had refused to hear the case and he had refused the gift.[6] Rabbi Nachman's misplaced sense of honor led justice astray as he privileged the man Rabbi Anan had sent. This infraction could not be laid at Rabbi Anan's feet, could it? Why was Rabbi Anan reprimanded or punished while Rabbi Nachman was not?

It seems that Elijah's task is not to monitor gross violations of justice, but rather to patrol the boundaries of acceptable behavior at the high end of moral action. While Rabbi Nachman's violations were egregious, they were also obvious. Rabbi Anan was being held accountable for not having attended to the possible ramifications of his acceptable behavior. This is at least one of Elijah's tasks.[7] How does this impact our understanding of the Elijah story with which we started?

The Hasid

Before proceeding home, as it were, to try to clarify the text with which we began, I am going to tarry a bit with the Hasid. Luckily, there is a section of a chapter of Mishnah from the tractate known as Ethics of the Fathers (*Pirkei Avot*) that references the Hasid. I will quote a number of those statements.

There are four types of character in human beings:

1. [One that says] "mine is mine, and yours is yours": this is a commonplace type; and some say this is a Sodom-type of character.
2. [One that says] "mine is yours and yours is mine": is an unlearned person (*am ha'aretz*).
3. [One that says] "mine is yours and yours is yours": is a pious person [Hasid].
4. [One that says] "mine is mine, and yours is mine": is a wicked person. (Ethics of the Fathers, chapter 5, Mishnah 10)

There are four kinds of temperaments:

1. Easy to become angry, and easy to be appeased: his gain disappears in his loss;
2. Hard to become angry, and hard to be appeased: his loss disappears in his gain;
3. Hard to become angry and easy to be appeased: a pious person [Hasid];
4. Easy to become angry and hard to be appeased: a wicked person.

(Mishnah 11)

There are four types of charity givers:

1. He who wishes to give, but that others should not give: his eye is evil to that which belongs to others;
2. He who wishes that others should give, but that he himself should not give: his eye is evil toward that which is his own;
3. He who desires that he himself should give, and that others should give: he is a pious man [Hasid];
4. He who desires that he himself should not give and that others too should not give: he is a wicked man. (Mishnah 13)

There are four types among those who frequent the study-house (*bet midrash*):

1. He who attends but does not practice: he receives a reward for attendance;
2. He who practices but does not attend: he receives a reward for practice;
3. He who attends and practices: he is a pious man [Hasid];
4. He who neither attends nor practices: he is a wicked man.

(Mishnah 14)

These texts are relatively straightforward and they yield the following. A Hasid is one who travels the extra distance to practice piety. The Hasid is not one to skimp on the rigors of righteousness. This returns us to our story with an even greater quandary. Elijah reprimanding the Hasid represents a strong argument for the fact that there must be untoward possible ramifications to the righteous behavior that, of all people, the Hasid should have known. Rashi points us in the right direction: "crying out."

Heeding the Cry

Exodus 22:20–23 is one of those texts that everybody seems to know. *Seems* is the operative word in that last sentence.

> You shall not wrong a stranger or oppress him, for you were strangers in the land of Egypt.
> You shall not ill-treat any widow or orphan.
> If you do mistreat them, I will heed their outcry [*tza'akah*] as soon as they cry out [*tza'ok yitz'ak*] to Me, and My anger shall blaze forth and I will put you to the sword, and your own wives shall become widows and your children orphans.

The customary interpretation of these verses, especially in circles sensitive to issues of social justice, is that the lesson of oppression is compassion. You were slaves in Egypt, you knew what it was like to be marginal and mistreated, therefore you will not wrong a stranger. This interpretation misses the significance of verse 22 (which uses forms of the verb "cry out," *tza'ak*, two times) and verse 23. I want to suggest a different way of understanding these verses.

The narrative of redemption in the book of Exodus[8] starts at the end of chapter 2 with the following.

> A long time after that, the king of Egypt died. The Israelites were groaning under the bondage and cried out [*vayitz'aku*]; and their cry for help from the bondage rose up to God. God heard their moaning, and God remembered God's covenant with Abraham and Isaac and Jacob. God looked upon the Israelites, and God took notice of them.

The series of actions that lead to redemption—in the very next chapter God commissions Moses—are crying out (verse 23), and hearing the cry (verse 24). Once God heard their *tza'akah*/cry,[9] then God remembered the covenant and took notice of them.

In complete contrast to this story, we read in chapter 5 of Exodus of the Israelites' earliest interaction with Pharaoh after Moses's first confrontation with Pharaoh.

> Then the foremen of the Israelites came to Pharaoh and cried [*vayitz'aku*]: "Why do you deal thus with your servants? No straw is issued to your servants, yet they demand of us: Make bricks! Thus your servants are being beaten, when the fault is with your own people." He replied, "You are shirkers, shirkers! That is why you say, 'Let us go and sacrifice to the LORD.' Be off now to your work! No straw shall be issued to you, but you must produce your quota of bricks!" (Exod. 5:15–18)

When the Israelites cry out to Pharaoh (the text uses again the verb *tza'ak*) in their anguish, Pharaoh *ignores them*, calls them shirkers, and places higher work demands upon them. This is the beginning of the end of Pharaoh. Pharaoh did not listen to the cries of the Israelites, but God did, and therefore God unleashed God's fury onto Egypt and made their wives widows and their children orphans—and worse.

This, then, is the meaning of Exodus 22:20–23. You were in Egypt. You know that there are two ways to react to the cry of the oppressed. You can react like God and hear the cry and bring about redemption, or you can react like Pharaoh and ignore the cry and bring God's wrath upon yourself. Exodus 22:20–23 puts the choice of justice in its starkest form—you can choose to imitate God or to imitate Pharaoh.

I would like to suggest that Rashi had this teaching in mind when he commented on the Talmudic discussion that we started with. He was answering some of the very same questions we posed. What was so important about this Elijah story that it would be introduced to contradict a law of the Mishnah? What was it that the Hasid did, or failed to do? Reading the story with and through Rashi we realize that Elijah's displeasure was aimed at the fact that a gatehouse can serve to undermine the moment that generates ethical, just, and therefore redemptive action. Elijah was not worried that a Hasid would ignore a poor person who presented himself on his doorstep. Nor was Elijah worried that if the Hasid happened upon a poor person in the street that the Hasid would ignore him. Elijah was worried that the act of building the gatehouse would prevent the Hasid from *hearing the cry* of the poor person, thereby preventing the possibility of a just, ethical response.

We end, then, at the beginning. The beginning of redemption is acting justly. The beginning of just action is hearing the cry of the poor. We do not need to know people intimately to hear their cry. We do need to have access to them—and we need for them to have access to us.

We are living, however, within a web of social and cultural projections of the world that are based in a fear of the other. Mike Davis has called this the ecology of fear in which people construct their lives around the need to feel secure—gated communities, threatening oversized cars, and so on.[10] I am not diminishing the real threats that we face—those drive-by shootings I mentioned above occurred within blocks of my house. I do, however, want to strongly agree with Rashi's Elijah that security does not trump justice.

If we think about our urban spaces with this fundamental principle in mind—choose to imitate God and not Pharaoh—we inexorably must choose justice over excessive security. We must choose not to hassle the homeless guy in the R.V., even if it may have an impact on our property values. We must choose decriminalizing homelessness over creating a business zone in our downtowns. Above all, we must figure out ways to turn our cars, our ears, and our minds toward the people in the areas of our cities where we do not go. When we are able to hear their cries, we can respond justly.

In the early twelfth century, the Spanish rabbi Meir HaLevi Abulafia, a close associate of the royal house, wrote an excursus on our Talmudic text. He understood the question the text poses: if we set up our urban spaces such that the poor can enter, then other darker forces can enter, too:

> Yet, here, what benefit is there? And what harm is removed from the courtyard with this gatehouse? For certainly when the poor can enter, so too can thieves enter! Still, this makes no difference. (*Sefer Yad Ramah, Bava Batra* 13)

Still, this makes no difference. There is a point at which justice must be everyone's priority.

A Jewish Vision for Economic Justice

RABBI JILL JACOBS

Rabbi Jill Jacobs is the director of education for the Jewish Funds for Justice. Her writings have appeared in magazines, journals, and websites, including *Conservative Judaism*; *Tikkun*; *The Reconstructionist*; *Lilith*; the *Forward*; *Women in Judaism: A Multidisciplinary Journal*; and MyJewishLearning.com. Jacobs was named one of the fifty most influential Jews of the year by the *Forward* newspaper in 2007.

Depending on whom you ask, Judaism advocates either a socialist redistribution of wealth or a laissez-faire capitalist system. Partisans of the former generally begin by pointing to the biblical institution of the *Yovel*, or Jubilee year, in which land returns to its original owner; proponents of the latter usually note the Rabbinic permission for merchants and employers to set whatever prices and wages the market will bear. A close reading of Deuteronomy 15:4–12 suggests, however, that Jewish law rejects both of these extremes and envisions a controlled free market system that attempts to balance an openness to entrepreneurship with a desire to protect the weakest members of society from economic hardship.

The book of Deuteronomy includes what is, arguably, the clearest articulation of a biblical vision of economic justice:

> There shall be no needy among you—for Adonai will surely bless you in the land which Adonai your God gives you for an inheritance to possess it if you diligently listen to the voice of

Adonai your God, and observe and do the commandment that I command you this day. For Adonai your God will bless you, as God promised you; and you shall lend unto many nations, but you shall not borrow; and you shall rule over many nations, but they shall not rule over you. If there is among you a needy person, one of your brethren, within any of your gates, in your land which Adonai your God gives you, you shall not harden your heart, nor shut your hand from your needy brother; but you shall surely open your hand unto him, and shall surely lend him sufficient for his need in that which he wants. Be careful lest there be a hateful thing in your heart, and you say, "The seventh year, the sabbatical year, is coming" and you look cruelly on your brother, the poor person, and do not give him, for he will call out to God and this will be counted as a sin for you. Rather, you shall surely give him, and you shall not fear giving him, for on account of this, God will bless you in all that you do and in all that you desire. For the poor will never cease from the land. For this reason, God commands you, saying, "You shall surely open your hand to your brother, to the poor and the needy in your land." (Deut. 15:4–12)

This passage includes a few particularly striking elements. First, the usually terse biblical text seems overly loquacious in its description of the poor person as "one of your brethren, within any of your gates, in your land." For those of us whose standard of living has risen above subsistence levels, it is tempting to imagine the poor as somehow different from us. The two-time usage, in this biblical passage, of the word *achikha*, "your brother," compels us to consider even the most destitute member of society as our sibling.

The next phrase, "within any of your gates, in your land," could be read as limiting Jewish responsibilities to only those people who live within our own city within the land of Israel. Yet Rabbi Moshe ben Nachman (a.k.a. Ramban; Spain, 1194–1270) points us in the other direction, commenting: "The meaning of 'in your land' refers to all of your settlements—in the land of Israel and outside of the land of Israel. And the meaning of 'your poor person in your land' is that this phrase refers both to your poor brethren and to all of the poor of your land."

Read expansively, the Deuteronomic commandment holds us responsible for the well-being of everyone who, by the broadest of definitions, might be considered a member of any of our communities.

Second, the text directly ties the treatment of the poor with the inheritance and possession of the land of Israel. It is no accident that the Torah ties the laws of *tzedakah* to the inheritance of the land of Israel. Conscious of the human potential for greed, the Torah chooses the moment in the story when real property ownership begins to establish protections against extreme wealth disparity. In particular, the institution of the *Shmitah* (Sabbatical) year and the *Yovel* (Jubilee) aim to lessen the economic stratification of society. During this *Shmitah* year, debts are forgiven and the land is left unplanted. In the *Yovel* year, slaves are freed and land returns to its original owner. The wealth is not, however, redistributed equally, since the original owners did not receive equal grants. The aim of these sabbaticals is not to create a socialist economy, but to remind Jews that "the land is [God's]" and can never fully belong to a human owner (Lev. 25:23). The accumulation of wealth is, by nature, temporary.

Perhaps the most striking element of the Deuteronomy passage is the apparent contradiction between verse 4, "There shall be no needy among you," and verse 11, "For the poor will never cease from the land." We expect the omnipotent God of the Torah to keep promises; we are therefore surprised to hear God promise to eradicate poverty and then, almost in the same breath, admit that this promise will never be fulfilled.

Noting the conditional nature of the promise to eradicate poverty "if you diligently listen to the voice of Adonai your God," most traditional commentators understand the passage as a prediction that the Jewish people will never fully obey the commandments.[1] However, such an interpretation contradicts a basic principle of rabbinic exegesis—the idea that every word of the Torah is divine and meaningful. Second, this suggestion raises an even more fundamental theological problem: if human beings are to hold ourselves responsible for observing the commandments of the Torah, we need to believe that God, at least, believes that we are capable of following these commandments. It would seem a betrayal of trust for the Torah to set out expectations that God already knows we will not fulfill.

Many commentators thus seek an alternative resolution of the apparent contradiction between the assurance that "there will be no needy among you" and the warning that "the poor will never cease from your land." Ramban, for example, writes, "It is impossible that the poor will permanently disappear ... not every generation, forever, will observe all of the commandments to the point that there is no longer any need for commandments concerning the poor." With this explanation, Ramban portrays the biblical text as optimistic, but realistic. According to his reading of this passage, the Jewish people will generally observe the commandments, but will not always do so perfectly. Even if one generation succeeds in temporarily eradicating poverty, the possibility remains that poverty will resurface in another generation. Thus, the Torah anticipates a perfected world, but plans for an imperfect one. Unlike some other commentators, Ramban assumes that some generations *will* succeed in ending poverty, but he realizes that the possibility that poverty will resurface can never entirely disappear.

We can extend Ramban's argument even further. A common debate among those involved in anti-poverty work today concerns the relative value of social action, with its emphasis on direct service, and social justice, with its emphasis on organizing for systemic change. Advocates of social action focus on the fact that today "the poor will never cease." They argue that the hungry need to be fed *today* and that the homeless need somewhere to sleep *tonight*. Those who prefer social justice, on the other hand, look forward to the day when "there will be no needy among you." They point out that soup kitchens and shelters will never make hunger and homelessness disappear, whereas structural change may wipe out these problems.

The Deuteronomic response to this debate is a refusal to take sides. Rather than advocate exclusively either for long-term systemic change or for short-term response to need, this passage articulates a vision that balances the pursuit of full economic justice with attention to immediate concerns. In this reading, the text in question becomes a charge to work for the structural changes that will eventually bring about the end of poverty without neglecting the pressing needs of those around us.

With this framework in mind, we can take a look at an instance in which the Rabbis of the Talmud interfere with the market in order to create a more just economic system.

Employers and Workers

The Rabbis posit the existence of two competing human impulses: the *yetzer ha-tov* (good impulse) and the *yetzer ha-ra* (evil impulse). A person who follows the *yetzer ha-tov* obeys divine commandments and acts ethically in the world, while a person who gives in to the *yetzer ha-ra* allows himself or herself to be ruled by appetite and desire. Justifying God's decision to create humans with the *yetzer ha-ra*, one midrash comments that "without the *yetzer ha-ra*, no one would ever build a house, or get married, or have children, or do business."[2] In other words, the *yetzer ha-ra* is an essential component of human ambition and is therefore necessary for the sustenance and development of the human community.

This midrash reflects the overall Rabbinic attitude toward the marketplace. While acknowledging the inherent dangers of greed and competition, the Rabbis also recognize the necessity of desire for economic development. As we will see, Jewish law establishes restrictions aimed at preventing this competitive drive from overwhelming any sense of responsibility toward other members of one's community.

The Torah understands workers to be a class of people who, like orphans, widows, and strangers, are in need of special protection. Two parallel verses thus aim to prevent exploitation by mandating the prompt payment of workers:

> Do not oppress your neighbor and do not rob him. Do not keep the wages of the worker with you until morning. (Lev. 19:13)

> Do not oppress the hired laborer who is poor and needy, whether he is one of your people or one of the sojourners in your land within your gates. Give him his wages in the daytime, and do not let the sun set on them, for he is poor, and his life depends on them, lest he cry out to God about you, for this will be counted as a sin for you. (Deut. 24:14–15)

In a poignant commentary on the Deuteronomy verse, Rabbi Moshe ben Nachman explains, "For he is poor—like the majority of hired laborers, and he depends on the wages to buy food by which to live ... if he does not collect the wages right away as he is leaving work, he will go home, and his wages will remain with you until the morning, and he will die of hunger that night." Inherent in a class-based system is the danger that the more powerful will profit from the desperation of the least powerful. Indeed, in contemporary America and elsewhere in the world, day laborers commonly experience the situation hinted at by the Torah, in which employers fail to pay in full or in part for a day's work.

Beyond prohibiting outright exploitation, Jewish law also makes some attempt to create an economic system that does not, in itself, lead to vast disparities between rich and poor. One hint of this desire for a balanced economic system emerges from Ramban's comment, cited above. In noting that a person who does not receive wages on time will "die of hunger that night," Ramban takes for granted that a person who *does* receive payment on time *will* be able to provide sufficiently for himself and his family and will not die of hunger. This assumption also forms the premise for Maimonides's designation of the highest level of *tzedakah* as "the one who strengthens the hand of his fellow Jew by giving him a gift or a loan or entering into partnership with him or finding him work in order to strengthen his hand so that he will not need to ask in the future."[3] For Maimonides, a person who has permanent employment or a share in a business will never find it necessary to ask for *tzedakah*. Neither Ramban nor Maimonides indicates familiarity with a class of "working poor," those who work full time but do not earn enough to provide for their families' basic needs. Rather, both expect that even the poorest worker will be able to live off of his or her wages.

While neither Ramban nor Maimonides refers to legislation aimed at preventing workers from falling into poverty, Jewish law offers significant precedent for regulating the market in order to protect the livelihood of workers. This tendency begins with a statement in the Tosefta, an early layer of the Jewish oral tradition, that permits "the people of the town" to stipulate wages, prices, and measurements, and they may inflict punishment on those who refuse to abide by the community standard.[4] Later interpretations of this statement, in the Talmud and later law codes, permit groups of workers, such as guilds or unions, also to set wage standards for individual industries.[5]

For the most part, Jewish labor laws favor the worker, who is understood to occupy the more vulnerable position. Rabbi Shillem Warhaftig, a contemporary expert in this area of Jewish law, explains, "The purpose [of Jewish labor laws] is to protect the weaker side in these relationships—the worker who is exposed to injustice and exploitation by the stronger party—the employer. We can say that the labor laws attempt to correct the socio-economic discrimination that exists in society against workers by instituting a legal discrimination against employers."[6] Rather than allow the market to run its course, Jewish law interferes in order to create a somewhat more equitable system. Workers, in most cases, still have less power than their employers, but they are at least protected from outright exploitation.

Some legal texts institutionalize the ability to adapt to changing market conditions. For the most part, Jewish law allows workers to quit their jobs midday without repercussion. This permission stems from the Talmudic assertion that "the Children of Israel are [God's] servants and not servants to servants."[7] In other words, human beings cannot become effectively enslaved to other human beings. However, in cases in which the market favors workers, rather than employers, employees may be forbidden from quitting early, or they may face penalties for doing so.[8] Here, we have a case in which the law changes according to the realities of the market. If employers will have little trouble finding new workers, then workers may leave midday; if employers are unlikely to find new workers and will suffer severe and irreparable economic loss while undertaking a search, then workers are penalized for leaving.[9] In order to correct the economic disparity that the free market creates, the law establishes provisions aimed at protecting whichever party the economic climate makes more vulnerable.

The regulation of the market system seeks to create a structure that will not allow extremes of economic inequality, while the laws of *tzedakah* aim to ameliorate the suffering of individuals who fall through the cracks in the system. For contemporary Jews, traditional Jewish law offers a model for our own struggles to define and to create economic justice. We cannot ignore the immediate needs of those who are hungry, homeless, or otherwise in need of material or spiritual sustenance. At the same time, we should constantly work toward a society in which poverty ceases to exist. Jewish law pushes us not toward a full redistribution of wealth, but rather toward the creation of a system that allows for free market competition, while also ensuring that the success of some does not come at the expense of the well-being of others.

Why a Labor Movement Matters

ARIEH LEBOWITZ

Arieh Lebowitz is the communications director at the Jewish Labor Committee and coeditor of *Archives of the Holocaust*, Volume 14: Robert F. Wagner Labor Archives, New York University—Records of the Jewish Labor Committee.

After she had retired, my mother mentioned to me that one of her earliest jobs was with the Textile Workers Union of America, right off of Union Square, in Manhattan. It was the first time she had mentioned her work there, or, indeed, any involvement in the labor movement. She had also, it turned out, been a member of District Council 37 of the American Federation of State, Council and Municipal Workers when she worked, years later, as a secretary. The health benefits secured by her union continued into her retirement and were very important the last years of her life.

Her story reminded me that the days of Jewish immigrant labor are not all that distant. Though most American Jews now are middle class,[1] that has been a relatively recent development, going back to the 1950s. The generation gap has been long enough, however, for many of us to have forgotten that the American Jewish rise from "rags to riches" is largely a story of labor unionism.

When we wonder today why there is a growing divide between rich and poor; why so few people have health care and so many of us are worried about retirement; why the poor seem to remain poor and have such trouble getting ahead—we only need to compare the strong labor movement of our parents' and grandparents' generation with the weakened movement today. History—and Jewish law—tell us that the key to economic justice is empowering workers.

Unions in American Jewish History

From its earliest days, the U.S. labor movement has had deep roots in America's Jewish communities, large and small, from coast to coast.[2] The great mass of immigrants who traveled from Eastern and Central Europe to these shores from 1881 to 1924 were generally poor, working-class folks. As with most newcomers, the majority made their homes in communities teeming with fellow Jewish immigrants, such as New York, Chicago, Philadelphia, Boston, and Baltimore.

Many of these Jews brought with them a heady mix of socialism, trade unionism, and political activism from the "old country," and these movements took root in the New World, where they served the new immigrants well. The most important of these was the General Jewish Labor Union of Lithuania, Poland and Russia, often known as the Jewish Labor Bund.[3] The Bund was formed in 1897 as a secular political and social movement of Jewish working men and women to better their own condition through organizing into unions and building socialism. Wages, working conditions, and combating anti-Semitism were central to the movement's agenda.

In the twentieth century, Jews have been deeply involved in the American labor movement. The Triangle Shirtwaist Factory fire of 1911, in which 146—mostly Jewish and Italian—women died, led to a successful effort by the predominantly Jewish International Ladies Garment Workers Union to pass legislation that mandated workplace safety protections. Many of the greatest American labor leaders—Emma Goldman, Samuel Gompers—have been Jews, and today, Jews lead some of the largest and most powerful unions, including Andy Stern at SEIU and Bruce Raynor at UNITE HERE.[4]

Even while Jews retain a historical connection to the American labor history, Jews have largely moved out of the working class and are underrepresented in the union rank and file. The question for the Jewish community today is how we can translate our historical connection and traditional values into our new roles as owners and managers, and as activists joining in solidarity with workers.

Workers' Rights in Jewish Law

Today, in our work for justice, it is critical that we know what the Jewish tradition has to say. A number of the Bund's early leaders came from traditional backgrounds, and one can find any manner of links among traditional Jewish texts, the political ferment of the Haskalah (Jewish Enlightenment), and the Jewish labor movement.

Jewish law on labor begins with the Bible itself. Torah tells us:

> Do not oppress your neighbor and do not rob him. Do not keep the wages of the workers with you until morning. (Lev. 19:12)

and:

> Do not oppress the hired laborer who is poor and needy, whether he is one of your people or one of the sojourners in your land within your gates. Give him his wages in the daytime, and do not let the sun set on him, for he is poor, and his life depends on them, lest he cry out to God about you, for this will be counted as a sin for you. (Deut. 24:14–15)

Rabbi Jill Jacobs has argued that these texts teach us several things.[5] First, workers are understood to be poor and deserving of our protection. Second, both Jews and non-Jews must be protected as workers. Third, the texts, in their very existence, assert that there must be specific legislation to prevent the oppression of workers. Fourth, the texts further recognize the essential power and wealth imbalance between employee and employer, and the employee's dependence on wage.

Building on these biblical texts, an entire class of Talmudic labor law deals with conditions of work, establishing rights that in many instances foreshadow modern trade union practices. Michael Perry, in his paper *Labor Rights in the Jewish Tradition*, points out that Talmudic regulations demand prompt payment of wages, give the benefit of the doubt to workers in disputes over wages, and prohibit in-kind payment instead of payment in money.[6]

There are Talmudic laws on the hours of work, including the requirement that workers have a day of rest, be paid for hours spent walking to work, and be prohibited from working at night after working a "day shift." Workers are entitled to eat the food that they harvest. Employers are liable for work-related injuries caused by negligence, and workers are prohibited from accepting unsafe working conditions.

Labor issues are not politicized in Jewish law, as they are in secular law. Orthodox as well as Reform Jews agree on the need to protect workers. For example, the Orthodox labor scholar, Rabbi Shillem Warhaftig, wrote:

> The purpose [of Jewish labor laws] is to protect the weaker side in these relationships—the worker who is exposed to injustice and exploitation, by the stronger party—the employer. We can say that the labor laws attempt to correct the socioeconomic discrimination that exists in society against workers by instituting a legal discrimination against employers.[7]

Jewish tradition also protects the right of workers to engage in collective bargaining. Rav Kook, the first chief rabbi of Israel, argued that it is unjust both to *hire* a nonunion worker or to *be* a nonunion worker. He writes:

> Within the workers' organization, which is formed for the purpose of guarding and protecting the work conditions, there is an aspect of righteousness and uprightness and *tikkun olam*. The workers' organization may sue both the employer and the worker who causes this problem, for unorganized labor brings damage and loss of money to workers. For the unorganized worker works under worse conditions—both in regard to wages and in regard to working hours, etc. And this is likely to make working conditions worse in general.[8]

Even the right to strike is consistent with the worker's right to assert his independence by stopping work at any time without penalty, although there is a tradition of support for binding arbitration to settle disputes. Modern rabbis have condemned strikebreaking on the grounds that it violates several strong Talmudic prohibitions against threatening the livelihood of fellow workers.

The Jewish bottom line is that workers should always have the advantage in employer-employee negotiations.

Challenges to Workers' Rights Today

Of course, the workers don't always "have the advantage." And, despite the relative affluence of many Americans, there are a lot of people in our own country working today under conditions that need to be improved.

Employers today pay such low wages that many workers struggle to put food on the table. Twenty-eight million people work full time, but earn less than $18,000 per year, the poverty line for a family of four.[9] Many are forced to take second and third jobs; the Bureau of Labor Statistics estimates that 5.6 percent of Americans (7,556,000) hold multiple jobs, with 300,000 working two full-time jobs.[10] Some have suggested that the actual rate may be closer to 15 to 20 percent, especially when we consider undocumented workers, whose statistics are not recorded but who occupy many of our country's lowest-wage jobs.[11]

When people have impediments to freely join unions, and to negotiate fair contracts and decent working conditions, from New York to Thailand to Bangladesh to Baton Rouge, the situation confronting working men and women and their families is sometimes quite bleak. On May 10, 1993, for instance, a major fire took place at the Kader Industrial (Thailand) Co. Ltd. Factory, near Bangkok, in the Nakhon Pathom province of Thailand. There, 188 workers were killed, in the world's worst accidental loss-of-life fire in an industrial building in recent history. And when fire broke out on November 25, 2000, in the Chowdhury Knitwear and Garment Factory on the outskirts of Dhaka, Bangladesh, the gates were locked so workers couldn't get out. Women and girls threw themselves from the fourth story of the burning building or stampeded down the stairways, pressing futilely against the chained gates. Fifty-one people died, among them eight children under the age of fourteen.

Elana Levin has noted that a study from the Political Economy Research Institute at the University of Massachusetts-Amherst indicated that the worst states to work in based on "terms of average pay, employment opportunities, employee benefits, percentage of low-income workers, fair treatment between genders," and other factors all have one thing in common: the bottom-ranking states are all so-called "Right to Work States"—that is, states that have laws discouraging unionization and undermining the unions that already exist. Louisiana was at the absolute bottom of the list. (Note: This study was done before Hurricane Katrina.)[12]

On the other hand, when workers organize to form unions, they have a chance to escape poverty, to give a better life to their children, and to have more time to make positive contributions to their communities. According to the U.S. Bureau of Labor Statistics, median weekly earnings in 2004 for union workers were 28 percent higher than for nonunion workers, and for the service industry, which contains many of the lowest-paying jobs such as cleaning, security, and restaurant service, earnings were 68 percent higher for union workers than for nonunion workers.

Some feel that an economic justice agenda can be pursued separately or even without the benefit of a union movement. Efforts to support workers by pushing legislation that would increase the minimum wage, government action to crack down on sweatshop labor, boycotts of goods or services that are produced by workers deprived of basic rights, affordable housing, basic health care, decent education for all, and other like concerns—these actions on their own are all, of course, worth supporting.

Notwithstanding the importance of these vehicles for improving specific conditions of workers' lives in the workplace and in their communities, unions are unique in enabling workers to have their own collective voice in their workplace, through which they can exert some collective control over their working lives. In a sense, unions are vehicles for self-determination through which basic economic and related challenges can be addressed.

As Regala Soto, a hotel housekeeper said of her work to gain a better contract at the Weston in Los Angeles, "We're fighting for respect, because they don't respect us. We're struggling for health care. On the salary they give us, we can't achieve the American dream. My American dream is that I can send my children to university.... The union is all of us together. [At a recent rally] so many woman came with their children. Politicians came. Pastors came. Police came. Everyone came to help us have a new beginning. It was beautiful."[13] For Regala and others, unions gives workers dignity, power, and a voice in the workplace.

Social justice, at heart, is about creating a mechanism for deep and widespread change. In the economic realm, the labor movement is that mechanism.

Opportunities for Change

How can we best support the labor movement?

First, we must support the right of workers to form unions, free of employer influence or intimidation. One good legislative solution is the Employee Free Choice Act, which would guarantee recognition of a union as the workers' representative when a majority of workers at a specific workplace sign union cards indicating that this is their choice—hence the term "card-check recognition." The JPCA, EPCA, and JFSJ have already signed on.

Second, we must support the signing of noninterference pledges by management in workplaces where campaigns for union recognition are taking place, as did the United Hebrew Trades, the New York division of the Jewish Labor Committee, during a campaign in support of workers at the Yellow Rat Bastard stores in New York. We also must call for meaningful penalties against firms engaging in unfair labor practices, support the right to union representation and collective bargaining, and support the right to arbitration if management and the union can't agree on a first contract.

Third, when employers try to exercise their power over employees, we must exercise our power in the marketplace over employers as consumers and religious people. Religious communities must stand with workers at rallies and vigils, on the picket line, and in meetings with management. We must commit ourselves to hiring union companies and contractors for business, and publicly avoid patronizing institutions that abuse their workers.

A Jewish colleague of mine, Adam Neiman, active professionally in marketing clothes, sneakers, and other goods not produced under sweatshop conditions, somehow ties a lot of this together. In a unique and unlikely *shidduch* ("match"), he has linked a Turkish cotton mill with a unionized Palestinian textile company in Bethlehem employing Palestinian Christians and Muslims. In a recent interview in *Sojourners Magazine*, he said:

> The most important part of making sure that working peoples' interest is secured is a strong labor movement. There is no substitute. This is something that the fair trade movement hasn't really dealt with, and it's incredibly important that they do. Otherwise, fair trade becomes just a niche that will satisfy a handful of guilt-ridden, upper-middle-class consumers in the West. But it will be only a drop in the bucket as far as dealing with the core causes of world poverty....
>
> Pity doesn't recognize the humanity, the equality, of working people. They don't want pity. They don't want a special break—they want an even break. The way you get an even break in an economic democracy is for the workers to have a place at the table.[14]

And If Not Together, How?

Jews and Immigration in the United States

DARA SILVERMAN

Dara Silverman is the executive director of Jews for Racial and Economic Justice (JFREJ) (www.jfrej.org). Prior to her work at JFREJ, Silverman worked with United for a Fair Economy, and the Ruckus Society. Silverman co-founded Tekiah: A Jewish Call to Action in Boston and coauthored the *Love and Justice in Times of War Haggadah*.

If I am not for myself, who will be for me?
If I am only for myself, what am I?
And if not now, when? (Rabbi Hillel)
And if not together, how? (Addition by Adrienne Rich)

Since the first waves of Jewish immigrants began landing in the United States in 1654, Jews have been both the beneficiaries as well as the targets of the U.S. government's shifting policies on immigration. Today, when the U.S. Jewish population comprises mainly established citizens rather than new immigrants, we have the opportunity to continue to support comprehensive immigration reform from both a personal and a political perspective.

One of the core stories of Jewish communities throughout the world is that of the wandering Jew. Beneath that mythology, there is a real history of displacement and eviction, as Jews were targeted and persecuted based on our ethnic identity and religious beliefs. Each of us carries deep within us this story, whether it was lived out in our own lives or the lives of our parents or grandparents, or as a cautionary tale we have learned about what may happen to Jews in any new place that we may go. In response to that history of persecution, our mandate through Jewish text and history is always to remember to "welcome the stranger, because you were once a stranger in Egypt" (Exod. 23:9).

Jewish Immigration

Until the twentieth century, Jews were strangers in the United States. The first wave of Jewish immigrants settled here between 1654 and 1820, fleeing religious intolerance in their home countries.[1] Between 1820 and 1880, the second wave of Jewish immigrants, 250,000 strong and almost entirely composed of Ashkenazi (Eastern European) and German Jews, came to the United States. While the first wave of Jewish immigrants had to struggle for citizenship and basic rights, the second wave came into cities with already established Jewish populations. A third wave of Jewish immigration (1880–1920) came from around the world, as Sephardi (primarily from Spain and Portugal) and Mizrahi Jews (from the Middle East, Asia, and North Africa) fled the collapse of the Ottoman Empire while Ashkenazi Jews fled the waves of pogroms sweeping Russia and Eastern Europe. In this third wave, more than 2 million Jews immigrated to the United States, and Jews began establishing themselves as insiders in the United States rather than the outsiders they had been.

Despite—or perhaps because of—the growing role of Jews in U.S. culture and economy, the U.S. government sought to restrict Jewish immigration in the 1920s. In 1921, the Emergency Quota Act was introduced and passed by Congress, which limited the number of immigrants to the United States to less than 3 percent of each nationality based on residency figures from 1910. The explicit aim of this act, supported by the Ku Klux Klan, among other organizations, was to keep out immigrants from Southern and Eastern Europe—mainly Jews and Catholics (in 1924, an "improved act" reduced those numbers to 2 percent of each nationality based on census figures from 1890, which further skewed immigration quotas against Eastern Europeans).

Restrictions finally eased after World War II, when 250,000 survivors of the Nazi Holocaust arrived. Since then, the United States has seen smaller waves of Egyptian, Syrian, Lebanese, Yemenite, Hungarian, Cuban, Algerian, Liberian, Moroccan, Czech, Polish, and Iranian Jews, along with a substantial wave of more than 140,000 Jews from the former Soviet countries between 1985 and 1990. Even today, up to 50,000 Jews immigrate to the United States each year. Many of them settle in New York City and Los Angeles and the surrounding areas, though not exclusively.

Non-Jewish Immigration

So what does it mean for Jews in the United States, this age-old immigration story as deep in our bones as the ability to nosh? As we are taught again and again in Jewish communities, in the Torah and the Talmud, "Have one law for the stranger and the citizen among you" (Num. 15:15). Now that Jews are largely United States citizens and other peoples—Mexicans, Brazilians, Pakistanis, Vietnamese—the strangers, it behooves us to continue to support these families as they make the same journey our ancestors made.

Today in the United States, more than 26.4 million people, or 9.7 percent of the total population, are foreign-born, compared to 15 percent in 1915.[2] People around the world are seeking new lives as the newly global economy—driven largely by neoliberal economic policies embraced and driven by the United States—results in the loss of farming, factory, and local employment opportunities throughout the world. As an example, in El Salvador, out of a total population of 5 million, more than 800 people leave each day for the United States. Eighteen percent of the country's Gross National Product (GNP) is from remittances wired to El Salvador from relatives, primarily in the United States and Canada.

In 1915, the Statue of Liberty opened her arms to all who were looking for a new start. Since 1917, however, quotas have limited legal immigration; one result is an increase in undocumented immigration, as individuals do what they must for themselves and their families to survive. Those same quotas that limited the number of Jews who could come to this country during Hitler's reign now limit the number of Haitian, Afgani, or Iraqi refugees attempting to escape the conflicts we helped provoke in those countries.

Over the past twenty years, the struggle for immigration has been reframed by conservative voices, policy makers, and politicians. Very few public voices are reminding Americans of the talents and economic power generations of immigrants have brought to this country through their lives and experiences. The real need to offer immigrants sanctuary from government oppression in their home countries is rarely mentioned. Instead, the focus of twenty-first-century immigration debates is primarily on security, borders, and terrorism, which is continually inserted into discussions of immigrant communities.

A Jewish Lens on Immigration

When Jews focus on immigration issues, the legal concept we most often turn to is *pidyon shevuyim*, the mitzvah of redeeming captives. In stories from ancient times, captives were literally ransomed. In the contemporary context, individuals may be imprisoned metaphorically rather than literally. Some "captives" face real danger in their home countries, and the only possible form of redeeming them and their families is to grant them asylum elsewhere. For example, women under threat of female genital mutilation are sometimes granted asylum outside their countries. Others face economic imprisonment, unable to feed their families unless they can emigrate elsewhere. Many of the undocumented in the United States fall into this category.

The need to fulfill the mitzvah of *pidyon shevuyim* is large. Yet many Jews interpret the mitzvah in limiting ways. Some take the mitzvah to be limited to the Jewish community, and work primarily to support Jews in Ethiopia or New Orleans and elsewhere who experience anti-Semitism, oppression, or hardship. While Jews should and will be focused on supporting other Jews, the mitzvah is not only limited to redeeming Jewish captives. Rather, the demand that we treat the stranger as we would treat ourselves requires that we also work to create immigration opportunities for any who require asylum.

Other Jews limit the mitzvah of *pidyon shevuyim* to service projects, primarily offering literacy classes to immigrants or volunteer hours at food banks and shelters that serve the immigrant population. Service is a crucial component of the work that needs to be done in the world, both for the individual spirit and when our government has abdicated so many responsibilities for supporting children and families in need. At the same time, it fulfills a different role from the core concept that Jews, both religious and secular, have followed for generations, which states, "You shall not return a slave to his master who seeks refuge with you from his master. They shall live with you in any place they may choose among the settlements in your midst" (Deut. 23:16). Or as the great Brazilian educator Paulo Freire stated, "Washing one's hands of the conflict between the powerful and the powerless means to side with the powerful, not to be neutral."

In light of these words, it is crucial to join with immigrants, both Jewish and non-Jewish, to fight for comprehensive immigration reform that supports immigrant families who in turn strengthen this country. For Jewish communities, our mandate is to speak, act, and fight for immigrant justice, standing shoulder to shoulder with immigrant communities who are demonized and targeted daily in the papers, on the airwaves, and on our streets.

What You Can Do

At Jews for Racial and Economic Justice (JFREJ) where I work, we believe we must stand with immigrants not only at rallies and actions but in the long-term work of building an immigrant rights movement that will win real changes for immigrants in New York and across the country. Our ongoing campaign, Shalom Bayit: Justice for Domestic Workers, in partnership with Domestic Workers United, a New York–based organization, won passage of the first ever citywide domestic workers bill of rights in the country, creating standards for housekeepers and nannies.

We are now working together to pass a statewide bill of rights. This work is hard and slow, but what we have found, in discussion groups, house meetings, and text studies from all corners of the Jewish community, is that Jews deeply feel the link between our ancestors' immigrant stories and the stories of the immigrants in our communities today. Across the religious spectrum, Jews are more likely to support comprehensive immigration reform that prioritizes family unity and pathways out of poverty.

There are hopeful signs of similar partnerships on the horizon across the country. The New Sanctuary Movement, led by Clergy and

Laity United for Economic Justice of California (CLUE-CA), and Interfaith Worker Justice, is building on the legacy of Central American solidarity work of the 1980s to have churches, mosques, and synagogues open their doors to immigrant families threatened with deportation. The Industrial Areas Foundation (IAF), Direct Action and Research Training Center (DART), and PICO networks of congregation-based community organizations have organized churches, mosques, and synagogues in support of immigrant rights. The work of hundreds of local organizations, such as the Border Action Network in Tucson, Arizona; DARE in Providence, Rhode Island; Mothers on the Move in New York; and countless others have created the backbone for this growing movement for immigrant justice.

As Jews, we are grounded in our history, our tradition, and our *rakhmones* (in Yiddish, compassion) for the immigrant experience, both of Jews from centuries past and today, and for the non-Jewish strangers among us. We must use that understanding to challenge our legislators to stand for what we know to be right, a comprehensive immigration program that supports the new families and children with whom we will build a new world together.

Gracious Giver of Wisdom
Recovering America's Great Public School System

RABBI MARLA FELDMAN AND JOSHUA SETH LADON

Rabbi Marla Feldman is the director of social action for the Union of Reform Judaism (URJ) and Central Conference of American Rabbis (CCAR). She has co-founded several grassroots organizations including the Detroit Coalition for Literacy. Her modern midrashim have been published in the *Journal of Reform Judaism*, as well as in several collections.

Joshua Seth Ladon is a master's student in Jewish philosophy at the Tel Aviv University as well as a Melamdim teaching fellow at the Shalom Hartman Institute.

It is no surprise that the Jewish community has become known as the "People of the Book." Our tradition is largely a written one, infused with literature from the biblical and Rabbinic periods, the Middle Ages, and the modern era. Each successive generation has relied on the knowledge of their predecessors to continue the development of law and scholarship.

The obligation to study in Jewish tradition cannot be understated. According to Midrash (*Midrash Rabbah*, Song of Songs 1:4), when God offered the Ten Commandments to the Children of Israel at Mount Sinai, God required a guarantee. The Israelites offered the patriarchs as their pledge, but God said that was not sufficient. They offered the assurance of the prophets, but that too was deigned insufficient. Only after offering their children as a guarantee did God give the Israelites the Torah.

The Rabbis echo this midrash. In the Bablyonian Talmud, Rabbi Hamnuna says: "Jerusalem was destroyed only because they neglected [the education of] school children." In the same passage, the other Sages agree and amplify Rabbi Hamnuna's emphasis on the importance of study. For example, in the same passage, Resh Lakish says in the name of Rabbi Judah the Prince: "School children may not be made to neglect [their studies] even for the building of the Temple" (*Shabbat* 119b).

Half a millenium later, Maimonides reinforces this societal obligation to educate the young in the *Mishneh Torah*, "It is a commandment on each and every wise person to teach every student, even though they are not their children, since the students that one teaches are called one's children." These Rabbinic passages speak very clearly to the obligation of the *community* to provide for the education of its children. In addition, they offer a warning that neglecting the youth will have dire consequences for society at large, and we ignore that message at our own peril.

Jewish tradition and public society seem well-matched in the United States, which has a long tradition of providing public education to all of its citizens, regardless of wealth, faith, ethnicity, or ability. The United States' establishment of public education was founded on the belief that educational opportunity is the basis of the American dream. It is the great equalizer for all children, rich and poor, immigrant or native-born, gifted or challenged, and a hallmark of American democracy. Yet despite these lofty goals, a quality education remains elusive for far too many youth, and we fail to provide them with the skills they need to succeed in America. As a society, we can do better. It is time to put the American public school system back on track.

Challenges Facing Public Schools

The United States Department of Education provides about 5 to 10 percent of the funds spent on schools in America, focusing on need-based financial aid, education for gifted and disabled students, and support for children with low English proficiency.[1] Even with this tight focus, many critical federal education programs such as Head Start are significantly underfunded.[2] State education funding contributes about 45 to 50 percent of school funds based on an annual per-student calculation. This allocation does not account for the actual higher costs of providing an appropriate education for certain children, such as those from impoverished communities and non-English speakers. Local governments provide the remaining funds, primarily through property taxes in a given school district.

Because up to 50 percent of school funding is provided through local property taxes, and because wealthy areas have more expensive properties and can afford higher tax rates than low-income areas, wealthier districts end up with more support for the school systems than poorer districts. This discrepancy is made all the worse given that schools in low-income communities actually require more funds to provide quality education to their at-risk populations. Since research has shown that education directly correlates to future earnings, children in poor districts lose twice: first by receiving a lower-quality education than their wealthier peers; then again when their lack of education causes them to be less competitive in the working world.[3] In order to give children in low-income communities equal access to quality education, more funding must be made available, particularly to those schools with higher percentages of at-risk youth. It is not enough, however, to throw money at schools. We must channel money into effective initiatives with proven successes. Across the political spectrum, parents, policy experts, and teacher advocates consistently call for:

> *Better academic standards.* America needs clear and consistent standards that articulate what students should know by a certain age, and encourage schools to meet those learning goals. Unfortunately, many students, especially at poorer schools, have been learning with unarticulated standards. Without consistent standards, one group of students might receive similar grades as another group, but actually learn significantly less.[4]

> *School accountability.* Schools should assess students according to rigorous, universal standards. Testing helps people see how students are progressing, and helps tailor curricula to students' needs. Tests should assess not only specific content, but also skills and concepts. Nevertheless, tests should not become the only means to assess students.

> *Smaller class size.* There is overwhelming evidence that smaller class size, especially in the early grades, leads to greater school achievements. One study of class size in Tennessee explored the impact of small class size on student progress. Students were followed from kindergarten through high school. By the time the students reached

eighth grade, children who had attended smaller classes in kindergarten through third grade were at least one full year ahead of their peers academically.[5]

Teacher training and incentives. Research has shown that academic achievement in public schools is related to the quality of the teachers.[6] Nevertheless, 22 percent of new teachers nationwide leave the profession within three years.[7] In order to keep more high-quality teachers, we must increase teacher salaries and provide incentives for talented people to remain in the teaching profession.

The George W. Bush Administration attempted to address some of these educational needs with its "No Child Left Behind" (NCLB) initiative, which placed more responsibility for student success on schools. However, NCLB measured student success only through fact-based standardized tests, and punished the schools that needed the most improvement. By focusing on numbers rather than people, NCLB rewarded test-taking rather than skill-building and placed even more burdens on the poorest schools.

Solutions

Addressing the crisis of American public education is no simple task. It requires a variety of approaches addressing multiple challenges, including funding inequities, assessment issues, and the differing issues that face school districts in urban, rural, and other at-risk communities. Just as each student is unique, "one size fits all" is not an approach that will best serve our nation's schools. Nonetheless, America needs comprehensive education policy with strong goals and effective execution.

Citizen advocacy is crucial. Our leadership must hear a strong, united voice that prioritizes educating America's youth. While there are both supporters and detractors of NCLB, the six largest associations of educators have joined together to call for a reauthorization of NCLB with very specific additions and changes. Revisions to NCLB might include:

Better academic standards. NCLB's goal of having every child learning at grade level by 2014 is not working consistently from state to state.[8] Testing helps people see how students are progressing, and helps tailor curricula to students' needs.

School accountability and comprehensive assessments. At present, NCLB not only tracks progress primarily through tests, but also focuses its testing too heavily on fact retention rather than on concepts or skills. This may steer the neediest schools in the wrong direction, making them focus on test preparation rather than real learning, which, often, the current tests do not assess. Students learn in different ways, and educators must have the latitude to reach out to the various types of learners in America's classrooms. Tests should reflect multiple types of learning, including a greater focus on skills and critical thinking, and should not be the only means for assessing states' educational achievements.[9] According to the National Education Association, "Other measures states could include are: district-level assessments, graduation rates (for high school), attendance rates, school-level assessments, performance or portfolio assessments, and the percent of students participating in rigorous coursework, which may include dual enrollment, honors, AP, or IB courses."[10] In addition, schools that show significant progress but need more improvement to start with should be rewarded for their efforts, not shut down because they have not met federal standards as quickly as other, better-funded schools.

Smaller class size. Though class size has been touted by NCLB as an important goal,[11] schools have consistently failed to increase the teacher-to-student ratio in the classroom. NCLB must rededicate itself to reducing class size.

Teacher training and incentives. NCLB specifies that all teachers need to be certified as "highly qualified" in the subjects that they teach, which often does not actually happen. In order to attract qualified, certified teachers, especially to schools in low-income neighborhoods, we must provide higher teacher salaries, benefits such as college student loan forgiveness and housing subsidies, and better teacher-training opportunities. We must also create targeted recruitment programs and improve teaching conditions and safety in schools. Reform of NCLB should include budget allocations for these programs.

Parents certainly will want to ensure that their children's school is providing the best education possible, but all members of society have a vested interest in producing well-educated citizens who can face the challenges of the twenty-first century. As the Rabbis warned us, if we fail to school our children, it will lead to our ruin. The reverse is also true. We learn in the Talmud, "One who teaches a child Torah is considered to have taught that child and that child's children and grandchildren, to the end of the generations" (Babylonian Talmud, *Kiddushin* 30a). When we commit ourselves to improving education today, we commit ourselves to our future.

The Possibility of Change
An Argument for Restorative Justice

RABBI SHARON BROUS AND DANIEL SOKATCH

Rabbi Sharon Brous is the founding rabbi of IKAR, an innovative spiritual community devoted to the integration of religious practice and social justice. She was ordained at The Jewish Theological Seminary of America and holds a master's degree in religion and human rights from Columbia University. Brous was named one of the fifty most influential Jews of the year by the *Forward* newspaper in 2006 and 2007.

Daniel Sokatch is the executive director of Progressive Jewish Alliance (www.pjalliance.org), a California-based Jewish social justice organization. He was trained as an attorney and holds a master's degree from the Fletcher School of Law and Diplomacy at Tufts University.

In 1995, a year after California adopted a strict "three-strikes" law, Jerry Dewayne Williams, a man with prior convictions for robbery, attempted robbery, drug possession, and unauthorized use of a vehicle, was convicted of felony petty theft for taking a slice of pepperoni pizza from a group of children on a pier in Redondo Beach, California.[1] For his crime, Williams was sentenced to twenty-five years to life in prison.

This case reveals the punitive and retributivist nature of the current American criminal justice system, which is all too often overburdened, overwhelmed, and wildly ineffective. Especially in the case of juvenile offenders, the system is failing at the most basic level. Rather than diverting young offenders from future criminality through rehabilitation, our juvenile justice system often serves as a university of criminality—one whose rotating door admits youthful, minor offenders and graduates them, years later, as hardened young adult criminals.

Many working for justice in both the religious and legal worlds increasingly believe a better, fairer system should be based on the model of restoration rather than retribution. Restorative justice is rooted in a recognition that the strict focus on retribution, on punishing and jailing perpetrators, fails to adequately address the deepest wounds of criminal activity, just as it fails to recognize the potential for change in people who commit crimes. Restorative justice calls for a more comprehensive response to crime, providing not only legal, but also social and spiritual mechanisms for both victims and offenders to make amends and heal. There are deep spiritual and religious foundations to the concept of restorative justice, which has benefited in recent years from a good deal of attention by Christian scholars and practitioners in particular, and merits a Jewish exploration as well.

We believe that the Jewish tradition can make a significant contribution to an alternative paradigm—a restorative justice that reflects core Jewish values of *tzedek*—justice, *teshuvah*—return, and *rachamim*—compassion. As Jewish social justice activists, we believe that it is our obligation to work toward the realization of a fairer, better criminal justice system, one that reflects the best of both the Jewish tradition and American democratic values.[2]

Tzedek: Redefining Accountability

Biblical Judaism is rife with examples of retributivism, including the famous principle: *ayin tachat ayin*—"an eye for an eye" (Exod. 21:23–27 and Deut. 19:19), also known by the Latin *lex talionis* ("law of retaliation"). This law is rooted in proportionality and reciprocity, offering victims equal and fair retaliation against offenders. Other examples of retributivist justice abound in Torah, including repeated calls for the penalty of death, instituted both by Divine and human hands, for infractions ranging from violation of the Sabbath to insulting one's parents.

Nevertheless, retributivism is not Judaism's final word on the treatment of crime and criminals. The Rabbinic tradition works to transform these seemingly explicit commands into ethical precepts, articulated in the Torah to teach us values rather than concrete prescriptions on dealing with criminal behavior. An eye for an eye, for example, is read *not* as a permission for reciprocal punishment, but rather as a call for equitable monetary compensation in the aftermath of a crime.[3]

Rather than sanction violence or retribution in response to violence, the Rabbis understand that *tzedek* justice and accountability are demonstrated through restoration after a crime and they require payment for multiple categories of loss: pain, lost wages, medical expenses, and humiliation,[4] all of which serve to restore the victim's body and spirit. This restoration allows for the individuals, the community, indeed the entire social fabric to begin to heal after an offense. The Rabbinic understanding that *tzedek* can be made manifest through restoration—physical, monetary, and emotional—is rooted in the three-fold commitment to the pursuit of truth, justice, and peace,[5] which can be achieved only through the right balance of justice and mercy.[6]

Teshuvah: The Power of Change

A cornerstone of the movement from retribution to restoration is the belief that transformation and renewal are possible, both for individuals and for communities. Rabbi Akiva taught: "Just as vessels of gold and silver, though they are broken, may be mended, so too a disciple of the wise, though he has gone rotten, may be mended."[7] What was evil can become good. What was broken can again be made whole. Change is always possible, and despair is, by definition, antithetical to the religious life.[8]

Fundamental to the Jewish concept of humankind is that human beings are not born good or evil, but are endowed with the innate capacity to do both good and evil and endowed with free will—the ability to make choices in their lives.[9] It is precisely because human beings have free will that they are required to go through the process of real change before being granted forgiveness. Just as a person can choose to commit an offense, so too can he choose to make *teshuvah*, literally "to turn" or "return."

An offender cannot be forgiven for offenses committed against another person until he has appealed directly to the victim.[10] This creates the possibility of true reconciliation, as victim and offender sit face to face to take part in the healing process. The victim cannot be sidelined—in fact the tradition teaches even God cannot grant forgiveness for offenses that one person commits against another, until the victim is appeased.

Jewish law understands that the repercussions of an offense are manifold. In some cases, for example, monetary compensation is a prerequisite of forgiveness even when the offense brought the perpetrator no monetary benefit.[11] Only after there has been material restitution can there be spiritual or emotional restoration. Nevertheless, Maimonides warns that legal remedies are no substitute for meaningful reconciliation through *teshuvah*. He contends that one who has undergone the rigors of the justice system, either by making appropriate monetary restitution or receiving corporal punishment or even a death sentence, has not "atoned" through her punishment. In order to return, she still must make *teshuvah*.[12]

Reconciliation with a perpetrator is predicated on the notion that the *teshuvah* is sincere. But how does a community, victim, or offender himself evaluate *teshuvah* to make such a judgment? Maimonides insists that sincerity is demonstrated not by a vague feeling possessed by the offender, but by the certainty that were he again faced with the identical circumstances in which he originally sinned, with all of the other factors again in place, he would choose this time not to commit the offense. And his motivation is not fear of possible repercussions, but rather sincere and complete transformation of heart and conscience.[13]

Tokhecha: Rebuke as a Religious Obligation

Teshuvah, as a system, depends on the offender's willingness to return. Rabbinic literature, however, is sensitive to the likelihood that victims may be confronted by hostile or indifferent offenders who have no interest in engaging in the spiritual transformation or moral regeneration of *teshuvah*. As a result, certain mechanisms were devised to facilitate a person's awareness of his offense and desire to return.

The victim has an affirmative obligation to notify the offender that she has been hurt, giving the offender the opportunity to make *teshuvah*. "You must not hate your brother in your heart," the Torah warns. How is this avoidable? "You shall surely rebuke *(hokheach tokheach)* your neighbor, and not bear sin because of him" (Lev.

19:17). A victim may not remain silent, allowing her hurt to swell into a consuming hatred. Rather, she must speak out, offer *tokhecha*, and name her offender as well as the injustice she has suffered. This frees the victim from the paralysis of victimhood, and simultaneously gives the offender the opportunity to make amends.

The victim is warned that rebuke must be offered with sensitivity and compassion. The purpose of the rebuke, the Rabbis make clear, is *not* to embarrass or antagonize, but rather to open the door for serious reflection and *teshuvah*.[14] The process of *teshuvah* must allow the offender the ability to "save face," otherwise he has no incentive to make himself vulnerable to the victim or the community in the first place. Ideally, upon hearing of the victim's suffering, the offender should be moved to make *teshuvah*,[15] which is ultimately beneficial for the victim, the offender, and the social fabric. In this way, *tokhecha* becomes a critical dimension of communal and social life.[16]

Rachamim: To Be Pliant Like a Reed

What if a victim is resistant to a perpetrator's attempts to make *teshuvah*? Maimonides argues that even after offering monetary or other appropriate compensation, the offender remains obligated to try repeatedly to appease the victim. In one case, Maimonides states that an offender is required to continue to seek forgiveness, even a thousand times, until it is granted.[17] For their part, victims are strongly encouraged to find *rachamim*—compassion and empathy for offenders—and allow them to complete their *teshuvah*. Jewish law, in fact, limits a person's freedom to eternally reject sincere pleas for forgiveness. Under normal circumstances, a person may initially refuse to grant the offender forgiveness, in which case the offender must return to the victim two more times. If, after the third sincere request for forgiveness the victim still refuses, then the sin falls upon the one who refused to forgive.[18]

What are the responsibilities of the community vis-à-vis the former offender who has made *teshuvah*? Jewish law mandates that once an offender has completed *teshuvah*, and therefore becomes a *ba'al teshuvah*, the community must accept and reinstate him, confident that justice has been served. Rabbi Elliot Dorff, author of *The Way Into Tikkun Olam* (*Repairing the World*) (Jewish Lights), writes: "*Teshuvah* is not just 'repentance' (from the Latin root meaning 'to pay back'). It is a full-blown return to the right path and to good standing with the community and, indeed, with God."[19] The Talmud states that even if a person transgresses his entire life, but does sincere *teshuvah* on his last day, he is forgiven.[20] Similarly, it is taught that to remind a *ba'al teshuvah* of deeds for which he has already done *teshuvah* is to commit a serious transgression.[21]

Scholars have argued that this principle has certain limitations. When dealing with a person who has a particularly violent history, or has committed a high-recidivism crime like pedophilia, it is better not to give that person the opportunity to commit the offense again.[22] Typically, however, when the repentant offender does not pose a serious physical threat to the community, sincere *teshuvah* is the key to social reintegration. The *ba'al teshuvah* is reinstated socially as well as spiritually. In fact, the *ba'al teshuvah* is honored for having broken the cycle of violence, choosing instead the path of peace and moral regeneration. Maimonides writes:

> [The *ba'al teshuvah*] receives a great reward, because he has tasted the taste of sin and yet separated himself from it, and conquered his [evil] inclination. The Rabbis said: In the place where the *ba'alei teshuvah* stand, even the completely righteous cannot stand.[23]

Applying Principles

How can these core Jewish values be translated into a working model that would address some of the shortcomings of the criminal justice system in the United States? In 2003 the nation's first and only Jewish restorative justice project, the Jewish Community Justice Project (JCJP), was introduced by the California-based Progressive Jewish Alliance (PJA).[24] This project is an attempt to build a model of responsible criminal justice activism rooted in the Jewish tradition's approach to *teshuvah*. The limitations of the juvenile justice system present an enormous challenge to America's urban centers. Many youthful offenders begin criminal careers with relatively small, nonviolent offenses. With proper intervention, they could be diverted from further criminal activity and could escape the cycle of crime, punishment, poverty, and despair. JCJP is an effort to offer an alternative, and provide an opportunity for volunteers to help young people change their lives.

JCJP serves willing victims and nonviolent first or second-time offenders with the goal of healing, restoring peace, and encouraging restitution. The offenses addressed through JCJP are most often property crimes, although some assault and battery cases have been mediated through the program as well. Embodying a commitment both to criminal justice reform and to the Jewish approaches to criminal justice and restoration, JCJP operates in cooperation with the judicial system to bring victims and offenders face to face in a restorative process.[25] Annually, "classes" of twenty or so volunteers are given extensive training in principles of mediation as well as Jewish perspectives on *teshuvah*. Mediators are then called to sit with victim and offender and to facilitate the process of *teshuvah*.

Key elements of the mediations, all rooted in core principles of *teshuvah*, include:

1. *Accepting responsibility:* The offender hears directly from his or her victim, and is encouraged to take responsibility for the harm caused. The mediator and victim help the offender recognize and acknowledge the injustice that has been committed and that there are ramifications to one's actions.
2. *Restoring equity:* The offender must recognize that some action is required, and then participate in deciding what needs to be done to rectify the offense. The victim must be prepared to accept the agreed-upon restitution. Critically, the restitution in mediated cases is generally significantly higher than court-ordered restitution for juvenile crimes.
3. *Affirming humanity.* Guided by a commitment to the possibility of change in all people, the offender and the victim decide how future behavior will be different.

The program has proven to be remarkably successful. Victims are given the opportunity to face their offenders. Young offenders are told not that they are lost causes who will inevitably end up hardened criminals, but that they are human beings who have used poor judgment and caused pain but have the capacity to change. And the community—in the form of the JCJP mediators—helps facilitate reconciliation, restitution, and healing. This has resulted in a dramatic decrease in recidivism. Remarkably, 82 percent of the young people who go through JCJP do not repeat offend.

Today, more than two-thirds of America's prison population is made up of racial and ethnic minorities. And one in eight black men in their twenties is in prison on any given day. The devastation that the endless cycle of crime and punishment has wrought on our most vulnerable communities attests to the urgent need for new models of criminal justice as well as a new commitment to responsible activism to realize those models.

JCJP is an example of an attempt by a Jewish social justice organization and a community of activists to implement core Jewish principles and teachings. The various elements of the JCJP program—from the broad philosophical commitment to the principle that people have the capacity to change, to the details of the implementation of *teshuvah* and *tokhecha* in a legal process—are all rooted in Jewish notions of responsibility, repentance, and forgiveness. This project serves as a model for how activists can build structures that answer real societal needs based on a commitment to essential Jewish teachings. Initiatives like this one give us the opportunity to put our values into practice, to roll up our sleeves and work to build better cities and a better nation for all.

PART V
KLAL YISRAEL:
CREATING AN
INCLUSIVE
COMMUNITY

The Significance of Sex
Social Order and Post-Mythic Religion

JAY MICHAELSON

Jay Michaelson is the founder and executive director of Nehirim (www.nehirim.org), an organization that builds spiritual and cultural community for LGBT (lesbian, gay, bisexual, transgendered) Jews. He is also chief editor of *Zeek: A Jewish Journal of Thought and Culture*; a columnist for the *Forward*; a PhD candidate in Jewish thought at the Hebrew University of Jerusalem; and author of *God in Your Body: Kabbalah, Mindfulness and Embodied Spiritual Practice* (Jewish Lights).

According to our best statistics, fewer than 3 percent of Americans identify as gay or lesbian. Why, then, is homosexuality the moral-political issue of the moment, provoking as much heated debate as was once inspired by abortion, civil rights, and equal rights for women? How has such a small group—6 million Americans, at most—come to be seen as, alternatively, a threat to our nation's social fabric, or the persecuted minority most in need of protection today?

Clearly, on the Right, homosexuality is a litmus test; like abortion before it, gay rights is a stand-in for a wide range of social issues, from the death penalty to environmentalism, feminism to censorship. And since homosexuality is still something unknown, threatening, and forbidden to many people, the sight of two women marrying one another can be a galvanizing political image. Yet even if it is just a litmus test—or, as some argue, a calculated strategy of fear-mongering—there seems to be something different about gay rights that is not merely reducible to the latest effort to raise funds or "Wag the Dog."

What's different about homosexuality is that it poses a fundamental religious question, not merely about the separation of church and state, but about what religion itself is supposed to be. By threatening a core principal of "mythic" (that is, revealed, nonrational, traditional) religion, namely, that sexual order reflects divine order, it forces religionists to either deny sexual equality, deny religious truth, or redefine religion in a post-mythic way. This is why progressives endlessly talk past our more conservative coreligionists—to the great detriment of the causes we seek to advance—and why when we talk about gay rights, we are really talking about the kind of religion there ought to be in the world.

The Idea of Order vs. Key West

In progressive circles, anti-gay rhetoric is usually characterized as hysteria. How could more marriage and commitment "threaten the institution of marriage"? How could a few men kissing unravel "the fabric of our society"? Progressives usually ascribe such sentiments to homophobia, thus implying that they are outbursts so outrageous, and so nonsensical, that they prove that gay-hatred is nothing but fear.

Such an assessment is oversimplified. Of course, homophobia is a real phenomenon: as a gay-identified man, I experience it all the time—in discrimination, in the tension I see in the faces of people to whom I come out, in the uncharacteristically fundamentalist misuse of biblical text by people who otherwise are hardly fundamentalist. But homosexuality *is* deeply threatening to one of the cornerstones of Western religion: the division between order and chaos. The triumph of order over disorder is the founding myth of the Bible, in which God divides light from darkness, brings order out of chaos, sets up laws to divide good from evil, and, in the Christian form, demarcates the sin that the passion of Christ forgives. Ordering chaos is the essence of "right and wrong"—surely the central value of ethical monotheism.

Nowhere is this more pressing than in the domain of sexuality. Here lie the deepest taboos of civilization itself; the power structures of patriarchal families, tribes, and nations; and the anarchic energies of eros, so akin to those of religious ecstasy. The patrolling of sexuality is thus the cornerstone of ethical order more generally—and homosexuality subverts it. In the Jewish context, consider Rabbi Steven Greenberg's reading of the Levitical prohibitions on male homosexuality in light of misogyny, maleness, and penetrative sexuality, a reading that essentially translates Leviticus 18:22 as meaning "Don't make a woman out of a man." Consider the prohibitions on male homosexuality in light of biblical, and later Talmudic and kabbalistic, ideas of wasting seed, subverting progeny, and, as a consequence, undermining the social order itself. These and countless other examples suggest that what is at issue is not simply a sexual act between two men (in the Jewish tradition, bans on lesbianism did not appear until the medieval period) but rather a deeper conception of social order, natural order, and divine order.

Consider the Jewish example, in which distinctions are everywhere. Jews are to be separate from non-Jews. The deathly (*tameh*) is to be separate from the pure (*tahor*). Meat is to be separate from milk. And, as Foucault has shown in his *History of Sexuality*, the regulation, policing, and control of pleasure is perhaps the fundamental exercise of any society's power—*a fortiori* when it is yoked to family, nation, and tribe. If the containment of eros is the cornerstone of Western religious civilization, then by de-linking sexual pleasure, sexual expression, and sexual being from inherited cultural norms, gay liberation (which, by its own internal logic, demands women's liberation—no doubt threatening to its opponents) threatens Western religious civilization itself. Order is civilization, and subverting order is subverting civilization.

More than that: it subverts God's word itself. Consider the frequency with which terms like "natural" and "unnatural" appear in biblical and popular rhetoric. In the New Testament, for example, Paul complains how Roman "women exchanged natural relations for unnatural, and the men likewise gave up natural relations with women and were consumed with passion for one another" (Rom. 1:27). In contemporary discourse too, homosexuality is called "unnatural"— often by people who think nothing of wearing clothes, living in air-conditioned homes, eating factory-made foods, contributing to global climate change, and engaging in a variety of other unnatural acts. In the mythic religious view, not merely the order of civilization but the order of nature itself is upended by non-procreative sexuality.

Nor does the pluralistic-liberal position of "separation of church and state" assuage these concerns, because the ordering process of religion is public as well as private. For most progressives, religionists of whatever political persuasion are welcome to hold all the superstitious, nonsensical, or even offensive ideas they want, as long as in our public society, governed as it is by the Bill of Rights and the principles of constitutional democracy, such ideas are bracketed so that we can all coexist within a religion-neutral "public square." This, however, is a minority opinion. For most religionists—and remember that 95 percent of Americans believe in a personal God, and the estimated 40 percent of Americans who are Evangelicals were the deciding vote in reelecting our first Evangelical president in 2004—religious order is a matter of public as well as private concern.

Surely this is what religious progressives believe as well. Saying "religion doesn't matter" betrays the hope (indeed, one of the points of this volume) that religion does have something useful to say about politics—for example, that lightening the yoke of the oppressed is a divine mandate. Would we say that a society that tolerated slavery posed no religious issue, as long as we ourselves were not slaveholders? If not, then we, too, believe that religion ought to say something about public life, not merely the private lives of our coreligionists.

In sum, liberated sexuality—homo and hetero—is a challenge to the deep structure of Western religious thought, one that cannot be reduced to hysteria or bias. Indeed, as we will now see, what it is really about is what the word *religion* is to mean.

Not Ideas About the Thing, but the Thing Itself

From our twenty-first-century perch, all the biblical *sturm und drang* of the previous section may seem quaint—or perhaps dangerously outmoded. Gay marriage erodes civilization? As anyone who has been to a same-sex wedding knows, a chuppah with two grooms is the great "So What?" of our times. And, obviously, it is possible to read biblical text, and Western religion, in a way that affirms the sanctity of love in all its varieties.

Yet transhistorical, mythic religion does not sit on that perch. In its mythic world, by which I mean a world defined not merely by reason and empirical knowledge but also by the norms set down in sacred text, the deepest impulses of Western religion are alive and well, and the effort to erode or circumscribe them really is the culture war of which the Radical Right (and Radical Islam) complains: a campaign to stamp out "religion" itself.

Consider the religious arguments for the liberation of gays and lesbians that have multiplied like loaves and fishes in the past few years. Some of the more appealing ones include:

God made me according to God's will, sexuality included.

God loves all of us.

Plenty of other biblical sexual proscriptions are ignored as our thinking has evolved (e.g., intercourse during menstruation, intermarriage). And some approved activities have fallen into disrepute (e.g., sex with slaves, polygamy, levirate marriage).

The Bible doesn't really prohibit homosexuality, only male anal sex under certain conditions (coercion, cultic practice, etc.).

These and other such arguments can form the basis of progressive Jewish positions on the issue of gay rights. But they have had, and will continue to have, only limited success, in large part because they are all really saying that religion itself is to be taken on a post-mythic, rather than conventionally mythic, basis. That is:

God made me according to God's will, sexuality included, *despite what the Bible seems to say.*

God loves all of us, *despite what the Bible seems to say about sexual choices.*

Plenty of other biblical sexual proscriptions are ignored as our thinking has evolved, and some approved activities have fallen into disrepute, *despite what the Bible seems to say.*

The Bible doesn't really prohibit homosexuality, only male anal sex under certain conditions, *despite what the Bible seems to say.*

In other words, progressives and traditionalists are talking past each other, using a common religious vocabulary to refer to two entirely different systems of thought. The moral voice of the Religious Right is mythic: the Torah is true, Jesus died for your sins, miracles happen, and God is watching. But the voice of the Religious Left is post-mythic: the Torah is important, Jesus died to teach forgiveness, miracles happen every day, and God is everything. Unfortunately, the mythic voice tends to sound more convincing, because it is more convinced.

Traditionalists, when they speak of religion, are referring to a mythic-stage world of absolute truth (Ken Wilber's developmental model of religion is quite useful on this point[1]). They relate to religion through taboos and objective values, and feel guilt at violating them. To them, noncoercive, non-mythic spirituality (grounded as it often is in personal, experiential, and mystical practices) is deeply threatening to normative, mythic, rule-oriented religion because it threatens to detach the experience of religion from the fixed rules and myths that enable religion to be a form of social ordering and control. Without taboo, without "values," and without guilt, what is left of religion?

Post-mythic religious progressives, in contrast, relate to religion through the pursuit of justice, spiritual experience, community, and kinship. They elevate the truth of individual subjective experience over the way sacred text has been interpreted by others. They regard the stirrings of the soul as at least co-equal with the demands of Scripture. What for traditionalists is religious anarchy is, for progressives, religious genius. And conversely, the cherished foundations of mythic religion may be, for progressives, backward, misogynist, racist, and the like.

Thus, while religious progressives may use the same vocabulary as traditionalists—God, Torah, Israel, forgiveness, sin, holiness, responsibility—their meanings are often diametrically opposed. (Incidentally, this is not a matter of Orthodoxy and Reform; it's quite possible to be an Orthodox post-mythic Jew by "wrestling with problem texts," or perhaps "reinterpreting" them—both marks of post-mythic religion.) They do not share the belief that mythic religion is the only source of enduring values. They may recognize the deep psychic power of taboos about order and disorder, but at the end of the day, they don't believe that overturning some of mythic religion, or bracketing it, or reinterpreting it, will really end the world. Surely it's nowhere near as important as the dignity of human beings alive today. In fact, religious progressives likely believe that real religion, the kind God *really* wants, *requires* us to reinterpret, reread, and revolutionize.

To traditional, mythic religionists, all this is nothing less than the destruction of the religious-mythic worldview itself—which looks like the end of religion. Liberated homosexuality in particular is a challenge not only to Western religion's ordering of chaos, but also to its insistence on an objective truth as mediated through Scripture. And unfortunately, the bedrock certainty of mythic religion is far easier to communicate than the multivalences, negotiations, and tensions of post-mythic religion.

Is there a way out? I think there is—but to explain, I want to take a cue from Wilber and observe that the progression from mythic to post-mythic takes place on personal, as well as societal, levels—and thus speak from my own experience.

There is no question in my mind, as a religious queer Jew, that the Divine Presence shines in same-sex families (including my own), and that God is eclipsed in the closet—that is, that the mythic picture of reality is simply not true on the literal level. I say this not from theory but from experience. I lived as an adult in the closet for more than a decade, and as the director of an LBGT Jewish organization, I hear from closeted Jews on a weekly basis. As I have written elsewhere, the "closet" is entirely too cozy a metaphor for the net of deception, self-hatred, repression, and denial that constitutes the life of a hidden homosexual. Try it for a day. Lie to everyone you know about something that is of the utmost importance to you. Scold yourself, bitterly, every time you feel an urge to eat, sleep, or use the restroom. Repress those urges until you are starved, exhausted, and wracked with pain. And then, if you like, repeat it every day until finally, something breaks.

For me, as for many gays and lesbians who wrestled with their identity prior to "coming out," the something that breaks is nothing other than the bulwark of traditional religion: the subservience of the self to God mediated by authority. At the time, I feared that the whole edifice would fall with it—Shabbat, kashrut, prayer, and the rest. Instead, what emerged, for me, was a new openness, an honesty that allowed me to appreciate the divine realities in my own life, an ability to relax and allow the light of the Infinite to enter.

Today, thanks to the crucibles of my own life journey and the serious practice of meditation, including several multiweek retreats, I know, as much as I know anything, that the loving God that emerges from the great Emptiness, the God of Abraham, Isaac, and Jacob, could not possibly wish for Her creations to distort, repress, deny, and mutilate themselves. It takes but a moment's reflection, when the mind is quiet, to know that for a certainty. I became, in other words, a mystic. I left behind the mythic world that had become a prison, and, to my surprise, a new one opened up. A new stage—as Wilber defines it—in which the mythic structures of the past are not so much refuted as surpassed. They still remain, with all their majestic force and power, but as forms, as narratives—not as science.

However, it's important to observe, as Wilber also does, that mystical states are not enough—there must be a move to a different *stage*. After all, Evangelicals and far-right-wing settlers also have powerful religious experiences. They may experience the same states as I do, but they interpret them according to their different stages: different categories of myth, nation, and Scripture. Thus they reach different, even terrifying, results. God loves us, therefore God *really* wants gay people to repent and become straight. Allah loves us, therefore Allah *really* wants the evil empire to be destroyed. The land is holy, therefore the land must be ours. The naive belief that spiritual practice will naturally lead to "compassionate" liberal political values is simply not true.

Mystical states are relatively cheap. Chant a mantra for four hours, or dance ecstatically, or meditate, or take psychedelic drugs, and you'll enter one yourself. To be sure, altered mind states, religious and otherwise, are often delightful, and potentially transformative— but the type of transformation they effect depends not on the state alone, but also on the *stage* of one's religious development.

In contrast, stages are expensive, and generally result in leaving behind everything you once thought was true—whether it's a God who rewards and punishes, or the belief that only one religion can be true, or the deep-seated notion that sexual order reflects divine fiat. One such moment happens in *Huckleberry Finn:* Huck has been told all his life that if he hides runaway slaves, he's going to go to hell. But now he's gotten to know Jim, a runaway slave, as a human being. What does he do: conform with his mythic religion, or listen to his heart? Huck's decision—"Well, I guess I'll go to hell then"—is the epitome of moving from one stage to the next. The old mythic structure is discarded, and the real work of conscience begins.

Will America really "discard" its mythic structures in this way? If the past is any guide, then it will happen only through a human reality strong enough to force ideas until they break. Kids in Alabama being sprayed by fire hoses, the gay teenager who kills himself, Rosa Parks, Matthew Shepard—these are not theories and theoreticians. They are people and narratives strong enough to dislodge ideas.

The question is not whether Judaism (or Christianity) is liberal or conservative. With proof-texts, everything is possible: bring in Leviticus, and I'll bring David and Jonathan. Cite from Joshua, and I'll quote Isaiah. Rather, the question is *how* we read, *how* we interpret even our deepest spiritual experiences. How do we take the achingly beautiful poetry of our religious tradition and read it in the achingly beautiful realities of lives far too subtle for certainty?

Not by waving the flag of civil liberties, or by demanding that people fence in their religion. Not by closeting our spiritual selves, even as we "out" our sexual ones. Only by being the kinds of people—publicly, with our whole messy selves on view—that can directly force the change that Huck Finn experienced. Facing myth, we must answer with reality. Studies of American views on sexual orientation have shown that whether one supports gay rights and gay marriage is directly related to whether one actually knows gay people—out gay people, that is. This is how the Dalai Lama moved from an initial anti-gay position to an accepting one: by meeting gay people directly. It's how heterosexual philanthropists and activists have made sexual equality a priority: by appreciating gay people as people, or by coming into contact with the tragedy of homophobia. It doesn't work for everyone—witness Dick Cheney—but it works for most.

Luckily, the time is right: the rhetorical structures of contemporary American religious discourse are precisely about personal narrative, personal experience, and personal transformation. Although my or your particular relationship with God is hardly the province of typical liberal discourse, it is, for better or for worse, increasingly common in American public life. We have become the nation of Oprah—but this can work to our advantage.

The transformation we progressives are asking from our traditionalist counterparts is a deep one: it is to move from literal to figurative, from certain to uncertain, from simplicity to complexity. And yes, even from order to chaos—or at least, to a place in which the neat dichotomization of reality no longer holds sway over the emotional life. Mythic religion will never accept sexual pluralism, because sexual pluralism undermines the idea of order and subverts authority. Such chaos looks like the end of religion. The tragic and beautiful truth is that it's really the doorway to a new beginning, practically begging to be unlocked. Or broken down, by the force of joy or tears.

Beyond Same-Sex Marriage
Social Justice and Sexual Values in Judaism

MARTHA ACKELSBERG, PhD AND JUDITH PLASKOW, PhD

Martha Ackelsberg, PhD, is professor of government at Smith College where she teaches applied democracy and women's studies. She is the author of *Free Women of Spain: Anarchism and the Struggle for the Emancipation of Women*, as well as numerous articles on women's community activism; gender and public policy; and women in Judaism.

Judith Plaskow, PhD, is a Jewish feminist theologian and professor of religious studies at Manhattan College. In addition to co-founding the *Journal of Feminist Studies in Religion*, she has written and edited several significant books in the field, including one of the first feminist dissertations in religious studies, *Sex, Sin, and Grace: Women's Experience and the Theologies of Reinhold Niebuhr and Paul Tillich*. Plaskow also wrote the first full-length Jewish feminist theology, *Standing Again at Sinai: Judaism from a Feminist Perspective*. Her most recent work is a collection of essays, *The Coming of Lilith: Essays on Feminism, Judaism, and Sexual Ethics, 1972–2003*. Plaskow is past president of the American Academy of Religion.

In the spring of 2004, in the immediate aftermath of the *Goodridge* decision (the Massachusetts Supreme Judicial Court ruling that asserted that gays and lesbians could not be denied the right to marry in Massachusetts), we published a brief article titled "Why We Are Not Getting Married." In it, we tried to affirm the historic significance of the court's ruling and at the same time to advocate a vision of society in which marriage is neither the only model for a fulfilling adult life nor the only context in which people can be assured of meeting their basic needs.[1] We hoped we were at the beginning of a shift in political and social consciousness toward greater acceptance of gays and of gay marriage, and in that context, we wanted to speak a cautionary word. Two years later, as the New York Court of Appeals and the Supreme Court of the State of Washington have both ruled that gays and lesbians do not have a right to marry in those states, we still feel strongly that there should be a *right* to marriage for gays and lesbians *and* that that is not the end of the story.[2] In fact, the need to place the issue of gay marriage in a broader context and to maintain the tension between supporting the right to marry and looking beyond it is even clearer now than it was in 2004.

In both the U.S. political setting and the Jewish community, the gay marriage debate is being fought out in fairly predictable terms. On the one side, gay marriage is figured as an attack on a basic social institution ("the family"), an attack with potentially grave consequences for the long-term stability of U.S. society and for the future of the Jewish people. On the other, it is presented as a simple issue of civil rights/ minority rights: gays, it is argued, are just like everyone else, and deserve the opportunity to marry should they choose to do so. We agree that the right to marriage is a fundamental civil right, and that gays and lesbians should have the option to marry. We also believe that the concept of Jewish marriage should be expanded to include all those who wish to enter into long-term committed relationships. Nevertheless, we would argue that neither side has adequately addressed the ways in which focusing on gay marriage obscures and distracts attention from larger changes that have taken place in the United States over the past fifty years in the realm of sexuality specifically, and of public policy more generally. In this article, we explore some of the issues at stake in the gay marriage debate that need to be discussed both within the Jewish community and in the larger society.

The Legal Arguments

Hernandez v. Robles, the July 2006 decision of the New York Court of Appeals, provides many examples of the "gay marriage as a threat to the foundations of our society" point of view. The opinion followed earlier decisions of the U.S. Supreme Court in stating that "marriage is fundamental to the very existence and survival of the human race,"[3] and relied on the claim that in all societies in all times and places, marriage has been understood as a relationship between a man and a woman. It asked whether a "rational legislature" could legitimately limit that right to opposite-sex couples, and argued that it could, because marriage is deeply tied to the procreation of children and is crucial to the welfare of children—both in offering them stability and in providing models of adult sex roles.

Strikingly, at the same time that the court affirmed marriage as essentially heterosexual, it seemed deeply worried about the fragility and unreliability of heterosexual relationships. Indeed, it argued that the legislature could legitimately privilege heterosexual relationships precisely to protect against familial instability. As the concurring opinion stated, "It is not irrational for the Legislature to provide an incentive for opposite-sex couples—for whom children may be conceived from casual, even momentary intimate relationships—to marry, create a family environment, and support their children." In fact, it continued, the "Legislature has granted the benefits (and responsibilities) of marriage to the class—opposite-sex-couples—that it concluded most required the privileges and burdens the institution entails due to inherent procreative capabilities."[4]

Plainly, from a progressive perspective, these arguments are absurd. As the dissenting opinion points out, not only has marriage taken many different forms over the centuries and in different cultures, but also extending marriage to gay men or lesbians does nothing to discourage it among heterosexuals: "While encouraging opposite-sex couples to marry before they have children is certainly a legitimate interest of the State, the *exclusion* of gay men and lesbians from marriage in no way furthers this interest. There are enough marriage licenses to go around for everyone."[5] Further, the dissent pointed out that the ability or intention to procreate is not a prerequisite for marriage—and also that many gay and lesbian couples are raising children. Finally, the dissenters argued (as had the majority in *Goodridge*) that a concern for the welfare of children should rightly lead to *extending*, rather than limiting, the right to marriage: "Depriving these children [of same-sex parents] of the benefits and protections available to the children of opposite-sex couples is antithetical to their welfare.... The State's interest in a stable society is rationally advanced when families are established and remain intact irrespective of the gender of the spouses."[6] As sex columnist Dan Savage commented in an op-ed piece written shortly after the Washington decision, "Both courts found that making heterosexual couples stable requires keeping homosexual couples vulnerable. And the courts seemed to agree that heterosexuals can hardly be bothered to have children at all—or once they've had them, can hardly be bothered to care for them—unless marriage rights are reserved exclusively for heterosexuals."[7]

A Deeper Anxiety

Thus, discernable just below the surface of the majority opinions in both the New York and the Washington cases is a profound anxiety about the changes in family patterns and in sexual behaviors that have occurred in the past several decades. Gay marriage has become the symbol of, and focus of concern about, sweeping changes in family forms and sexual values. These include later age at first marriage; the increasing acceptance of nonmarital sex; the practice of living together before (or instead of) marriage; the move toward more egalitarian forms of marriage; the growing numbers of single people at all stages in the life cycle; the increases in the number of single-parent families and of female-headed families; the increasing visibility of gay, lesbian, and transgendered people; and the marketing of sexuality and of a wide range of sexual practices and paraphernalia.

As Jeffrey Weeks so succinctly puts it, "There no longer appears to be a great continent of [sexual] normality surrounded by small islands of disorder." Instead, there are many islands, great and small, each with its own unique features, all shifting in relation to each other and in their overall configuration.[8] Battling gay marriage is part of a much broader agenda on the part of the Right that entails rejecting all these changes in patriarchal, hierarchical social relationships. We suspect that part of the "traction" that right-wing positions have in the larger culture has to do with their tapping into the deeper (and often unacknowledged or unaddressed) concerns about living in a time of shifting sexual norms. But even for liberals, who defend the notion of gay marriage, focusing debate on the status and behaviors of gay people still functions as a substitute for dealing with the changes that affect every family and every community in the country. Thus, both right-wing opponents and liberal supporters of gay rights and gay marriage treat gay people as emblematic of broader changes in which they are simply participants.

It is interesting to see how this dynamic plays out in the Jewish community, because Jews are disproportionately represented in the changes in sexual behavior we have named. They are more likely to approve of premarital sex and cohabitation than either Americans belonging to other religious groups or those with no religious affiliation, and they are the most likely group to enter into their first union through cohabitation. Jews marry later than other Americans: according to the 1990 National Jewish Population Survey, only half of Jews were married by ages 25 to 34, as compared to two-thirds of the general white population. As the Jewish divorce rate—though still lower than the general divorce rate—rises, singleness is no longer a brief way station between childhood and adulthood, but an ongoing way of life for large numbers of Jews. Perhaps because Jews remain single longer, they constitute the highest percentage of Americans who have had five or more sexual partners, again including those with no religious affiliation.[9] Yet, all the Jewish denominations have devoted far more communal time and energy to debating the status of gays and lesbians in the Jewish community than they have to discussing sexual norms more generally.[10]

On the one hand, questions surrounding the acceptance of homosexuality seem to demand special treatment in the Jewish context because they pose a particularly clear and explicit challenge to the authority of tradition. The fact that the Torah contains two verses explicitly prohibiting anal intercourse between men makes the issue of gay marriage a particularly important test case for the continuing relevance of traditional sexual values in contemporary society.

On the other hand, the injunctions against male same-sex sex are part of a broader Halachic and narrative tradition that has treated heterosexual, patriarchal marriage as the only legitimate structure for adult Jewish life.[11] Jewish feminists have been challenging this vision for more than three decades, analyzing and criticizing notions of women's sexuality as male property, arguing for a more expansive understanding of what constitutes fully realized adulthood, and supporting the democratization of communal decision-making structures to include those who never have been part of the formulation of Jewish communal norms. In our view, the issue of gay marriage cannot be separated from this larger project, which includes rethinking the roles of women, the meaning of intimate relationships, the structures in which we bear and raise children, the hierarchical organization of our communities, and a host of other questions.

Marriage in Context

Placing the issue of gay marriage in this wider context provides an opportunity to explore the ways in which many debates about sexuality among Jews are, at bottom, debates about conflicting values *within* our tradition. Even when we focus narrowly on sexual norms, we can still find profound tensions between different strands in Jewish sources. As Rachel Adler points out, the Jewish wedding ceremony expresses both an understanding of marriage as a patriarchal property transaction (*kinyan,* male acquisition of the bride) and a more expansive vision of marriage as about companionship, wholeness, and creativity (the *sheva brachot,* seven blessings). Similarly, the Sages were deeply torn about whether it was more important to produce biological children or to cultivate disciples to whom to transmit Torah knowledge.[12]

As we think about redefining sexual ethics and values for the twenty-first century, do we want to give priority to particular injunctions and prohibitions derived from a patriarchal vision of society and the family, or do we want to highlight values such as companionship and a broad understanding of generativity that have equally deep roots in Jewish tradition? Moreover, when we place sexual questions in the context of fundamental Jewish principles, we must ask ourselves how values such as kindness to strangers, creation in the image of God, and pursuit of justice, etc., relate to the realm of sexuality.

Rabbi Lisa Edwards, in a sermon on *Aharei Mot* (the Torah portion that contains the prohibition of male anal intercourse in Leviticus 18), brilliantly juxtaposes the prohibition against same-sex sex with broader values of communal inclusion articulated in the same *parashah:*

> We are your gay and lesbian children: "You must not seek vengeance, nor bear a grudge against the children of your people"
> (Lev. 19:18)

We are your lesbian mothers and gay fathers: "Revere your mother and your father, each of you"

(Lev. 19:3)

We are the stranger: "You must not oppress the stranger. You shall love the stranger as yourself for you were strangers in the land of Egypt"

(Lev. 19:34)[13]

As progressive Jews, we want to argue that, rather than endlessly debating the behavior of a small minority, Jewish communities need to engage in wide-ranging discussions of sexual values that make clear that *all* in the community have a stake in the conversation.

But changes in sexual behaviors and values constitute only one level on which the issue of gay marriage functions as a lightning rod for broader questions. The gay marriage debates are also taking place in a political, social, and economic context in which the social supports that, since the New Deal, have offered U.S. citizens at least some protection from economic catastrophe are being eroded. Social Security, unemployment insurance, aid to the blind and disabled, and, more recently, Medicare and Medicaid are all under attack. Current threats to the Social Security system and to Medicare and Medicaid, the collapse of many corporate pension plans (Enron being, perhaps, the most notable), and growing awareness of the numbers of U.S. citizens without access to health care have led many to fear being thrown back onto personal/familial resources alone—resources that are ever more inadequate as the population ages, the costs of health care and long-term care rise, and the availability of quality child care remains, as ever, largely nonexistent or unaffordable. In a context in which two incomes are virtually essential for the attainment of middle-class status, women of the "boomer" generation in particular are increasingly caught between the demands of the workplace and the need to care for children and/or frail parents.

It may be that for the Right, traditional marriage represents the one institution that counters the individualism and isolation of a world where mutuality and communal responsibility appear to be eroding. In Christopher Lasch's words, marriage seems to be the only "haven in a heartless world." In this view, to countenance gay marriage would be to give in to the "permissiveness" that is taken to have resulted in the weakening of familial and communal bonds. Liberals, on the other hand, have argued that gays and lesbians should have access to the rights and privileges of marriage precisely *because* of the benefits that status provides: the *Goodridge* decision noted more than a thousand federal benefits, and the New York decision referred to more than a hundred benefits under New York law. Thus, many supporters of gay marriage argue that it should be understood as a civil rights/equal protection issue (a perspective taken up by the dissenting justices in both New York and Washington).

Both perspectives, however, make access to social supports contingent upon marriage, a position that marginalizes and ignores the situation of those who, through choice or circumstance, organize their lives differently. Although marriage is meaningful and positive for many people, tying social benefits to marriage (however defined) ignores the *many other* ways in which people organize their households: senior citizens living together, adult children living with and caring for their parents, queer couples who decide to raise a child jointly, blended families, and caregiving and partnership relationships that have been developed to provide support systems to those living with HIV/AIDS.[14] Seeking expanded benefits through marriage accepts the privatization of responsibility of caring for children, the elderly, the ill, and the disabled. Moreover, a focus on gay marriage as a "stand-alone issue" leads us to neglect our *social* responsibilities to provide adequate health insurance, child care, adult day care, etc., that would allow people to live with dignity and enable all adults who want to work to be able to do so. Everyone is "dependent" at some point in his or her life; we are all entitled to care in such situations, and we should not have to rely on family members (usually women, and often under stress themselves) to provide such care.

Alternative Models

It is disappointing that liberal Jews should focus on access to marriage for gays and lesbians without taking account of this larger social-economic context, because the history of Jewish communal life provides many alternatives to the isolated nuclear family model. The existence of institutions such as *hachnassat kallah* (dowry societies), *hevrei kadishah* (burial societies), *maot hittin* (Passover food groups), and free loan societies, for example, that flourished in the shtetls of Eastern Europe and among immigrants in the United States, serve as evidence of the Jewish community's awareness that families cannot always support their members. They attest to the assumption of a *communal* responsibility to meet the needs of individual members.[15] Why are *these* values not being articulated as a Jewish response to debates around same-sex marriage and access to benefits?

It seems that there is a double narrowing that takes place around issues of sexuality. On the one side, gays and lesbians become the repositories for collective anxieties about changing sexual values; at the same time, sexual questions are, themselves, isolated from broader issues of social and economic justice and the supports necessary for *everyone* to lead Jewishly and humanly fulfilling adult lives. We believe that the Jewish community should use this historical moment—in which same-sex marriage is on the national agenda—to bring together the streams of sexual ethics and of social justice. At a time when conservatives and fundamentalists have had a virtual monopoly on the use of religious language in the public arena, progressives, both Jews and others, must articulate visions that emerge out of their traditions of what it means to live just and healthy adult lives. What kinds of religious, social, and political changes would be necessary to enable full inclusion of *everyone* in the lives of our communities? What is the responsibility—and what are the *opportunities*—for progressive Jews to engage with issues of both sexual *and* social justice in the Jewish community and in the larger society?

As Jews, we certainly need to address these questions within the context of the Jewish community. What would it take to incorporate fully as members of the Jewish community those whose households take a variety of different forms? We know many lesbian and gay Jewish parents who celebrate Shabbat and holidays with their children and live rather exemplary contemporary Jewish lives. We also know many single Jews (especially women) who similarly observe traditions, and celebrate holidays, but are marginalized by mainstream synagogues and Jewish communal organizations. Are their lives less valid or valuable than those of heterosexual married couples? How can the

Jewish community support the many different ways in which people find companionship and intimacy, work to pass on values to future generations, and organize themselves to meet their own and others' needs? How do we recognize and celebrate the presence of gay, lesbian, bisexual, and transgendered persons in our communities in ways that go beyond expanding the privileges of married coupledom to a slightly larger cohort?

We are struck that, although Jewish feminists placed many of these issues on the communal agenda more than thirty years ago, significant problems remain to be addressed. Although Jewish communities increasingly recognize the presence of "singles," the primary mode of doing so is to create opportunities for them to meet others to marry. Jews who are divorced or widowed often continue to find themselves alienated from the community at precisely the time when they need it most. Single parents and gay and lesbian parents often feel marginalized by the definition of family communicated by synagogues, religious schools, and Jewish community centers. Moreover, despite the supposed centrality of "the Jewish family" in communal programming, few Jewish events offer provisions for child care, and the establishment of child-care centers is still not a priority for Jewish communities. On top of all this, the increasing demands of work—and the Jewish community's adoption of 24/7 expectations for Jewish professionals—have, if anything, made it even more difficult to formulate "family-friendly" policies, whatever the definition of "family."[16]

But these issues within the Jewish community cannot be separated from larger questions of social justice. The current debate over gay marriage offers Jews an opportunity not just to support the extension of civil rights to gays and lesbians but also to raise the broader issues of social acknowledgment of diverse family structures and of social provision for all. We would like to see the Jewish community support the legal recognition of a wide range of relationships, households, and families, and all the children within them.[17] We would like to see it take on issues such as universal health care, a living wage, and the right to adequate and dignified support in one's old age *in the context of the marriage debates*—rather than supporting gay marriage as a way to extend (increasingly minimal) benefits to a slightly larger group. Yes, gays and lesbians who wish to marry should have the right

to do so, and the Jewish community should defend that right. But ultimately, we should be working toward a society in which we all get the
social and other supports that we need, regardless of marital or other
relationship status. At this moment when there is so much focus on
gay marriage, we want to see the Jewish community actively advocate
for the vision of a society in which basic rights are not tied to marriage, and in which there are many ways to organize one's intimate life,
marriage being only one of them.

Priority Lists

A Dialogue on Judaism, Feminism, and Activism

RABBI REBECCA ALPERT, PhD, AND DANYA RUTTENBERG

Rabbi Rebecca Alpert, PhD, is assistant professor of religion and women's studies at Temple University. She is the author of *Like Bread on the Seder Plate: Jewish Lesbians and the Transformation of Tradition*, and the coauthor of *Exploring Judaism: A Reconstructionist Approach*.

Danya Ruttenberg is author of the forthcoming *Surprised by God: How I Learned to Stop Worrying and Love Religion* and editor of the anthology *Yentl's Revenge: The Next Wave of Jewish Feminism*. She is a contributing editor to *Lilith* magazine and *Women in Judaism: A Multidisciplinary Journal*. Ruttenberg will receive rabbinic ordination from the American Jewish University.

This is a dialogue between two women of different generations who chose the same path. Rebecca grew up in the 1950s in a largely secular home. In the Reform Judaism of her childhood, Judaism was a force for justice, but young women didn't have b'not mitzvah. Danya grew up in the 1980s in a Reform household with a classic suburban bat mitzvah, heavy on the "bat" and light on the "mitzvah."

Rebecca became one of the first six women in the world ordained as rabbis, and she spent her years in the rabbinate working on feminist issues within the Jewish community, creating ceremonies for naming baby girls and supporting the first battered women's shelter in Israel. When she came out as lesbian in 1986, she was no longer comfortable working professionally in the Jewish community,[1] finding instead a position in academia where she could pursue her Jewish feminist work from a different perspective.

206

Danya began her adulthood energized by feminist issues. She became an activist, doing everything from escorting women to abortion clinics to running sexual assault workshops. Judaism remained important to her, however, and long before she entered the seminary, Danya was writing about the challenges of being a "third wave" Jewish feminist. She has continued to be engaged in Jewish feminism ever since.

We both have been active in a Jewish feminist movement, engaged in the internal battles for women's rights in the Jewish world. We agree that what led us to that place was, at least in part, a secular feminist imperative to work on issues of justice. We also agree that just as feminism made us look at the Jewish world and discover inequity, we also have been moved by a Jewish imperative to do justice work in the outside world. In the conversation that follows, we explore the tensions—and convergences—between secular and Jewish feminisms and discuss the very real contribution Jewish feminists can make to social justice within and outside of the Jewish community.

In the conversation that follows, Rebecca's comments are in regular type; *Danya's are in italics.*

In rabbinical school in the 1970s I was shocked by how few of my classmates shared my perception about the connections between the work of women's liberation and our newfound opportunity. They wanted to be rabbis, not women rabbis. Most did not see themselves as the beneficiaries (or even sisters) of the women who were protesting the Miss America Pageant, sitting in at the *Ladies Home Journal*, starting rape crisis centers, and organizing consciousness-raising groups. We knew that many of the "women's libbers" were Jewish, but what did they have to do with our struggles in the Jewish community for recognition and equality? Didn't those women have contempt for Judaism, which they critiqued as the inventor of patriarchy? What did we have in common with them?

Unlike some of my rabbinical school colleagues, I remained mindful of my debt to secular feminists, but I decided that fighting for women's rights in the Jewish community was what mattered most to me, and there was much to be done within the Jewish world. So I left the work of changing the wider world to the women's liberation movement and challenging the anti-Semitism in that movement to secular Jewish feminists.

When I was in my early twenties, just out of college and beginning to get interested in Judaism, I used to say, "I'm a Jew and I'm a feminist, but I'm not a Jewish feminist." For me, at the time, that statement spoke both to my perceptions of what Jewish feminism was, and what I perceived my own agenda to be. My feminist concerns were global— fighting for reproductive rights, workplace parity, a world free from sexual violence, gay and lesbian equality, as well as racial and economic justice for everyone. Judaism was personal—the treasure trove that fed my soul. While I was aware that it had taken some feminist battles in years past to create the kind of egalitarian environment in which I was so comfortable, I didn't feel compelled to take up that work and push it further.

And yet, as service to the Divine became an increasingly central concern, I began to feel a real need to enter the Jewish conversation. I had noticed that a lot of young women were, like me, drawn to Judaism but not without issues and difficulties about finding their home in it—issues that we hadn't seen addressed in the literature thus far. The anthology Yentl's Revenge *emerged from this and, gradually, my work turned to questions about the gender trouble (and gendered possibilities) in my religious world. Somewhere in there I got over whatever discomfort I had had with the label "Jewish feminist."*

It's not that I ever forgot other kinds of questions and battles— it's just that I began to regard Judaism as a site of feminist inquiry as worthy as other sites. My home turf became a place I felt that I had an obligation to try to fix, and to which I felt that I might even be able to make a contribution. If we don't address the problems of agunot ("chained women"), of Halachic inconsistencies and double standards, of gaps in leadership and representation in the Jewish world, who will?

Ever since the 1980s, I have gone in the opposite direction, focusing more and more of my time and energy on feminist issues outside the Jewish world. Often, when I meet Jews focused only on the Jewish community, I wonder what happened to my childhood roots that taught me that being Jewish meant making the whole world a better place. Perhaps Reform and secular Judaism of the 1950s and 1960s were out of touch with the rest of the Jewish world past and present, but maybe that isn't such a good thing. What rings always in my ears is Hillel's question, "But if I am only for myself, what am I?" which I've always loosely interpreted to say, if we are only for ourselves as Jews, what are we?

I agree that there are plenty of situations in which we have more power than we often care to admit—and it's quite literally a sin if we don't put it to use. The Talmud (Shabbat 54b) teaches that "Whoever can forbid his household [to commit a sin] but does not, is considered liable for [the sins of] his household; [if he can forbid] his fellow citizens, he is considered liable for [the sins of] his fellow citizens; if the whole world, he is considered liable for [the sins of] the whole world." I agree that we have a religious imperative to work for the interests of people beside ourselves, whether or not it bears fruit in our local community.

And yet, with all this internal/external talk, we have to be careful. It's easy enough to set up a tension between work that's only internal to the Jewish community and work that has broader, more global implications. But in some ways, it's a false dichotomy, particularly if we're asking the right kinds of questions. Questions about why not everybody can afford those High Holy Day tickets can (and should) lead to other questions about the distribution of wealth in a community, in a city, in America. Questions about the inclusion of Sephardi and Mizrachi voices in the mainstream Jewish world can and should lead to other questions about race dynamics and perceptions of power within the American Jewish community, among both Jews and non-Jews in Israel, and in secular America. Organizations like Women in Black and Rabbis for Human Rights are hard at work on reducing suffering in the Israeli/Palestinian conflict. Can anyone with a conscience about the Holocaust manage to ignore the crisis in Darfur? We don't always make the connections that are there, waiting, between issues "just" in the Jewish community and those in the big world. That's one of our biggest problems and greatest failures.

But who are "we" in this case? Jews? Or Jewish feminists? Does the Jewish commitment combine with the feminist commitment to make

Jewish feminists responsible for ALL social justice issues in the world? I'm not sure that's the best use of Jewish feminist energy today, nor do I think we need to go it alone. Although much of the religious Jewish community is focused on internal issues, there are powerful efforts in the Jewish secular world that respond to the Jewish imperative to do justice. The American Jewish World Service leads the fight to end the genocide in Darfur; the Religious Action Center is a Jewish voice in Washington that lobbies on issues from the minimum wage to gay marriage; Jews for Racial and Economic Justice, the Shalom Center, and the *Tikkun* community represent us on the war, global warming, immigration, and fighting the "religiophobia" on the Left; and Jewish Funds for Justice support these efforts financially. But these are not feminist efforts, per se. Who's going to work on women's issues in the wider world from a Jewish perspective?

So why Jewish feminists? Why not Jewish social activists/*tikkun olamniks*? I think if Jewish feminists are going to get into the act based on a Jewish feminist commitment, then we should be working on issues that affect women. A Jewish voice is conspicuously absent from work on secular women's issues. Jewish feminists can make a real contribution in the areas of reproductive rights, labor, child care, education, housing, immigration, prison, and the myriad other things that make women's (and especially poor, or incarcerated, or immigrant women's) lives harder. Women are still disproportionately burdened with caring for family members, old and young, and for household chores. Men and women who seek to emigrate from Latin American countries face dangers, but it's only the women who get raped in the process. Access to abortion (and even contraception, in some cases) is seriously restricted for poor and rural women in the United States. I'd like to see these issues on the Jewish feminist agenda, and I'd like to see us use our rituals, religious insights, and communal power in support of those issues.

I'm with you, I agree with you. We have a strong network of Jewish feminists in place and we should use it on secular—or at least not specifically Jewish—women's issues. I come back, however, to my concern that we not separate out the Jewish and secular worlds too much. Activists can start from a specific issue in the Jewish world and build from there. If we instead ask activists to work on unrelated issues both within and outside the community, we end up asking too much of people. We risk burnout. As one friend of mine said, she barely has time to shake things up in her synagogue, where she can make a meaningful difference—what on earth could she do to fix the situation in Darfur?

It all sounds like too much because we tend to think that "synagogue" and "Darfur" are two different issues, instead of related issues. The solution is to relate them. There are plenty of structures in place—religious coalitions that would be thrilled to have a Jewish voice, secular events that could benefit from a ritual/Jewish component, Jewish programs that can be tied into some of the more urgent things happening out there. We don't have to reinvent the wheel, we just have to pay better attention than we often do on how to bring our tools and our resources to some of the many tasks at hand.

Like you, I want to connect the Jewish and secular feminist worlds. I believe that the solution to the problem has to come from within the Jewish community. We have learned too well the lesson of identity politics, that we must do things for ourselves, both for the sake of our pride and because no one else would do it for us. Of course, that was necessary, and still is. But in focusing inward on ourselves, we have turned our back on the world.

Why don't we, as Jewish feminists, always take the extra steps of inquiry? To some degree, there's the privilege rut that we have to get out of—working only on issues that directly affect us or people we know, people we like, issues that don't ask us to consider where we have power and what we might be able (and obligated) to do with it. I think many of us are used to seeing ourselves as parts of minority/disadvantaged groups (Jews, women) even though some of us are dripping in white privilege, economic advantage, and/or some other kind of power that might be useful in the big world. As one woman once snarked to me, "The reason that [a particular group of Jewish feminists] are still on about body image is that, as rich Ashkenazi women from the suburbs, that's the only thing they have left to feel oppressed about." Whether or not she was being entirely fair, it's still a statement worth considering. If that's true, can't we do better?

We do have to make priorities. I believe that our priorities have been mostly about shaking things up in synagogue, and throwing up our hands when it comes to issues outside the community. Maybe it's time to reorient those priorities. We need to begin to feel the connections between being Jewish and the state of the world. Take the unnamed group that's working on body image, for example. Their problem is not their interest in this issue, just their isolation. It's not only Jewish women who have eating disorders; why should we only be dealing with our own? We could use our energy (and financial resources) to support local treatment programs, encourage rabbinic leaders to volunteer in those programs, do some legislative lobbying around bills that get diet soda out of school cafeterias, take the good stuff that has been written about healthy bodies from a Jewish perspective and get it circulated to a wider audience. And then maybe broaden the discussion about food and bodies to join with Jewish organizations like MAZON and the American Jewish World Service that work on the issue of world hunger.

How would we reorient our priority list? Do you think that we, as Jewish feminists who span a wide range of ideologies, theologies, and perspectives, can come together and unite over our differences and come up with a few issues that seem most pressing? There have been times when we've barely managed to get it together to work on issues of our (theoretically) collective self-interest.

I used to think that much of our problem as Jewish feminists was that we couldn't get together and agree on an agenda, and that one of the biggest weaknesses of our movement is that we don't have a central address, a "Jewish Feminist Organization" that, like the Religious Action Center of the Reform movement, could coordinate our activities. It's still something I dream about, but you're probably right—our differences in religious orientation, age, and priorities may prohibit that from ever taking place. However, not working together does give us the opportunity to let a thousand flowers bloom. And it might be exciting if different groups of Jewish feminists figure out how to take issues they're working on in the community and see how they translate outside, like the women working on body image, for example.

What do we have to offer that secular feminism doesn't already have covered? One thing that I see, at least, is the way in which a religious practice can help sustain and nourish the self on both an individual and a communal level. As the writer Carol Lee Flinders once observed:

> *Since women have been so burnt by organized religion, it seems that we no longer have access in large numbers to the energy and the drive that comes from spirituality. In the secular women's movement, I see a deep grief and weariness. It's clear to a lot of women who have been battling a long time that they're up against something deeper than they thought they were up against thirty years ago.[2]*

In order to have the resources to continue with very difficult, very painful work, I think more women are starting to see that they're going to have to take care of themselves spiritually. Jewish feminists can be a crucial part of reconnecting secular work to the sacred.

Exactly. There was one moment that serves as an example of what I'd like to see at the top of the Jewish feminist agenda. It took place one Saturday morning when I was an escort at the local abortion clinic. Together with a group of Jews and in between our escorting, as much to drown out the noise of the protesters as anything, we began to chant parts of the Shabbat morning service. In that moment, my worlds came together in a way I just think they should and hope they will again. It's this kind of fusion of ritual and values that will give us a particular voice.

And yet, I won't say that we should stop working within the Jewish community entirely—there's still way too much to do, especially for those of us who situate ourselves within a Halachic context. But there's much to be said about how we do the work that we do, and what else we decide is a priority. For pete's sake, we have, at this point, a tremendous series of networks in place from thirty-plus years of making things happen. Aren't we remiss in not using them? And when we think about what we could be doing with our resources and power, isn't it criminal not to?

Created Beings of Our Own
Toward a Jewish Liberation Theology for Men, Women, and Everyone Else

RABBI ELLIOT ROSE KUKLA

Rabbi Elliot Rose Kukla received his ordination at Hebrew Union College in 2006. Currently a fellow in clinical pastoral education at the University of California at San Francisco (UCSF) Medical Center, he previously served as the rabbi of Danforth Jewish Circle. Kukla is the author of a number of articles on the intersections between Judaism and justice.

Rabbi Yosi says: "An androgynous he is a created being of her own." The Sages could not decide if the androgynous is a man or a woman. But this is not true of a *tumtum*, who is sometimes a man and sometimes a woman. (Mishnah, *Bikkurim* 4:5)

How I Met the *Tumtum*

The first time I met the *tumtum* I was twenty years old and studying in an Orthodox yeshiva. I was new to religious Judaism and I was falling in love with traditional texts fast and hard. I was captivated by the mysterious square Hebrew letters and the beautifully convoluted logic of the ancient Rabbis. In a class on the Mishnah, the earliest layer of Jewish oral tradition, I found a startling text buried in a sheaf of handouts. The topic was the rules governing someone who takes an ascetic vow. The Rabbis said this vow will be valid if, and *only if*, a son is born to him. However, if the baby turns out to be a daughter, a *tumtum*, or an *androgynos*, he is not bound by this vow (Mishnah, *Nazir* 2:7).

As soon as I read this perplexing text I called over my teacher and excitedly asked her: "Who is this *tumtum*?" "Oh," she answered, "the *tumtum* is a mythical beast that is neither male nor female—kind of like a unicorn—that our Sages invented in order to explore the limits of the law." Even though I knew next to nothing about Jewish texts and traditions, I had a feeling that my learned teacher might be wrong. I instantly identified with the *tumtum*. I had spent a lifetime feeling homeless and adrift between the modern categories of "male" and "female." When I met the *tumtum*, I finally came home.

The Rabbis of the Mishnah, who lived in the first two centuries of the Common Era, identify at least four possible genders/sexes:[1] the *zakhar* (male) and the *nekevah* (female), as well as two sexes that are neither male nor female—the *tumtum* and the *androgynos*. They also had two other categories for gender identity that don't appear at birth, but develop later in life. The *saris* is born male but later develops female traits; the *aylonit* is born female, but later develops male traits. All these genders appear frequently in classical Jewish texts[2]—the *tumtum* appears 119 times in the Babylonian Talmud alone! And yet gender diversity is seldom discussed as an integral part of Jewish sacred texts or as a spiritual resource of our tradition.

It has now been more than a decade since I first met the *tumtum*. In a sense, I have come a long way. Squat Hebrew letters are no longer mysterious to me; they are now my intimate friends, my constant companions. In spring 2006 I came out as transgender and was ordained as a rabbi at the same time. However, in other ways, not much has changed since that first encounter. I still recognize the *tumtum* whenever we meet in the text, and I am still surrounded by voices that deny that the *tumtum* and I really exist.

What's at Stake?

The invisibility of the *tumtum* is connected to the fact that modern society holds that there are two (and only two) ways of being human. From before we are born people ask, "Is it a boy or a girl?" From the moment of birth onward, most facets of our lives—the clothes we are told to wear, the activities we are supposed to like, the careers and hobbies we are encouraged to pursue, the loving relationships we are expected to have—are guided by the answer to this crucial question. The past few decades of feminist organizing have deeply questioned whether we can (or should) see gender as an essential way to divide up humanity. And yet most of us twenty-first-century people were still raised to believe that whether we are a girl or a boy is a simple, and unchangeable, fact.

There are countless people who are excluded in varying degrees and ways by this rigid understanding of gender. There is the eight-year-old boy who was suspended from school for wearing his ballet tutu to class in upstate New York, the flight attendant in Atlanta who is currently suing her employer for firing her because of her refusal to wear makeup, the butch lesbian who was shouted at and harassed in a women's restroom in a synagogue in Los Angeles, and the more than forty transgender people worldwide who were murdered in the past year alone in gender-based hate crimes.[3]

The term *transgender*, or *trans*, is a broad category that encompasses many different types of gender diversity. Anyone who can't or doesn't want to "match" the appearance, roles, or behaviors of the gender that he or she was assigned at birth might identify as trans. Some transgender people choose to use surgeries and/or hormone therapies so that their bodies better express their inner gender identities, others may want to take these steps but can't afford them, and still others have chosen not to modify their bodies at all. Some transgender people identify wholly with one preferred gender category (male or female) that is not the category they were originally assigned at birth. For example, a person may have been considered "male" at birth but clearly understands herself to be female and wants to live completely as a woman. However, there are also some transpeople who identify as neither male *nor* female, or as both male *and* female, or who inhabit an alternate, nonbinary, gender identity.

All transgender people pay a high social price for living as the unique persons that God made us. Transphobia, the fear of gender variance in society, impacts all parts of life. Children who do not gender-conform are often met with physical, verbal, and sexual cruelty and are sometimes forced to drop out of school, while youth are frequently disowned by their families and lose economic support systems. Transgender adults face significant obstacles to accessing employment, health care, police protection, and other essential services. Today, trans and gender-nonconforming communities live in relative poverty, habitually alienated from social services, spiritual care, or support. And, as is the case with anyone experiencing multiple oppressions, transpeople who are also people of color, poor or working class, disabled, or otherwise marginalized in our society are exponentially affected by transphobia.[4]

Gender rigidity impacts all of us, even if we are not transgender. Ronnie Paris Jr., a three-year-old boy, was beaten to death by his father in 2005 for not acting "masculine" enough. Ronnie's story illustrates how the belief that there are only two ways to be human leads to multiple types of violence and oppression. It limits and circumscribes everyone's potential. "Who would you be," asks transgender activist Pat Califia, "if you had never been punished for gender inappropriate behavior? What would it be like to walk down the street, go to work, or attend a party and take it for granted that the gender of the people you met would not be the first thing you ascertained about them? What would happen if we all helped each other to manifest our most beautiful, sexy, intelligent, creative, and adventurous inner selves, instead of cooperating to suppress them?"[5]

Created Beings of Our Own

Faith traditions have a role to play in the expansion of society to help create a world in which everyone's multifaceted and complicated gender identity can develop without the threat of violence or humiliation. Religion grounds and contextualizes human experience; congregational life offers individuals concrete sustenance and support. When I was in rabbinical school, I organized with a group called Clergy and Laity United for Economic Justice (CLUE). One of the communities I had the opportunity to get to know was a congregation in East Los Angeles composed almost entirely of Episcopalian Latina transgender women who use the power of their faith to come together and offer one another support in fighting for access to health care, housing, and basic legal protections, as well as lobbying for other political advances that will improve the life of low-income people of color of all genders.

In general, Jews are much less comfortable framing our struggles for liberation in the language of faith or spirituality. However, I believe that Judaism offers us the resources to ground the growing gender liberation movement in a rich theology. Differently gendered individuals already are integrated into the world of Jewish sacred texts if we only look for them, and they play leading roles in our spiritual history. The Midrash, for example, teaches that Adam, the first human being, was an *androgynos* (*Bereshit Rabbah* 8). In the Babylonian Talmud (*Yevamot* 64a) the radical claim is made that both of the first Jews, Abraham and Sarah, were actually *tumtumim* who later transitioned genders to become male and female. According to some of the most influential texts of our tradition, the first human being and the first Jews were gender-nonconforming people!

The reason that my first Mishnah teacher told me that the *tumtum* was a mythical creature is because most modern readers approach Jewish sacred texts with the presumption of finding a system of binary gender that is virtually identical to today's mainstream understanding that there are two (and only two) *opposite* sexes. According to this view, the *tumtum* must be either a mythical creature or a statistical aberration. However, as writers on the history of sex differences, including Thomas Laqueur, Alice Domurat Dreger, and Anne Fausto-Sterling, have pointed out, a binary approach to sexing the body is relatively new.[6] They argue that the separation of people into two sexes was part of a larger cultural desire in the eighteenth and nineteenth centuries to regulate and control society. The idea of opposite sexes was just one expression of an increased emphasis on binary social and economic hierarchies at a time when modern emancipation movements were questioning these distinctions. Victorian science found "evidence" for the inherent differences between men and women, working class and owning class, and white people and people of color in order to justify subjugation and maintain neatly defined categories for human experience.

Judaism speaks in a different voice. Although Jewish Sages often tried to sort the world into binaries, they also acknowledged that not all parts of God's Creation can be contained in orderly boxes. Distinctions between Jews and non-Jews, Shabbat and the days of the week, and purity and impurity are crucial to Jewish tradition. However, it was the parts of the universe that defied binaries that interested the Rabbis of the Mishnah and the Talmud the most. Pages and pages of sacred texts are occupied with the minute details of the moment between fruit and bud, wildness and domestication, innocence and maturity, the twilight hour between day and night. We read in the Babylonian Talmud:

> Our Sages taught: As to twilight, it is doubtful whether it is part day and part night, or whether all of it is day or all of it is night.... Rabbi Yosi said: "Twilight is like the twinkling of an eye as night enters and the day departs, and it is impossible to determine its length." (*Shabbat* 34b)

We might have thought that the ambiguity of twilight would have made it dangerous or forbidden within Jewish tradition, since twilight marks the end of one day and the start of the next. But, in fact, our Sages determined that dawn and dusk, the in-between moments, are the best times for prayer (Babylonian Talmud, *Brachot* 29b). Jewish tradition acknowledges that some parts of God's Creation defy categories and that these liminal people, places, and things are often the sites of the most intense holiness. After all, the word for holiness in Hebrew, *kedusha*, literally means "set aside" or "out of the ordinary."

Chapter 4 of Mishnah *Bikkurim* offers a long discussion of the ways in which the *androgynos* is "in some ways equivalent to men, in some ways equivalent to women, in some ways equivalent to both men and women and in some ways equivalent to neither men nor women" (Mishnah, *Bikkurim* 4:1). Throughout this discussion, our Sages take care to define the ways that the *androgynos* deserves protection and the ways in which life is holy for the *androgynos*. Reuben Zellman, a transgender activist and rabbinical student, writes:

> Twilight cannot be defined; it can only be sanctified and appreciated. People can't always be defined; they can only be seen and respected, and their lives made holy. This Jewish approach allows for genders beyond male and female. It opens space in society. And it protects those who live in the places in between.[7]

At the end of Mishnah *Bikkurim*, Rabbi Yosi makes the radical statement that the *androgynos* is actually "*bria b'ifnei atzmah hu*"[8] (he is a created being of her own).

This Hebrew phrase blends male and female pronouns to poetically express the complexity of the *androgynos*'s identity. The term *bria b'ifnei atzmah* is a classical Jewish legal term for exceptionality. The *koi*, an animal that is neither wild nor domesticated, is referred to by the same phrase (Tosefta, *Bikkurim* 2). This term is an acknowledgement that not all of Creation can be understood within binary systems. It is a recognition of the possibility that uniqueness can burst through the walls that demarcate our society. It is also a theological statement—it is a proclamation that God creates diversity that is far too complex for human beings to understand. There are parts of each of us that are uncontainable. Every one of us must be appreciated as a "created being of our own."

This Must Be the Place

> Home is where I want to be, but I guess I'm already there.
> —*Talking Heads, "This Must Be the Place"*

Transgender people are often homeless, both literally and metaphorically. Transphobic employment discrimination leads to rampant poverty and homelessness. Discrimination in the health care system means that many transpeople can't afford the surgeries or medications needed to feel truly at home in their bodies. Transgender people also often feel spiritually homeless because our realities have been effaced from sacred traditions and human histories.

In order to create a just society for people of all genders, we need to create new and infinitely diverse "homes" in the fullest sense of the word. Home as an ideal represents the place in the world where we are the safest. Home is a synecdoche for belonging. It is spiritually, as well as practically, significant to me that one of the first world-changing acts of resistance that came out of the LGBT (lesbian, gay, bisexual, transgender) liberation movement was transgender activists Sylvia Rivera and Marsha P. Johnson's building a safe home for transgender youth in the 1970s.

Like the feminist and gay rights movements, trans liberation creates changes in society that open up more options in the social universe for men, women, transgender people, intersex people, and everybody else. On *Kol Nidre*, I delivered a sermon at my synagogue on the power of diversity. Afterward, in the swirling crowd, I felt someone tug at my jacket. I turned around to find a nine-year-old boy in shiny lavender sneakers. "I really liked your sermon," he whispered before disappearing into the crowd. Later, his mom told me that he had been hassled about his shoes at school all week, but after hearing my sermon he had decided to keep wearing them. I don't really think it was my words that impacted him, but the visual power of a gender-nonconforming rabbi on the bimah. It took years of struggle by feminist, gay, and trans activists in previous generations to allow that moment to happen.

When our struggles for liberation build upon the past, we lay a solid foundation for a more expansive future. Classical Jewish sacred texts, composed in the first centuries of the Common Era, provide anyone who can't or won't conform to modern binary gender a solid connection to another time, space, and community—a spiritual home. I believe that gender multiplicity in the texts of Jewish antiquity when read through a contemporary feminist lens do not just offer the reader *more* options for finding a home with a gender. Seeing ourselves as "created beings of our own" provides an opening toward infinitely diverse gender identities that are still authentically connected to our histories and communities. Twenty-first-century transgender liberation follows in the footsteps of the ancient Rabbis. It also builds upon the past few decades of feminist and LGBT organizing, which have created more space in society to express what it means to be male or female and to push at the limits of gender-based hierarchies.

The injunction to see one another as "created beings of our own" is the basis of a liberation theology for men, women, transgender people, and everyone else: God wants and needs difference, and holiness comes from diversity, as opposed to sameness. This theology can liberate all of us from the boundaries that circumscribe our lives. It asks us to throw away the expectations that our bodies or our souls are containable within two categories. It allows us to see each and every other person as a uniquely created being. And it commands us to move through the world embodying infinitely diverse manifestations of God's own image.

Multiracial Jewish Families

A Personal and Political
Approach to Justice Politics

MARLA BRETTSCHNEIDER, PhD

Marla Brettschneider, PhD, is associate professor of political science and women's studies at the University of New Hampshire, where she also coordinates the queer studies program. She served as the executive director of Jews for Racial and Economic Justice (JFREJ) from 2002 to 2004. Her books include *The Family Flamboyant: Race Politics, Queer Families, Jewish Lives*; *Democratic Theorizing from the Margins*; and *Cornerstones of Peace: Jewish Identity Politics and Democratic Theory*.

M y daughter Paris is two years old. She stands in front of the hallway mirror gazing at herself. She repeats a new phrase she has learned: "Jewish girl. Paris is a Jewish girl." What image of herself is created with these new words to accompany her constantly changing reflection? What does she see now that she may not have seen about herself before?

She asks about other members of our family. "Toni Jewish?" Toni is her younger sister, about eight months old. I say, "Yes, Toni is Jewish." She asks me about myself, "Mama Jewish?" I answer, "Yes, I am Jewish." I say to my daughter, "African-American." She tries to sound it out, but the word *African-American* is more difficult for her to pronounce than *Jewish*.[1]

In my personal life, I'm a light-skinned European-heritage mom of two African-American kids. In my professional life, I'm a political theorist accustomed to examining diversity politics in the U.S. in general, and in the U.S. Jewish community in particular. Looking at my own family through the lens of critical race theory, I feel called both to reexamine the ideas of "whitening" and "white privilege" in the U.S. Jewish community and to transform the tale of U.S. Jewish racialization by recognizing the narratives of non-European Jews. With the growing ranks of Jews of African, Latina/o, Asian, Arab, and Native American heritage, it is time for a new telling of the U.S. Jewish story.

Jews of Color—Uncategorized, Unrecognized

According to the Library of Congress, my African-American Jewish daughters hardly exist. The very possibility of Black Jews has been virtually erased in the U.S. racial "coding" of Jews in subtle and insidious ways. For example, a subject search in my university library's catalog with the title "Black Jews" yields nothing, despite the fact that there are many books by women who are Black and Jewish, and that use the words *Black* and *Jewish* in their titles. This is because there is no Library of Congress subject heading for "Black Jews." When I search for "Black Jews," the system tells me to use the category "Black Hebrews" or "Black Israelites." These terms refer to a web of African and African-American communities who, for better or worse, are not generally identified as Jews by the mainstream Jewish community—and happen not to include my daughters.

In a post-1960s political challenge to library categorizations, activist librarians succeeded in shifting numerous cataloging methods. As heir to this legacy, the term *African-American Jews* did eventually become introduced as a Library of Congress subject heading, though rarely and unevenly utilized. In most local libraries, when one looks up "African-American Jews" the system suggests instead "African-American Jewish Relations" to which it directs the searcher to its more "proper" category: "African-Americans' Relations with Jews."

When we essentialize one another as either Jewish *or* Black, we cannot imagine the multiple identities African-American Jews and all of us actually experience. Usually, the closest we come to talking about African-Americans and Jews in the same sentence is to talk about the changing historical relationships between African-Americans and Jews as two separate groups. Though these discussions often have the best intentions of building bridges between communities, the conversational frame often serves to reinscribe fixed notions of who Jews and Blacks are, foreclosing the possibility of imagining Black Jews, such as my daughters Paris and Toni.

In contrast to a stereotyped image of the U.S. Jew as European/Ashkenazi, current demographic estimates (these figures are hotly debated) suggest that this description extends to perhaps less than three-quarters of the 5 million strong U.S. Jewish population. About 10 percent of U.S. Jews identify as Sephardi. Another 2 percent—approximately 100,000 Jews—identify as Mizrahi, having migrated from North African and Middle Eastern countries. One recent study by demographers Tobin, Tobin, and Rubin estimates that there are approximately 400,000 Jews of color in the U.S.—Asian/Latina/African-American Jews—accounting for about 7 percent of the Jewish community. This study finds an additional 1.7 million people of color in the United States who have a familial or ethnic connection to Judaism, or an ancestral connection, but may not identify "Jewish" as their primary religious/ethnic affiliation.[2]

With this kind of diversity, it doesn't make sense to talk about Jews as one ethnic/racial group. When we do, we leave out not only self-identified Jews of color but also people who might identify as Jews but don't because they feel they do not fit in with the Jewish stereotype. For example, in my many years of teaching at a school that has, at least historically, been proud of its reputation as "lily white," I have encountered less than a handful of self-identified Jewish students. As the years pass, however, I have found more and more white students, coded in class as "Christian," who tell me privately that they have a Jewish parent, but are not being raised as Jews.

This bit of news is likely not particularly surprising to many Jews, nor would it be to many demographers of the Jewish community. But I live multiple lives, and find other realities outside of the predominantly white Christian University of New Hampshire. For example, each time I teach a course at Lehman College, the CUNY campus in the Bronx where we live, there is usually at least one African-heritage Jamaican student who notes that one grandparent is Jewish. Though these students can talk about some things Jewish, they do not identify themselves religiously as Jewish. Or on any given day of my urban life engaged in raising my children, I will meet a Latina, an Asian, an African-American, or a mixed-heritage person who tells me the story of being raised Jewish, though he or she does not necessarily "identify" as such. A Mexican waiter in a taco shop shows me his Jewish star tattoo.

Of course, as a light-skinned Jew walking around the city with two beautiful African-American daughters, I may get more regular introductions to the array of Jews of color than do most Jews of European descent. But if we as a community don't look more carefully, we risk excluding others, misunderstanding ourselves, and limiting our work for social justice.

The Politics of Whiteness in the Jewish Community

In the late 1980s, Melanie Kaye/Kantrowitz reminded us of the racial/national/ethnic diversity in the U.S. Jewish community and the costs of our increasing erasure of this reality.[3] She offered a conceptual frame of an "off-white" or "colored" status to move beyond a bifurcated black-white grid that did not explain the realities of Jews in the United States. She called upon individual Jews and the Jewish community to assess and take responsibility for the white-skin privilege many had come to experience and take for granted.

In the late 1990s, Karen Brodkin took many of Kaye/Kantrowitz's insights and resituated them to tell a history of the "whitening" of U.S. Jews as a specifically class-based phenomenon.[4] She told how European immigrants of the last century, with the help of labor unions, were directed into certain professions and how the clustering in such professions contributed to the changing racial assignments of U.S. Jews (from nonwhite to white). She took Kaye/Kantrowitz's work and told a new story, in Brodkin's words, of "how Jews became white folks." Brodkin's powerful analysis gained wide popularity within the Jewish Left (and the U.S. Left, in general). Often the popular version of Brodkin's work accepted that "Jews" *had*, in fact, *become* "white folk." In reality, the current position of Jews and our "privilege" in the United States is far more complex.

For white-identified and light-skinned Jews, taking responsibility for "white privilege" in a profoundly racist society is a significant requirement of justice politics. At the same time, such efforts can reinforce, rather than disrupt, the centrality and significance of "whiteness." In many of the ways that Brodkin's analysis has taken hold on the U.S. Left, Jewish and otherwise, the result too often has been a reinscribing of whites and whiteness at the center of race-based analysis. There are several problems with this tendency. First, a race-critical analysis needs to help us listen to the experiences of people of color and work in solidarity to end problems of racism that affect us all. Rather than expanding the chorus of voices we value, focusing on white privilege instead frequently keeps white-identified people thinking only about their own experiences of whiteness and their own guilt about their privilege.

Another reason that the "Jews as white folks" analysis needs to be reformulated is that it does not explain the experiences of many Euro-heritage and even light-skinned Jews in the United States. Yes, this work of taking responsibility for white-skin privilege is important in my work as an activist in New York City, where there are so many Jews in the urban power structure. But it didn't help my sister, slightly darker skinned than I, who was repeatedly targeted for random bag searches on the subway in a post-9/11 New York City with Mayor Bloomberg's "If you see something, say something" campaign. How many Jews, careened to positions of privilege with their newfound status of whiteness, have been caught in such anti-Arab profiling?

Further, the "Jews as white folks" perspective does not influence my "off-white" status in places such as New Hampshire. Here, often "well-meaning" students write both overt and veiled anti-Semitic comments on student evaluations that directly affect my job, livelihood, and capacity to do my work in the world. For example, in a class in which I included one Jewish author among the readings, students wrote in course evaluations, "This class was too Jewish" and "Did she have to push the Jewish thing so much?" I may not get stalked by the clerk in a convenience store the way my African-American students do. At the same time, there are some who don't see me as "white" either, even if they are not fully aware of the Jewish aspect of their prejudice. When people roll their eyes when I ask for correct change, tell me to tone down the loud, "pushy," intellectual way I talk, I understand that urban Jewish identity is not fully welcome here.

The "Jews as white folks" analysis does little to foster coalitions, which are critical to political work for justice. To be successful, each group in the coalition needs to understand its own complex relation to power, so that the coalition together can maximize its work and play to each group's various strengths. When Jews lose their capacity to name our multiple relations to power—even to specifically racialized modes of power—then our capacity for justice work is diminished.

But this is only a portion of the need for new stories. A central reason we need new stories of a multiracial Jewish community is because, like my daughters Paris and Toni, a large percentage of us are not Euro-heritage. These people are us, and they are our partners, cousins, neighbors, children, and friends. There may be two African-American Jews in my family, but four of us live in our mixed-race nuclear family (and still more belong to our mixed-race *extended* Jewish family). Let's face it, issues of racism directly affect a huge percentage of the U.S. Jewish community. This fact is simply lost in the "Jews are white folks" analysis.

Important as it is, the mantra of "taking responsibility for white-skin privilege" also serves to marginalize many Jews of color, those Jews with no white-skin privilege. When Jewish individuals and organizations assume that Jews' only role is to take responsibility for racial privilege and support *other* groups dealing with racism, we ignore the experience of Jews of color who likely experience racism both in the wider world and in the Jewish community. The portrayal of "Jews as white folks" in these cases actually reinscribes white supremacy—this time with Jews doing its bidding—by denying the existence and political aspirations of so many Jews of color.

Jews of color, who want to do their political work in any given instance *as Jews*, are constantly forced to take responsibility for the white identity other Jews have taken on. Jews of color are forced to acquiesce to presumed white paradigms of justice politics in Jewish organizations. This is not always inappropriate as, certainly, even Jews of color "benefit" in complex ways that any Jew might from the organized Jewish community's access to power, in part based on its relatively new racial status as white or off-white. However, we, as a community, have not yet created wholistic or workable paradigms for Jews of color for their own identities both as Jews and as people of color in political and organizational work. In fact, given the way organizational conversations about race and white privilege ignore the existence of Jews of color, despite decades of racial justice work in the Jewish community, it seems we have barely begun to explore the possibilities for Jewish engagement in social justice work, particularly race-based justice politics.

The images of Jews as white and middle class—with all the power these bring—come at a cost. In the past, Jews were classified in U.S. census figures as "nonwhite," as barely "American." Now we're the "model minority," honorary white folk. Yet one doesn't easily change status from uncouth, low-class Jew to country club Hollywood mogul, from nonwhite second-class citizen to white power broker. You've got to keep up the image by constantly assimilating, by continually reproducing the image. Some of the ways that we do this in an ongoing way is by daily acting as middle-class white folks (in the Western, Christian paradigm), by ignoring Jews of color, and by denying our own sense of Jewishness, and our own definitions, our own experiments in Jewish cultural tradition.

Regardless of all the (relatively unconscious) white privilege at galas and Jewish fundraisers for the Democratic Party or high-profile Jewish neoconservatives, the more we recognize racism as a Jewish issue at the core of communal concerns about Jewish continuity and identity formation, the more we are able to recognize how critical work against racism is to the creation of vibrant Jewish lives, thriving Jewish institutions, and vigorous Jewish communities. Doing anti-racism work is one of the most significant ways for Jews to claim our Jewishness in the United States today. The story of who Jews are and what we can create is not yet finished. It is through this work that we will continue to figure out what kind of Jews we want to be, and what kind of Jews we might become.

Differently Abled
The Lesson of Rabbi Elazar

Abigail Uhrman is a doctoral student in education and Jewish studies at New York University and a graduate of the University of California at Los Angeles. She serves as a language specialist at the Solomon Schechter School of Manhattan.

He rolled onto the grass, accompanied by his wife and two sons. His family put their blanket down, and set up their picnic lunch. The boys soon left to play catch in a nearby patch. The parents stayed behind, relishing the sunshine. I sat maybe ten feet away, watching as the happy family settled into their afternoon routine. My own heart, however, felt heavy. All I could think of was the father's wheelchair. He was unable to lie down next to his wife, unable to run to the field and play with his sons.

I was surprised by the feelings that had welled up in me. Like the man at the park, my father is in a wheelchair. My own experience has taught me not to think too much of his disability. Some dads are short, others tall. Some dads have dark hair, others light. Some can walk, and some can't. Usually, I understand that a wheelchair is just one part of the wonderful package that is my dad. And like my own dad, that other father with his wife and sons—he too is a whole person, deeply nuanced and complex; yet I couldn't seem to transfer the awareness of my dad to this man. Instead, I observed him from a distance, preoccupied with his wheelchair, incapable of seeing his full humanity, and reduced him to what he lacks.

For so much of our lives, we operate based on our assumptions about who others are: he is white; she is black; he is gay; she is blind; he is in a wheelchair. Through our labels, we create stories about who they are, whence they come, and what they need. In Martin Buber's *I and Thou*, Buber refers to this type of relationship between people as "I-It": a relationship of utility in which we interact only as members of preconceived categories. "I-You," in contrast, is a relationship in which we see and appreciate the Other with the totality of our being. "He is no longer He or She," Buber explains, "limited by other He's and She's, a dot in the world grid of space and time, nor a condition that can be experienced and described, a loose bundle of named qualities. Neighborless and seamless, he is You and fills the firmament." The Other becomes an equal, of infinite value.

And yet, Buber acknowledges not only the reality of the "I-It" relationship but also its necessity. These categories allow us to make sense of our lives. They can even enable us to help one another and, at times, may even save lives. In an article in *The New Yorker*, Jerome Groopman explores this premise in doctors' diagnoses and treatment of patients.[1] "Most physicians already have in mind two or three possible diagnoses within minutes of meeting a patient," Groopman argues. "To make diagnoses, most doctors rely on shortcuts and rules of thumb—known in psychology as 'heuristics.' Heuristics are indispensable in medicine; physicians, particularly in emergency rooms, must often make quick judgments about how to treat a patient, on the basis of a few, potentially serious symptoms." In medical practice, as elsewhere in life, the stories we tell about others can provide vital clues. They can even allow us to be sensitive to the needs of others— opening the door for an elderly woman, helping a blind man cross a busy street, or giving food to the person on the street corner who is hungry.

If our interactions with others are confined to such narratives, however, we can go terribly wrong. "Just as heuristics can help doctors save lives, they can also lead them to make grave errors," Groopman explains. "When people are confronted with uncertainty—the situation of every doctor attempting to diagnose a patient—they are susceptible to unconscious emotions and personal biases, and are more likely to make cognitive errors." A sole focus on a particular story, the labeling of someone as this or that, may hamper a doctor's ability to consider alternate possibilities.

Outside the doctor's office, our narratives can similarly fail us, leading us toward stigma or discrimination. We presume to understand people and what they need with little, if any, real information about their lives. Does that elderly woman want me to open the door for her? Does that man need help crossing the street? Is food what that person on the street corner wants? Are our assumptions insulting, hurtful? Our challenge, therefore, is to learn to balance internalizing the larger social narratives and deconstructing these narratives to see people for who they are.

The Jewish tradition gives us some insight into the pitfalls of creating false assumptions about others based on superficial categories. A Talmudic story in *Ta'anit* 20a features a certain Rabbi Elazar and his interaction with another man. Journeying back from the house of his master, Rabbi Elazar is joyous about the wealth of knowledge he has just learned. On his way, he encounters a man the story calls "terribly ugly." The man greets Rabbi Elazar with due respect, for he is a renowned rabbi and scholar, but Rabbi Elazar responds with repulsion: "Is everyone as ugly as you where you come from?" In disbelief, the man replies, "Tell the Creator who made me what an ugly, empty vessel I am!" Immediately, upon hearing the man's rebuke, Rabbi Elazar realizes his grave mistake, having insulted God's creation. The rabbi falls to the ground and begs the man for forgiveness.

Rabbi Elazar has learned that others can teach him that which his Master cannot—how to treat others with dignity—and that even all his studies cannot inoculate him against behaving poorly. Yet, the lesson is not finished. In Rabbi Elazar's eyes, the man is still different from himself, now to be admired, revered, but only from a distance, from below as he lies begging on the ground, looking up. Although the rabbi's apology is certainly an improvement over his insult, his effort demonstrates that he has not yet seen the man fully. He still does not see him as an equal.

Thus the tale continues on to Rabbi Elazar's second lesson. In a surprising twist, after Rabbi Elazar's heartfelt appeal, the man refuses to accept his apology. Unwilling to give up, Rabbi Elazar follows the man to his village in hopes of being forgiven. Upon reaching the village, the townspeople greet Rabbi Elazar, "Rabbi! Master!" Following this warm welcome, however, the man replies with disdain, "If he be a rabbi, let there be none other like him in all of Israel." After some prodding from his fellow townspeople, the man reluctantly forgives Rabbi Elazar, but only on the condition that he not act likewise again.

The text then shares a teaching from Rabbi Elazar: "A man should be soft as a reed and not hard as a cedar." The man, capable of teaching Rabbi Elazar much about acting with loving-kindness, is himself flawed. He refuses to forgive Rabbi Elazar; he is "hard as a cedar," unbending and rigid, and not "soft as a reed," merciful and magnanimous. Only in this final exchange does Rabbi Elazar finally begin to treat the man as an equal. Neither worse than he is (uglier) nor better than he is (beyond reproach), the man he has met is a "You," a person full of imperfections and yet one who is also inherently valuable and unique.

The story of Rabbi Elazar ends at this point. There is no prescription for how to emulate this teaching. Perhaps this is in part because we can never see people wholly separate from the narratives we impose upon them. Whenever we meet others, we create a narrative about them. What matters is not the act of creating this story, but what we do with it. When we see someone who is unlike us—someone in a wheelchair, if we are able; someone standing, if we are in a wheelchair—do we then leap to assumptions that bar us from seeing that other person's potential? Do we bend over backward to erase all difference and in doing so negate the imperfections that make us most human? Or do we take the story we have created as just a beginning whose end we don't yet know, an opportunity to begin our exploration of the You we have just met?

There are many opportunities for Jewish communities to apply Rabbi Elazar's lesson. It is true that many Jewish communities are trying to become more accessible, from ensuring that people in wheelchairs can attend services to providing sign language interpreters at events, but there is so much more to be done. Along with these practical, physical changes, we make an effort to learn Rabbi Elazar's lesson. We must learn to regard all community members without an assumption of pity or condescension. For a just approach to increasing accessibility, we must include all community members in policymaking that affects them—both on issues of accessibility and in general. In this way, we strive to ensure that we are encountering all the members of our communities on their own terms, based on their own voices and needs, not based on our own assumptions.

As my afternoon in the park taught me, having a father in a wheelchair has not equipped me to suspend my presumptions any better than I would if I had a father who could walk. When I saw the man with his family at the park, I was still uncomfortable. I pray that one day soon, that will change. Meanwhile, I know that it is what I—what we—do next that makes the difference.

PART VI
**SEEKING PEACE:
ISRAEL, PALESTINE,
AND AMERICAN
JEWRY**

Warriors, Prophets, Peacemakers, and Disciples

A Call to Action in the Face of Religiously Inspired Violence

RABBI MELISSA WEINTRAUB

Rabbi Melissa Weintraub is the co-founder and co-director of Encounter (www.encounterprograms.org), an organization that provides Jewish diaspora leaders with exposure to Palestinian life. A graduate of Harvard University, The Jewish Theological Seminary, and the Wexner Graduate Fellowship, Weintraub has published several articles on human dignity, war ethics, and human rights.

Imagine the gay pride parade in Jerusalem, 2005. A pageant of colliding worlds: jubilation and violence, ecstasy and anger, ostentation and fear.

Thousands of gay and straight supporters from all over Israel stream through the major thoroughfares of the holy city. Most appear representative of down-to-earth Jerusalem gay culture: moms and dads attending strollers, straight allies and friends. A visible minority has come in from Tel Aviv for the occasion—flamboyant drag queens decked in rainbow flags and thongs and little else, chanting antireligious and anti-occupation slogans in the same breath. Some parody religious Jews openly; a few women don the religious dress of the ultra-Orthodox—with fake beards and long black coats—and carry signs saying, "Make war, not love." One of them chants into a megaphone in English, "Two, four, six, eight, God is good, God is great!"

And on all sides, a sea of Orthodox and ultra-Orthodox protesters—forcefully stemmed by riot police and barricades—some dropping stink bombs and hurling urine; others shouting derogatory slogans about homosexuality, immorality, and AIDS: one managing to break through the blockades to stab and wound three participants before being whisked away. "I acted in God's name," he later told police interrogators. "I came to murder on behalf of God."

I walked on the periphery of the parade, between the participants and the protesters, carrying signs with sayings from the Talmud.

"*Kvod ha-briot docheh lo ta'aseh*," said one of my signs. "Concern for human dignity trumps all other religious obligations." Discard all of our teachings—the Talmudic Rabbis assert—set aside our very authority, and the way of life it is meant to preserve, before humiliating another human being. For the human being is created in the image of God—and God is at stake in human relations, harmed and violated through acts of cruelty or degradation. *To shame or insult another human being, created in God's likeness, is to shame and insult none other than God.*

I was surprised when a religious protester offered this in response: "Exactly! Whose side are you on?" *Kvod ha-briot docheh lo ta'aseh*. "Concern for human dignity trumps all other religious obligations," and these people are publicly degrading their bodies in shameless nakedness—parading their abhorrent immorality through the streets of the holiest city on earth. The human being is created in the image of God, and God is at stake in human relations, harmed and violated through acts of degradation. *To shame and insult the human body, created in God's likeness, is to shame and insult none other than God.*

This interpretation of my sign threw me, to say the least. I had come thinking my mission was obvious: to interject a bit of subversive, redemptive confusion into everyone *else's* tidy schemes by championing gay rights in the language of faith. I had come to vex the assumptions of the religious protesters and (primarily) secular participants alike. To demonstrate to the religious that values like "tolerance" and "welcoming diversity" could be anchored in religious values and texts. And to demonstrate to the secular that religion could be a force for compassion and social inclusion and not only repression.

But I suspect I walked away as confounded as anyone I encountered.

"*Whose side are you on?*" The perplexity and vulnerability of this question has become the headline of my personal call to action—and my charge to all those who wish to mobilize Judaism and other world religions for the sake of healing and peace-building in the face of religiously inspired violence.

We must be Gibborai Torah—*Exegetical Warriors.*
We must be Nevi'im—*Prophets.*
We must be Shomrei Shalom—*Peacemakers.*
And we must be Talmidim—*Disciples.*

We Must Be *Gibborai Torah*—Exegetical Warriors

The Jerusalem Talmud claims that "the Torah may be expounded with forty-nine arguments by which something may be declared unclean and forty-nine arguments by which the same thing may be declared clean." Explains Rabbi Yannai: "Had the Torah been given in the form of clear-cut decisions, the people of Israel would have had no leg to stand on" (Jerusalem Talmud, *Sanhedrin* 84b).

What purpose for human agency and creativity—implies the Talmud—if not to struggle and compete over the eternal question of how best to live? Had we been granted unequivocal guidelines for conduct—what good are our complex and groping minds in the negotiation of truth, the quest for meaning, the imperfect assertion of will?

So, instead, we were given this great, amorphous book to ground our unending, irresolvable battles over meaning, morality, legitimacy, and desire.

I have seen many throw up their hands in the face of this interpretive pluralism and indeterminacy. "If I can make an argument for gay rights drawing from Jewish tradition, and someone else can turn around and make an equally valid argument *against* gay rights, what's the point? I have my sources, and he has his. Why engage in this project at all?"

Why indeed. The director of a leading Israeli human rights organization once told me that she believed she would have no audience for materials anchoring human rights in Jewish values. *No audience for anchoring human rights in Jewish values in the Jewish state!* For this we wandered two thousand years?

I told her: "Your resistance is self-fulfilling. If a human rights organization in Israel frames its arguments exclusively in the terms of *secular* and *international* law, and *ignores* the insights and principles of *Jewish* law, it *predetermines* its audience. Publish articles about proportionality, combatant/civilian distinctions, and collective punishment in Jewish tradition; integrate your reports on beatings and home demolitions with Jewish teachings on the renunciation of guilt by association; the passionate protection of the innocent; and the absolute abhorrence of violence and punitive revenge."

As I continue to tell my colleagues, the Rabbis of the Talmud vigorously engaged in this kind of wrestling over the meaning of our tradition. Take the penultimate psalm in *Tehilim*, the book of Psalms, which pleads for divine involvement in military victory and revenge:

Let the faithful exult in glory ...
with praises to God in their throats
and two-edged swords in their hands,
to impose retribution upon the nations,
punishment upon the peoples,
binding their kings with shackles,
their nobles with chains of iron
executing the doom decreed against them. (Ps. 149:5–9)

A midrash transposes the context for these verses from the battlefield to the *Beit Midrash* (the House of Study), where Rabbis vie ferociously over their various interpretations of Torah. In a commentary that deftly integrates three militaristic passages from Psalms, the Song of Songs, and the book of Numbers, the midrash declares: "[What does the Torah mean by] 'Expert in war'? (Cant. 3:8) Namely, in the battle of Torah, as it says: 'The Book of the Wars of the Lord'" (Num. 21:14) (*Numbers Rabbah* 11:3).

What are "the Wars of the Lord"—*Milhamot Hashem*—the Torah's version of "holy war"? They are, according to the midrash, battles over the interpretation of tradition, the exegetical rivalry that determines the truths each generation will tell, the manner in which each generation will live. What does it mean to be expert in war, a two-edged sword in one's hand? It is to become a *gibbor Torah*, a hero or soldier of Torah, to engage in the hermeneutical jousting and play over which the Talmudic Rabbis achieved their notoriety.

I have taught this text as an example of the ways the Rabbis systematically displaced the Torah's martial traditions by either reframing them as figurative or retrojecting them into the distant past. But one student challenged me: "This text is hardly de-valorizing violence! It is, rather, glorifying it—recognizing the harsh, verbally violent atmosphere of the *Beit Midrash*. It bespeaks recognition that the project of negotiating our tradition is a semiviolent one—and celebrates this process in all its gruesome messiness."

What does it mean to serve as a *gibbor Torah*, an expert in the battle of Torah? Even that, apparently, is a matter of interpretation.

But whether this text is or is not valorizing violence, it *is certainly* lauding—well before the postmodern era—the complex, fraught, and necessary give-and-take of a tradition elastic enough to accommodate multiple truths and sensibilities, and the refusal of this tradition to settle into univocal, dogmatic assertion. "'Behold, My word is like fire,' declares the Lord, 'and like a hammer that shatters rock'" (Jer. 23:29). Comments the Talmud: "As a hammer [stroke] scatters many sparks, so a single Scriptural passage yields many senses" (Babylonian Talmud, *Sanhedrin* 34a).

Our malleable tradition will always be fought over—that is what makes it immortal. Precisely because it *does not* take sides—because it contains "many senses," and will always be used both by those who are "with" us and by those who are "against" us—we must become "expert in war," enter into the fray, armed to the hilt and alive with our consciences, our exegetical tools, and our religious commitment. Precisely because we cannot monopolize our tradition, we must battle over its meaning with all our souls and might—neither ceding it to those who disagree with us, nor skimming it to seek superficial religious confirmation of our preexistent views. Rather, we must forcefully weave our values out of the fabric of our living traditions so that any Torah-loving traditional Jew might also, on some level, be compelled to wonder whose side we are on, and whether our truths just might also be his or her own.

We must be exegetical warriors.

We Must Be *Nevi'im*—Prophets

When we simply *know* which side we are on, *we must be prophets.*

I'd like to ask you to picture another difficult scene.

This is the hardest scene for me to conjure up, and I do so with trepidation. Why tell *this* story—why air our foulest communal laundry? Why not rather disseminate stories of Jewish nobility and goodness? My answer: to be a prophet (and we *must* be prophets), we must tell our most troubling stories, and not only our most heroic ones.

So I will now pull up the curtain on one of the most troubling scenes I have confronted as a contemporary Jew.

An interdenominational group of twenty rabbinical students is walking down *Shuahada* Street in the Jewish section of Hebron.

The street is hauntingly still—a veritable ghost-town of deserted shops, with little evidence of the bustling Arab marketplace that surged here just a few years ago. Your eyes are drawn to graffiti slogans spray painted in Hebrew on the sealed shop doors. *Death to Arabs. Muhammad is a pig. Revenge.* Groups of extremist, national-religious Jews pass you in their cars, periodically slowing down, rolling down their windows to leer at you. Perceiving you as foreign diplomats or journalists, or worse yet, Jewish Leftists, a few of them menacingly toy with their guns. Two Druze border policemen trail behind you, uninvited, in their Jeep; they follow you, glued watchfully to your every move, wherever you turn. When the Jews reach for their guns, they draw *their* guns protectively in return.

Flash to a scene down the street—an elementary school with bright-eyed kids giggling and playing ball in the courtyard. Murals of hearts, trees, and butterflies decorate the sky-toned walls. On closer glance, something strange emerges. A number of internationals, unarmed but in uniform, are standing guard. They are Europeans and Americans, you are told, here to accompany Palestinian children to and from school every day, to protect them from the bands of Jews that lie in wait to ambush the children on their walk.

Inside the school, you watch a video of one such attack. Jewish children and their parents, their tzitzit dangling, their *payos* flying in the wind, waiting at the bottom of the steps you've just ascended, fists clenched, stones, garbage, and bags of feces in hand. Palestinian little girls ducking and screaming as the stones, kicks, and blows land. A few Israeli soldiers observe the scene nonchalantly without interfering. Fariel abu Haikal, the daughter of the fiery headmistress who just welcomed you with sage tea, appears in the video, her face streaming with blood. She turns to one of the soldiers: "Do you see?" she pleads in Hebrew. "I see," he says, then puts his hand over the camera, apparently so that no one else will.

After watching the video, someone in the group asks the headmistress how often this happens. "Not *every* day," she responds. "Most often they come on Saturday afternoons, on the Sabbath, after they're done praying, and whenever there's a Jewish festival."

> I loathe, I spurn your festivals, I am not appeased by your solemn assemblies.... Spare Me the sound of your hymns, and let Me not hear the sound of your lutes. But let justice well up like water, righteousness like an unfailing stream. (Amos 5:21–24)

We must be prophets. And to be a prophet—to confront the ugliness in one's *own* community as well as the beauty it eclipses—is to be at once heartbroken and full of hope.

I am heartbroken because I have stared into the most noxious and shameful corners of my own community—and witnessed the tradition that shapes my daily activity and prayer used to defend brutality toward little girls walking home from school.

And I am also full of hope, because, in the last two years, more than 350 Jewish religious leaders have journeyed to Palestinian communities through a program I cofounded called Encounter (www.encounterprograms.org). And I have watched innumerable on-the-spot shifts in perspective as participants have gained exposure to hitherto unknown realities, renegotiated perceptions of "self" and "other," struggled with emotions of pain, rage, shame, and fear, and sought constructive channels of response.

I am heartbroken because I see how easy it is to condemn and disown the violence of our extremists, and how much more difficult to acknowledge the more structural ways we sabotage prospects for living in a peaceful world. How we create and maintain grievances that—

while not justifying or explaining away extremist violence *against* us—help trigger and fuel it.

And I am full of hope because I know growing numbers of Jewish leaders who will not be sold on hypocrisy and party lines, even when it means criticizing the acts of our coreligionist brothers and sisters—not just preaching tolerance, but actively countering *in*tolerance where it rears its head in our name.

We must be prophets.

We must lead the way in both word and deed, holding ourselves accountable for our communities' contributions to the stalemate and injustice all around us.

Too many of my Palestinian colleagues and friends are petrified to speak out against their own militants and extremists intent on torpedoing every prospective avenue out of the morass. Too many of my Christian colleagues and friends condemn the evils of the Israeli occupation without taking responsibility for Christian implication in violence—historical and contemporary—in conflict situations throughout the world. And too many of my Jewish colleagues and friends think the extremists and peace-saboteurs are all on *"their"* side, while we are to be forever exonerated for our own destructiveness by our perceived perennial victimhood. Too many of my fellow Jews have been sold on the blame-assigning myth of "no partner for peace" and its companion strategy of unilateralism, and thereby hardened to the good faith and reasonable unmet needs of the human beings over whom we continue to rule.

We must help our communities to engage in the holiest work of the religious life, and the apex of the Jewish calendar: *teshuvah*. Repenting through self-examination, truth-telling, and remorse; restoring our betrayed potential for harmonious living; turning inward to again turn outward, toward our fellow human beings and toward God.

We must be gibborai Torah, *exegetical warriors*, who will battle for *our* religious values, truths, and readings of tradition.

We must, at times, be nevi'im, *prophets*, willing to proclaim our truths where they matter most, where they break hearts and bring hope.

And in this battle over the destiny of our tradition, we must be *Shomrei Shalom*, guardians of peace.

We Must Be *Shomrei Shalom*—Guardians of Peace

A few years ago I heard Rev. Gene Robinson—the first openly gay bishop of the Episcopal Church—give a stunning presentation at a Fellowship of Reconciliation conference, the gist of which was: wage reconciliation, not war.

What is this "reconciliation" that Rev. Robinson called on us to wage? *Not right thought or belief, not winning, but rather the restoration of relationship.* Do you know the difference—challenged Rev. Robinson—between activism and reconciliation?

Activism assumes that our cause is worthy and in service of justice, but ultimately demands victory of *our* "good" over *their* "evil." Reconciliation is not about "us" and "them," or "good" and "evil," but rather about *respect* and *relationship*—the attempt to reunite with the estranged. It is about asking ourselves how we will treat each other in the struggle. It is not about being nice or liking one's enemies, but about treating them with infinite honor and respect. "That is hard enough to do with those we love," Robinson acknowledged. It is all the more difficult with those by whom we have felt dishonored, let alone our "real enemies."

But the religious challenge before us remains: *can we find a way to prostrate before the God in each and every human being*? Can we part ways and divide property in a way that ensures relationship afterward? Can we bite our tongue rather than say the thing that might score us points in the debate and salvage our pride, but damage our relationships?

I would like to share two unlikely people, besides Rev. Gene Robinson, who have modeled peacemaking for me.

The first: an Israeli man named Yisrael who once helped me to move several boxes of books while I was in the process of writing an article for Rabbis for Human Rights–North America, arguing for the prohibition of torture in Jewish law. Yisrael and I got to talking about the work of Rabbis for Human Rights as well as the medieval legal commentaries I had just been immersed in. It turned out that he was a national-religious settler and a Kahanist—meaning that he subscribed to the philosophy of Meir Kahane that the deportation of Palestinians is the only possible solution to the Palestinian-Israeli conflict. And you better believe he had passages from the Talmud to back him up. But—

exegetical warrior that I strive to be—I had some passages on hand for my point of view as well. As his van pulled up to my Jerusalem apartment, he said matter-of-factly, "You know, I don't see things the way you do, but—if my Rav and wife will permit it—I'd love to learn some Torah with you. I have to admit I'm hoping that if we do, you'll come around to agreeing with me, but if not, that's okay too."

The second: Sheikh Talal Sidr, one of the founders of Hamas, who, when deported to Lebanon in the 1990s, heard the voice of Allah come to him in the middle of the night and say: "You've been a warrior for blood. Now become a warrior for peace." Sheikh Sidr was tragically incapacitated by a stroke before bringing his message to complete harvest. But last year—in fulfillment of a promise he made just before his stroke—his children, grandchildren, and close associates welcomed twenty rabbinical students into their living room. After hummus and cardamom coffee, Muslim and Jewish prayers, chitchat and exchanges of gifts, Sheikh Sidr's children, grandchildren, and associates conveyed, in a roundabout fashion, a message difficult but critical for our group to hear: *separate the sin from the sinner.* Hamas is a complex, multifaceted organization. The individuals that choose for various reasons to affiliate with Hamas, whether now or in the past, are complex, multifaceted individuals. And the switch from "terrorist" to "fighter for peace" is less dramatic and unlikely than one might think.

We must be *shomrei shalom*, guardians of peace, as receptive as we are prophetic, as compassionate as we are censuring, knowing the potential in our brothers and sisters, redemptive in our critique.

We must see the individual faces of our adversaries *within* and *beyond* our communal gates, never allowing the overgeneralizing gaze of propaganda to dim our curiosity about each singular person before us, in his or her mixed emotions, latent possibilities, and flux. We must remember that making room for another's point of view, suffering, and needs denies no measure of our own, and will, in fact, create more room for our needs and views as well.

We must talk to *everyone*, and I mean *everyone*, knocking down every door with an invitation to conversation and exchange, remembering Gene Robinson's teaching that *peacemaking* is not about "us" and "them," or "good" and "evil," but rather about *respect* and *relationship*—the attempt to reunite with the estranged.

Facing the religious protesters at the gay pride parade, facing Jewish and Palestinian extremists in Hebron, facing my own rage and fear in these settings, I ask myself: Can I be an exegetical warrior, a prophet, *and* a peacemaker all at once? Can I find ways to assert my readings of Jewish tradition and the call of my conscience without contributing further to the demonization and polarization afflicting North America and Israel, as well as many other parts of the world?

Can I *choose sides*, carry my banners, march in my parades, and declare my solidarities as dictated by my conscience and my faith—and still listen vigilantly to those who stand on the other side of the picket line, with an open mind and a ready heart, with curiosity and attention as well as arguments, questions as well as answers?

Can I be not only an exegetical warrior, a prophet, and a peacemaker, but also a *Talmidah,* a disciple, ready to admit my confusion, and journey out beyond my rehearsed scripts and habituated thinking into the unpredictable encounter with the other?

We Must Be *Talmidim*—Disciples

Whose side am I on when I crusade for human dignity at a gay pride parade?

Whatever meanings we attribute to our traditions, we are not in control. As exegetical warriors and prophets, we will try to mediate the meanings of our texts. But try as we might to manage them, our unruly texts will resist us, and speak in ways we cannot dictate or anticipate. And our interlocuters and adversaries, *especially if we really listen,* will surprise us, overflow our expectations, and initiate us into the holy threshold of uncertainty.

On Encounter trips—as we bring Jewish leaders to Palestinian communities, usually for the first time—we tell participants that our greatest hope as organizers is that each of them will walk away confused about something they thought they knew.

> And it shall come to pass in the Fulfillment of Days ...
> They shall beat their swords into plowshares
> And their spears into pruning hooks. (Isa. 2:2, 4)

And on that day, we will turn to each other in confusion, and say, *Wait! Whose side are you on?* Are you with us or against us? Should we identify or dis-identify with each other? Are we antagonists, or compatriots? *Who are you, we, I, us, and them anyway?*

On that day, we will meet over the text, and ask: how *do* we share and learn and battle over our traditions, our ancient ways of ordering death, desire, and chaos? And the ensuing confusion will open something in us—something closed and rigid will come unhinged—and we will sense, through our encounter, how much we don't know; how sweeping and great reality is; how much more expansive than our special interests, our campaigns, and our sense of right and wrong.

We will *not* forego our shrewd exegetical warrior, our stinging prophet, or our compassionate peacemaker. We will *not* (God forbid!) shrink into detached relativism or defeated nihilism! But we will also be *Talmidim*, disciples, aspiring toward our visions and marching in our parades while keeping in mind how utterly small we are, however on the cusp of understanding, and never quite there. We will ask, not only, Whose side are *you* on? And whose side am *I* on? But also, what Heaven includes us, what God loves us both? And what can we learn from each other that will befuddle and enlighten us still more?

We will wrestle with each other as warriors. We will challenge each other as prophets. We will prostrate before each other as guardians of peace. We will learn from each other as disciples. And old traditions will be kept. And new traditions will be born. And peace and justice will reign. *Lo yisa goi el goi herev, lo yilmedu od milhama.* "Nation shall not lift up sword against nation, neither shall they study war any more."

Adapted from an address delivered at The Global Congress of World's Religions after September 11, Montreal, Canada, Sept. 11–Sept. 15, 2006

Plotting the Middle Path to Israeli-Palestinian Peace

The Role of American Jews

DIANE BALSER, PHD

Diane Balser, PhD, is the former executive director of Brit Tzedek v'Shalom (www.btvshalom.org) and is currently co-chair of Brit Tzedek's Advocacy and Public Policy Committee. She is also a professor of women's studies at Boston University.

Many American Jews have long been in the vanguard of progressive politics in the United States. The traditional Jewish impulse toward social justice—rooted in our texts, manifested in our political and social history, and shaped by the great questions of the modern day—has compelled American Jews to the forefront of the contemporary world's definitive struggles, a modern response to the imperative to work toward *tikkun olam*, repair of a broken world. The establishment of unions, the civil rights movement, the fight for women's rights—each of these chapters in American history found Jews disproportionately leading the battle and persevering in the face of enormous difficulty.

For at least the first two decades of Israel's existence, support for the Jewish state was considered part and parcel of the progressive Jewish agenda. Zionism was one of many national liberation movements to come to international attention in the wake of World War II, its ethical and egalitarian aspirations—to become, as its first prime minister David Ben-Gurion described, "a light unto nations"—enshrined in Israel's Declaration of Independence:

The State of Israel will be open for Jewish immigration and for the Ingathering of the Exiles; it will foster the development of the country for the benefit of all its inhabitants; it will be based on freedom, justice and peace as envisaged by the prophets of Israel; it will ensure complete equality of social and political rights to all its inhabitants irrespective of religion, race or sex; it will guarantee freedom of religion, conscience, language, education and culture; it will safeguard the Holy Places of all religions; and it will be faithful to the principles of the Charter of the United Nations.

As we supported the rights of others to self-determination, many progressives within the American Jewish community were proud and happy to support the national liberation of our own people.[1]

Of course, there was a potentially perilous naiveté involved in this support, in that most American Jews, along with most of the Western world, failed to understand the level of suffering and sheer disenfranchisement that the establishment of Israel meant for the Palestinian people. The oft-repeated Zionist adage "A land without a people for a people without a land" captured the imagination of so many of our parents and grandparents in their quest for sanctuary, but now resonates tinnily for we who have seen a very different reality borne out. While some recognized early on the serious implications for Israel's future of the massive displacement of Palestinians following the 1948 War, for many this understanding dawned slowly, only in the post–Six-Day War world, as Israel's occupation of the West Bank and Gaza Strip increasingly took root. Without wishing to deny the right of the Jewish people to its own state, many of us came to comprehend the cost this state has entailed for another people. Particularly since the first Palestinian intifada began in December 1987, many American Jews have begun to try to bring their attachment to their own people's national project in line with the understanding that Palestinian rights must not be denied.

The question of Israel's place on a progressive agenda is further complicated by the complex nature of Israel's relationship with the United States. Largely by virtue of its reliance on the United States for foreign aid and particularly military aid, as well as for diplomatic cover in an often hostile international environment, Israel has become, at least publicly, the standard bearer for the increasingly troubled and troubling American policies in the Middle East.

The effort to put pro-Israel activism back on the progressive agenda will require us to formulate, organize, and put forward a third political and cultural path for supporting Israel, independent of the right-wing/neoconservative U.S. foreign policy agendas, and stepping clear of left-wing denial that Jews need a homeland. It will comprise an understanding of the importance of a Jewish homeland to meet both the needs of Jewish survival and the demands of broader justice, as well as an understanding of the urgent necessity of such a state to ally itself with a Palestinian state along its border, with which it lives in peace.

In this chapter, I will argue that a progressive Jewish movement must reclaim and reframe the sometimes forgotten progressive ideals that were essential to the establishment of the State of Israel, both as the central path to ensuring Jewish survival and as the core of our fight for international social justice—a struggle that reflects the most basic of Jewish ethics.

Our own struggle as progressive American Jews—to cultivate a collective agenda-driven identity that is at once independent and closely interconnected to and engaged in the world around it—would then fittingly mirror our aspirations for Israel as a peaceful and secure Jewish homeland that is both integrated in and integral to the Middle East and the international community as a whole. Isolation from other peoples—particularly oppressed peoples—has historically been key to the vulnerability of Jews throughout the world and in Israel in particular. The vision of an Israel of the future is one that lives in cooperation with its Arab neighbors, not a militarized, isolated ghetto in the middle of a hostile Arab world. By cultivating a strong Jewish presence in Israel and the United States that lives in a multicultural, multinational world, we will create a political home for those in the progressive movement who would advance the principle of two states for two peoples, and help progressive Jews develop greater confidence in their Jewish identity, from which to reach out to potential allies among Muslims, Arabs, African-Americans, and all peoples of color.

The Elephant in the Room

Israel has long stood at the center of the American Jewish community's agenda. It often appears that unquestioning support of official Israeli government policy, and a unified, community-wide defensive stance (with only slightly nuanced differences of opinion), reflects the reality of American Jewish thought.

However, the actual significance of Israel for the majority of American Jews is not as clear-cut as this would suggest. In the period leading up to, during, and immediately after Israel's establishment in 1948 (as well as in the immediate aftermath of the 1967 Six-Day War), there was a broad consensus of admiration for Israel across the United States, but most particularly in the Jewish community. This expressed itself in genuine engagement in such questions as the right of Soviet and Ethiopian Jewry to immigrate to Israel, in a wide array of tactics from letter-writing campaigns to fund drives.

In stark contrast, though, many in the Jewish community today appear to have distanced themselves from issues relating to Israel. Indeed, this trend has become strong enough that many in Jewish institutional life have begun to show concern about the ongoing connection between the American community and the Jewish state. A recent poll of young Jewish adults conducted by the American Jewish Committee showed that, across the board, knowledge of the Holocaust continues to play a key role in shaping Jewish identification, while Israel itself appears much less important in positively affecting Jewish identity.[2] This confounds the reasonable expectations of many scholars who had argued that the impact of the Holocaust would decrease from generation to generation, and that the centrality of Israel would grow as the country itself flourished.

However, a growing minority has appeared on the scene, people who support a secure Israel and encourage its relationship with the Diaspora, but who also question Israeli policies regarding the Israeli-Palestinian conflict. Polls consistently demonstrate that the majority of Americans Jews support a two-state solution to the conflict. Further, for some time American Jews have been particularly critical of Israeli settlement policy, which encourages Israelis to settle in the occupied territories regardless that, in most formulations of a two-state solution,

SEEKING PEACE: ISRAEL, PALESTINE, AND AMERICAN JEWRY

this land is promised to the Palestinians. Interestingly, many liberal Jewish organizations have responded to this growing unease by simply avoiding the issue of Israel altogether, so as not to force difficult decisions and potential division on their membership.

This ambivalence in the broader Jewish community also informs the progressive Jewish movement. Some progressive groups have placed Israel-related matters at the center of their concerns; others support progressive causes within Israel, but refuse to deal with foreign policy. It may seem safe to assume that the majority of "progressives" (left of liberal) are peace advocates, but only a very few have made solving the Israeli-Palestinian conflict a top political priority. Often, there are pressures to push discussions of the conflict to the margins, regardless of what individual opinions may be within any given organization. There are many progressive and liberal Jews who feel torn and would prefer not to deal with the complexities of maintaining a relationship with Zionism—yet for most, Israel remains the elephant in the room.

Why Israel?

Israel was created as a Jewish state for the purposes of self-determination for the Jewish people as a nation, as a base of unity out of which to stand up for ourselves, and as a safe refuge from anti-Semitism.

But today, why do we still need a Jewish state? The right-wing religious justifications for a "Greater Israel" based on religious covenant and the bringing of the Messiah are not politically or morally viable. So how do we counter the left-wing claim that the very idea of a Jewish state and pro-Jewish policy is counter to social justice and equality for all?

We answer that every nation has borders, and almost every nation struggles with issues of racism and ethnic oppression. There may be a day that nation-states will no longer prevail, but in today's world, if other states are given the right to exist, Israel should not be held to a completely different standard. It is neither pragmatic nor desirable to demand that Israel cease to exist as a Jewish state.

Both peoples—Israelis and Palestinians—deserve national homelands. It is wrong for those on the Left to think these two peoples can jump over the stage of national self-determination and statehood. Some day, the world may change in such a way that national and/or ethnic minorities are less vulnerable to oppression, and then, maybe a Jewish or a Palestinian state won't be necessary. But a two-state solution is the workable and needed solution in today's world.

Social Justice and the Jewish State

The reluctance to discuss Israel is indicative of a substantial historic shift for the American Diaspora. In the past, particularly in the aftermath of World War II, Zionism was a thriving social/political movement. The progressive wing of Zionism (sometimes taking the form of Socialist Zionism) inspired many Jews and non-Jews alike. The struggle for broader social justice and for the establishment of a Jewish state often went hand in hand.

Some early Zionist writing did address tensions between Jews and Arabs in Eretz Yisrael, seeking to resolve these tensions in large part to protect the moral fiber of the nascent Jewish state, but also to recognize the needs of the people who had been living on the land well before and during the establishment of the Yishuv, the Jewish settlement of Israel in the early part of the twentieth century.

Clearly, however, the association between social justice issues and the establishment of a Jewish state has in the meantime become problematic. Israel now does exist, but not in the visionary form that many Jews believed it would take.

Indeed, for the majority of American Jews—who make up the largest share of white liberal opinion on almost every other issue— Israel is something of an exception to the liberal rule. The dominant position of the American community vis-à-vis Israel has for some time now tended to mirror the American neocon agenda: isolation and non-negotiation, "fighting the war on terrorism," as it were, by military means rather than by relying on creative diplomacy. Prevailing conventional wisdom suggests that there is only one way to stand by Israel: provide unquestioning support for Israeli government policy, almost regardless of what the Israeli people themselves may say.

Many non-Jewish progressives do not understand why we appear so uncritical of Israel, or why the established Jewish lobby now works so closely with the American neoconservative movement. Our non-Jewish friends do not understand why we fail to show more compassion for the Palestinians, and often seem frightened that if they question Israeli policy, they will be labeled anti-Semitic. Unfortunately, the tendency on the Left is then to focus entirely on the oppressive nature of the occupation and cast Israel as an American lackey, carrying out militaristic U.S. foreign policy. In some regards, there is indeed a double standard applied to Israel, an expectation of better behavior from Jerusalem than may be expected elsewhere.

A Third Way

The notion of two states for two peoples—with its implicit acceptance of a Jewish state and both national narratives—is rarely espoused on the Left; the American antiwar movement is rife with anti-Israel sloganeering that fails to differentiate between bad government policy and the Israeli population. As a result, many Jews have been driven yet further away from progressive thought.

Even those Jewish progressives who do not deal with Israel or the conflict directly find that this tension intrudes in other ways. For instance, the excellent work done by Jewish organizations on the Darfur crisis has been undermined by allegations that the issue became a Jewish cause because Jews found a place where an Arab entity is so clearly in the wrong; in some cases, groups that engage with Israel through social justice issues come under pressure from Jewish donors to stay away from any work that might touch on the Israeli-Palestinian conflict.

Ultimately, however, if we are to be true to ourselves, our convictions, and our history, we can go neither right nor left. A growing number of American Jews have, in fact, begun to forge such a third way, one that acknowledges that social justice requires both the well-being of the Jewish state, and the establishment of a just peace between Israel and the Palestinians.

Brit Tzedek v'Shalom, the Jewish Alliance for Justice and Peace, is one organization based on these principals. Since its inception in 2002, Brit Tzedek has emerged as the largest American Jewish grassroots organization that is both pro-Israel and pro-peace. Along with other

Jewish peace organizations, Brit Tzedek has taken on the task of building a counterpoint to the traditional Israel lobby in Washington.

If this counterpoint is to become a true counterweight, however, we will need to be both assertive and creative. We will need to articulate clearly the position that Israel's future security depends on reclaiming a strong social justice agenda, and that further, Israel will need to establish itself as a strong ally for a Palestinian homeland with which it lives in peace. We can no longer fight for the self-determination of one people without committing ourselves to the self-determination of *both* peoples.

We will need to organize liberal and progressive Jews around these principles, and reconnect the notion of *justice for Jews* with *justice for all*. This will entail challenging progressive movements the world over to integrate the eliminating of anti-Semitism into their agendas, as part and parcel of the effort to eliminate racism.

American Jews who support a negotiated, two-state solution to the conflict are well positioned to play a pivotal role in mobilizing support for an active U.S. engagement in facilitating such a resolution. The presence of a strong Jewish voice that is at once pro-Israel and anti-occupation mitigates fears in the general population that expressing criticism of Israeli government policies is tantamount to anti-Semitism, thereby broadening the possibility for building coalitions between Jews and those who share our concerns.

We will further need to pressure the U.S. government and Congress to take on a major role in resolving the Israeli-Palestinian conflict and the larger regional conflict, with all of its implications. Many of our elected officials are under the mistaken impression that the traditional Israel lobby represents a monolithic Jewish "vote"—if we are to serve as an effective alternative to that lobby, we will have to boldly challenge this assumption and bring our message directly into the halls of power in Washington.

Nevertheless, despite the need for American activism to shift Israel policy, our ultimate goal is not that Americans dictate Israel policy. In Israel's long history of relationship with international superpowers, first with Great Britain, then with the Soviet Union in the Eastern Bloc, and now with the West, Israel's dependence on outside support has been both a blessing and a curse.[3] In the 1950s and '60s, Israel developed a tighter alliance with the West and ultimately became dependent on the United States for military protection. Today, Israel is seen as representing the United States's interests in the region, and Israel often accepts that role. On a short-term basis, this alliance has given Israel military protection and power, but on a long-term basis it has created antipathy for Israel in the region. It has also created latent hostility from at least some Israelis who would like to have control over their own policies and direction. By representing Western interests, Israel becomes a *target* in the Middle East, a historical role that is part of the experience of Jews.

Thus, it is critical that American Jews work not only for long-term peace in the Middle East but also for real self-determination for the peoples there. We must work both to change American policy and to change the power relationship between the United States and Israel once Israel—and Palestine—have gained their own footing.

Changing American Jewish Discourse

All of this means that the Jewish progressive movement must play a leading role in redefining the conversation about Israel within the American Jewish community and the country at large. In giving voice to opinions many hold but fear expressing, we will act to normalize these opinions and broaden the parameters of acceptable discourse.

Jews need to be able to fight for what is right in Israel regardless of whether it is aligned with American policy. Possibly from the beginning of Israel's existence, support for Israel and other Jewish political issues have been bolstered not only by the organized Jewish power but also by the political winds of the day. American Jews gained ascendance in the Soviet Jewry movement of the 1980s not only because they were right, but also because their activism was politically consistent with American anti-Soviet foreign policy. Unlike the Jews who stayed silent as the United States failed to intervene in World War II or accept Jewish refugees from Nazi Germany, unlike the Jews who failed to stand up for themselves (as Jews) during the McCarthy era, Jewish activists today must form an independent political force for justice. As we advocate for just solutions in Israel, we must have the courage and perseverance to organize for change regardless of the popularity of the cause or its consistency with existing American policy.

As things stand today, the conversation among American Jews regarding Israel generally centers on encouraging people to travel there, or defending Israel against threats both military and rhetorical. Those who would take a different tack often fail to do the work necessary to change the tone across the board, and few have access to in-depth information about Israel, its domestic issues (poverty, new immigrants, tensions between Mizrahi and Ashkenazi Jews, the minority Arab population), and political debates. In the aftermath of the 2006 war with Hezbollah, for instance, debate broke out immediately among Israelis of different political stripes regarding the efficacy of the war, the true significance of its outcome, and the implications for Israel's future. Yet little of this was evident in American Jewish discourse, where a reflexive support for official Israeli positions continues to mark the community's reactions to the hostilities.

If nothing else, the 2006 war in Lebanon brought home the fact that military might cannot be the solution to all of Israel's problems. After the bombs cleared in Beirut, Israel was still at risk from Hezbollah, and the country itself was divided on whether the war was necessary or effective. Simply put, discussion about the efficacy of the Lebanon war or Israel's reliance on military force in general would require a paradigm shift of frightening proportions. For years, pride in Israel's ability to defend itself served to ease the pain of our losses over centuries of Diaspora, and soothe fears raised by ongoing anti-Semitism. How do we understand an Israel for which straightforward military victory is no longer a foregone conclusion? So much of the Israeli national narrative is rooted in the notion of the powerful Jewish warrior—while some in Israel have clearly become comfortable with questioning that part of the narrative, perhaps the Diaspora continues to hold on to that narrative too tightly.

Yet on the other hand, while clear-cut victories may be a thing of the past, future military engagements are likely to have a global impact unlike any since the end of the Cold War. To the extent that Iran and Syria are involved with funding and arming Hezbollah, for instance, even the most limited of conflagrations, such as Hezbollah's kidnapping of two Israeli soldiers in the summer of 2006, has the potential to engulf the entire region in conflict. Conversely, to the extent that Iran continues to work toward achieving nuclear capability, the United States will likely view any military actions by those close to Iran as a threat to its own larger interests; some experts speculated during the Second Lebanon War that the Bush Administration was only too happy to have Israel pounding away at Shiite targets, as a roundabout way to strike Iran.

For all these reasons, the progressive Jewish movement must push for substantive discussions about Israel's diplomatic future. We must ask questions that our wider community still finds painful, in order to broaden the scope of legitimate opinion. In this, we need to examine our relationship to Israel's struggle for security in an increasingly volatile world, question the extent to which Israel's foreign policy is determined by the American neocon agenda, and shift the conversation to an examination of Israel's true long-term interests. If Israel's conflict—with the Palestinians or the broader Arab world—can no longer be managed through periodic military engagement, how can Israel's long-term interests be met? How can Israel's legitimate desire to live in peace and security be achieved, if it cannot truly defeat its enemies through military means?

To this end, the progressive Jewish movement must clearly articulate the potential for Israel to find diplomatic solutions to decades of violence. Bottom line, what's called for is education: publications, media reports, conferences, and simple conversation. We need to reach everyone from the White House down to our next-door neighbor with the fact that a majority of Palestinians are now looking for a two-state solution; that a majority of Israelis believe that talks should be held with any and all Arab parties willing to hold such talks; and that resolving the Israeli-Palestinian conflict stands at the very center of the rest of the region's tensions—and thus at the heart of American and Israeli interests.[4] We must be unequivocal: a stable Palestinian state and cooperative relationships between Israel and her neighbors are not only possible—they are crucial to both Israel's well-being and that of Jews worldwide.

Imitatio Dei and/as
Shared Space
A Jewish Theological Argument
for Sharing the Holy Land

SHAUL MAGID, PhD

Shaul Magid, PhD, is the Jay and Jeannie Schottenstein Professor of Modern Judaism at Indiana University, Bloomington. He is the author of *Hasidism on the Margin* and the forthcoming *From Metaphysics to Midrash: History, Myth, and the Interpretation of Scripture in Lurianic Kabbala*, as well as many articles. Magid is a founding member of Jews Against the War.

This essay is founded on the claim that the worsening situation in Israel/Palestine is an opportunity for both progressive Zionists and for those who may not call themselves Zionists but who care deeply about Israel, Palestine, and social justice to revisit some of the theological underpinnings of the Zionist project. Current discussion focuses narrowly on territory—the way Jews and Judaism construct the land in relation to, and as a foundation for, national revival and survival. These political and strategic arguments against dividing or sharing Eretz Yisrael and the theological agenda of the religious Right, both in Israel and in the Diaspora, have effaced the more nuanced theological positions that informed early progressive Zionism.

What follows is an exercise inspired by a Zionist spirit that no longer flourishes in the Diaspora in any discernable way. In some fundamental sense, the right-wing "settler movement" and its supporters have co-opted contemporary Zionist discourse in the Diaspora. The settler movement is fundamentally messianic, believing that growing the State of Israel will proactively bring the Messiah, but it sells its agenda to a secular audience by couching its messianism in the language of "security"—the "settlers" are the new pioneers who are on the front lines protecting Israel. The movement thus conflates—or disguises—Zvi Yehuda Kook's religious messianism with Vladimir Jabotinky's militant revisionism, a secular Zionism founded on the principles of unapologetic land conquest and militarism. Creative progressive Zionism, once the heart of the movement, has disappeared.

What has disappeared from contemporary Zionism in the Diaspora is the utopian but secular Zionism that was from the start devoted to creating a "new society" that would share territory with its Arab neighbors. That's too bad, because the secular Zionist ideologues and activists of the early twentieth century, many of whom were influenced by Ahad ha-Am, made two claims worth reexamining: one, they rejected what Judaism understood as a traditional "religion" as the exclusive backbone of Jewish identity; and two, they rejected Herzl's vision of normalization. These idealists did not want to be religious in any normative sense, and indeed they didn't want to be "normal" at all (which they interpreted as bourgeois) but revolutionary, utopian, and experimental.[1]

In the early- to mid-twentieth century this progressive Zionism was very compelling and had a real voice at the table. That is not the case anymore. In this brief essay I return to the most well known of the representatives of progressive Zionism, the Jewish theologian Martin Buber. Buber called for a binational state of Jews and Arabs before 1948 and, in the wake of statehood, advocated for a Near East federation of states that could constitute a region with common interests and goals.[2] He also fought strenuously for the repatriation of Arab refugees after 1948,[3] an idea that is now considered almost anti-Semitic! I will use selections of Buber's writings coupled with a section of a homily on Passover by the nineteenth-century Hasidic master Rabbi Jacob Leiner of Izbica (nineteenth-century Poland)[4] to make a theological case for sharing Eretz Yisrael as an act of *imitatio Dei*.

Hebrew Humanism

Any effort that even suggests binationalism immediately will evoke the ire of traditionalists, apologists, and imperialists on all fronts. And for good reason, because the exegetical attempt to argue for joint tenancy is daunting. Both the Jewish and Palestinian traditions contain strong sentiments of a zero-sum game when it comes to territory. While each tradition also contains elements of old-fashioned humanism, those moments are often drowned out by a divinely ordained winner-take-all perspective. Perhaps this is partly because in the ancient and early medieval world where their scriptures and canons were born, politics was, in fact, a zero-sum game—you were either the conqueror or the conquered, ruler or vassal, or so our sacred texts would have us believe. In the Jewish tradition, which views sovereignty largely in the frame of redemption, this zero-sum game is even more pronounced. The political world we live in, however, is quite a bit different, requiring us to think about the ways in which these texts need to be reread and, if necessary, revised in order to serve as live models for contemporary civilization.[5]

In his essay "Hebrew Humanism," Buber addresses this very challenge.[6] "We must at this point ask a question which is essential even though it is specifically modern. We must ask whether a human pattern which was evolved under an entirely different set of historical conditions can be valid for our own times; whether it can help us realize humanity in an era which is utterly different in character. The answer is in the affirmative, provided we can separate the timeless elements in this pattern, the elements that are valid for all time, from those which are conditioned by its epoch" (243, 244). For Buber, the process of distinguishing between the timeless and the conditioned in classical Jewish literature is the foundation of Hebrew humanism. His "biblical Judaism" is thus unabashedly a constructed category, "a return to the linguistic tradition of our own classical antiquity"(244), but also a subjugation of that linguistic tradition to the humanistic ethos of contemporary civilization.

This sentiment has even become part of more traditional Jewish discourse. In the recent essay "Monotheism and Humanism," the philosopher Hilary Putnam (reading Jonathan Sacks's *The Dignity of*

Difference) writes, "[Jonathan] Sacks is quite right that the monotheistic religions have to revise (or at least add to) their theologies explicitly, that there has to be, to use a very American metaphor, an 'amendment to the constitution' of each of the major religions, particularly, for our purposes, to those of the three 'Abrahamic' faiths."[7] Putnam and Sacks's concern is the way in which each views the religious other as "other" after 9/11. I borrow this observation and apply it to the more focused question of peoplehood, nationalism, territory, and the relationship between them. Thus for me, part of the "amendment" must address the way each views the land, *this* land, as its exclusive real estate. For Jews, this amendment would mandate that the covenantal promise of the land requires sharing it with another. This theological model of Jewish responsibility would not only tolerate permanent and sovereign Arab presence in Eretz Yisrael but also make it a theological desideratum. The seeds of such an argument lie in Buber's writings on Zionism.

Reframing Zionism

In his essay "Zion and the Other National Concepts,"[8] Buber notes that the choice of the term *Zionism* to define the modern movement of returning Jews to Eretz Yisrael is quite significant. Biblically, the term does not refer to a people or even to a place. Rather, for Buber, the term *Zion* refers to a specific place that is God's alone (*The Lord is great and much acclaimed in the city of our God, His holy mountain, fair-crested, joy of all the earth* [Ps. 48:3]). The ostensible secular political movement of Zionism is thus a movement imbued with "religious" significance from its inception. The territory of Zion is already a theologically sacrosanct place. Once a nation inhabits and achieves sovereignty in a territory that plays such a strong role in its ethnohistory, the nation's secular political goals can never be totally severed from its mythic genealogy.[9]

Once this genealogy is established, the difficult task is to make sense of the nature of the land's religious significance and determine how one may work to embody it individually and collectively. Buber suggests that the essential consequence of the name *Zionism* implies that the Jews are more caretakers than owners of Eretz Yisrael. "This land was in no time in the history of Israel simply the property of the people; it was always at the same time a challenge to make of it what God intended to have made of it."[10] Buber argues here that territoriality more generally is based on inhabiting, and not owning, a land. "It seems to me that God does not give any one portion of the earth away, so that the owner may say as God says *For all the earth is mine* (Exod. 19:5). The conquered land is, in my opinion, only lent even to the conqueror who has settled on it—and God wants to see what he will make of it."[11]

Buber's observation on private property rights is a subversive (and perhaps intentional) rejection of Rashi's first comment on Genesis, where he justifies beginning the Torah with the Book of Genesis, that is, Creation, because Creation affirms that God created the world and can thus give any portion to anyone God sees fit. Rashi's was a transparent attempt to justify Israel's claim to a territory that Rashi knew in the eleventh century had been populated by other peoples before and after the Israelites. Implied in Rashi's comment is the very problem of the claim—i.e., that Israel could successfully convince the people inhabiting Canaan that the land they were living on was promised to Israel by God.

Buber responds to Rashi by returning to the emphasis in Genesis on stewardship. According to Buber, Israel's mission is not to own the land but to be a caretaker of it, a position that has certain conditions. Israel's obligation becomes a charge to make the land a place that mirrors its divine owner, thereby making the dwellers on that land a people who reflect the land's only true sovereign. In short, for Buber, dwelling in the land should be—must be—an act of *imitatio Dei*. And, as the Hebrew prophets taught, failing to embody that religious precept forfeits the right to dwell in that sacred place.

Imitatio Dei

Buber argues the fact that Eretz Yisrael is inhabited by another people is not an obstacle but a challenge to embody that divine call in the modern world. But the modern return of the Jews to "Zion" (His mountain), a return not founded on conquest but a "gift" from the world to the Jews (it was the U.N., after all, that created the State of Israel as a Jewish state), requires us to rethink the divine mission of dwelling in God's land previously accomplished via conquest and divine fiat. Annihilating or creating vassals of the indigenous population as in biblical times is thankfully no longer a viable option. Rejecting the medieval notion of the "descent of the generations," Buber argues that changed conditions "sometimes allow[s] [us] to make amends for lost opportunities in a quite different situation, in a quite different form, and it is significant that this new situation is more contradictory and the new form more difficult to realize than the old, and that each fresh attempt demands an even greater exertion to fulfill the task—for such is the hard but not ungracious way of life itself."[12]

For Buber, insularity (individual or collective) is a profane act. The sacred act is always one of relationality—coming out of one's hiddenness to greet the other in spite of precarious circumstances (one needn't "obligate" relationality in friendly circumstances).[13] This "coming out" of Israel is not only coming out of its collective cocoon—a natural state for a people who have lived under siege for most of their history—but also knowing when to break through the confines of an old paradigm and create a new spirit to meet a new situation. Modernity (and Zionism) has created the context for Jews to extend their relationality to the larger world and, in the case of Israel, to the population that lives in its midst. For Buber, *imitatio Dei* is an act that emulates the personality of God. Buber writes, "One may understand the personality of God as his act."[14] To act in a way God acts is to mirror God's personality, to embody the precepts of *imitatio Dei*, imitating God (*Sifra, Kedoshim* on Lev. 19:2).

But more needs to be said of this "divine nature" we are commanded to emulate. For this I turn to the mid-nineteenth-century Hasidic master Rabbi Jacob Leiner of Izbica. His comment appears in his gloss to the Passover Haggadah, a Rabbinic text read at the annual Passover seder. The Haggadah contains numerous Rabbinic liturgical inventions coupled with literary (midrashic) readings of biblical verses focused on the story of the Israelite Exodus from Egypt. One of the early liturgical flourishes in the Haggadah reads as follows:

> "Blessed be the Place (*makom*), Blessed is He. Blessed be the one who gave Torah to Israel His people." The use of the term *place* to describe God is based on a Rabbinic midrash from the third century CE (*Genesis Rabbah*, chapter 61). The midrash

reads, "Why is it that we use place as a name of God? It is because God is the place of the world but the world is not His place." Rabbi Jacob Leiner comments, "This means that God gave a place to all of His creations, even the most lowly, and their existence remains His concern, as the Talmud teaches, 'in the very same place that you find God's greatness you find His humility.' ... (Babylonian Talmud, *Megillah* 31b).

No good act or thought by a human being is lost on God—God has a place for all of them.... Yet God first had to create [the idea of] 'place' (*makom*), for if there was no place where would they exist?... This is why God is called 'place' because He gives a place for all His creatures."

(Leiner, *Haggadah shel Pesach*)

The concept of place here suggests a seeming infinitude of space. As there is never any space void of God there is never a place that excludes, by definition, God's creatures or divine presence. The statement in the Haggadah suggests that the God who gives the Torah to Israel is the God who creates infinite space for all of Creation. The Torah takes up some of that space but, as the word of God, must also have the potential to create space for those in need. Here the creation of space or accommodation for the stranger in one's midst is more than a divine command, it is an act of *imitatio Dei*.

Consequences for the State

One could justifiably argue that the stance against Jews sharing Eretz Yisrael does not deny the Palestinians a place, it just denies them *this* place. But this place is also a part of their ethnohistory, which, regardless of its origins and trajectory, has as much legitimacy as the ethnohistory and territoriality of the Jews.[15] To reject that is to make an exceptionalist argument that undermines Israel's reentrance into the global community of nations. The dilemma is not "who was there first" but that "both were there" and have legitimate national histories and interests that include this real estate.

Early Zionism was quite aware of this dilemma (taking it far more seriously than much of contemporary Zionism does) and responded to it through various forms of legislation. For example, on March 10, 1953, the Israeli Knesset passed the Land Acquisition Act, making it "legal" for the new State of Israel to acquire "absentee properties," land abandoned by Arabs during the 1948 War, some of whom, we now know, did not leave voluntarily but were expelled by Israeli forces.[16] Other properties, belonging to "non-absentee Arabs," could be legally confiscated if they were needed for security *or* other "developmental projects." In short, the State of Israel took upon itself the right to determine *this* place as *its* place in instances that were not solely about the security of its citizens.

Buber pressed hard against this move. In a letter[17] dated March 1953, Buber pleaded with the new government to allow Arabs to return to their lands in the absence of a real security threat. His plea went unanswered. Buber's argument was based on "moral conscience," but there is no real distinction between morality and true religiosity in his theological worldview of Judaism. A "religious" offering that is unethical or, in modern parlance, unjust, is what the prophets call blasphemy or, in extreme cases, even idolatry!

The question as to whether Israel should be simply a nation-state among others (this was largely Theodore Herzl's position) or something different weaves through the entire history of Zionism. In comments[18] made to the new prime minister, David Ben-Gurion, in 1949, Buber said, "I heard one more important thing from the Prime Minister this evening. He said, 'Not a *nation* like all the others.' Might not one add, 'Not a state like the rest either'?" States act according to the *raison d'etat*, Buber continues, because "they chose the path in which the good of the state seems to lie at that moment, no less and no more." That is, Buber's response to Ben-Gurion is that the Zionist experiment is precisely an experiment in combining Hebrew humanism with statecraft—can Israel live up to its own tradition and not succumb to the self-serving nature of the modern nation-state?

While it may be true that "every civilization finds it necessary to negotiate compromises with its own values," each civilization must constantly reassess those values, weigh the price of that compromise, and consider whether in the long term the compromise undermines the very mission the civilization wishes to achieve. On this point it is worth mentioning another early Zionist ideologue, Aaron David Gordon, who argued that, like an individual, an exemplary nation must create itself "in the image of God." Gordon argued that Israel must become an *Am-Adam* (a "people-humanity"), whose institutions and relationship to the world reflect a morality born from a history of suffering. Like Buber, Gordon believes it is the suffering of Israel at the hands of despotic regimes that is the condition for the creation of a Jewish host society that acts otherwise.[19]

Toward a Solution

Sadly, the history of Israel's conflicts with its Arab neighbors and the subliminal influence of Kook's religious Zionist vision moved Zionism in another dangerous direction. When the theological realm collapses into the political—as it has in the settler ideology of Rabbi Zvi Yehuda Kook and his disciples—the *raison d'etat* becomes a divine command. When the holiness of the land (a divine proclamation) becomes the holiness of the state (a human creation), we all too easily move in the direction of theocracy veiled as stateism (where the state, even in its secularity, becomes the embodiment of divine will). But this undermines the very notion of God, and the land, as the embodiment of God as "place." Theocracy, even if manifest in the secular concept of stateism, is predicated on exclusion and exclusivity, especially when rooted in ethnicity. Buber's fear of a nationalism that sees the state as its final goal was an integral part of his Zionism. He argued that the realization of Zionist aspirations needn't result in a Jewish state: "The demands for an Arab state or a Jewish state in the entire Land of Israel falls into the category of political 'surplus' of the desire to achieve more than what is truly needed."[20] Buber argued that the Jews could, and must, reenter history in cooperation with the Arab population.[21]

Yet as early as 1958, and even before, he noted the failure of his idealistic project because Jewish-Arab solidarity was not created *before* the state, when it could have been done on a more level playing field. States create hierarchies of power that often are a threat to those under its domination. Naturally, Buber laments, after the founding of the state, mass immigration and Zionism were perceived by the indigenous Arab population as a "hireling of imperialism," a perception he thought was mistaken yet understandable. His stinging conclusion is haunting. "Our *historical* reentry into our land took place through a false gateway."[22]

I have suggested that a dimension of Zionism long forgotten may hold the resources of a theological alternative that begins with the notion that no one, not even the Jewish or the Palestinian people, has ever or can ever own this land. The land is the land of God, who provides infinite space for God's Creation. While the political notion of a one-state solution or binationalism may no longer be viable for Jews at this time, it may reemerge in the future as a land of two peoples.

The guiding principle of Buber's vision is that the land is for two peoples. Whether they choose to divide it between them, or to share it as one, theologically the point is for the peoples to accept the existence of the other.

Perhaps the reemergence of such a "binationalist" perspective would demand that each side's territorial claim must be founded on the "religious" obligation (born from a strong reading in each religious tradition) that this land—Eretz Yisrael as the Promised Land for the Jews and for Palestine, part of the Islamic Umah for Muslims—*must* be shared with the non-Jew and non-Muslim. Rather than compromise or accommodation, dividing the land under this view would be seen as an example where the generosity of the human spirit takes hold of a tradition and, combined with deep respect for the tradition and the idealistic audacity against it, moves tradition forward.

If Israel views itself as the caretakers of the land—their divine mission, in Buber's view—whose owners always make space for those who need it, the religious precept of *Imitatio Dei* would require us as Jews to share that space, even the holy city of Jerusalem, to make it a "divine place"—a place "God intended to have made of it."

For Yehuda and Miriam, caretakers

Everything Falls Apart

JOEL SCHALIT

Joel Schalit is an Israeli-American writer and editor. The former co-director of the world's longest-running online periodical, *Bad Subjects*, he also served as the managing editor of *Tikkun*. The author of *Israel vs. Utopia* and the memoir *Jerusalem Calling*, he is also the editor of *The Anti-Capitalism Reader*.

Among academics, politicians, and pundits, it's well known that the very same ideas that have been condemned as being examples of self-hating extremist leftist propaganda in the Diaspora have been freely discussed, and often adopted, by the mainstream in Israel. For example, it was the Diaspora Left who, after the Six-Day War, revived the original U.N. plan to divide Israel and Palestine into two states: that "two-state" solution, however revised, has now been adopted by the Israeli establishment. Likewise, the withdrawal from Gaza was at first suggested by certain members of the Israeli Left, but later became the position of more than 60 percent of all Israelis.

Today, when a new Jewish Left is forming in the Diaspora in opposition to many of Israel's policies, the question of how to understand criticism of Israel by the Diaspora is getting a new look. The 1990s and early 2000s witnessed the formation of numerous like-minded Jewish progressive advocacy organizations focused on Israeli politics, ranging from Rabbi Michael Lerner's Tikkun Community to Brit Tzedek v'Shalom, Ameinu, the Israel Policy Forum, and Jewish Voice for Peace.[1] Such organizations slowly have become a permanent part of the American Jewish mainstream, despite their perennially small membership rosters.[2] Their persistence may be less surprising in light of a paper by researchers Steven M. Cohen and Ari Kelman, who found that only 28 percent of the American Jews surveyed defined themselves as "Zionist."[3] It's not a far step from this observation to the Right's contention that left-wingers are, in fact, anti-Zionist and leading the well-meaning Jewish Diasporic citizenry astray.

Yet, that conclusion does not follow from the data. Almost all of the Jews in Cohen and Kelman's survey, whether Zionists or not, do consider themselves "pro-Israel." What this data points to is the decline of traditional forms of Israeli politics in the Diaspora, not a rise in hostility toward Israel. Jews no longer feel the need to identify as "Zionist" in order to be "pro-Israel," because Israel is a permanent part of their cultural identity—even if they disagree with the Israeli government's policies. In essence, Israel has become "normalized" within the Diaspora's identity (as it is for Israelis), even though the country may no longer be considered central to what it means to be religiously Jewish. From this context stems the freedom to adopt the progressive positions espoused by the peace- and justice-oriented Israel advocacy groups.

Along with this normalization of pro-Israel identity for Diaspora Jews has come an increasing unwillingness to refrain from criticizing the Jewish state. Where Diaspora critics of Israeli policies were once silenced by accusations that they were self-hating Jews, they now fight back by referencing the lively debate on the same policies in Israel itself. For example, Rob Eshman, the editor-in-chief of California's largest circulation Jewish periodical, the *Jewish Journal of Los Angeles*, has complained: "From the biblical prophets down through modern times, we are a people who have canonized those who scold and chastise the established order, who envision a different world.... The tradition of sharp criticism turned on one's own people still lives—in Hebrew. The Israeli press has always been far more contentious toward Israel than American Jewry. Nothing [Tony] Judt or [Tony] Kushner has proposed hasn't already been written in Israel."[4]

Another prominent American Jew, J.J. Goldberg, the editor of the *Forward*, has made the same point: "There are vast numbers [of Jews] who call themselves progressive or liberal," he told an interviewer, "who are pro-Israel, pro-Jewish, who are [*laughs*] generals in the

Israeli Army." The logic here is clear: if Army generals can criticize the politics of civilian leaders, why can't civilians abroad do the same?[5]

The Big Picture

What's at stake in such comparisons between Diaspora and Israeli speech is more than the content of the specific arguments in play. What's at stake is the relationship between the Diaspora and Israel itself. The invocation of Israeli self-criticism by the Diaspora Jewish Left is symptomatic of the collapse of traditional distinctions drawn between Israel and the Diaspora. It's a desire to elide the difference between what it means to be a citizen of Israel and the ways in which Diasporic Jews experience the "birthright" of potential membership in the Jewish state.

The more that non-Israeli Jews are encouraged to feel attached to and to be involved in Israel's life, the more they are going to feel as though they can participate in its politics in the same ways that they participate in the political spheres of their own home countries, whether that be Germany, the United Kingdom, Australia, or the United States. They will feel encouraged to do so not only by immigrating to Israel, but also by doing so from within the confines of their own home states abroad. Logically speaking, what such a sense of citizenship entails for members of the "foreign Jewish Left" is exactly what has encouraged such strong identification with the Israeli state among the Diaspora Jewish Right. In the place of veneration for Jerusalem, the holy places, and the Jewish character of the Israeli state, we find an equally reverential attachment to Israeli media and culture, and the high level of public debate that takes place in Israeli society over such burning issues as religion, gender, citizenship, and economics.

Ironically, even though Israel may have become a pariah state politically to the Diaspora Left, its tradition of self-criticism—by its liberal civil servants, by its left-wing activists, and by specific, internationally distributed representatives of its media—are shining beacons of political virtue in the eyes of non-Israeli Jewish liberals. In a sense, they embody the political and moral conscience that the Israeli government and its foreign policy appears to have lost in the years following the Six-Day War. Of course, one might legitimately argue that valuing these aspects of Israeli life on such profound grounds constitutes the same kind of fetishization of Israel as that practiced by the Diaspora Jewish Right—only in reverse. But, given the gravity of the situation Israel finds itself in today, there is indeed something positive about the value that progressive Jews in the United States and Europe bestow upon these aspects of Israeli culture. Most important, they reflect an ironic investment in the state, which, however problematic, is still treated as something worth redeeming for whatever reason might be offered—cultural, political, or religious.

Secondly, the comparison of Diasporic to Israeli discourse demonstrates a desire to reform Israel as a state, to correct its deficits, in accordance with the standards of what it means to live in a European-style, multicultural social democracy. Thus, through their criticisms of Israeli foreign policy, Diaspora Jews assume that such a country can indeed be created in an Israeli context, even if they are not prepared to specify whether they prefer a one- or a two-state solution to the Palestinian-Israeli conflict, or a market-based or government-dominated public sector as a means of redressing the country's increasingly high levels of social inequality.

It could be said that right-wing Jews fear the growth of the organized Jewish Left precisely because they recognize that its ideological sensibilities are more in tune with those of the larger Left zeitgeist. Progressive-leaning Diaspora Jews want for Israel the same kinds of political and cultural positions they want at home: an end to war, religious traditionalism, racism, and social inequality. Such views can prove threatening to a religious and conservative status quo that prefers a state in which Arab and non-Jewish Israeli citizens are given a second-class status.

That's why *Occupied Minds* author Arthur Neslen explained in a January 2007 interview in *Tikkun* that putting an end to Israel's occupation of its remaining Palestinian territorial assets is a much bigger deal than simply withdrawing from captured enemy land. To advocate withdrawal is to call into question the character of the modern Israeli state and everything that comes along with it.[6] In the same way, one may legitimately infer that tolerating even the semblance of an open political discussion about Israel in the Diaspora is a sign that the Diaspora has finally become competitive, so to speak, with Israel.

Regardless of whether they are Zionist or not, non-Israeli Jews are conditioned to believe that their lives in the Diaspora remain incomplete because they continue to live outside of their native element. The benefit in learning about politics, specifically about democracy, is that these lessons are always universally binding. If all Jews remain citizens of the same greater nation, imagine what kind of impact injecting more of *this kind* of Israel into the Diaspora would have on Israel. Or, to put it another way, a healthy Diaspora means a more democratic Israel.

The Challenge of
Making Peace

STEPHEN P. COHEN, PhD

Stephen P. Cohen, PhD, is a leader in the practice and theory of unofficial diplomacy known as Track Two Diplomacy. Cohen founded the Institute for Middle East Peace and Development in 1979 and has served as its president ever since. He is the national scholar of the Israel Policy Forum and in the last few years has served as a visiting professor at Princeton University and Lehigh University.

The American Jew in the twenty-first century faces a complex set of imperative responsibilities for the pursuit of peace in the Middle East and the world at large. As an American, he or she lives as a citizen of an America that faces danger in the world system and itself poses a danger to the world's peace. When America brandishes its sword of military dominance too easily without first assuring wide understanding among the community of nations, it puts on display the weakness of others. This show of dominance plays a sharp role in other people's perceptions that they must act as soon as possible to balance the threat and shift the ratio of fear.

One response is terrorism, which requires highly motivated young people to be willing to die while killing others. The other response is more conventional; it involves the perpetual effort to buy or steal more effective weapons, more sophisticated weapons, and weapons of greater firepower. The willingness, even enthusiasm, for doing violence grows exponentially as people are humiliated by their weakness and inability to protect their families. The perception of being overpowered, dominated, and overwhelmed generates hatred, acts of violence, and self-styled revenge.

To reverse course, American national identity, national purpose, and America's role in the world needs a thorough reassessment and refurbishment. The Jews of America must play an effective role as part of the American cultural, intellectual, and financial elite in helping to have an impact on that reshaping of national identity and national public expression. We must return to respecting others if we are to have any hope of having that respect be returned.

No less challenging is the role of the Jews of America in the struggle for peace between Israel and the Palestinians and between Israel and the rest of the Arab states and peoples. Though American Jews must understand that they are not citizens of the State of Israel and do not carry the rights and responsibilities of that citizenship, they do carry a unique level of responsibility nonetheless. First, as American citizens we play a significant role in helping to determine America's role in the conflict and the extent of its efforts in brokering any peace agreements. Most deeply, American Jews do carry the burden and opportunity to help shape the definition of what it means to be a Jewish state in the twenty-first century. One primary question is how it can be defined or whether Israel can be shaped into a pluralistic state which is fully democratic but that also maintains its special place in the life of the Jewish people. Can we reach a point where a Palestinian citizen could actually say, "I choose to live in this state of Israel as it gives me unique opportunities and quality of social, economic and cultural life for all its citizens"? To succeed as a democracy, Israel must be as comfortable a place for Arab citizens who wish to participate in Israeli-Jewish society, as Christian societies like France, the United Kingdom, and even Italy have been for Jews.

This reshaping of Israeli legal and institutional life must be aided and then monitored and assessed by the institutions of American Jews who are active participants in the American democratic system and therefore should be able to be helpful participants in the Israeli reform process. To do so, they must come to understand Israel and its multi-layered problem of Arab citizen opportunity, identity, and level of comfort while not pretending that there is no security problem.

The ultimate dimension of American Jewish responsibility for world peace is the most subtle and penetrating. The great threat of conflict and violence among Jews, Muslims, and Christians points to an important challenge to the ethical role of monotheism in contemporary civilization. Can monotheists assure each other that their joint claim of serving the One God will not be a cause for competitive mutual rejection and destructiveness? How can they recast their teaching and worship to place more emphasis on their common Abrahamic origins, and their sacred descent from God's creation, and recognition of each other as equals in the creation, all in service of the One God even if they have strong theological differences? How can the adherents of each religion learn to respect each other while maintaining loyalty to their own religious beliefs and practices, and each religion's uniqueness?

This interfaith danger and its antidote through interfaith respect is an arena in which Americans—through all of our civil society, institutions, and our widespread and deep diverse religious life—can play an important role for the whole world. If America could become understood as the place of unique respect across faith loyalties, this could be one important, perhaps even vital, step in America's regaining of its world role. In this American problem, which is also a world peace problem, American Jews would do themselves proud if they could be interfaith leaders bringing new energy to Israeli Judaism in fulfilling its interfaith responsibilities and in helping to shape American civil society and public policy to take on major efforts in such interfaith communication.

PART VII
THE SEVENTY NATIONS: GLOBAL CONCERNS

Am I My Brother's Keeper If My Brother Lives Halfway Around the World?

RUTH MESSINGER AND AARON DORFMAN

Ruth Messinger is the president and executive director of the American Jewish World Service (AJWS). Prior to assuming this role in 1998, Messinger was in public service in New York City for twenty years, including having served as Manhattan borough president. In 1997, she became the first woman to secure the Democratic Party's nomination for mayor. Messinger is currently a visiting professor at Hunter College. For the past four years, Messinger has been named one of the fifty most influential Jews of the year by the *Forward* newspaper.

Aaron Dorfman is the director of Jewish education at the American Jewish World Service (AJWS). Before joining AJWS, Aaron completed the Wexner Graduate Fellowship with a master's degree in public policy from the Kennedy School of Government at Harvard University, and a year of study at the Pardes Institute of Jewish Studies in Jerusalem.

In March of 1991, a tsunami struck Bangladesh and killed 138,000 people. Both citizens and governments in the West scarcely registered the disaster, and the few who did scarcely acted. The news media barely covered the story, and NGOs (non-governmental organizations) provided limited international humanitarian response. Likewise, the Jewish community's reaction was muted. The disaster was too far away to connect with. CNN was a nascent network; there was no Internet, nor were there tourists with video cameras to record the damage. The essayist Annie Dillard described a conversation with her daughter that tries to make sense of our apathy:

At dinner I mentioned to my daughter, who was then seven years old, that it was hard to imagine 138,000 people drowning. "No, it's easy," she said. "Lots and lots of dots, in blue water."[1]

Lots and lots of dots in blue water. It's a childish image, but how far is it from our own? Annie Dillard recounts the image because it helps to explain why we were unable to connect with what happened. These people are so far away and so anonymous, their problems are so different from our own, that we can't imagine ourselves in their circumstances. And because we can't imagine ourselves in their circumstances, we don't act.

Fast-forward thirteen years. A tsunami once again strikes in the Indian Ocean, killing 225,000 people. This time, the international response is overwhelming. More humanitarian aid was committed by governments and individual citizens in response to the 2004 tsunami than has ever been for any other natural disaster in human history.

The disasters were nearly identical, but the world's responses were radically different. Why?

We watched the 2004 tsunami on television. As the giant waves struck Phuket, Thailand, wealthy European and American tourists, video cameras in hand, stood on hotel room balconies, filmed the waves washing over the beaches and sweeping people away, and transmitted those images almost instantaneously to viewers around the world. You can still watch the videos on YouTube.

A skeptic might argue that we could empathize with the mostly white and relatively affluent tourist-filmers, that their similarity to us accounts for the difference in response. But we think it was something else. The first time, the area hit was a poor one and didn't support a tourist industry. No tourists = no video cameras = no images on the evening news = limited access for an international audience = little humanitarian aid.

The second time, we watched what happened nearly in real time. And in watching, we were brought into the lives of people halfway around the world; we could see their humanity, if only for a moment. But in that moment, we became obligated to them as fellow human beings. The essence of the distinction rests on this shift: these people, so dissimilar from us, so foreign, had entered our universe of obligation.

The Universe of Obligation

The universe of obligation is a way of understanding how we decide which people in the world we feel responsible for and what we owe them.

The specific term gained currency in the aftermath of the murder of Kitty Genovese in New York in 1964. On her way home from waiting tables late one night, Kitty Genovese was killed outside her apartment in Queens, despite repeatedly calling for help. The next day, when police canvassed the neighborhood to see whether anyone had witnessed the crime, thirty-eight people indicated that they had watched the attack take place and had chosen, essentially, to do nothing.

The public uproar that followed the news reports on the thirty-eight witnesses prompted Abe Rosenthal, then a reporter for the *New York Times*, to write, "How far away do you have to be to forgive yourself for not doing whatever is in your power to do?... How far is silence from a place of safety acceptable without detesting yourself as we detest the thirty-eight?"[2] How far, in other words, do you have to be from someone who is in need for that person to be outside your responsibility? Or, conversely, to what extent does seeing, witnessing, or having clear knowledge of suffering or injustice bring those affected inside our universe of obligation?

Expanding Our Universe of Obligation: Jewish Perspectives

Judaism has a broad, deep, and detailed tradition of social justice and social responsibility, ranging from *tzedakah* to *bikkur cholim* (visiting the sick) to *pikuakh nefesh* (saving a human life). What is less clear in Jewish teaching and tradition is how to prioritize among the seemingly infinite needs that surround us. That process of prioritizing is the process of constructing our universe of obligation.

There are a variety of Jewish sources that speak to this endeavor. There are voices in our tradition that, informed by Jewish historical experiences of persecution, construct the universe of obligation narrowly, in ways that prioritize the needs of Jews—serving the Jewish poor, providing aid and succor to Israel, supporting Jewish education. There are perspectives that recommend that we cast our net of responsibility more widely, but only to serve the narrower Jewish interest: giving to non-Jews as a way of building up a reservoir of goodwill in order, ultimately, to protect and defend Jewish interests. And there are some voices in the Jewish tradition that suggest we should prioritize based solely on need, regardless of the ethnic, religious, or national identification of the beneficiaries. None of these traditions is sufficient to the task at hand: balancing the sense of obligation that comes from seeing the needs of the developing world with both the limitations of our ability to address those needs and the competing demands on our fixed resources.

Fortunately, Judaism demands of us to continuously apply ancient concepts to contemporary problems. In *Pirkei Avot* 1:1, we read:

> Moses received the Torah from Sinai and transmitted it to Joshua; Joshua to the elders; the elders to the prophets; and the prophets handed it down to the men of the Great Assembly. They said three things: "Be deliberate in judgment, raise up many disciples, and make a fence around the Torah."

This seminal Mishnaic passage acknowledges the evolutionary nature of the Halachic process, that the law is passed from generation to generation and that each generation is bound to apply the law deliberately. This sentiment is echoed, albeit nontraditionally, in a review of Israeli Supreme Court Justice Menahem Elon's four-volume work on Jewish law, the second volume of which "studies the legal sources of Jewish law, namely, exegesis and interpretation, legislation, custom, precedent, and legal reasoning. These are the creative processes and modes of growth that enable the law to take account of changing circumstances and adapt to changing needs."[3]

This adaptive flexibility of the law is one of the great challenges and responsibilities of Jewish life. The Torah, the Talmudic Rabbis, and the writers of the medieval codes of Jewish law could never have anticipated the Internet or the 747, but the traditions they bequeathed us are living ones, meant to be adapted and renewed. Making this responsibility explicit, the Rabbis interpreted the line in Leviticus 18:5, "Keep my laws and my judgments, and you shall live by them, I am God," to mean, "You should live by them, and not die by them."[4] As our world changes and the moral and ethical demands on us shift, we must be willing to revisit the old "laws and judgments" and apply their underlying principles to the challenges we confront.

The values that underlie Jewish traditional rules offer us a powerful set of motivations and guidelines for how to respond to the new circumstances wrought by globalization. In Deuteronomy is a series of esoteric rules with surprising salience in the context of the universe of obligation. Chapter 21 spells out the laws governing the *met mitzvah*—a term for the body of a murder victim found in the wilderness. According to the Torah's teaching, the authorities should measure the distance from the body to the nearest town. Then the elders of whichever town is nearest must attend to the body, sacrifice a heifer near the scene of the crime, and recite a particular formula: "Our hands did not shed this blood, nor did our eyes see it done."[5]

At first blush, it's an unusual statement. Why would the community's elders be asked to declare their innocence of a crime that we would never have suspected them of committing? It's as if we expected the mayor of New York City to tend to the body of a murder victim found floating in the Hudson and publicly declare, "I didn't do it." Early Rabbinic authorities also noted this peculiarity and commented on it in the Mishnah: "But could it be that the elders of a Court were shedders of blood?"[6]

Instead, the Rabbis explain, the Torah is demanding that the town elders proclaim publicly that they did not *know* that the victim was out there, in the wilderness, lacking sustenance or protection: "He came not into our hands that we should have dismissed him without sustenance, and we did not see him and leave him without escort!"[7] *We did not know*, the town elders must swear. The implication is that, had they known, the person would have entered their universe of obligation, and they would have taken care of him. In other words, knowing that people are suffering thrusts those people into our universe of obligation.

Acting Based on Our Expanded Universe of Obligation
What do we do if we accept the notion that our universe of obligation includes people who live far away and whose plight we have come to know?

Rabbi Jonathan Sacks, the chief rabbi of Great Britain, poses this question eloquently:

David Hume noted that our sense of empathy diminishes as we move outward from the members of our family to our neighbors, our society and the world. Traditionally, our sense of involvement with the fate of others has been in inverse proportion to the distance separating us and them. What has changed is that television and the Internet have effectively abolished distance. They have brought images of suffering in far-off lands into our immediate experience. Our sense of compassion for the victims of poverty, war and famine, runs ahead of our capacity to act. Our moral sense is simultaneously activated and frustrated. We feel that something should be done, but what, how, and by whom?[8]

As Sacks correctly notes, it is easy to experience what social psychologists call "compassion fatigue," the reduction in our capacity for empathy that results from oversaturation with images of suffering. The need is indeed overwhelming, but we cannot retreat to the convenience of being overwhelmed. As we read in *Pirkei Avot*, "It is not necessary for you to complete the work, but neither are you free to desist from it."[9]

What, then, can we do?

Responsible Consumption

Any idea where the coffee you drank this morning was grown? Did your orange juice come from Latin America? Were your clothes manufactured in a developing country? All of us are global consumers, purchasing items that have arrived in our stores as a result of transnational economic interconnectedness. And most of us are also global investors: anyone who owns a share of a mutual fund is likely a part owner of some multinational corporation.

These economic interconnections create specific responsibilities for us as consumers. According to Maimonides, the great twelfth-century scholar and codifier of Jewish law:

One may not buy from a thief the goods he has stolen, and to do so is a great transgression because it strengthens the hands of those who violate the law and causes the thief to continue to steal, for if the thief would find no buyer he would not steal, as it says, "He who shares with a thief is his own enemy." (Prov. 2:24)[10]

As Maimonides articulates, when we pay for a product whose origins are unjust, we enable the injustice to continue and become tainted by the injustice. In a world in which our purchases may go through many hands before reaching ours, we are tainted not only when the seller acquires the goods in an unjust way, but also when any part of the chain of production perpetuates an injustice. For example, if a commercial coffee plantation abuses its workers, our purchase of that coffee represents a form of doing business with a thief. We ought not to be let off the hook because the thief happens to be operating behind a retailer, a domestic distributor, an importer, and an exporter. Intentionally or not, our purchase of unjustly produced goods enables the injustice to continue. And, of course, the opposite is also true: underlying this contention is that every economic transaction is an opportunity to pursue justice and, in the process, to become more just ourselves.

This means that we need to investigate the origins of the goods we buy and not buy things that were produced unethically. It means that we must ensure that the products we buy are produced using fair and safe labor practices. And it means that we must invest in companies whose practices meet our standards of ethical and responsible businesses, and when appropriate, invest in the companies we criticize in order to help change their policies through shareholder activism.

In practical terms, if the diamonds that sparkle in our jewelry are "conflict diamonds" whose international trade fuels many of Africa's wars, we have an obligation not to buy them and instead to support conflict-free diamonds. If Central American farmers work to produce the coffee that we consume, we have an obligation to ensure that they receive sufficient income to support themselves and their families and that their worksites meet basic standards of health and safety. And if we own shares of stock in a company that funds a regime that is violating human rights, we have an obligation to pressure that company to change, and if necessary, divest from that company as a way of signaling our disapproval until such a time that the regime is no longer in violation or the company has distanced itself from the regime.

By refraining from purchasing items that fuel strife, by committing to purchase fair-trade goods, and by making socially responsible investments, we can move along a continuum toward responsible consumption.[11] Furthermore, the very act of making these commitments enhances both our own awareness of the consequences of our economic decisions and models socially responsible consumption to friends and peers.

Finally, we must exercise our power as consumers and investors not only through purchasing and investment decisions, but also through direct pressure on corporations. As corporations invest incredible sums of money in their brand names, activists have grown ever more effective in changing corporate policies by raising the profile of unjust corporate policies. For example, in 2002 students from around the country transformed the paper industry when they convinced Staples to multiply its recycled product offerings tenfold.[12] In 2004, Rainforest Action Network pressured Citigroup not to invest in logging projects involving the destruction of ancient rainforests.[13] In 2006, in collaboration with worker efforts nationwide, religious groups from coast to coast used their consumer power to boycott hotels with poor labor practices, which helped lead to victories in wages and benefits for hotel workers around the country.[14]

Responsible *Tzedakah*

The commitment to *tzedakah* is prevalent throughout Jewish tradition. As Maimonides writes:

> We are obligated to be more scrupulous in fulfilling the mitzvah of *tzedakah* than any other positive mitzvah, because *tzedakah* is the sign of the righteous person, the seed of Abraham our ancestor, as it is said, "For I know him that he will command his children to do *tzedakah*." (Gen. 18:19)[15]

According to Maimonides, *tzedakah* is far more than just one of the mitzvot; it is the sine qua non of membership in the Jewish people and the very act that binds us to our forefather Abraham. In doing *tzedakah*, we reconnect ourselves to the very essence of what makes us Jewish.

But for those of us committed to giving *tzedakah*, how do we prioritize where to give? Most of us live in a world of zero-sum charitable dollars. Contributions to the developing world compete with requests from local Jewish organizations, domestic charities, and entities working with Israel. Given that we have to make choices, why should we use our precious *tzedakah* dollars to support people in the Global South?

The Talmud in *Gittin* speaks directly to this challenge:

> Our Rabbis taught: We sustain the non-Jewish poor with the Jewish poor, visit the non-Jewish sick with the Jewish sick, and bury the non-Jewish dead with the Jewish dead, for the sake of peace [literally: for the ways of peace].[16]

The Talmud directs us to treat the non-Jews who have entered our universe of obligation just as we do the Jews.[17] By committing at least some of our *tzedakah* resources to international development, humanitarian relief, and the expansion of human rights around the world, we are both embracing the fundamental Jewish social justice value of *tzedakah* and applying it in a way most consonant with its original formulation—to both Jews and non-Jews. Peace itself depends on it. And while the phrase "for the sake of peace" is often read as self-serving—that we, a distinct minority, should care for the majority in order to keep them from having reason to hate us—there are valid alternate readings of the line. The first is that providing aid and succor to people suffering from poverty, illness, and death is a way of filling the world with goodness and peace. The second, and the reading preferred by the Rambam, is that the traditional equating of Torah with peace implies that "for the sake of peace" is simply a poetic way of saying, "for the sake of Torah." In other words, we must care for the non-Jewish poor, the non-Jewish sick, and the non-Jewish dead because the Torah itself demands it.

Responsible Exercise of Political Power

Deuteronomy teaches: "When you build a new house, you shall make a parapet for your roof, so that you do not bring bloodguilt on your house if anyone should fall from it."[18] The rule is simple—a flat roof, where people might congregate, can be a dangerous place, so we must build a railing so that no one falls off.

Maimonides reads the principle more metaphorically: first, by including not just the homeowner but all who encounter a threat, and second, by expanding the idea of the rooftop to any danger we might come across. "Not just the owner," he writes, "has a positive commandment to remove it.... If one does not remove [the obstacle] but leaves it while it is still a potential danger, one transgresses a positive commandment and negates a negative commandment, 'Thou shall not spill blood.'"[19]

Where the dangers are contained and easy to address, personal action, like building a parapet, is sufficient. There are some dangers, however, that individual actions cannot remedy. Responsible consumerism and generosity of *tzedakah* and deed are two critical ways to realize our obligation to the developing world. But effecting change at the scale necessary to solve the complex and systemic problems of the Global South requires not just individual acts but the will and participation of governments.

Too often, though, the task of moving governments feels insurmountable.

Lots and lots of dots in blue water. We opened the essay with that image as a way of capturing the prevailing view of the distant, anonymous, and overwhelming need of the developing world. But in the context of the responsibility of our political power, it takes on another meaning. Sometimes, we, too, feel like lots of dots in a sea of political inertia. With so many potential voters, one ballot doesn't matter, we say. With so much noise, our elected officials won't notice whether we send another letter or make another phone call.

The Deuteronomy text doesn't permit us to indulge our sense of apathy or frustration. And, as it turns out, we shouldn't feel so powerless. After the genocide in Rwanda, the late Senator Paul Simon said, "If every member of the House of Representatives and Senate had received 100 letters from people back home saying we have to do something about Rwanda, when the crisis was first developing, then I think the response would have been different."[20]

Senator Simon's ruminations confirm what we hope, as citizens still committed to the democratic enterprise, to be true: every voice matters. But our obligation goes beyond the personal duty of active citizenship. We, American Jews, have enormous power and political voice not just as individuals, but as a community. And with that power and voice comes equally great obligation. As the Babylonian Talmud explains, anticipating by thousands of years John F. Kennedy's admonition that "of those to whom much is given, much is required":

> Whoever can prevent his household from committing a sin but does not, is responsible for the sins of his household; if he can prevent his fellow citizens, he is responsible for the sins of his fellow citizens; if the whole world, he is responsible for the sins of the whole world.[21]

The Talmud teaches us that the greater our power, the greater our responsibility to exercise that power. And the realpolitik of American democracy teaches us that if we choose to use that power, we can affect policy. When the American public has focused its attention on the genocide in Darfur— for example, at the April 2006 Save Darfur Rally to Stop Genocide that AJWS spearheaded—the Bush Administration has consistently stepped up diplomatic pressure on the government of Sudan. When public pressure has waned, so has the Administration's attention.

The universe of obligation, then, comprises three pillars: responsible consumption, responsible *tzedakah*, and the responsible exercise of political power. On these three responsibilities the world rests.

Moving Past Pity

As we continue to expand our universe of obligation to include our neighbors in the developing world, we will continue to confront the enormous suffering that resides there. Faced with the images of endemic poverty and disease, it is easy to feel overcome by pity for those people and their plight.

But pity is a dangerous response.

"Pity," Hannah Arendt explains in *On Revolution*, "can be enjoyed for its own sake, and this will almost automatically lead to a glorification of its cause, which is the suffering of others."[22] In other words, feeling pity feels good, and if it feels good, we're inclined to perpetuate the circumstances that engendered the feeling. Susan Sontag takes the criticism a step further. "So far as we feel sympathy," a word which is used as Arendt used pity, "we feel we are not accomplices to what caused the suffering. Our sympathy proclaims our innocence as well as our impotence. To that extent, it can be (for all our good intentions) an impertinent—if not an inappropriate—response.[23]

Pity, or sympathy, as Sontag so eloquently lays bare, has a palliative effect on our conscience. It lets us feel our humanity. As Sontag understands, when we view images of people in pain, we are moved, even anguished, by their suffering. But even as we are anguished, we are also comforted by our own sympathetic response: if we feel pained by suffering in the developing world, we must be people of conscience. Our discomfort, as Sontag intuits, feels like the best evidence of our goodness.

Our tradition offers a model for responding to the people of the developing world without the pity that Sontag and Arendt teach us is ultimately self-serving. The central command of the Passover seder is to see ourselves as if we have been freed from Egypt. We don't sympathize with the experience of slavery or pity the Hebrew slaves; we find ways to relive their oppression. And we don't just imagine freedom; we're told to embody it. Some Haggadot even include mirrors on the page where this text is found.

The message of the seder, then, is to see ourselves as intimately connected to our own history of oppression and liberation, and to connect our narrative with the struggles for liberation of other oppressed peoples. This becomes a recurring theme in the Bible—take care of the widow, the orphan, and the stranger, we are commanded, because you once were slaves in Egypt.

But the message is deeper. When we become aware of the suffering of others, they enter our universe of obligation. And when they enter our universe of obligation, our own moral identity becomes inextricably tied up in their fate. Acting from a place of that awareness minimizes the possibility of pity and enhances our ability to act. As Lila Watson, an Australian Aboriginal activist, puts it, "If you have come here to help me you are wasting your time. But if you have come here because your liberation is bound up with mine, let us work together."

A Jewish Response to Globalization

Rabbi Micha Odenheimer

Rabbi Micha Odenheimer is the founding director of Tevel b'Tzedek, a new Israeli-based nonprofit whose first project is a work-study program on poverty, environment, and globalization for Israeli and Diaspora Jews based in Kathmandu, Nepal. A contributing editor to *Eretz Acheret*, his articles have been published widely in newspapers and magazines in the United States and Israel.

Although history is full of surprises, my bet is that the globalization of the economy will be remembered in centuries to come as the most significant development of our era. The definition of economic globalization is the integration of all the economies of the world into a single international market. In today's model, this means the control and domination of the world's economy by giant, politically powerful multinational corporations. Increasingly, these corporations decide what we grow and eat, what information we encounter, and even which laws will govern our increasingly small world. The struggle to determine the shape that economic globalization will take is thus a sacred struggle for the human future.

As Jews, we belong to a tradition that has fought against a market-centered vision of social life. For us, globalization clearly presents a grave challenge and an unprecedented opportunity. The globalization of the economy is a process that began five hundred years ago with European colonialism, but the end of World War II, the concomitant expansion of American economic power, and more recently, the fall of Communism and the subsequent international trade and banking agreements imposed by the World Trade Organization mark astounding new phases in the totality of its scope. The process of globalization has gained exponentially in velocity at the very moment at which the majority of Jews are, for the first time, fully empowered citizens of democratic countries—first and foremost the United States and Israel—that are key participants in the global economy. We thus have the opportunity, the freedom—and the urgent responsibility—to influence the future face of humankind.

The predominant voices in the mainstream media claim that globalization creates economic growth that will eventually wipe out poverty and increase democracy. But what I have witnessed in fifteen years of reporting from Africa, Asia, the Middle East, and the Caribbean does not allow me the comfort of believing that globalization, in its present form, is good for the poor and oppressed. In country after country, I have seen how the viselike logic of profit maximization crushes the poor and destroys their culture and dignity.

From Thailand to Mexico, farmers living in semi-communal villages have been forced off their land by a combination of violence, trickery, and the degradation of their environment and have been forced to sell their labor to factories, mining companies, or plantation owners. This process has been driven by governments, usually corrupt ones, that take huge "development" loans from Western powers and must now produce what can be sold for dollars in order to service these loans. Economists who judge economic success in terms of "growth" and Gross National Product have not devised ways to measure what it means to lose forever the chance to fish in a clean river, to raise children in a safe environment and transmit to them your ancient culture, or to grow food on your own land. Nor do their statistics account for the hundreds of billions of dollars' worth of nonrenewable natural resources that have been extracted from developing countries over the past few decades, or the cost of the devastating pollution that is the byproduct of growth.

What does Judaism have to teach about all this? The notion that economic power must be diffused and democratized runs through the Torah like a spine, beginning with the Garden of Eden narrative. Whatever else the multilayered story of Adam and Eve in the Garden of

Eden is about, it can be read as a symbolic account of the emergence of humankind from prehistory, marked by innocence and nakedness, into the long era of "By the sweat of thy brow thou shall eat thy bread."

Food Is the Original Capital

Adam and Eve's eating of the fruit of the Tree of Knowledge is connected, on a compressed, symbolic level, to the end of the hunter-gatherer period and the beginnings of agriculture. One of the great differences between gaining one's food supply through agriculture and acquiring it as a hunter-gatherer is that staple foods offer a diet that is less varied, but always safe, while hunter-gatherers, who typically utilize hundreds of kinds of plants and fruits, must always be aware of the possibility of poison. On the simplest level, God's warning to Adam that if he eats from the fruit of a certain tree he will "surely die" might be read as an allusion to this constant presence of danger in a hunter-gatherer's food supply.

Over the past century, archaeological anthropologists have traced the ways that the beginnings of agriculture often turned on the human ability to transform a specific species from a poisonous to an edible state through, for example, the chance discovery and the subsequent cultivation of a harmless mutation of a poisonous fruit or plant. Perhaps this transformation is encoded in the snake's assurance: "No, you shall surely not die." And if, as Kafka says, Adam and Eve's punishment was not immediate death, but consciousness of mortality, would not this consciousness coincide with the kind of conception of time necessary for the long-term calculations of horticulture and the domestication of animal species?

Whatever the merit of these interpretive conjectures, one fact is clear: the emergence of agriculture created, for the first time, the possibility of surplus, of the storage of food. *Food is the original capital.* Storage prevents starvation during lean times, and also facilitates the possibility of permanent human settlements with populations far larger than that of the largest hunter-gatherer collectives, which never exceed 150 to 200 people. But with the possibility of surplus and the resultant growth of the population came bureaucracy, social class, specialization, hierarchy, and oppression.

The Economic Meaning of Egypt

The vector leading from the end of hunter-gatherer society to the hierarchical centralization of power and concomitant exploitation can be seen as defining the narrative arc of the book of Genesis. Opening with the parable of Eden, the last third of Genesis is devoted to the Joseph story, which brings to denouement the book's thematic leitmotifs, such as jealousy between siblings, recognition, and mistaken identity. The artistic and emotional power of the Joseph story is so great, and its culmination so heartrending, that it is easy to lose sight of the fact that it ends with the enslavement of the Egyptian people to Pharaoh through the instrument of the storage of food. We are barely done wiping the tears from our eyes from Joseph's reunion with his brothers and father when the Torah tells us the following:

> And there was no bread in all the land, for the famine was sore.... And Joseph gathered up all the money that was found in the land of Egypt, and in the land of Canaan, for the corn which they bought and Joseph brought the money into Pharaoh's house. And when money failed in the land of Egypt, and in the land of Canaan, all the Egyptians came unto Joseph and said, Give us bread.... And Joseph said, Give your cattle.... When that year was ended, they came unto him the second year, and said unto him, We will not hide it from my lord, how that our money is spent; my lord also hath our herds of cattle; there is not ought left in the sight of my lord, but our bodies, and our lands: And Joseph bought all the land of Egypt for Pharaoh; for the Egyptians sold every man his field, because the famine prevailed over them: so the land became Pharaoh's. And as for the people, he made slaves of them from one end of Egypt to the other. (Gen. 47:13–16, 18–21)

Could the subsequent enslavement of the Israelites have been accomplished without the prior centralization of power and resources in the hands of Pharaoh? In Jewish tradition, Joseph is known as Yosef ha-Tzaddik, "Joseph the righteous one," both for his feat of chastity in refusing the advances of Potiphar's wife, and for saving his family and the Egyptian people from starvation. But the Torah has complex undercurrents running through it. According to Jewish educator Joshua Lauffer, there are some striking affinities between the snake—in our reading, the catalyzing agent in the transformation of human society from hunter-gatherer to agricultural means of production—and Joseph, who utilizes the capacity for concentrating and storing the wealth that agriculture unlocks in order to create an unprecedented conjunction of wealth and political power.

In its promise to Eve, the snake says, "You will be as God (*Elohim*), knowing good and evil." As Lauffer points out, unlike the heroes of previous stories in Genesis—Noah, Abraham, Isaac, or Jacob—Joseph never speaks to God or hears God's voice. Instead, he seems to function as a virtual stand-in for God, recalling the serpent's prediction, "You will be as God." "For doth not God (*Elohim*) have the answers," Joseph says to his fellow prisoners. "Tell [the dream] to me" (Gen. 40:8).

Moreover, in describing his predictive powers (the same powers that enable him to store food and thus power for Pharaoh), Joseph uses the root *n-kh-sh*—the very same letters as those that form the word *snake*—doubling the word for emphasis. "Did you not know," he asks his brothers—"*SheNakhesh YeNakhesh Ish asher Kamoni*"—that a person like me would surely divine [what you have done]?" (Gen. 44:14). Here the narrative, through the voice of Joseph himself, conflates prediction and manipulation—Joseph here claims to have foreseen a theft when actually he has presided over a frame-up. In the interpretation of Pharaoh's dream, Joseph takes the "knowledge of good and bad" that the snake predicts for Adam and Eve and realizes this knowledge within the realm of time—good and bad, fat and thin, become good years and bad years, fat years and thin years. Knowledge of good and evil is revealed as manipulation, calculation, planning, and strategy.

The juxtaposition of slavery and accumulation—the concentration of capital that is a sign of an oppressive society—continues in the book of Exodus, in which the Children of Israel are forced to build "storage cities" for Pharaoh. In the description of Israelite slavery, the Torah uses some of the same vocabulary that will be used to describe the struggles of the poor within Israelite society. The suffering of the slaves is called *oni*—poverty. And their taskmasters, those assigned to extract their labor, are called *nogshim*, the same word as that used later in the Torah to describe a person attempting to squeeze money from the indebted poor. Thus, accumulation and the concentration of capital come to be associated with oppression and poverty.

What Manna Means

Redemption, along with the giving of the Torah, is marked by a new means of sustenance. The Israelites are lifted out of the by now seemingly inevitable economy and culture of hoarding through the story of the manna. In the narrative arc we have begun to follow, the manna is a crucial watershed. The Sages rightly saw the manna as creating a preparatory, material basis for divine revelation. "The Torah was not given," says the Talmud, "but to the eaters of the manna."

What is the essential quality of manna? It is a sustenance unmediated by a human economic system. It cannot be stored or hoarded. Left overnight, it spoils, corrupts, and crawls with worms. Each and every person is charged with gathering just enough manna to eat for one day. The Torah calls this *"d'var yom b'yomo"*—"each day's matter on that day" (Exod. 16:4). Pharaoh uses this very expression after imposing heavier burdens upon the Israelites after Moses's initial intervention on behalf of the beleaguered people. There, "each day's matter" refers to the arbitrary quota of bricks that each person was to produce—bricks for a giant storehouse (Exod. 5:13). In the story of the manna, to emphasize the revolutionary nature of the Exodus—in which Egyptian reality is stood on its head—the phrase is used again, but this time it refers not to the gross accumulation of resources, but to the modest amount of sustenance each person needs for that particular day.

Time, instead of becoming reified ("Time is money and money is time"), is renaturalized, measured according to the rhythm of the human body and its biological needs. The measure of manna required by each person is an omer, which we are told is "a tenth of an *ephah*." This is the only place in which the Torah gives us a key to its system of measurement—to teach us, it would seem, to keep actual human need at the basis of all our calculations.

To emphasize the centrality of the manna principle in Judaism, God commands Moses, at the very end of the manna narrative, to place a jar with exactly one omer of manna in the Ark of the Covenant, alongside the tablets of the law, in the holy of holies. The story of the manna evokes the idealized essence of the hunter-gatherer era. In its immediacy, in the total economic equality it represents, and in its negation of accumulation and stockpiling, it repudiates those cultures in which economic and political power are centralized and conjoined through the storage of food and other forms of capital. The presence of the manna, and thus of the trace memory of hunter-gatherer society, is felt in numerous ways in the Torah's legislation: in the injunction against the planting or storing of fruits of the Sabbatical year, in the commandment to allow the poor the right to "gather" for themselves the remnants of a harvest, even in the prohibition against delaying the wages of a laborer—"on the same day you shall pay him what he is due"—as if the money, left in the employer's hands, would rot like the manna.

Seen in the light of the narrative arc stretching from Eden to the giving of manna, the meaning and direction of the economic justice legislation of the Torah becomes more readily apparent. The Torah's purpose is to create an "anti-Egypt," in which exploitation is not allowed free reign because land, wealth, and the means of production have not been concentrated in the hands of the few. Rather than the consolidation of land in the hands of one person, the Torah commands that the land of Israel be divided, so that each family has its own plot of land, of a size appropriate to the needs of the family. As with the manna, the principle of land distribution is, "To each according to his needs." The land is meant to provide each family with its own independent source of wealth and blessing and can only be sold in time of need, if the family has become impoverished. As if to emphasize the nature of this society as opposite that of Egypt, the priests are the only group not allotted land; ironically, in Egypt the priests were the only group that was allowed to keep its land in the face of Joseph's feudalization of the Egyptian economy.

The Torah allows for the sale of land under special circumstances. But the laws of the Jubilee (*Yovel*) mean that every fifty years, the wealth of society and its primary mode of production are redistributed and equality reestablished—the land returns to its original owners. The Jubilee is called freedom, *dror*, the very opposite of slavery. The Jubilee law is an attempt to legislate against the development of wealthy classes and impoverished, landless classes. It also ensures that land will not become a reified commodity. Instead of a constant increase in land value, the Jubilee law makes certain that land is priced according to its use value, "for it is a quantity of crops that he is selling to you." In other words, land, the major source of wealth and means of production in Israelite society, can never become a source of financial speculation.

The Jubilee is not the only legislation designed to correct the tendency of agricultural (and certainly industrial) societies to concentrate wealth and thus power. In four different places, the Torah also emphasizes the prohibition against taking interest on loans of money or food, expressed as a continuation of the laws of the Jubilee:

> If your brother grows poor, and his means fail with you, then you should strengthen him, though he is a stranger or a sojourner, that he may live with you. Take no interest from him, nor take any increase, but fear God, so that your brother might live with you. I am the Lord your God who brought you out of the land of Egypt, to give you the land of Canaan, and to be your God. (Gen. 25:35–38)

The Torah repeats the phrase *live with you* three times, suggesting that the prohibition against taking interest is a strategy aimed at creating a society based on at least rough social equality, without divisions into separate social classes. As Rabbi Shimon Federbush, a rabbinic luminary writing just before the creation of the State of Israel, says:

> At the foundation of the prohibition against taking interest is the Torah's desire to prevent the formation of a class of extremely wealthy people who have gained their riches at the expense of the economically weak. In doing this, the Torah legislates on the one hand against the possibility of the rich using interest to continuously enhance their wealth, and on the other hand, prevents the emergence of a class of people struggling under the weight of debts that continue to grow as the poison of interest causes economic collapse and finally even slavery.[1]

The Pharaoh of Globalization

How can we, as faithful Jews, fight against a form of globalization created to maximize the accumulation of wealth by multinational corporations? How can we raise up our brothers and sisters who are victims of this form of globalization, who are growing poorer, losing their ways of life, bearing the brunt of environmental destruction? Battling for a different kind of globalization will take clarity of purpose and strength of conviction. A clear and strong reading of the Torah's teachings on economic justice can serve as a crucial ethical and spiritual bulwark, a place to stand as we reach outward to make new alliances.

These teachings have far deeper and more complex psychological and economic implications than can be sketched in a single schematic essay. However, it is my contention that the overwhelming economic direction of the Torah, evidenced through the integration of its narrative and legal strands, is not only to insist on the equitable distribution of resources but also to stand against the kind of concentration of wealth that inevitably leads to abuses of power.

The entrance into the land of Israel, unfortunately, does not result in the establishment of the kind of society prescribed by the Torah. The prophets—Isaiah, Jeremiah, Ezekiel, Amos, Micah, Hosea, and others—spend much of their energy in the remaining books of the Tanakh railing against the exploitation of the poor at the hands of the rich. In particular, the prophets expose the nexus of political and economic power that perverts justice in order to serve the greed of the wealthy. The prevailing Western ideology—that the free market is really free of political influence and will eventually uplift the poor—would have evoked the bitter ire of the prophets.

Today, as modern Jews, it is our responsibility to bring Jewish ethical wisdom to bear on the analysis, exposure, and repair of the current international economic order. We will need to focus on the regulation of international corporations and the promotion of grassroots democracy, and on the nexus between the battle for a clean environment and the struggle for social justice. And we must not forget that the prophetic voice of justice emerges from a faith that human beings have within us the potential for something better, deeper, and ultimately more pleasurable—both as individuals and as a society. If we listen closely to the deepest layers of our tradition we will begin to realize this truth: none of us will be free until all of us are. When we gain awareness of how enmeshed we are with all of humanity, economically and thus ethically, we will begin the work, in partnership with other spiritual traditions, of creating a new ethic for the global age.[2]

"Silence Is Akin to Assent"
Judaism and the War in Iraq

Adam Rubin, PhD, is an assistant professor of Jewish history at Hebrew Union College–Jewish Institute of Religion in Los Angeles, California. He is a founding member of Jews Against the War. He is currently writing a book on the Jewish community in Palestine during the period of the British Mandate tentatively titled the *People of the Book: Sacred Texts, Hebrew Culture, and the Making of a Jewish Nation in Palestine, 1924–1948.*

The invasion of Iraq, launched on the basis of false premises, selective intelligence, and outright lies against a country that posed no threat to the United States and which had no connection to the terrorist attacks of September 11, 2001, has caused the deaths of several hundred thousand Iraqi civilians[1] and, at the time of this writing, over 3,700 American soldiers, more Americans than died in the September 11 attacks.[2] In addition, over 50,000 American soldiers have been injured, and more than 2 million refugees have fled Iraq.

The geopolitical consequences of the invasion have been disastrous. All sixteen government intelligence agencies concluded in a national intelligence estimate of August 2007 that the United States invasion of Iraq strengthened Al Qaeda and increased the threat of terrorism in this country. It strengthened Iran, inspired hatred of the United States across the globe, and cost more than $400 billion as of August 2007 (the ultimate cost will be more than a trillion dollars). According to Sen. Richard Durbin (D-Ill.), that $400 billion could have provided health care coverage for all of the uninsured children in

America for the entire duration of the war, new affordable housing units for 500,000 needy families, all the needed port security requirements to keep America safe, or complete funding for the No Child Left Behind program.[3]

In sum, there is no longer any doubt that the Bush/Cheney war in Iraq was an utter catastrophe. Former Vice President Al Gore called it "the worst strategic mistake in the entire history of the United States."[4] Many leading generals (whose pensions are protected in retirement) strongly criticized the war and called for a gradual U.S. withdrawal, and almost 1,000 active-duty soldiers, sailors, Marines, airmen, rank-and-file enlistees, and noncommissioned officers, along with high-ranking officers, submitted a petition to Congress demanding that the troops be brought home.[5] According to all available polls, by summer of 2007 a large majority of Americans wanted to bring our involvement in Iraq to an end, and an overwhelming majority of Iraqis themselves were opposed to the continued American occupation of their country.

Jewish Silence

Given all of these facts, it is difficult to understand the organized Jewish community's silence. At a time when our country has been mired in a catastrophic, immensely unpopular war, a sectarian conflict that has caused untold damage to our country's security and exacted an extremely high price in blood and treasure, when the great majority of American Jews have been opposed to the war (87 percent of the Jewish community voted for Democratic candidates in the last elections), the organized Jewish community has been remarkably silent. Progressive rabbis have spoken out—both the Reform and Reconstructionist movements issued official antiwar statements, as have progressive Jewish rabbis such as Arthur Waskow and Michael Lerner. Yet little has been heard from prominent Conservative or Orthodox movement rabbis, from important lay leaders, or from the many important Jewish religious and community organizations.

This silence is particularly mysterious in light of the damage that the war has done to Israel's interests by creating conditions for the emergence of a radical, fundamentalist Shiite state among the ruins of Iraq;

eliminating a counterweight to Iran, and increasing the strength and influence of that country, Israel's most dangerous enemy. Martin Van Creveld, a distinguished military historian at the Hebrew University in Jerusalem, recognized those dangers in an essay in 2007, calling for President Bush to be impeached and put on trial for "launching the most foolish war since Emperor Augustus in 9 BC sent his legions in Germany and lost them."[6]

Frustrated by the passivity of much of the organized Jewish community in the face of the overwhelming urgency of the situation in Iraq, and by a sense that the unwillingness to speak out represented a betrayal of the moral imperatives of the Jewish religious tradition, Jews Against the War (jewsagainstthewar.org) was founded in the spring of 2007. As of August 2007, it had received the signatures of over 1,300 rabbis, Jewish studies professors, lay leaders, and concerned Jews throughout the country.

A Jewish Response

The founders of Jews Against the War (including the writer of this article) were motivated to take action by the conviction that as Jews, citizens, and human beings, we all bear some measure of responsibility for our country's destructive policies in Iraq. This sentiment is given eloquent expression both by Abraham Joshua Heschel's belief that "In a democracy some are guilty but all are responsible.... The opposite of good is not evil, the opposite of good is indifference," and by the Talmudic notion that "One who is able to protest against a wrong that is being done in his family, his city, and his nation or the world and does not do so is held accountable for that wrong being done" (Babylonian Talmud, *Shabbat* 54b).

We are aware that Judaism is not a pacifist religion; Deuteronomy sets forth the laws of war, and lengthy sections of the books of Joshua, Judges, Samuel, and Kings are devoted to depictions of just and unjust wars. On the other hand, the Rabbinic tradition, drawing on the Hebrew Prophets, insists that even those wars that are permitted and necessary are evil, unleashing unrestrained violence and death and provoking the very worst in humanity. For example, in the legal world envisioned by the Rabbis, a *kohen* (priest) who kills an enemy during a war, even in self-defense, is not allowed to serve in the Temple; more-over, a king has to get permission from the high priest and high court to wage war. The Sages established a series of checks and balances to insure that leaders could not launch a war on a whim.

The modern period has also witnessed the emergence of impor-tant voices from within the tradition that affirm Judaism's aversion toward war and desire for peace. Hillel Zeitlin (1871–1942), a jour-nalist, mystic, and religious thinker, argued that "when a people is *forced* to conduct war, the murder of women and children is forbid-den, as is the destruction of trees that surround a city; a captive village must be treated with love and respect. The true spirit of the Torah is not 'You shall not let anyone live' (Deut. 20:16), but rather 'Do not provoke them to war' (Deut. 2:9)."

Isaiah writes: "Nation shall not lift up sword against nation, nei-ther shall they learn war anymore" (Isa. 2:4). Isaac Breuer (1883–1946), a leading figure of German Neo-Orthodoxy, insisted that "Every line of Holy Scripture is a protest against might. Indeed the genesis of the Jewish people itself is a divine demonstration against might. Egypt was mightier than Israel. But Israel dedicated itself … to the law of God."[7]

An even stronger condemnation of war and espousal of peace can be found in the writing of Aharon Shmuel Tamares (1869–1931), a rabbi and polemicist in Poland. Writing soon after the First World War and the pogroms that came in its wake, he characterized militarism as a new form of idolatry. In his view, modern people had turned to the sword as an antidote to the spiritual emptiness of extreme nationalism:

War is not a sudden chance occurrence, nor is it an isolated link unconnected to other links in the chain of life. Rather, it is the inexorable result of the base dedication of the nations. War, which is inherently irrational in character … represents that great crisis of immorality which discloses in retrospect all the sins of society and all the falseness plastered into the wall of civilization…. Men will reject war only when their hearts become filled with an abundance of love and concern for their fellow-men, all created in the image of God…. True peace would come to the world, the prophets insisted, only when

"The earth shall be filled with knowledge of the Lord." In other words, man must first be imbued with that condition of spiritual purity which knows and recognizes the inner worth and glory of man.[8]

While it is impossible to speak of one definitive "Jewish perspective" from within a religious tradition as variegated and multilayered as Judaism, the founders and supporters of Jews Against the War nevertheless assert our belief in the wisdom and relevance of the Jewish tradition regarding matters of war and peace, and are led by our reading of that tradition to the inescapable conclusion that the invasion of Iraq was not just and that the continued occupation extends this injustice. The Talmud teaches that silence is akin to assent. As long as this unjust war continues, we need to do everything within our power to end it.

Once Again
Genocide in Darfur

MARK HANIS

Mark Hanis is the founder and executive director of the Genocide Intervention Network (www.genocideintervention.net), an organization created to empower citizens with the tools to prevent and stop genocide. He is a Draper Richards fellow and an Echoing Green fellow.

What has been happening in Darfur, Sudan, for the last several years is genocide.

Sadly, I am familiar with genocide. All four of my grandparents were Holocaust survivors. I was raised for eighteen years in Ecuador in a small Jewish community in Quito—one hundred families—made up mostly of Shoah (Holocaust) survivors and their families. The elders of the community made a point of wearing short-sleeved shirts so that we could see the numbers tattooed on their arms. Virtually every door in the local synagogue had a sticker on it reading, "Six million, Never Again."

Yet "never again" has become "once again" in Darfur, the western region of Sudan, where an ongoing genocide has led to the murder of hundreds of thousands of people and the displacement of millions more. In the face of genocide, we have an obligation to act. As the book of Leviticus states, "Do not stand idly by the blood of your neighbor" (Lev. 19:16). Living as we do in an era of globalization, the people of Darfur are our neighbors.

Background to Genocide

In early 2003, two rebel groups, the Sudan Liberation Movement and the Justice and Equality Movement, attacked government positions in Darfur. The aim of this rebellion was to force President Omar Al-Bashir and his Khartoum administration to provide Africans in western Sudan with increased economic and political opportunities after years of neglect and alienation. Since taking power in 1989, Al-Bashir and his National Islamic Front have enacted exclusivist and oppressive measures against the non-Arab populations of the country (Christians and Animists in the south and African Muslims in the west).

In response to this uprising, the Sudanese government and its proxy militia, the Janjaweed, initiated a scorched-earth campaign in Darfur. This brutal onslaught has involved the indiscriminate murder of tens of thousands of rebel fighters and civilians, the destruction of hundreds of villages, and the rape and maiming of untold numbers of women and girls. The Sudanese government has also severely limited the flow of humanitarian aid to Darfur, depriving survivors of food, medicine, and shelter. To date, approximately 450,000 people have died as a result of the conflict, and over 2.5 million have been forced from their homes and are living in internally displaced persons (IDP) and refugee camps along the Sudan-Chad border.

While President Bush and other world leaders have named this crisis "genocide," the international community has thus far failed to stop President Omar Al-Bashir and his despotic regime from massacring the people of Darfur. As citizens of a free and democratic nation, we must do everything in our power to help end the genocide in Darfur.

The Three "P"s

I founded the Genocide Intervention Network (GI-NET) with my friend and classmate Andrew Sniderman at Swarthmore College in 2004. Inspired by Samantha Power's award-winning book *A Problem from Hell: America in the Age of Genocide*, we decided to create a fund to help support the undermanned and under-resourced African Union (AU) peacekeeping force in western Sudan. World leaders were doing very little to help protect the people of Darfur, and private citizens felt that donating money for humanitarian aid was the only way they could make a difference.

Since that time, GI-NET has evolved into a multidimensional organization. At present, we have three broad areas of activity: protection, political will, and permanency.

Protection: To date, GI-NET has raised over $250,000 for peacekeeping efforts. This includes the funding of a civilian protection program that safeguards women and girls from rape and assault when they leave refugee camps to collect firewood. Currently, we are working with the African Union in eleven IDP camps in northern Darfur to help protect civilians.

Political Will: Recognizing that the fight to stop genocide requires intensive political action, GI-NET has created several innovative tools to help people raise their voices to protest the bloodshed in Darfur.

- **1-800-GENOCIDE** is a toll-free service that connects callers directly to their representatives without being put on hold or having to dial multiple numbers. The hotline provides callers with talking points based on GI-NET's most up-to-date information.
- **Darfur Scores** is a scorecard that grades members of Congress on how engaged they have been in legislative efforts to address the genocide in Darfur. This grading system provides citizens with the information they need to lobby more effectively and pressure their representatives to take meaningful action.
- **The Sudan Divestment Task Force** assists individuals and organizations in researching their mutual funds to ensure that their money is not being invested in companies helping to fund the genocide. Members of the Task Force have worked with several colleges, universities, and states, helping them divest their pension funds from the most egregious companies doing business with the Sudanese government.

Permanency: Our unique goal as an organization is to establish the first permanent anti-genocide constituency. If we can achieve this goal, we can ensure that there will always be an informed and willing group of activists that can mobilize our government to intervene when the threat of genocide arises. We are very proud of the work of our student division, STAND: A Student Anti-Genocide Coalition, which serves as an umbrella organization for student groups across North America. These groups promote awareness, advocate for an end to the genocide in Darfur, and work to create a permanent anti-genocide student movement. There are now over seven hundred STAND chapters in colleges and high schools throughout the United States and Canada.

The solution to abolishing genocide has never been clearer: we must hold our leaders accountable for stopping these atrocities. Teenagers and adults, Democrats and Republicans—we *all* have the responsibility to help protect people facing genocide anywhere in the world. So get political, especially on the local level; we need to continue growing this grassroots movement throughout the country and around the world. Please consider joining GI-NET—the first permanent anti-genocide constituency—and help us fulfill the promise of "Never Again."

How to Split the Sea
Anti-Semitism and Social Change

APRIL ROSENBLUM

April Rosenblum, a native of Philadelphia, is the author of the widely distributed pamphlet "The Past Didn't Go Anywhere: Making Resistance to Anti-Semitism Part of All of Our Movements." She has also written for *Bridges*, *New Voices*, and *Afn Shvel*, the journal of the League for Yiddish.

It's very hard to move forward in a struggle for justice if a part of you always has to watch your back. If the Israelites had been forced to watch for the soldiers at their heels, instead of focusing on the way forward, can you imagine the bottleneck at the Red Sea?

Yet in a world that hasn't yet defeated anti-Semitism, this is the tension faced by Jews fighting for social justice. And it's not only *our* collective potential as justice workers that is hampered by anti-Semitism. Wider social justice movements suffer greatly as well. Whenever progressive movements get confused, and take part in anti-Semitic thinking, they are held back from building a real vision for social change.

For this dynamic to shift, Jewish communities—starting with those of us who are passionate about social justice—will have to play a central part in a sea change in the culture of the Left.

I grew up in the Left; that much I've always known. In Philadelphia, the activist community of which my parents were part was small enough that Democrats and radicals of all stripes worked together in coalitions to fight nuclear power, U.S. intervention in Central America, the advance of the arms race, and police brutality in our own backyards.

Yet it wasn't until I'd long been an activist myself that I realized I had grown up squarely inside a Jewish community. Looking back at photos from my 1980s childhood, I can tell now that the warm, smiling, dark-eyed activists I felt so safe around shared more than just politics with my family; they shared Jewish ancestry and backgrounds—be it the fairly recent religious heritage of my mother's side or the secular culture of my father's. But our being Jews was one thing that rarely got discussed around a table that was otherwise full of questions and penetrating conversations. Why is that?

Lots of factors are responsible for why Jewish identity often goes unspoken and unclaimed by activists in social justice movements: the rightward drift of parts of the organized Jewish community; the pressure for Jews to fit into the American mold of religion, not ethnicity, which isolated thousands of Jews who once would have been at home in secular Jewish communities; and the general effects of assimilation.

A factor less often identified is anti-Semitism. During peaks of anti-Semitism, Jews have sometimes had to cope by laying low—such as after World War II, when American Jews shuddered over the execution of the Rosenbergs, fearing that it might signal the start of wider targeting of Jews. Times like these have impacted Jews' ability to be politically active and their willingness to identify themselves as Jewish in their activism. When McCarthyism hit, Rifke Feinstein of the Congress of Secular Jewish Organizations remembers, "Whole communities of us [Leftist, Yiddish-speaking, secular Jewish schools and organizations] just tried to go underground, to disappear. But when it was over and we poked our heads up, no one else was there."

But if attacks from the outside world are bad, the anti-Semitism that Jews have periodically encountered inside our own movements has in some ways had an even greater impact on our morale. Each time that the Left engages in or tolerates anti-Semitism, a generation of Jewish activists is affected. Many pull back from progressive activism, as did countless American Jews who had lovingly defended the Soviet Union for its social advances, after revelations emerged about targeted anti-Jewish violence and repression there. Those who feel ready to stay in the Left after such events are often the ones who identify less strongly as Jews. No wonder, then, that by the time I was born, my mother could find dozens of Jews to hang out with, but few who reflected with her on being Jewish. Water, water, everywhere—but not a drop to drink.

The cycle adds to itself. The more anti-Semitism pushes out those of us who are appalled by it, the less those of us who are left know how exactly to stand up against it. When, around September 11, I first started to encounter anti-Semitic behaviors in the movements I cared about, I found myself speechless—and worse, so did my gentile friends, whom I trusted to speak out against harm to me, just as we worked to support one another to speak out against racism wherever we encountered it. Seeing my friends go silent inspired me to embark on a long-term effort to figure out why social justice movements have such a spotty track record when it comes to anti-Semitism, and what it will take to change that.

Opening a Path for Our Movements

From 2005 to 2006, I interviewed activists from across the United States—both Jewish and non-Jewish—who had made progress toward bringing understanding of anti-Semitism into the rest of their social justice work. I taught a nine-month training for non-Jewish activists to build their skills as allies to Jews, traveled to Latin America to observe more overt anti-Semitism firsthand, gave talks to synagogues and activist groups, and created a pamphlet for mass distribution to activists.

I found that social justice movements have had trouble understanding anti-Semitism partly because it looks different from the oppressions with which they're familiar. Oppressions such as racism against people of color enforce inferiority on their target groups in order to disempower them. Anti-Jewish oppression, on the other hand, can make its target look extremely powerful. It does so by drawing upon charges that have been evolving since the earliest days of Roman-era anti-Jewish theology: charges that Jews are mysterious or act secretly behind the scenes, have abnormal or supernatural amounts of power, are disloyal to the societies we live in, cause a disproportionate amount of harm in the world, are wealthy or greedy, or are the "brains" behind the action.

Anti-Semitism's job is to make the systems that create injustice invisible. It protects unequal power structures, diverting anger at injustice toward Jews instead. The process goes something like this:

Jews are isolated, especially from other exploited groups—people who might normally be expected to team up with us and defend us in times of danger.

Other oppressed groups are encouraged to channel their anger at Jews, which keeps them from identifying and fighting the real sources of their exploitation.

Jews are targeted for violence or other forms of attack, sometimes intentionally by local governments and other times spontaneously at the grassroots of society.

In search of some protection, Jews are pressured to cooperate with those in power, to stay quiet, and not to challenge the status quo, for fear of greater targeting.

Considering the pressures exerted on Jews, it's a wonder and a source of pride how really powerful we *have* been in fighting for social change.

In a world that's very difficult to change, anti-Semitism makes things seem easy to solve. It invites people to fix their gaze on an imagined group of greedy, powerful Jews at the root of the world's problems, and redirects their vision right past the systems that actually keep injustice in place: capitalism, weapons dealers, oil companies, you name it ... and the overwhelmingly non-Jewish people in power who benefit from systems of inequality.

That's the nature of anti-Jewish oppression: to cover up the roots of injustice. To make people think they've figured out who's really pulling the strings. This is one of the biggest reasons why it's important for social justice movements to figure out and confront anti-Jewish oppression, for the movement's own sake: because anti-Jewish oppression is designed as a way to keep people from understanding where the power lies. And it works.

To make things more complicated, anti-Semitism tends to move in cycles, allowing Jews to succeed during the good times. Attacks come in waves, yet each time things calm down and Jews are able to blend in or succeed in society again, it gives the appearance that anti-Semitism is "over." Prior to attacks in Germany and medieval Spain, for instance, Jews were among the most successful and well-acculturated minorities.

Without understanding this, social justice activists tend to see Jews as a group that's "made it" in the United States, and anti-Semitism as something that went out of business in the 1940s.

Yet the signs are clear that anti-Semitism is a real and present danger—most visibly outside the United States. Take Russia, where parliament members fought to have all Jewish organizations banned in 2005 on charges that Judaism is anti-Christian, extremist, and inhumane; that Jews ritually murder Christian babies; and that "the whole democratic world is under financial and political control of the international Jewry."[1] Or consider Malaysia, where former Prime Minister Mahathir bin Mohamad declared in 2003 to a world summit of Muslim leaders that "the Jews run this world by proxy. They get others to fight and die for them," and "have now gained control of the most powerful countries."[2]

Then there's the street-level violence targeted at individual Jews, from the now-famous case of Ilan Halimi, a twenty-three-year-old working-class Moroccan Jew who was tortured to death outside Paris in January 2006, to the many lesser-known people, like Mordechai Molozhenov, who was stabbed and beaten into a coma in the Ukraine in 2005. And while we remain relatively safe in the United States, it's hard not to be unnerved by a hit film restaging the "Passion plays," which sparked annual Easter massacres of Jews in medieval Europe, or theories arising amid growing public disenchantment with the Iraq war that it was fought for Jewish or Israeli interests.

How to Split the Sea

Social justice movements are not immune to the anti-Semitic ideas that affect our wider society—as anyone can tell you who's had a progressive friend forward conspiracy e-mails that place Jews or Israelis behind 9/11, or who has taken part in vital work to prevent war against Iran, but has been scoffed at for raising concerns about the anti-Semitism Iran's government promotes, or who has worked in coalition against an inhumane politician and overheard derisive references to the leader's Jewishness.

But our movements are also fertile places for change and improvement. I saw it firsthand as I interviewed Jews and non-Jews who have found creative ways to push the conversation forward—leading seminars at activist retreats, forming troubleshooting teams to confront people with anti-Semitic signs at local demonstrations, joining forces with Arab-American colleagues to teach an "Anti-Semitism and Anti-Arabism" course at a local community college, designing progressive *tashlich*[3] services over the High Holy Days at which Jewish activists reflect on what they want to change in the Jewish community and Gentile activists reflect on the need to resist anti-Semitism.

The first thing required to defeat anti-Semitism in social justice settings is for us to *stay in the movement*—no matter how difficult it gets. We can make this easier by building teams of Jewish social justice workers who share mutual concern about anti-Semitism, who support each other to keep bringing up the issue, and who stay involved in our movements when this struggle gets annoying or downright frightening.

At the same time, we must evaluate and discard some of our first instincts and timeworn tactics against anti-Semitism. One of our most common desperate measures is to rush to stop the spread of anti-Semitism by exerting whatever power we can muster from above. I've seen this play out on campuses, for instance, in efforts to get professors fired, student groups' funding cut, or events cancelled when we fear such people or organizations are anti-Semitic. Methods like these are doomed to fail, because anti-Semitism is built on a vision of Jews as all-powerful and in control. Tactics that clamp down on others perpetuate the cycle of anti-Semitism, compounding our situation instead of protecting us.

The same goes for our common response of "circling the wagons" to refute and suppress criticism of Israel—a natural response for many of us when we are afraid of attacks on Jews. When we foster an atmosphere in which Jews or Gentiles who criticize Israeli actions fear being automatically labeled as anti-Semites, we engage in a form of *lashon hara* ("evil tongue") that cuts us off from people who could, in fact, develop into our true allies.

We cannot defeat anti-Semitism by ourselves. We *can* do it by reaching out to non-Jewish allies from all backgrounds and asking them to be a part of changing our movements and our world by educating themselves and standing up against anti-Semitism. And that, in the end, may be our most formidable task. Not because people will say no—many are honored to be asked, and plenty recognize that it is in their own interests to free social justice movements from false ideas of who has power and where problems stem from—but because it's so hard for us to ask.

In a world where Jews have faced sometimes unspeakable brutality, it can feel impossible to ask for allies. To risk believing that somebody might actually show up—that feels as preposterous as it must have been to stand at the edge of the Red Sea and weigh the benefits of walking in, in the hope that it would open.

But the Midrash tells us that the sea opened because one Israelite did just that: walked in. As hundreds of thousands of Israelites stood between an army and an unmoving sea, one man, Nachshon ben Aminadav, stepped forward and began to move into the water. I imagine him walking tentatively forward, conscious of the stares of disbelief and scorn he was drawing, and recognizing that these steps that looked so foolish were the only way forward; going deeper and deeper, until the waters reached his nostrils and—suddenly!—broke open.

It feels crazy to ask for allies when they haven't exactly always shown up when we've needed them. Seas just don't *open*. But for us, as for our ancestors at the water's edge, there's only one way forward. So ...

Deep breath ...

Deep breath ...

Go.

Reopening the Tent of Abraham

Rabbi Phyllis Berman and Rabbi Arthur Waskow, PhD

Rabbi Phyllis Berman is the founder (1979) and director of the Riverside Language Program in New York City for adult immigrants and refugees. She is the coauthor of *Tales of Tikkun: New Jewish Stories to Heal the Wounded World* and *A Time for Every Purpose Under Heaven: The Jewish Life-Spiral As a Spiritual Journey*.

Rabbi Arthur Waskow, PhD, is the director of The Shalom Center (www.shalomctr.org), which voices a new prophetic agenda in Jewish, multireligious, and American life. A coauthor of *The Tent of Abraham: Stories of Hope and Peace for Jews, Christians, and Muslims*, Waskow is the author of *Godwrestling—Round 2: Ancient Wisdom, Future Paths*; editor of two volumes of *Torah of the Earth: Exploring 4,000 Years of Ecology in Jewish Thought* (all Jewish Lights); and many other books on public policy and Jewish thought and practice.

The world is falling helter-skelter down a steep incline toward a fatal cliff: an endless world war between the whole Muslim world and the West. A war between the different families of Abraham.

Sometimes it seems we are already over the edge of the cliff, but perhaps, God willing, *im yirtzeh Hashem, inshallah*, we're not quite there yet. Not quite.

Such a war would leave us all at constant risk of death and material impoverishment, bereft of security, ridden and riddled with fear and rage. To imagine a war between the families of Abraham, imagine: the bombed-out tip of Manhattan on September 11, 2001; the city of Baghdad during the summer of 2006; Qana on July 30, 2006; Kfar Giladi on August 6, 2006—all repeated and magnified worldwide.

What can this war between the families of Abraham, what the West calls its "war against terror," hope to achieve? Is the notion and practice of a "war against terror" even working for the West? In Iraq, every neighborhood that the U.S. war against terror destroyed bred more people furious with its destroyers and more skilled in how to kill them. In Afghanistan, the U.S. and NATO governments threw down the memory hole those oral manuals of war that had written upon their title pages the blood-red note, "Do not invade Afghanistan!— Signed, the British Empire, 1843, 1881, 1919. Signed, the Soviet Empire, 1989." It is becoming more and more likely that another such note, signed by the USA and NATO, will be necessary.

The "war against terror" also has not worked for Israelis, whose government follows a similar notion and practice. Each attack, like that in Lebanon in 2006, is bought at the cost of more threat, disloca- tion, and death in the Israeli interior, and more hostile foes forearmed into the future.

If the "war against terror" has failed, then surely the "other side" in this war must be winning? Is the notion and practice of a "war against the degenerate West" working for the Muslims among whom some unelected bands of warriors are carrying it out? Clearly not. Each attack on an office building, a pizzeria, a subway, an airport brings gigantic destructive retaliation against some part of the Muslim world, and more and more rigid restrictions on Muslim minorities in "Western" countries.

No one is winning, and no one will win, this war.

Why Do We Fight?

So why are we fighting? Not because the religious doctrines of Judaism, Christianity, or Islam require a war of each against each. While we must not blind ourselves to the reality that some parts of the sacred texts of all three communities can be read to allow such bloodshed, there have also been periods when the three have avoided bloodshed, and large majori- ties of the three communities today are horrified by the violence.

When we look for causes, in this moment we cannot ignore the intensifying struggles over oil and those beginning to arise over water. Yet even these, the "normal" reasons nations and warrior bands start killing, are self-destructive. The West's addiction to oil is a major fac- tor in wrecking the climatic system that has undergirded human civilization for ten thousand years. No matter which "great power" controls the oil—China, Russia, the USA, India—its overuse will poison us all. It will flood our coasts, dry up the snows and rivers that slake our thirst, scorch our farmlands.

But that knowledge, like the knowledge of most addicts that their drug of choice is killing them, does not in itself end the addiction. The "drug lords" of this oil-oholic addiction pretend there is no addiction, and that the only danger is not climate disaster but loss of access to the drug. And since the greatest pool of oil on the planet sits in the heartland of Islam, the desire to control the oil quickly turns to "Western" rage against Islam when it does not prostrate itself to this control, and Muslim rage against those who seek to tighten their control.

So—what to do? The alternative is to move toward peace, step by step. Beginning by halting the most egregious violence, ending the oil-oholic addiction that turns desire into rape, and reweaving the threads of international and transnational nongovernmental community that can inhibit, delay, and defuse the fears and rages that otherwise boil over into war.

Finding a Third Path

Reweaving these threads of connection will require action in three arenas: ending the addiction to oil, creating a public opinion in Muslim and Western countries that firmly rejects the resort to violence (whether by official armies or underground warrior bands), and transforming the religious relationships among Jews, Christians, and Muslims.

The third path is alien to, and best not undertaken by, official policymakers. Through it, "the medium becomes the message." Through it, we embody in the present the future that we intend to create. As Gandhi put it, "Be the peace that you seek," or as Martin Buber put it, "The means we use turn into the ends we actually achieve."

When we come together, whether with friends or strangers, especially when we are hoping to inspire compassion and connection, what we most want and need is to feel our hearts touched by one another, recognizing our shared humanness, actually recognizing the presence of the Other, in the other.

When we meet with people from spiritual and religious traditions other than our own, that sense of connection comes if our meeting is grounded in seeking to see the One Who is the Root and the Blossom of all our traditions. The image of God that appears in every human face is authentically divine precisely because each face is unique, reflecting the Infinite. So it is this uniqueness that we seek to see; in it is the One.

One aspect of that diverse uniqueness and the unity on which we agree becomes apparent when we share our intellects. We may learn a great deal from each other, even come to understand our own selves better, by explaining to each other the thoughts and practices of our own religious paths. And we may gain from discovering how much we agree and how we differ when it comes to pursuing justice, peace, and the healing of the earth. These are ideas, valuable and necessary. But even this is limited, if we restrict ourselves to it. Our own experience with interfaith work has taught us that intellectual dialogue will not be a strong enough foundation for change.

The Jewish mystics teach us that there are four worlds of reality: *asiya* (the physical world of action); *yetzira* (the emotional world of feelings); *briyya* (the intellectual world of ideas); and *atzilut* (the soul world of Oneness). The deeper task of meeting in an interfaith community is the sharing of our lives in all four worlds, not only the world of intellect. We must create a deep connection at the spiritual and emotional levels as well as at the intellectual and political levels if we are going to heal the broken families of Abraham.

Pitching the Tent

Through The Shalom Center, we have explored a model for interfaith meeting that participates in all four worlds. We call this kind of gathering "The Tent of Abraham, Hagar, and Sarah," drawing on the ancient teaching that the Abrahamic family kept its tent open on all four sides so as to welcome from any direction the hungry and the thirsty.

From these gatherings, we have learned that to incorporate the four worlds, events must offer these opportunities:

- Opportunities to hear the soul journeys of people whose paths may have been parallel to ours, so as to understand our interconnectedness.

- Opportunities to celebrate the One through the specific idioms of one another's religions. At one gathering, a Jewish participant led a service using chant and meditation rather than Hebrew, which few present would have understood.
- Opportunities to understand the ways in which our traditions are similar and different in philosophy, theology, and practice. A Christian participant pointed out that while communion is restricted to Christians, the *agape* meal is an authentic New Testament practice not limited to Christians and could be an act of prayer.
- Opportunities to eat, dance, and move together. A Muslim participant invited participants to move in the rhythmic *zikr* gestures that are part of Muslim spiritual practices, though different from the regular daily prayers.
- Opportunities to plan actions together that keep our Abrahamic families in peaceful connection with one another. From one such gathering came a decision to write a public statement on peacemaking signed by religious leaders from all the regions where Abraham traveled—from Babylonia (Iraq) and Canaan (Israel and Palestine), to Egypt and Saudi Arabia.

Celebrations Under and Beyond the Tent

One of the most powerful recent expressions of peacemaking became a call for a one-day fast for all Americans during Ramadan.[1]

It is not surprising that in order to turn in a profoundly new direction, Jews, Christians, and Muslims would return to the practice of fasting, a means of self-transformation that is a bright thread in all three traditions. It is also not surprising that we would turn toward our festivals as moments that call us to higher, deeper awareness of the One.

In each of our traditions, this deeper awareness at festival time has addressed society and "politics" as well as individual transformation. Christians have taken the ceremony of the Stations of the Cross—reenacting the painful journey of Jesus under arrest in Jerusalem—into the prison-scarred, drug-ridden, bullet-holed streets of American cities. Jews have turned the Passover seder into challenges to racism and sweatshops and the Tu B'Shvat seder into a challenge to earth-destroying corporations. Muslims have made Eid al-Adha, the Festival of the Sacrifice, into an obligatory opportunity to feed the poor.

One powerful way to bring the Children of Abraham, Sarah, and Hagar together is to join together during these seasons of celebration. We should be especially aware of times when these seasons converge, as they did in the years 2005, 2006, and 2007, when the Jewish sacred month of Tishrei and the Muslim sacred month of Ramadan occurred simultaneously. But there are ways we can share celebrations even when they do not overlap.

Once we have shared hearts as well as minds, we can find creative points of connection, ways of meeting together under the same tent.

Finding a Focus for Action

There are, for example, some areas where the three Abrahamic families can agree on goals or means for peacemaking in the Middle East. Most American Jews believed the Iraq war was a profound mistake, and in this way were in agreement with both the Roman Catholic Church and many Protestant denominations, as well as with many in the Muslim world.

Similarly, even in the matter of the Israeli-Palestinian conflict, many Christians and Jews are committed to a two-state solution, as are a heavy majority of American Muslims. Specifics might differ, but these communities share a similar goal.

Moving beyond such moments of sharing the observance of sacred time, the families of Abraham might also take concerted action for peace and justice, intended to change public policy.

The most obvious and perhaps the most urgent action might seem to be setting forth another path of peacemaking in the tangled wars and conflicts of the Abrahamic region, and of U.S. governmental policy toward that region. But for some, this may also be the most difficult arena to begin with, because there, in the broader Middle East, the collisions of Jews and Christians and Muslims with each other are harshest and hottest. In each of the various American communities that identify strongly with each of the Middle Eastern communities, there has been a mobilization of dug-in support for one or another position, and the generation of suspicion and anger toward each other.

This *tour d'horizon* of American religious opinion on the broader Middle East suggests an imaginable but difficult coalition among those Jews, Christians, and Muslims who urge the abandonment of terrorism, assassination, and war and encourage the cultivation of an ethic of nonviolence among the many conflicting parties in the Middle East; who support the emergence of a viable, democratic, peaceful, and independent Palestine deeply influenced by the Christian and Muslim values so vivid to those who live in the shadow of Bethlehem, the Church of the Holy Sepulchre, and the Dome of the Rock; who seek an Israel that sees the best vision of itself as an expression of Jewish and democratic vitality expressed not through expansionism but in the prophetic values of justice, creative self-renewal, and peace; who work for the achievement of a full peace among Israel, Palestine, and all the surrounding states and political groupings; and who insist on the disengagement of the U.S. military from Iraq.

To be able to mobilize strong public support, such a coalition would need to be aware of the practical realpolitik behind these policies, yet root itself most deeply in religious commitments to oppose oppression, war, violence, and injustice—values shared by great majorities in all of the Abrahamic faiths, and with some exceptions upheld by their sacred texts.

Such a coalition would need to face the truth that even those who could agree on these basic values and the future goals might deeply disagree about specific events in the present—an outbreak of war, a terrorist attack, the bombing of a city. Tribal loyalties may at least for a moment override more universal values.

Indeed, it might for some people and groups be easier, or more prudent, to begin the knitting together of an Abrahamic action coalition around protection and healing of the earth than around the making of peace in the Middle East. Since there is an overlap between the dangers of global scorching and a U.S.–Muslim world war, it only makes sense for Abrahamic compacts seeking Middle East peace to take our society's oil-oholic addiction into account.

Two other arenas that may lend themselves to early experiments in common action are empowerment of the poor and the protection of human rights, civil liberties, and equal justice for the weak—in the present American atmosphere, especially immigrants of Hispanic, Arab, and Muslim origins, as well as native-born American Muslims.

So we encourage groups or "Tents" of the Abrahamic communities that may arise in any American community, after going through the processes we have suggested of learning to understand and trust each other, and celebrating together each other's holy seasons, to choose some issue and some level of shared social action to change public policy—whatever level of action and focus of change meets their own situation.

NOTES

Part I: Judaism, Justice, and American Life

Can Social Justice Save the American Jewish Soul?

1. Comment of Rabbi Joseph Soloveitchik, in Abraham Besdin, *Man of Faith in the Modern World* (Hoboken, NJ: KTAV, 1989), 67–69.
2. *Ma'amrei HaReAYaH* *("Teachings of Rav Kook")*, p. 252, cited in Rav Yehuda Amital, "The Significance of Rav Kook's Teaching for Our Generation," in *The World of Rav Kook's Thought*, ed. Benjamin Ish-Shalom and Shalom Rosenberg (New York: Avi Chai Foundation, 1991), 434.
3. For a fuller discussion of "secular" Jewish identity, see S.M. Lipset and E. Raab, *Jews and the New American Scene* (Cambridge, MA: Harvard University Press, 1995), 66, 175.
4. In one section, the National Jewish Population Study breaks down the numbers as follows: 28 percent highly affiliated, 28 percent moderately affiliated, and 44 percent unaffiliated. However, these numbers were based exclusively on memberships in JCCs, synagogues, or other Jewish organizations. In another section, under "Jewish Connections," the same survey revealed more than 70 percent observing Hanukkah, 67 percent observing Passover, and 65 percent reading Jewish content books and magazines. In other words, if the criterion is not rigidly defined as just dues-paying membership, a significant portion of the category that the study labels "unaffiliated" is better classified as "potentially affiliated." That is how I arrive at these rough estimates.
5. "One of" because I believe that there are three elements to a renaissance Jewish agenda that has a chance to attract young and marginally affiliated Jews, the other two being spirituality and serious Jewish learning. My book, *Finding a Spiritual Home: How a New Generation of Jews Can Transform the American Synagogue* (Woodstock, VT: Jewish Lights, 2000), makes the case for spirituality. The case for how the new Jewish agenda needs to replace the older, defense/survival agenda can be found in my article, "Hold the Eulogy: Jewish Renaissance on the Rise," in *Conservative Judaism*, no. 56 (2004).
6. The study, "American Jews and Their Social Justice Involvement: Evidence from a National Survey," was released in 2000 and used to launch Amos, which got some initial foundation support and functioned for a few years with a board and small staff. But the organization struggled to define its mission and find its niche in the American Jewish community and folded after the initial grants expired. Interviews

with Heather Booth, November 19, 2004, and Leonard Fein, September 24, 2004. It should be noted that the study's findings about the centrality of social justice to Jewish identity were consistent with findings of a major study twenty-five years earlier of the Jews of "Lakeville." See Marshall Sklare and Joseph Greenbaum, *Jewish Identity on the Suburban Frontier* (Chicago: University of Chicago Press, 1979), ch. 3.

7. Ari Lipman, "From Woodrow Avenue to Woodrow Avenue: The Path of an Organizer and a Jewish Community," *Reconstructionist*, vol. 68, no. 1 (Fall 2003), 24–32.

8. Joseph Soloveitchik, *Fate and Destiny: From the Holocaust to the State of Israel* (Hoboken, NJ: KTAV, 1992), 57–60. I am indebted to Barry Shrage for suggesting this excerpt.

What Does Tikkun Olam *Actually Mean?*

1. For more on the idea of *tikkun olam*, see: Elliot N. Dorff, *The Way Into* Tikkun Olam *(Repairing the World)*, (Woodstock, VT: Jewish Lights, 2005), and Gilbert S. Rosenthal, "*Tikkun Ha-Olam*: The Metamorphosis of a Concept," *The Journal of Religion* 85.2 (2005): 214–40.

2. M. *Gittin* 4:2–7, 9; 5:3; 9:4; M. *Eduyot* 1:13. See also T. *Ketubot* 12:2; T. *Gittin* 3:5, 7–9; 6:9, 20; T. *Bava Batra* 6:20–21.

3. B. *Gittin* 45a.

Divine Limitation and Human Responsibility

1. To learn more about the Lost Boys of Sudan, see Alphonsian Deng, Benson Deng, and Benjamin Ajak, with Judy A. Bernstein, *They Poured Fire on Us from the Sky: The True Story of Three Lost Boys from Sudan* (New York: Public Affairs, 2005).

2. See Martin Buber, *Tales of the Hasidim: The Early Masters*, translated by Olga Marx (New York: Schocken Books, 1991 [1947]); and Elie Wiesel, *Souls on Fire: Portraits and Legends of Hasidic Masters* (New York: Simon & Schuster, 1982).

3. The texts of the *Kedushat Levi* were originally delivered as Yiddish sermons—the spoken language of the Jews of Eastern Europe, but were written in Hebrew—the sacred language of the Jewish tradition. This translation is my own.

4. Interestingly, Levi Yitzhak makes no comment about the erotic nature of his imagery—God disrobing at the Sea—despite the fact that the midrashic text he quotes does speak of God and Israel as lovers in the continuation of the teaching.

5. For more information on the mystical concept of *tsimtsum*, see Arthur Green, *These Are the Words: A Vocabulary of Jewish Spiritual Life* (Woodstock, VT: Jewish Lights, 2000), 35–36.

6. Though I find this text meaningful, I am aware that its strong male and militaristic imagery may be an obstacle for some readers. For a detailed discussion of this issue, see Judith Plaskow, *Standing Again at Sinai: Judaism from a Feminist Perspective* (New York: Harper & Row, 1990), 121–170.

7. Theodicy ("God's justice," Greek) is the attempt to reconcile experiences of evil and suffering with belief in a benevolent, just, and omnipotent Deity.

8. David J. Wolpe, *The Healer of Shattered Hearts: A Jewish View of God* (New York: Henry Holt, 1990), 151.

9. Versions of this story or complementary tales about Levi Yitzhak's spiritual audacity are recorded in many sources, including in Wolpe's book, 154–155.

10. For a helpful introduction to Jewish theology, including the issue of theodicy, see Neil Gillman, *The Way Into Encountering God in Judaism* (Woodstock, VT: Jewish Lights, 2000).

Preaching What I Practice

1. Organizing is the work of using "people-power" to motivate decision-makers to act justly. "Grassroots organizing" involves mobilizing regular people, often from traditionally disadvantaged groups, to build the necessary power to shape their lives and the lives of others. "Jewish organizing" harnesses the power of the Jewish community and Jewish tradition to strengthen and inspire organizing work.

2. To learn more about Mothers for Justice, please visit www.ccahelping.org.

The Legacy of Abraham Joshua Heschel

1. John Rawls, *A Theory of Justice* (Oxford University Press, 1999), Passim.

2. Abraham Joshua Heschel, "Existence and Celebration," in *Moral Grandeur and Spiritual Audacity*, ed. Susannah Heschel (New York: Farrar, Straus and Giroux, 1997), 31.

3. You can read more about the Global Marshall Plan—and my answers to the standard objections to it—in my book *The Left Hand of God: Healing America's Political and Spiritual Crisis* (New York: Harper SanFrancisco, 2007).

Religious Leadership and Politics

1. See for example the chapters on social justice in *Life Is with People* (Madison, CT: International Universities Press, 2006), Mark Zborowski's evocative description of the shtetl and Jewish communal life in the pre-Holocaust era.

2. See for example Marc Saperstein's *Jewish Preaching in Times of War, 1800–2001* (Oxford, UK: Littman Library of Jewish Civilization, 2007).

3. Most seminaries are improving, and some do better than others. The heads of the three major seminaries all have long-standing commitments in this area. Richard Joel built the Tzedek Hillel program in recognition of the importance of social justice in shaping Jewish identity. Arnie Eisen has written extensively in his books on this dynamic. David Ellenson has been courageously outspoken on a number of social justice issues. The new Davidson Chair in Social Justice at HUC–JIR will greatly expand such courses and training. The Reconstructionist Rabbinical College has worked to integrate these themes into its curriculum and several of the

newer seminaries/yeshivot—for example, American Jewish University, Yeshivat Chovevei Torah, and Boston's Hebrew College—have made a greater effort to integrate these themes and skills into the general curriculum.

Part II: Renewing Creation

Rereading Genesis

1. Lynn White, "The Historical Roots of Our Ecological Crisis," in *Science* 155, (10 March 1967).

2. Wendell Berry, environmental writer and farmer, appalled by this anti-environmental reading of Genesis, demanded, "How, for example, would one arrange to 'replenish the earth' if 'subdue' means, as alleged, 'conquer' or 'defeat' or 'destroy'?" Berry contends: "The ecological teaching of the Bible is simply inescapable: God made the world because He wanted it made. He thinks the world is good and He loves it. It is His world; He has never relinquished title to it. If God loves the world, then how might any person of faith be excused for not loving it or justified in destroying it?" Wendell Berry, *What Are People For?* (San Francisco: North Point Press, 1990), 99.

3. The historical context is this: in all the biblical commentaries over the last 2,000 years, the Rabbis rarely even mentioned dominion, undoubtedly because Jews rarely "owned" their own land for most of history, and consequently were not in a position to dominate nature. What little the Rabbis did say about dominion—most rabbinic commentary focuses on the "be fruitful" half of the verse—was framed in the context of governance of nature, never control. They compared humanity's dominion of nature on the sixth day to God's governance of the luminaries on the fourth day. Humanity's charge is to preserve the order and integrity of Creation, maintaining all the diverse kinds of organisms. The prototype of dominion was Adam's stewardship of the Garden of Eden (Gen. 2:15).

4. Lewis Hyde. *The Gift: Imagination and the Erotic Life of Property.* Vintage, 1983.

5. Aviva Zornberg, *The Beginning of Desire* (Philadelphia: Jewish Publication Society, 1995).

6. Rashi, *Commentary on Genesis* 1:26.

7. Provocative verses in the Bible have generated thousands of years of rabbinic debate. But, other than the comment by Rashi, the Rabbis are, by and large, silent on the question of "dominion" and "mastery of the earth." Since, throughout history, Jews were rarely allowed to own land, the rabbis undoubtedly found the idea of mastering the earth and the creatures irrelevant to their circumstances.

8. Rav Saadia Gaon, Commentary on Genesis 1:26. The Christian theologian Claus Westermann highlights the unfolding development of a distinctively human civilization replete with technological discovery and artistic refinement. Claus Westermann, *Creation* (Philadelphia: Fortress Press, 1976).

Judaism, Oil, and Renewable Energy

1. Press release of May 10, 2006, cosigned by fifty-seven NGOs, including Amazon Watch and Amazon Alliance, addressed to the president of Colombia. It can be found on the Web at www.amazonwatch.org/newsroom/view_news.php?id+1253.
2. There are many sources on the U'wa conflict, almost all biased toward one side or another. This is mainly drawn from a paper titled "Environment, Indians, and Oil" by Theodore Macdonald, published in *ReVista: Harvard Review of Latin America*, Fall 1998. Macdonald's aim was to help oil companies avoid such difficulties in the future, so although it leans toward the oil companies, it is detailed and candid in its descriptions. Another good source, on the U'wa side, is a news story from March 29, 1999, by Yadira Ferrer, titled "U'wa—Caught in the Crossfire," published online by The Latin American Committee of New Zealand and available on the Web at www.converge.org.nz/.ac/articles/news990506a.htm.
3. "Gas Flaring in Nigeria: A Human Rights, Environmental and Economic Monstrosity." A report by Environmental Rights Action/Friends of the Earth Nigeria and The Climate Justice Program. Amsterdam, The Netherlands. June 2005. 9.
4. Ibid.

Part III: The Temple of the Spirit

Redemption for Radicals

1. Saul Alinksy, *Reveille for Radicals* (New York: Vintage Books, 1989), 15.

The Blood of Our Neighbors

1. *U.S. Census Bureau News*, 8/29/06 press release.
2. Ibid, 9/28/2000 press release.
3. "Most Support U.S. Guarantee of Health Plans," *New York Times*, 3/2/07, p. 1.
4. http://jspot.org/?p=1355. Out of 8,600 Jews surveyed, 87 percent felt that health care was a key national priority, more than any other issue listed.
5. Deuteronomy 21:7.
6. Mishnah *Sotah* 9:6.
7. Drs. S. Woolhandler, Terry Campbell, and D. Himmelstein, "Costs of Health Care Administration in the United States and Canada," *New England Journal of Medicine* 349 (21 August 2003): 768–775.
8. Actual names are changed, to protect privacy.
9. www.highmark.com
10. Scholars now believe this famous oath, often recited by new medical graduates, may actually have been written by Marcus Herz, a German physician to Moses Mendelssohn. Whoever wrote it, it reflects Jewish values.
11. *Mishneh Torah, Sefer Hamada* IV:23.
12. Americans are in less agreement about whether the government should give affordable health care to noncitizens, especially undocumented immigrant workers. From

a Jewish perspective, we believe that the repeated commandments to have one law for the citizen and the stranger compel us to seek quality care for citizens and noncitizens alike.

The Global AIDS Crisis

1. UNAIDS "2006 Report on the Global AIDS Epidemic," abstract.
2. Laurie Garret, "The Challenge of Global Health," in *Foreign Affairs*, February 2007.
3. "Is Uganda's HIV prevention success story 'unravelling'?", Michael Marco and Edwin J. Bernard, 22 August 2006, www.aidsmap.com/en/news/E7A3F648-945A-405D-BF00-89BA7E7FDCDF.asp.
4. Moses ben Maimonides, *Hilckot Rotzeach V'shmirat Hanefesh* 1:14.
5. "Missing the Target," International Treatment Preparedness Coalition (ITPC), 28 November 2006, www.aidstreatmentaccess.org.

A Jewish View of Embryonic Stem Cell Research

1. For more on these and other fundamental assumptions of Jewish medical ethics, and for the Jewish sources that express these convictions, see Elliot N. Dorff, *Matters of Life and Death: A Jewish Approach to Modern Medical Ethics* (Philadelphia: Jewish Publication Society, 1998), chapter 2.
2. Genesis 2:15.
3. National Institutes of Health, *Stem Cells: A Primer*, May 2000, pp. 1–2. This material was originally published online at www.nih.gov/news/stemcell/primer.htm. The National Institutes of Health has since removed the link, but the material can be accessed at Spanish, German, and other sites. A much shorter description is now available at stemcells.nih.gov/info/faqs.asp.
4. "Simply water": B. *Yevamot* 69b. Rabbi Immanuel Jakobovits notes that "forty days" in Talmudic terms may mean just under two months in our modern way of calculating gestation, since the Rabbis counted from the time of the first missed menstrual flow while we count from the time of conception, approximately two weeks earlier. See Immanuel Jakobovits, *Jewish Medical Ethics* (New York: Bloch, 1959, 1975), 275. The fetus after the forty-first day is described as being "like the thigh of its mother" in B. *Hullin* 58a, where the status of the fetus is a dispute between Rabbi Eliezer and Rabbi Joshua; B. *Sanhedrin* 80b, where the position that the fetus is the thigh of its mother is just assumed; and elsewhere (e.g., B. *Gittin* 23b; B. *Bava Kamma* 78b).
5. *Proceedings of the Committee on Jewish Law and Standards of the Conservative Movement, 1980–1985* (New York: Rabbinical Assembly, 1988), 37, with supporting papers for that stance on pp. 3–35.
6. Robert Spirtas, Steven C. Kaufman, and Nancy J. Alexander, "Fertility Drugs and Ovarian Cancer: Red Alert or Red Herring?" in *Fertility and Sterility* 59:2 (February 1993), 291–293. The 1988 congressional report also stated that a num-

ber of other possible complications are caused by commonly used drugs to stimulate the ovaries, including early pregnancy loss, multiple gestations, ectopic pregnancies, headache, hair loss, pleuropulmonary fibrosis, increased blood viscosity and hypertension, stroke, and myocardial infarction; see U.S. Congress, Office of Technology Assessment, *Infertility: Medical and Social Choices*, OTA-BA-358 (Washington, D.C.: U.S. Government Printing Office, 1988), 128–129. The demonstrated risks are not so great as to make such stimulation unwise for a woman who needs to do this to overcome her own infertility or even to donate eggs once or twice to infertile couples, but they are sufficient to demand that caution be taken and that the number of eggs donated be limited. Here, where the eggs will be used not for producing a child but for medical research, undertaking such risks seems even less warranted.

7. Dorff, *Matters of Life and Death*, 106–107.

8. *Hastings Center Report* 29:2 (March-April 1999), 30–48; 36:1 (January–February 2006), 16–33.

9. For more on Judaism's view on communal responsibilities in the distribution of health care, see Elliot N. Dorff and Aaron L. Mackler, "Responsibilities for the Provision of Health Care," in *Life and Death Responsibilities in Jewish Biomedical Ethics,* ed. Aaron L. Mackler (New York: The Jewish Theological Seminary of America, 2000), 479–505, and Dorff, *Matters of Life and Death*, chapter 12.

10. See Stephen J. Gould, *The Mismeasure of Man* (New York: W. W. Norton & Company, 1996), and George J. Annas and Michael A. Grodin, *The Nazi Doctors and the Nuremberg Code: Human Rights in Human Experimentation* (New York: Oxford, 1992).

11. For a thorough discussion of this blessing and concept in Jewish tradition, see Carl Astor, "... *Who Makes People Different": Jewish Perspectives on the Disabled* (New York: United Synagogue of America, 1985).

The Brownsville Legacy

1. Margaret Sanger, *Birth Control Review*, April 1918. In the *Margaret Sanger Papers*, Smith Collection, Reel S70.

2. Fertility was actually lower among Jews than other immigrant groups, suggesting that Jewish women practiced some form of birth control, but these means remained insufficient.

3. Sanger, *Birth Control Review*, April 1918. In the *Margaret Sanger Papers*, Smith Coll., Reel S70.

4. Margaret Sanger, *Margaret Sanger: An Autobiography* (New York: W. W. Norton and Co. 1938), 214.

5. Though Sanger reached out to the Italian immigrant community as well as to the Jewish immigrant community, Italians were not as receptive to the birth control movement due to cultural and religious factors.

6. Sanger, *Birth Control Review*, April 1917.

7. Americans for UNFPA, "Women's Health," www.americansforunfpa.org/NetCommunity/Page.aspx?&pid=223&srcid=223 (accessed May 9, 2007).

8. Americans for UNFPA, "UNFPA: Promoting the Human Rights of Women," www.americansforunfpa.org/NetCommunity/Document.Doc?&id=6 (accessed May 9, 2007).

9. Save the Children, "State of the World's Mothers 2002: Mothers & Children in War & Conflict," May 2002.

10. Until.org, "Vital Statistics," www.until.org/statistics.shtml (accessed May 9, 2007).

11. Rachel Biale, *Women and Jewish Law* (New York: Schocken Books, 1984), 198–218.

12. David M. Feldman, "This Matter of Abortion," in *Contemporary Jewish Ethics and Morality: A Reader*, eds. Elliot N. Dorff and Louis E. Newman (New York: Oxford University Press, 1995), 383–384.

13. Mishnah *Ohalot* 7:6 states, "If a woman has [life-threatening] difficulty in childbirth, one dismembers the embryo within her, limb by limb, because her life takes precedence over its life. However, once its head (or its "greater part") has emerged, it may not be touched, for we do not set aside one life for another."

14. Including abortion for reasons of maternal mental health, as well as physical health. See Feldman, "This Matter of Abortion," 389.

15. Sanger, *Autobiography*, 413–414.

Looking Inward

1. Abuse is an ongoing pattern of power and control in a relationship, where one person systematically controls the other—through fear, intimidation, or threats. Abusers use verbal and emotional violence (insults, name calling, humiliation, isolation from friends/family/community, making someone feel bad about who she is, and other forms of psychological manipulation). The abuser may also use financial, sexual, or physical means of controlling his partner. Physical violence can include hitting, choking, grabbing, shaking, confining, throwing things, stalking, destroying personal property, sexual coercion, or the abuser's threats to harm himself, his partner, family members, or pets. Because studies show that in adult heterosexual relationships 95 percent of the victims are women, I cite women as my primary example of abused partners.

2. National Coalition Against Domestic Violence: www.ncadv.org; Family Violence Prevention Fund: www.endabuse.org.

3. Forty-four percent of cities surveyed named domestic violence as the primary cause of homelessness (The U.S. Conference of Mayors, 1999, "A Status Report on Hunger and Homelessness in America's Cities," p. 39). On average, 50 percent of homeless women and children are homeless due to domestic violence (studies by the Ford Foundation, 1990; ACLU Women's Rights Project, "Domestic Violence and Homelessness," 2004).

4. M. Straus, R. Gelles, and C. Smith, *Physical Violence in American Families: Risk Factors and Adaptations to Violence in 8,145 Families*, 1990. The U.S. Advisory Board on Child Abuse and Neglect states that 50 percent of men who assault their partners also frequently assault their children; and suggests that domestic violence may be the single major precursor to child abuse and neglect fatalities in this country. (*A Nation's Shame: Fatal child abuse and neglect in the United States: Fifth report*. Department of Health and Human Services, Administration for Children and Families, 1995.)

5. Examples include: "A wife should never raise her voice against her husband, but should remain silent even if he beats her—as chaste women do" (Yehudai Gaon, 8th c; Pumbedita); "A husband may strike his wife if she transgresses the law ... he can only beat her if she doesn't heed his warning" (Solomon Luria, 16th c); *Yam Shel Shlomo* on *Bava Kamma*, 20b#9); "A man who strikes his wife commits a sin, just as if he were to strike anyone else. If he does this often, the court may punish him, excommunicate him ... but if she is the cause of it ... then he is permitted to beat her" (Rabbi Moses Isserles, *Darkei Moshe*, 16th c.); "A Jew must honor his wife more than he honors himself. If one strikes one's wife, one should be punished more severely than for striking another person. For one is enjoined to honor one's wife, but is not enjoined to honor the other person" (Rabbi Meir of Rotenberg, 13th c, *Even haEzer* 297); "A man is forbidden to force his wife to have sex" (Talmud, B. *Eruvin* 100b); "A man is forbidden to beat his wife, and is moreover liable for any injury caused by him. If he is in the habit of beating her continually or insulting her in public, he should be forced to divorce her" (R. Israel of Krems, 15th c). For comprehensive citations of text and responsae that discuss spouse abuse and other violence against women, see also Diane Gardsbane, *Embracing Justice: A Resource Guide for Rabbis on Domestic Abuse* (Washington, D.C.: Jewish Women International, 2002); Naomi Graetz, *Silence Is Deadly: Judaism Confronts Wifebeating* (Latham, MD: Jason Aronson Press, 1998); and *A Portrait of Domestic Abuse in the Jewish Community: Key Findings from the National & Chicagoland Needs Assessments* (Jewish Women International, Washington D.C., 2004).

6. Organizations include the Family Violence Project of Jewish Family Service in Los Angeles, SHALVA (Shelter and Legal Advocacy for Victims of Abuse) in Chicago, the first kosher kitchen in a battered women's shelter (Rockland Family Shelter, NY) and Shalom Bayit in San Francisco. Leigh Hoffheimer and Rabbi Drorah O'Donnell Setel of Seattle wrote the first training curriculum on anti-Semitism and Jewish awareness/outreach for battered women's shelters.

7. For examples of these kinds of educational materials see *Love Shouldn't Hurt* (San Francisco: Shalom Bayit, 2007) and *When Push Comes to Shove: It's No Longer Love* (Washington DC: Jewish Women International, 2005).

Part IV: The Yoke of Oppression

Hearing the Voice of the Poor

1. The latter is a recent development. Only in the past has the California Supreme Court ruled that if the city does not have enough places to shelter the homeless population, then the latter cannot be fined and punished for vagrancy. Homelessness, the court declared, is not an action; it is a situation.

2. We can also infer from the use of the term *they coerce* rather than "it is an obligation" or some other form of the verb *chayav* that this is not an absolute obligation but is dependent on the specific circumstances whereby the other residents want to have a gate and a gatehouse.

3. We are also decamping to Sassanian Persia.

4. Rashi (1040–1105) is an acronym that means either Rabbenu Shlomo Yitzchaki or Rabbenu SheYichyeh.

5. Seemingly of the generation of the students of Shmuel, one of the two founders of the academies in Babylon in the fourth century. He is quoted as disagreeing with Shmuel, which means that at least for the transmitters of those teachings Rav Anan is considered to have been as much of an authority as Shmuel.

6. Although, in the end, after he refused to hear the case, he did accept the gift *gratis*.

7. The reason that Elijah merits this and the other tasks ascribed to him by the Sages is that a close reading of II Kings 2 can yield the fact that Elijah did not die, he merely went up by a whirlwind into heaven (11). Thus Elijah is available to return and perform specific functions on earth—such as dropping by our seders on Passover eve.

8. Which is actually called the Book of Redemption by medieval Jewish commentators.

9. *Tza'ak* and *za'ak* are the same thing in biblical Hebrew.

10. Mike Davis. *Ecology of Fear: Los Angeles and the Imagination of Disaster.* Vintage, 1999.

A Jewish Vision for Economic Justice

1. Rashbam (Rabbi Shmuel ben Meir, 1085–1158), for example, suggests that this prophecy cannot come true, as there are no fully righteous people who never sin.

2. *Breishit Rabbah* 9:7.

3. Mishnah Torah, *Matanot Aniyim* 10:7.

4. Tosefta, *Bava Metzia* 11:23.

5. See, for example, Rashba (Rabbi Shlomo ben Aderet, 1235–1310) *She'elot u'Teshuvot* 4:185; Rambam (Rabbi Moshe ben Maimon, 1135–1204) Mishnah Torah, *Hilkhot Mekhira* 14:10; and Joseph Caro (1488–1575), *Shulchan Arukh, Hoshen Mishpat* 231:28.

6. Warhaftig, *Dinei Avodah b'Mishpat ha'Ivri*, vol. 1, p. 2.

7. Babylonian Talmud, *Bava Kamma* 117b. This is a gloss on Leviticus 25:55, "For the Children of Israel are my servants."

8. Babylonian Talmud, *Bava Metzia* 86b, cf. Maimonides, Mishnah Torah, *Hilkhot Schirut* 9:4; *Shulchan Arukh. Hoshen Mishpat* 333:3.

9. The law assumes a situation in which workers are hired to harvest crops. If the workers quit, then the season's crop will be lost. In nonagricultural industries, it may be more difficult to prove that economic loss is irreparable. A business may lose profit one day, but regain these profits the next day. It is primarily in agriculture that taking a day off from work may destroy an entire year's profit.

Why a Labor Movement Matters

1. There are poor Jews, of course, often invisible to most of us. See, for example, Naomi Levine and Martin Hochbaum, *Poor Jews: An American Awakening* (New Brunswick, NJ: Transaction, 1974), or the 2004 Report on Jewish Poverty, commissioned by the UJA Federation of New York and that city's Metropolitan Council on Jewish Poverty, which estimated that 20 percent of New York's Jewish residents live in poverty or close to poverty guidelines set forth in the study; the report's data apparently suggested that Jewish poverty in New York has risen during the past two decades and will continue to rise. See also Benjamin Small, "Jewish Poverty: In Our Own Backyard," in *PresenTense*, April 10, 2006. New York is not alone: also in 2004, the Jewish Federation of Greater Los Angeles reported that nearly one in five local Jews earned less than $25,000 a year, with 7 percent living beneath the poverty line—see Marc Ballon, "Jewish Poor Fear Stigma of Poverty," *The Jewish Journal*, November 26, 2004.

2. The Jewish Labor Committee has a useful resource, "Readings on the American Jewish Labor Movement," available in print from their office, and online at www.jewishlabor.org.

3. Jack Jacobs, ed., *Jewish Politics in Eastern Europe: The Bund at 100* (New York: New York University Press in association with the Jewish Historical Institute in Warsaw, 2001).

4. The SEIU is the Service Employees International Union. UNITE HERE is a merger of two unions: the Union of Needletrades, Industrial and Textile Employees (UNITE) and the Hotel Employees and Restaurant Employees International Union (HERE).

5. Jill Jacobs, "Work, Workers, and the Jewish Owner," pending *teshuvah* for the Conservative Movement's Committee on Law and Standards.

6. Michael Perry, *Labor Rights in the Jewish Tradition* (New York: Jewish Labor Committee, 1993).

7. Warhaftig, *Dinei Avodah b'Mishpat ha'Ivri*, vol. 1, p. 2.

8. Quoted in Tzvi Yaron, *Mishnato shel HaRav Kook*, trans. Jill Jacobs (Jerusalem: Moreshet Press, 1986).

9. Michelle Conlin and Aaron Bernstein, "Working and Poor," *Businessweek*, May 31, 2004.

10. Bureau of Labor Statistics, *Monthly Labor Review*, 123:10 (October 2000).

11. Stephen C. Betts, *Multiple Job Research Project* (William Patterson University), unpublished research.
12. Elana Levin, "Here's to the people that brought you the weekend," *DMI blog*, October 27, 2005. www.dmiblog.com/archives/2005/10/ heres_to_the_people_that_broug.html
13. Regala Soto, Hotel Workers Rising video, www.changetowin.org/campaigns/ hotel-workers-rising.html.
14. "What Would Yeshua Wear? A Bethlehem factory produces fair trade clothing by unionizing workers," interview by Rose Marie Berger, *Sojourners Magazine*, May

And If Not Together, How?

1. "An Abbreviated Timeline of Jewish Immigration to the United States," compiled by Jenny Romaine at Jews for Racial and Economic Justice, Summer 2003.
2. National Network for Immigrant and Refugee Rights Basic Facts, www.nnirr.org/immigration/immigration_faq.html.

Gracious Giver of Wisdom

1. CBIA Education Foundation, "10 facts about K-12 Education Funding," www.cbia.com/ed/NCLB/10facts.htm.
2. Office of Speaker Nancy Pelosi, "President's Budget on Education: More of the Same Misplaced Priorities," majorityleader.house.gov/docUploads/ BushBudgetEducation%2Epdf?CFID=9815534&CFTOKEN=35072074 (accessed February 27, 2007).
3. Jennifer Cheeseman Day and Eric C. Newburger, "The Big Payoff: Educational Attainment and Synthetic Estimates of Work-Life Earnings," U.S. Census Bureau, July 2002, www.census.gov/prod/2002pubs/p23-210.pdf.
4. The Education Trust, "Fact Sheet: Standards," July 27, 2007, www2 .edtrust.org/NR/rdonlyres/82FA87DD-62D2-415E-8426-32FD14CF2EF8/0/ fact-sheetrev4.pdf.
5. U.S. Department of Education, "Reducing Class Size, What Do We Know?" March 1999, www.ed.gov/pubs/ReducingClass/Class_size.html#research.
6. Harold O. Levy, "NYC Public Schools Chancellor's 60-Day Report," March 15, 2000.
7. U.S. Department of Education, "Survival Guide for New Teachers," last modified September 14, 2007. www.ed.gov/teachers/become/about/survivalguide/ message.html.
8. U.S. Department of Education, "Mapping 2005 State Proficiency Standards onto the NAEP Scales: Research and Development Report," nces.ed.gov/nationsreportcard/ pdf/studies/2007482.pdf.
9. National Education Association, "Building Tests to Support Instruction and Accountability: A Guide for Policymakers," www.nea.org/accountability/ buildingtests.html

10. National Education Association, "NEA's Top Legislative Priorities for ESEA* [NCLB]," March 21, 2007, www.nea.org/esea/legpriorities.html.
11. U.S. Department of Education, "Preliminary Overview of Programs and Changes Included in the No Child Left Behind Act of 2001," www.ed.gov/nclb/overview/intro/progsum/sum_pg6.html.

The Possibility of Change

1. The *New York Times*, March 5, 1995.
2. An important source of writing on restorative justice has come from Christian thinkers. See Pierre Allard, and Wayne Northey. *Christianity: The Rediscovery of Restorative Justice*, ed. Harold Coward. (Albany, NY: State University of New York Press, 2001).
3. Babylonian Talmud, *Bava Kamma* 84a.
4. Babylonian Talmud, *Bava Kamma* 4a and 5b.
5. See especially Jerusalem Talmud, *Ta'anit* 4:2.
6. *Genesis Rabbah* 12:15.
7. Babylonian Talmud, *Hagigah* 15a.
8. See Babylonian Talmud, *Brakhot* 17a and Rabbeinu Yonah of Geronah, *Sha'arei Teshuvah*, especially 2:26.
9. He later states this explicitly: "Free will is given to all people. If one wants to turn himself to the path of goodness and to be a righteous person, he has the freedom to do so. And if one wants to turn himself to the path of evil, and be a wicked person, he has the freedom to do so." *Mishneh Torah* (hereafter M.T.), *Hilkhot Teshuvah* 5:1.
10. M.T., *Hilkhot Teshuvah* 2:9.
11. In the case of a woman who is raped, for example, the law demands that the perpetrator make monetary compensation to the victim for the indignity she suffered, for her blemish, for the statutory fine, and for her physical pain. Babylonian Talmud, *Ketubbot* 39a.
12. M.T., *Hilkhot Teshuvah* 2:9. See also Babylonian Talmud, *Bava Kamma* 92a. See M.T. *Hilkhot Teshuvah* 1:1.
13. M.T., *Hilkhot Teshuvah* 2:1 42 .
14. See Babylonian Talmud, *Arakhin* 16b, for Rabbinic rules of rebuke.
15. See Rabbeiun Yonah of Gerona, *Sha'arei Teshuvah*, 2:10. *Genesis Rabbah* 54.
16. *Genesis Rabbah* 54.
17. M.T., *Hilkhot Teshuvah* 2:9. In this case, the victim is the offender's teacher, and therefore merits unusual efforts at redress.
18. Maimonides states that a person should be quick to pardon and slow to anger: "When the one who wronged him asks for forgiveness, he should grant him forgiveness with a complete heart and a willing spirit. Even if he [the offender] distressed and wronged him very much, he [the victim] should not seek revenge or bear a grudge" (M.T. *Hilkhot Teshuvah* 2:9).

19. Elliot Dorff, "Elements of Forgiveness: A Jewish Approach," in *Dimensions of Forgiveness: Psychological Research and Theological Perspectives*, ed. Everett L. Worthington Jr. (Philadelphia: Templeton Foundation Press, 1998).

20. Babylonian Talmud, *Kiddushin* 40b. While this is the case, one must not deliberately transgress his whole life, knowing that he can ultimately do *teshuvah* and be forgiven before he dies. The Mishnah teaches: "One who says, 'I will sin and I will return, I will sin and I will return' does not have the opportunity to do *teshuvah*" (*Mishnah Yoma* 8:9). Similarly, Rabbeinu Yonah writes: "When one grows old and the strength of his desire [to sin] is weakened, he does not receive the reward for his *teshuvah* that [he would have received had he done *teshuvah*] with the intention of perfecting his heart, in his youth" (*Sha'arei Teshuvah* 2:33). See also Babylonian Talmud, *Avodah Zarah* 19a.

21. Mishnah, *Bava Metzia* 4:10.

22. Rabbi Elliot Dorff writes: "It is undoubtedly right and proper, for example, for pedophiles to remove themselves from children as much as possible. They will never be able to effect the full return as a result, but they can surely accomplish a great measure of return, and it is more important to protect innocent children from abuse than to enable pedophiles to achieve full return.... The community can and should limit [an offender's return] for its own protection." Dorff, "Elements of Forgiveness," 44–45.

23. M.T. *Hilkhot Teshuvah* 7:4.

24. PJA runs this program in collaboration with the Centinela Youth Service's (CYS) Victim-Offender Restitution Services. CYS and PJA provide mediation training for PJA volunteers; in exchange, each PJA mediator agrees to participate in twelve mediations involving juvenile offenders under the auspices of CYS's case management service over the course of one year.

25. The American judicial system defines crime as a violation of laws, with the state— not the individual—as victim. The individual actually harmed is treated almost as a spectator, and the many needs of that individual are often ignored. The state's response is the administration of punishment to the offender for violating the law. Restitution to victims, which occurs rarely, is an "add-on" and is not considered essential to the justice process.

Part V: *Klal Yisrael*

The Significance of Sex

1. Ken Wilber, *Integral Spirituality: A Startling New Role for Religion in the Modern and Postmodern World* (Boston: Shambhala Publications, 2006), Passim.

Beyond Same-Sex Marriage

1. Martha Ackelsberg and Judith Plaskow, "Why We're Not Getting Married," www.nyblade.com/2004/6-4/viewpoint/opinion/why.cfm.

2. This article was written before the opinion was handed down in the New Jersey same-sex case, *Lewis v. Harris*. While the outcome of that case was generally more favorable to gay and lesbian rights, the issues raised were similar to those discussed here.

3. *Hernandez v. Robles*, J. Graffeo concurring and quoting the Supreme Court's *Skinner* decision, 7.

4. Ibid., 20 and 21.

5. *Hernandez v. Robles*, Chief Judge Kaye dissenting, 9 and 19.

6. Ibid., 22.

7. Dan Savage, "Same-Sex Marriage Wins by Losing," *New York Times*, July 30, 2006, op-ed page.

8. Jeffrey Weeks, *Sexuality and Its Discontents: Meanings, Myths, and Modern Sexualities* (London and New York: Routledge, 1985), 213.

9. Evelyn Lehrer, "Patterns of Education and Entry into First Union Among American Jewish Women," in *Contemporary Jewry* 20 (1999): 106, 110–14. Cf. Lehrer's "Religion as a Determinant of Entry into Cohabitation and Marriage," in *The Ties That Bind: Perspectives on Marriage and Cohabitation*, ed. Linda Waite (New York: Aldine de Gruyter, 2000), 227–52. Sidney Goldstein, "Profile of American Jewry: Insights from the 1990 National Jewish Population Survey," in *American Jewish Yearbook* 92 (1992), 117.

10. We are aware that all of the non-Orthodox denominations have produced documents on sexual ethics in recent years, but it is striking that each arose from a consideration of homosexuality, rather than from an impulse to address changing sexual ethics more broadly.

11. See Judith Plaskow, "Authority, Resistance, and Transformation: Jewish Feminist Reflections on Good Sex," in *The Coming of Lilith: Essays on Feminism, Judaism, and Sexual Ethics, 1972–2003* (Boston: Beacon Press, 2005), 196–201.

12. Rachel Adler, *Engendering Judaism: An Inclusive Theology and Ethics* (Philadelphia and Jerusalem: The Jewish Publication Society, 1998), ch. 5, and Howard Eilberg-Schwartz, *The Savage in Judaism: An Anthropology of Israelite Religion and Ancient Judaism* (Bloomington and Indianapolis: Indiana University Press, 1990), 229–34.

13. Rabbi Lisa Edwards, "A Simple Matter of Justice" (sermon, April 29, 1993).

14. These examples were taken from "Beyond Same-Sex Marriage: A New Strategic Vision for All Our Families and Relationships," July 30, 2006, www.indybay.org/newsitems/2006/07/30/18293090.php.

15. See Martha Ackelsberg, "Jewish Family Ethics in a Post-halakhic Age," in *Imagining the Jewish Future: Essays and Responses*, ed. David A. Teutsch (Albany, New York: State University of New York Press, 1992), 149–64.

16. Stephen M. Cohen, Shifra Bronznick, Didi Goldenhar, Sherry Israel, and Shaul Kelner, "Creating Gender Equity and Organizational Effectiveness in the Jewish

Federation System: A Research-and-Action Project" (New York: Advancing Women Professionals and the Jewish Community, 2004), 12–13, 21.

17. Ackelsberg, "Jewish Family Ethics."

Priority Lists

1. I've written about this in my essay "On Being a Rabbi at the Margins" in *Lesbian Rabbis: The First Generation*, eds. Alpert, Elwell, and Idelson (New Brunswick, NJ: Rutgers University Press, 2001).

2. "Striking a Balance: Carol Lee Flinders on Spirituality, Politics, and the Spaces in Between." Interview by Danya Ruttenberg, *Bitch* magazine, no. 24, Spring 2004.

Created Beings of Our Own

1. The term *gender* has been used to denote social roles and behaviors, while the term *sex* indicates physiological differences. Both sex and gender can be complex for transgender and gender-nonconforming individuals. In recent years, theorists such as Michel Foucault and Judith Butler have pointed to the shifting nature of sex, as well as gender, across lines of history and geography. Butler and other contemporary feminists have suggested that the borders around sex have been drawn and redrawn in various times and places to meet a variety of social and cultural needs. This view posits that the sexing of our bodies, as much as the gendering of our roles, is culturally and historically construed. This contemporary feminist position is where I situate myself. I do not mean to deny that there are sexual characteristics that unite and divide bodies in every epoch, but I believe that it is impossible to say anything about sex differences that does not also encode messages about gender relations and power. For more information, see Judith Butler, *Gender Trouble: Feminism and the Subversion of Identity* (New York and London: Routledge, 1990), and Michel Foucault, *The History of Sexuality*, trans. Robert Hurley (New York: Vintage Books, 1985).

2. The *tumtum* appears 17 times in the Mishnah; 23 times in the Tosefta; 119 times in the Babylonian Talmud; 22 times in the Jerusalem Talmud; and hundreds of times in Midrash, commentaries, and Halacha. The *androgynos* appears 21 times in the Mishnah; 19 times in the Tosefta; 109 times in the Babylonian Talmud; and countless times in Midrash and Halacha.

3. For a complete list of the victims of hate crimes against gender-nonconforming individuals each year, see www.gender.org/remember/index.html.

4. For information and statistics on the impacts of transphobia and the way that it intersects with other oppressions in terms of poverty, incarceration, access to health care, employment, and other indicators, see the website of the Sylvia Rivera Law Project, www.srlp.org.

5. Pat Califia, *Sex Changes: The Politics of Transgenderism* (San Francisco: Cleis Press, 2003), 1.

6. Alice Domurat Dreger, *Hermaphrodites and the Medical Invention of Sex* (Cambridge, MA: Harvard University Press, 1998); Anne Fausto-Sterling, *Sexing the Body: Gender Politics and the Construction of Sexuality* (New York: Basic Books, 1990); Thomas Laqueur, *Making Sex: Body and Gender from the Greeks to Freud* (Cambridge, MA: Harvard University Press, 1992).

7. From a sermon at Congregation Sha'ar Zahav, San Francisco, CA, Rosh Hashanah 2006.

8. In the Tosefta and in other places, this phrase appears in the masculine form: *bria b'ifnei atzmo* (a created being of his own).

Multiracial Jewish Families

1. For further discussion of race dynamics in my family, see Marla Brettschneider, *The Family Flamboyant: Race Politics, Queer Families, Jewish Lives* (New York: SUNY Press, 2006).

2. Diane Tobin, Gary A. Tobin, and Scott Rubin, "The Growth and Vitality of Jewish Peoplehood: Ethnic and Racial Diversity," San Francisco: Institute for Jewish & Community Research, 2005, www.jewishresearch.org/projects_growth.htm (accessed 6/18/05). See also Diane Tobin, Gary A. Tobin, and Scott Rubin, *In Every Tongue: Ethnic & Racial Diversity in the Jewish Community* (San Francisco: Institute for Jewish & Community Research, 2005).

3. Melanie Kaye/Kantrowitz, *The Issue Is Power: Essays on Women, Jews, Violence and Resistance* (San Francisco: Aunt Lute Books, 1992).

4. Karen Brodkin, *How Jews Became White Folks and What That Says About Race in America* (New Brunswick, NJ: Rutgers University Press, 1998).

Differently Abled

1. Jerome Groopman, "What's the Trouble? How Doctors Think" in *The New Yorker* (Jan. 29, 2007).

Part VI: Seeking Peace

Plotting the Middle Path to Israeli-Palestinian Peace

1. While a greater attention to this point falls outside the scope of this article, it should be noted that there was also substantial dissent among progressive American Jews about the implications of Jewish statehood. The sources of concern varied widely, and included early critiques of the displacement of Eretz Yisrael's indigenous Arab population, questions about the impact of a nationalism on Jewish culture, concern for Israel's dependence on imperialist powers to ensure its survival, and fear that Israel's existence would lead Americans to perceive American Jews as a fifth column.

2. "Young Jewish Adults in the United States Today: Harbingers of the American Jewish Community of Tomorrow?" Survey by American Jewish Committee, April 15, 2006.

3. For example, in the case of Great Britain in the pre-state era, Jews benefited from British rule only to a point, and then felt the need to rebel against it. The British gave the Zionism movement early assurances of support, but withdrew that support when it did not coincide with their interests. The divide and rule policy—between Palestinians and Israelis—emerged during that time.
4. Poll conducted by Steven M. Cohen for Ameinu in 2005. From Ha'aretz Poll: American Jews back Gaza pullout, Palestinian statehood.

Imitatio Dei *and/as Shared Space*

1. Martin Buber, "Herzl and History," in *The First Buber: Youthful Zionist Writings of Martin Buber*, ed. and trans. Gilya G. Schmidt (Syracuse: University of Syracuse Press, 1999), 154–163.
2. Buber, "Israel and the Command of the Spirit," in *A Land of Two Peoples: Martin Buber on Jews and Arabs* (Chicago: University of Chicago Press, 2005), 252–257.
3. Buber, "A Protest against Expropriation of Arab Lands," in *A Land of Two Peoples: Martin Buber on Jews and Arabs* (Chicago: University of Chicago Press, 2005), 261-262.
4. Jacob Leiner, *Haggadah shel Pesach*.
5. Buber, "Two Peoples in Palestine," in *A Land of Two Peoples*, 194, 202.
6. Buber, "Hebrew Humanism," in *Israel and the World*, 240, 243–244, 252.
7. Hilary Putnam, "Monotheism and Humanism," in *Humanity before God: Contemporary Faces of Jewish, Christian, and Islamic Ethics*, eds. W. Schweiker, M.A. Johnson, and K. Jung (Minneapolis, MN: Fortress Press, 2006), 19, 22, 30. Jonathan Sacks, *The Dignity of Difference: How to Avoid the Clash of Civilizations* (New York and London: Continuum, 2003), 1–23.
8. Buber, *On Zion: The History of an Idea* (Syracuse: Syracuse University Press, 1997), xvii.
9. Anthony Smith, "Ethnohistory and the Golden Age," in *Chosen Peoples: Sacred Sources of National Identity* (New York and Oxford: Oxford University Press, 2003), 166, 189, and Smith, "Sacred Homelands," in *Chosen Peoples*, 131, 165.
10. Buber, *On Zion*, xvii, xxii.
11. Buber, "The Land and Its Possessors," *Israel and the World*, 227–233.
12. Buber, "Zionism and Other National Concepts," xi, xii.
13. Lawrence Kaplan, "Martin Buber on the Imitation of God," in *Daat* 56 (Summer 2005): v, xxi.
14. Buber, "Religion and Ethics," in *Eclipse of God* (New York: Harper and Brothers, 1952): 97.
15. Buber, *A Land of Two Peoples*, 196, and Rashid Khalidi, *Palestinian Identity* (New York: Columbia University Press, 1998).
16. Benny Morris, *The Birth of the Palestinian Refugee Problem Revisited* (Cambridge: Cambridge University Press, 2003).

17. Buber, "A Protest Against Expropriation of Arab Lands," 261–263.
18. Buber, "On the Moral Character of Israel: A Debate with Ben-Gurion," in *A Land of Two Peoples*, 239–244.
19. Aaron David Gordon, "*Avodatenu me-atah*," cited in Mendes Flohr, "In Pursuit of Normalcy: Zionism's Ambivalence toward Israel's Election," in *Many Are Chosen: Divine Election and Western Nationalism*, eds. W. Hutchinson and H. Lehman (Minneapolis, MN: Fortress Press, 1994), 221.
20. Buber, "Two Peoples in Palestine," 199.
21. Buber, "We Must Grant the Arabs Truly Equal Rights," in *A Land of Two Peoples*, 297–299.
22. Buber, "Israel and the Command of the Spirit," in *A Land of Two Peoples*, 255.

Everything Falls Apart

1. For more information on the rosters of U.S., membership-based, Jewish peace organizations, visit the websites of groups such as Brit Tzedek (www.btvshalom.org), the Tikkun Community (www.tikkun.org), and Jewish Voice for Peace (www.jewishvoiceforpeace.org).
2. The largest of these groups, Brit Tzedek v'Shalom, reported a membership of 19,000 in 2006.
3. Cited in Leonard Fine, "Define Zionism as the Right of Return," *Forward*, May 11, 2007.
4. Rob Eshman, "Shutting Jewish Mouths," *The Jewish Journal of Los Angeles*, February 2, 2007, www.jewishjournal.com/home/preview.php?id=17222.
5. On the Media, transcript of "A Zion in the Sand," National Public Radio, February 16, 2007, onthemedia.org/transcripts/2007/02/16/02.
6. "Covering Israel: A Conversation with Arthur Neslen," *Tikkun* (January/February, 2007): 48.

Part VII: The Seventy Nations

Am I My Brother's Keeper If My Brother Lives Halfway Around the World?

1. Annie Dillard, *For the Time Being* (New York: Vintage Books, 2000), 46.
2. A.M. Rosenthal, *Thirty-Eight Witnesses* (Berkeley and Los Angeles: University of California Press, 1999).
3. www.logos.com/products/prepub/details/3048.
4. *Sanhedrin* 74a.
5. Deuteronomy 21:7.
6. Mishnah *Sotah* 9:6.
7. Ibid.
8. Rabbi Jonathan Sacks, *The Dignity of Difference* (New York: Continuum International Publishing Group, 2003), 30.

9. *Pirkei Avot* 2:19.

10. Maimonides, *Mishneh Torah, Laws of Theft* 5:1.

11. For more information on where to find fair trade goods, see www.transfairusa.org. For more information about socially responsible investing, see www.socialinvest.org.

12. www.dogwoodalliance.org/content/view/52/113/#staplevictory.

13. www.democracynow.org/article.pl?sid=04/01/23/0453233.

14. See, for example, www.cluela.org/victories.html and www.thejewishadvocate.com/this_weeks_issue/news/?content_id=2765.

15. Maimonides. *Mishneh Torah,* Laws of Gifts to the Poor 10:1.

16. Babylonian Talmud, *Gittin* 61a.

17. The Talmud seems to be making this argument out of self-interest: because it's useful to us to have peace with non-Jews, we should bury their dead and feed their poor. But Maimonides rereads this text to say that the use of the term *for the sake of peace* is meant to be read as "for the sake of Torah." Maimonides, *Mishneh Torah,* Laws of Kings 10:12.

18. Deuteronomy 22:8.

19. Maimonides, *Mishneh Torah, Laws of the Murderer and Protecting Life* 11:4.

20. Samantha Power, *A Problem from Hell: America in the Age of Genocide* (New York: HarperCollins, 2007), 377.

21. Babylonian Talmud, *Shabbat* 54b.

22. Hannah Arendt, *On Revolution* (London: Penguin Books, 1963), 89.

23. Susan Sontag, *Regarding the Pain of Others* (New York: Picador, 2004), 102.

A Jewish Response to Globalization

1. Rabbi Dr. Shimon Federbush, "*Mishpat HaMelucha BeYisrael* (*The Laws of the Kingdom in Israel*) Published by Mosad Harav Kook, Second Edition, 1973 pg 129.

2. Parts of this essay first appeared in *Sh'ma*, January 2006.

"Silence Is Akin to Assent"

1. According to the most respected medical journal in Great Britain, *The Lancet*, researchers estimate 655,000 more Iraqis (as of 2006) had died since the war began than would have occurred otherwise. G. Burnham, et al., "Mortality After the 2003 Invasion of Iraq: A Cross-Sectional Cluster Sample Survey," *Lancet* 368 (2006): 1421–28.

2. The official death toll from the World Trade Center bombing was 2,752. See www.CNN.com posting on Wednesday, October 29, 2003, www.cnn.com/2003/US/Northeast/10/29/wtc.deaths. *The Associated Press* reported 3,724 U.S. military deaths in Iraq as of August 23, 2007, as reported on Forbes.com, www.forbes.com/feeds/ap/2007/08/23/ap4050488.html. An ongoing count of U.S. military fatalities is kept at icasualties.org/oif.

3. Comments by Senator Durbin made in remarks delivered on the floor of the Senate, January 8, 2007. A transcript can be read at www.thenation.com/blogs/edcut?pid=157755.
4. Gore made these comments throughout summer 2007. See *NBC Today*, December 6, 2006, interview with Matt Lauer.
5. www.appealforredress.org.
6. Martin van Creveld, "War Clouds Gather Over the Golan," *Forward*, March 9, 2007. www.forward.com/articles/war-clouds-gather-over-the-golan.
7. Isaac Breur. "The Philosophical Foundations of Judaism and Modern Law," in Jacob S. Levinger, ed., *Concepts of Judaism* (Jerusalem, 1974), 53–81.
8. A.S. Tamares, *Kenesset Yisra'el u-millhamot ha-goyim*, 1920.

How to Split the Sea
1. CNN, Friday, October 17, 2003. Speech to the 57-nation Islamic summit.
2. This quote is from a letter published in *Rus Pravoslavnaya* newspaper (March 2, 2005). Signed by A.N. Krutov, editor of *Russiley Dom*; K. Yoi Dushenov, the editor of *Rusi Pravoslavnaya*; and 5,000 others, including nineteen members of the State Duma.
3. *Tashlich* means "you will cast away." During a special service on the first day of the Jewish New Year, Jews gather at a body of flowing water to symbolically cast their sins into the water. It marks the start of the ten days of atonement leading up to Yom Kippur, the Day of Atonement.

Reopening the Tent of Abraham
1. Muslims observe Ramadan, the month of the revelation of the Qur'an, by fasting from sunrise to sunset every day, having an *iftar* (break-fast) meal after sunset, and turning their attention to God and to works of compassion for the poor. Close to the end comes Lailat al Qadr, the Night of Power. It marks the night in which God first revealed the Qur'an to the prophet Muhammad (peace be upon him). Some Muslims spend that whole night in prayer or in reciting the Qur'an, and Lailat al Qadr is considered a good time to ask for forgiveness.

As Ramadan ends and the next month begins, there is the Break-fast Festival, Eid al-Fitr. In Morocco, for a thousand years the Jewish community has brought the Muslim community the first food for Eid al-Fitr. That tradition might be enriched in America by bringing members of the two communities together to share a celebration feast. (Conversely, Moroccan Muslims brought Jews the first bread for the night after the last day of Pesach. This "ninth day" became an add-on festival called Maimouna, or Prosperity.)

CREDITS

This page constitutes a continuation of the copyright page. Every effort has been made to trace and acknowledge copyright holders of all the material included in this book. The editors apologize for any errors or omissions that may remain and ask that any omissions be brought to their attention so that they may be corrected in future editions.

Grateful acknowledgment is given to the following authors for permission to use material:

Foreword © 2008 David Ellenson

Can Social Justice Save the American Jewish Soul? © 2008 Sidney Schwarz

What Does *Tikkun Olam* Actually Mean? © 2008 Jane Kanarek

Divine Limitation and Human Responsibility © 2008 Or N. Rose

Preaching What I Practice: The Power of Jewish Organizing © 2008 Margie Klein

The Legacy of Abraham Joshua Heschel: Jewish Spirituality and Political Transformation © 2008 Michael Lerner

Religious Leadership and Politics © 2008 David Saperstein

Rereading Genesis: Human Stewardship of the Earth © 2008 Ellen Bernstein

Jewish Textual Practice and Sustainable Culture © 2008 Natan Margalit

Wonder and Restraint: A Rabbinical Call to Environmental Action © 2008 COEJL

Toxic Waste and the Talmud © 2008 Jeremy Benstein

Judaism, Oil, and Renewable Energy © 2008 Shana Starobin

Redemption for Radicals: Jewish Congregation-Based Community Organizing © 2008 Jonah Dov Pesner

The Blood of Our Neighbors: American Health Care Reform © 2008 Sandra Fox and Martin Seltman

The Global AIDS Crisis: Caring for the Sick by Standing with the Activists © 2008 Jacob Feinspan and Julia Greenberg

A Jewish View of Embryonic Stem Cell Research © 2008 Elliot N. Dorff

The Brownsville Legacy: Judaism and Reproductive Rights © 2008 Judith Rosenbaum

Looking Inward: Domestic Violence within the Jewish Community © 2008 Naomi Tucker

Hearing the Voice of the Poor © 2008 Aryeh Cohen

A Jewish Vision for Economic Justice © 2008 Jill Jacobs

Why a Labor Movement Matters © 2008 Arieh Lebowitz

And If Not Together, How? Jews and Immigration in the United States © 2008 Dara Silverman

Gracious Giver of Wisdom: Recovering America's Great Public School System © 2008 Marla Feldman and Joshua Seth Ladon

The Possibility of Change: An Argument for Restorative Justice © 2008 Sharon Brous and Daniel Sokatch

The Significance of Sex: Social Order and Post-Mythic Religion © 2008 Jay Michaelson

Beyond Same-Sex Marriage: Social Justice and Sexual Values in Judaism © 2008 Martha Ackelsberg and Judith Plaskow

Priority Lists: A Dialogue on Judaism, Feminism, and Activism © 2008 Rebecca Alpert and Danya Ruttenberg

Created Beings of Our Own: Toward a Jewish Liberation Theology for Men, Women, and Everyone Else © 2008 Elliot Rose Kukla

Multiracial Jewish Families: A Personal and Political Approach to Justice Politics © 2008 Marla Brettschneider

Differently Abled: The Lesson of Rabbi Elazar © 2008 Abigail Uhrman

Warriors, Prophets, Peacemakers, and Disciples: A Call to Action in the Face of Religiously Inspired Violence © 2008 Melissa Weintraub

Plotting the Middle Path to Israeli-Palestinian Peace: The Role of American Jews © 2008 Diane Balser

Imitatio Dei and/as Shared Space: A Jewish Theological Argument for Sharing the Holy Land © 2008 Shaul Magid

Everything Falls Apart © 2008 Joel Schalit

The Challenge of Making Peace © 2008 Stephen P. Cohen

Am I My Brother's Keeper If My Brother Lives Halfway Around the World? © 2008 Ruth Messinger and Aaron Dorfman

A Jewish Response to Globalization © 2008 Micha Odenheimer

"Silence Is Akin to Assent": Judaism and the War in Iraq © 2008 Adam Rubin

Once Again: Genocide in Darfur © 2008 Mark Hanis

How to Split the Sea: Anti-Semitism and Social Change © 2008 April Rosenblum

Reopening the Tent of Abraham © 2008 Phyllis Berman and Arthur Waskow

RIGHTEOUS INDIGNATION
ON THE WEB

Righteous Indignation is both a book and a communal organizing project. Our long-term mission is twofold:

- To provide progressive Jewish justice activists with the intellectual and spiritual resources to inspire and sustain their work
- To strengthen the Jewish community's capacity to engage in systemic justice activities by helping religious and secular organizations connect with one another and with Jewish and interfaith activists across the country.

The work we have begun in this book continues on our website at www.jewishjusticebook.com, where you will find a number of resources, including a list of local and national Jewish justice organizations; links to current and ongoing campaigns in the Jewish justice world; organizing resources for Jewish activists; a Jewish justice blog; and information about conferences, activist trainings, and networking opportunities.

We invite you to visit the website to obtain or to post information about Jewish justice work. We hope the website will facilitate continued conversation among members of the growing Jewish justice community.

ABOUT THE EDITORS

Rabbi Or N. Rose, educator, writer, and activist, is associate dean at the Rabbinical School of Hebrew College in Boston. He is also coeditor of *God in All Moments: Mystical & Practical Spiritual Wisdom from Hasidic Masters* (Jewish Lights), and the author of *Abraham Joshua Heschel: Man of Spirit, Man of Action*, a biography for children (Jewish Publication Society).

Jo Ellen Green Kaiser, PhD, has fostered Jewish thinking about social justice for over a decade as an editor at *Tikkun* and at *Zeek: A Journal of Jewish Thought and Culture*.

Margie Klein is a passionate activist and budding religious leader. Founder and director of Moishe House Boston: Kavod Jewish Social Justice House, she is a student at the Rabbinical School of Hebrew College. She is the founder of Project Democracy, a program that mobilized 97,000 students to vote in the 2004 election.

Bar/Bat Mitzvah

The JGirl's Guide: The Young Jewish Woman's Handbook for Coming of Age
By Penina Adelman, Ali Feldman, and Shulamit Reinharz
This inspirational, interactive guidebook helps pre-teen Jewish girls address the many
issues surrounding coming of age.   6 x 9, 240 pp, Quality PB, 978-1-58023-215-9 **$14.99**
  Also Available: **The JGirl's Teacher's and Parent's Guide**
  8½ x 11, 56 pp, PB, 978-1-58023-225-8 **$8.99**

Bar/Bat Mitzvah Basics: A Practical Family Guide to Coming of Age Together
Edited by Cantor Helen Leneman   6 x 9, 240 pp, Quality PB, 978-1-58023-151-0 **$18.95**

The Bar/Bat Mitzvah Memory Book, 2nd Edition: An Album for Treasuring the
Spiritual Celebration *By Rabbi Jeffrey K. Salkin and Nina Salkin*
  8 x 10, 48 pp, Deluxe HC, 2-color text, ribbon marker, 978-1-58023-263-0 **$19.99**

For Kids—Putting God on Your Guest List, 2nd Edition: How to Claim the
Spiritual Meaning of Your Bar or Bat Mitzvah *By Rabbi Jeffrey K. Salkin*
  6 x 9, 144 pp, Quality PB, 978-1-58023-308-8 **$15.99** *For ages 11–13*

Putting God on the Guest List, 3rd Edition: How to Reclaim the Spiritual
Meaning of Your Child's Bar or Bat Mitzvah *By Rabbi Jeffrey K. Salkin*
  6 x 9, 224 pp, Quality PB, 978-1-58023-222-7 **$16.99**; HC, 978-1-58023-260-9 **$24.99**
  Also Available: **Putting God on the Guest List Teacher's Guide**
  8½ x 11, 48 pp, PB, 978-1-58023-226-5 **$8.99**

Tough Questions Jews Ask: A Young Adult's Guide to Building a Jewish Life
By Rabbi Edward Feinstein   6 x 9, 160 pp, Quality PB, 978-1-58023-139-8 **$14.99** *For ages 12 & up*
  Also Available: **Tough Questions Jews Ask Teacher's Guide**
  8½ x 11, 72 pp, PB, 978-1-58023-187-9 **$8.95**

Bible Study/Midrash

**Abraham's Bind & Other Bible Tales of Trickery, Folly, Mercy
and Love** *By Michael J. Caduto*
Re-imagines many biblical characters, retelling their stories.
6 x 9, 224 pp, HC, 978-1-59473-186-0 **$19.99** *(A SkyLight Paths book)*

Ancient Secrets: Using the Stories of the Bible to Improve Our Everyday Lives
By Rabbi Levi Meier, PhD 5½ x 8½, 288 pp, Quality PB, 978-1-58023-064-3 **$16.95**

The Genesis of Leadership: What the Bible Teaches Us about Vision,
Values and Leading Change *By Rabbi Nathan Laufer; Foreword by Senator Joseph I. Lieberman*
Unlike other books on leadership, this one is rooted in the stories of the Bible.
6 x 9, 288 pp, HC, 978-1-58023-241-8 **$24.99**

Hineini in Our Lives: Learning How to Respond to Others through 14 Biblical Texts and
Personal Stories *By Norman J. Cohen*   6 x 9, 240 pp, Quality PB, 978-1-58023-274-6 **$16.99**

Moses and the Journey to Leadership: Timeless Lessons of Effective Management from
the Bible and Today's Leaders *By Dr. Norman J. Cohen*   6 x 9, 250 pp, HC, 978-1-58023-227-2 **$21.99**

Self, Struggle & Change: Family Conflict Stories in Genesis and Their Healing Insights for
Our Lives *By Norman J. Cohen*   6 x 9, 224 pp, Quality PB, 978-1-879045-66-8 **$18.99**

The Triumph of Eve & Other Subversive Bible Tales *By Matt Biers-Ariel*
5½ x 8½, 192 pp, Quality PB, 978-1-59473-176-1 **$14.99**; HC, 978-1-59473-040-5 **$19.99**
(A SkyLight Paths book)

The Wisdom of Judaism: An Introduction to the Values of the Talmud
By Rabbi Dov Peretz Elkins
Explores the essence of Judaism.   6 x 9, 192 pp, Quality PB, 978-1-58023-327-9 **$16.99**
  Also Available: **The Wisdom of Judaism Teacher's Guide**
  8½ x 11, 18 pp, PB, 978-1-58023-350-7 **$8.99**

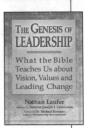

Or phone, fax, mail or e-mail to: JEWISH LIGHTS Publishing
Sunset Farm Offices, Route 4 • P.O. Box 237 • Woodstock, Vermont 05091
Tel: (802) 457-4000 • Fax: (802) 457-4004 • www.jewishlights.com
Credit card orders: (800) 962-4544 (8:30AM–5:30PM ET Monday–Friday)
Generous discounts on quantity orders. SATISFACTION GUARANTEED. Prices subject to change.

Congregation Resources

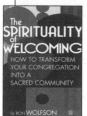

The Art of Public Prayer, 2nd Edition: Not for Clergy Only By Lawrence A. Hoffman
6 x 9, 272 pp, Quality PB, 978-1-893361-06-5 **$19.99** (A SkyLight Paths book)

Becoming a Congregation of Learners: Learning as a Key to Revitalizing
Congregational Life By Isa Aron, PhD; Foreword by Rabbi Lawrence A. Hoffman
6 x 9, 304 pp, Quality PB, 978-1-58023-089-6 **$19.95**

Finding a Spiritual Home: How a New Generation of Jews Can Transform the
American Synagogue By Rabbi Sidney Schwarz
6 x 9, 352 pp, Quality PB, 978-1-58023-185-5 **$19.95**

Jewish Pastoral Care, 2nd Edition: A Practical Handbook from Traditional &
Contemporary Sources Edited by Rabbi Dayle A. Friedman
6 x 9, 528 pp, HC, 978-1-58023-221-0 **$40.00**

Jewish Spiritual Direction: An Innovative Guide from Traditional and Contemporary
Sources Edited by Rabbi Howard A. Addison and Barbara Eve Breitman
6 x 9, 368 pp, HC, 978-1-58023-230-2 **$30.00**

The Self-Renewing Congregation: Organizational Strategies for Revitalizing
Congregational Life By Isa Aron, PhD; Foreword by Dr. Ron Wolfson
6 x 9, 304 pp, Quality PB, 978-1-58023-166-4 **$19.95**

Spiritual Community: The Power to Restore Hope, Commitment and Joy
By Rabbi David A. Teutsch, PhD 5½ x 8½, 144 pp, HC, 978-1-58023-270-8 **$19.99**

The Spirituality of Welcoming: How to Transform Your Congregation into a
Sacred Community By Dr. Ron Wolfson 6 x 9, 224 pp, Quality PB, 978-1-58023-244-9 **$19.99**

Rethinking Synagogues: A New Vocabulary for Congregational Life
By Rabbi Lawrence A. Hoffman 6 x 9, 240 pp, Quality PB, 978-1-58023-248-7 **$19.99**

Children's Books

What You Will See Inside a Synagogue
By Rabbi Lawrence A. Hoffman and Dr. Ron Wolfson; Full-color photos by Bill Aron
A colorful, fun-to-read introduction that explains the ways and whys of Jewish
worship and religious life.
8½ x 10½, 32 pp, Full-color photos, HC, 978-1-59473-012-2 **$17.99** For ages 6 & up (A SkyLight Paths book)

The Kids' Fun Book of Jewish Time
By Emily Sper 9 x 7½, 24 pp, Full-color illus., HC, 978-1-58023-311-8 **$16.99**

In God's Hands
By Lawrence Kushner and Gary Schmidt 9 x 12, 32 pp, HC, 978-1-58023-224-1 **$16.99**

Because Nothing Looks Like God
By Lawrence and Karen Kushner
Introduces children to the possibilities of spiritual life.
11 x 8½, 32 pp, Full-color illus., HC, 978-1-58023-092-6 **$16.95** For ages 4 & up

Also Available: **Because Nothing Looks Like God Teacher's Guide**
8½ x 11, 22 pp, PB, 978-1-58023-140-4 **$6.95** For ages 5–8

Board Book Companions to Because Nothing Looks Like God
5 x 5, 24 pp, Full-color illus., SkyLight Paths Board Books For ages 0–4

What Does God Look Like? 978-1-893361-23-2 **$7.99**

How Does God Make Things Happen? 978-1-893361-24-9 **$7.95**

Where Is God? 978-1-893361-17-1 **$7.99**

The Book of Miracles: A Young Person's Guide to Jewish Spiritual Awareness
By Lawrence Kushner. All-new illustrations by the author
6 x 9, 96 pp, 2-color illus., HC, 978-1-879045-78-1 **$16.95** For ages 9 and up

In Our Image: God's First Creatures
By Nancy Sohn Swartz 9 x 12, 32 pp, Full-color illus., HC, 978-1-879045-99-6 **$16.95** For ages 4 & up

Also Available as a Board Book: **How Did the Animals Help God?**
5 x 5, 24 pp, Board, Full-color illus., 978-1-59473-044-3 **$7.99** For ages 0–4 (A SkyLight Paths book)

What Makes Someone a Jew?
By Lauren Seidman
Reflects the changing face of American Judaism.
10 x 8½, 32 pp, Full-color photos, Quality PB Original, 978-1-58023-321-7 **$8.99** For ages 3–6

Children's Books
by Sandy Eisenberg Sasso

Adam & Eve's First Sunset: God's New Day

Engaging new story explores fear and hope, faith and gratitude in ways that will delight kids and adults—inspiring us to bless each of God's days and nights.

9 x 12, 32 pp, Full-color illus., HC, 978-1-58023-177-0 **$17.95** *For ages 4 & up*

Also Available as a Board Book: **Adam and Eve's New Day**

5 x 5, 24 pp, Full-color illus., Board, 978-1-59473-205-8 **$7.99** *For ages 0–4 (A SkyLight Paths book)*

But God Remembered

Stories of Women from Creation to the Promised Land

Four different stories of women—Lillith, Serach, Bityah, and the Daughters of Z—teach us important values through their faith and actions.

9 x 12, 32 pp, Full-color illus., HC, 978-1-879045-43-9 **$16.95** *For ages 8 & up*

Cain & Abel: Finding the Fruits of Peace

Shows children that we have the power to deal with anger in positive ways. Provides questions for kids and adults to explore together.

9 x 12, 32 pp, Full-color illus., HC, 978-1-58023-123-7 **$16.95** *For ages 5 & up*

God in Between

If you wanted to find God, where would you look? This magical, mythical tale teaches that God can be found where we are: within all of us and the relationships between us.

9 x 12, 32 pp, Full-color illus., HC, 978-1-879045-86-6 **$16.95** *For ages 4 & up*

God's Paintbrush: Special 10th Anniversary Edition

Wonderfully interactive, invites children of all faiths and backgrounds to encounter God through moments in their own lives. Provides questions adult and child can explore together.

11 x 8½, 32 pp, Full-color illus., HC, 978-1-58023-195-4 **$17.95** *For ages 4 & up*

Also Available: **God's Paintbrush Teacher's Guide**

8½ x 11, 32 pp, PB, 978-1-879045-57-6 **$8.95**

God's Paintbrush Celebration Kit

A Spiritual Activity Kit for Teachers and Students of All Faiths, All Backgrounds

Additional activity sheets available:

8-Student Activity Sheet Pack (40 sheets/5 sessions), 978-1-58023-058-2 **$19.95**

Single-Student Activity Sheet Pack (5 sessions), 978-1-58023-059-9 **$3.95**

In God's Name

Like an ancient myth in its poetic text and vibrant illustrations, this award-winning modern fable about the search for God's name celebrates the diversity and, at the same time, the unity of all people.

9 x 12, 32 pp, Full-color illus., HC, 978-1-879045-26-2 **$16.99** *For ages 4 & up*

Also Available as a Board Book: **What Is God's Name?**

5 x 5, 24 pp, Board, Full-color illus., 978-1-893361-10-2 **$7.99** *For ages 0–4 (A SkyLight Paths book)*

Also Available: **In God's Name video and study guide**

Computer animation, original music, and children's voices. 18 min. **$29.99**

Also Available in Spanish: **El nombre de Dios**

9 x 12, 32 pp, Full-color illus., HC, 978-1-893361-63-8 **$16.95** *(A SkyLight Paths book)*

Noah's Wife: The Story of Naamah

When God tells Noah to bring the animals of the world onto the ark, God also calls on Naamah, Noah's wife, to save each plant on Earth. Based on an ancient text.

9 x 12, 32 pp, Full-color illus., HC, 978-1-58023-134-3 **$16.95** *For ages 4 & up*

Also Available as a Board Book: **Naamah, Noah's Wife**

5 x 5, 24 pp, Full-color illus., Board, 978-1-893361-56-0 **$7.95** *For ages 0–4 (A SkyLight Paths book)*

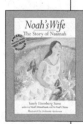

For Heaven's Sake: Finding God in Unexpected Places

9 x 12, 32 pp, Full-color illus., HC, 978-1-58023-054-4 **$16.95** *For ages 4 & up*

God Said Amen: Finding the Answers to Our Prayers

9 x 12, 32 pp, Full-color illus., HC, 978-1-58023-080-3 **$16.95** *For ages 4 & up*

Current Events/History

A Dream of Zion: American Jews Reflect on Why Israel Matters to Them
Edited by Rabbi Jeffrey K. Salkin Explores what Jewish people in America have to say
about Israel.   6 x 9, 304 pp, HC, 978-1-58023-340-8 **$24.99**
  Also Available: **A Dream of Zion Teacher's Guide** 8½ x 11, 18 pp, PB, 978-1-58023-356-9 **$8.99**
The Jewish Connection to Israel, the Promised Land: A Brief Introduction for
  Christians *By Rabbi Eugene Korn, PhD* 5½ x 8½, 176 pp, Quality PB, 978-1-58023-318-7 **$14.99**
The Story of the Jews: A 4,000-Year Adventure—A Graphic History Book
  Written & illustrated by Stan Mack 6 x 9, 288 pp, illus., Quality PB, 978-1-58023-155-8 **$16.95**
Hannah Senesh: Her Life and Diary, the First Complete Edition
  By Hannah Senesh; Foreword by Marge Piercy; Preface by Eitan Senesh
  6 x 9, 368 pp, Quality PB, 978-1-58023-342-2 **$19.99**; 352 pp, HC, 978-1-58023-212-8 **$24.99**

The Ethiopian Jews of Israel: Personal Stories of Life in the Promised
Land *By Len Lyons, PhD; Foreword by Alan Dershowitz; Photographs by Ilan Ossendryver*
Recounts, through photographs and words, stories of Ethiopian Jews.
10½ x 10, 240 pp, 100 full-color photos, HC, 978-1-58023-323-1 **$34.99**

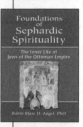

Foundations of Sephardic Spirituality: The Inner Life of Jews of the Ottoman Empire
  By Rabbi Marc D. Angel, PhD 6 x 9, 224 pp, HC, 978-1-58023-243-2 **$24.99**
Judaism and Justice: The Jewish Passion to Repair the World
  By Rabbi Sidney Schwarz 6 x 9, 250 pp, HC, 978-1-58023-312-5 **$24.99**

Ecology/Environment

A Wild Faith: Jewish Ways into Wilderness, Wilderness Ways into Judaism
By Rabbi Mike Comins; Foreword by Nigel Savage
Offers ways to enliven and deepen your spiritual life through wilderness experience.
6 x 9, 240 pp, Quality PB, 978-1-58023-316-3 **$16.99**
Ecology & the Jewish Spirit: Where Nature & the Sacred Meet
  Edited by Ellen Bernstein 6 x 9, 288 pp, Quality PB, 978-1-58023-082-7 **$16.95**
Torah of the Earth: Exploring 4,000 Years of Ecology in Jewish Thought
  Vol. 1: Biblical Israel: One Land, One People; Rabbinic Judaism: One People, Many Lands
  Vol. 2: Zionism: One Land, Two Peoples; Eco-Judaism: One Earth, Many Peoples
  Edited by Arthur Waskow Vol. 1: 6 x 9, 272 pp, Quality PB, 978-1-58023-086-5 **$19.95**
  Vol. 2: 6 x 9, 336 pp, Quality PB, 978-1-58023-087-2 **$19.95**
The Way Into Judaism and the Environment
  By Jeremy Benstein 6 x 9, 224 pp, HC, 978-1-58023-268-5 **$24.99**

Grief/Healing

Healing and the Jewish Imagination: Spiritual and Practical
Perspectives on Judaism and Health *Edited by Rabbi William Cutter, PhD*
Explores Judaism for comfort in times of illness and perspectives on suffering.
6 x 9, 240 pp, HC, 978-1-58023-314-9 **$24.99**
Grief in Our Seasons: A Mourner's Kaddish Companion *By Rabbi Kerry M. Olitzky*
  4¼ x 6¼, 448 pp, Quality PB, 978-1-879045-55-2 **$15.95**
Healing of Soul, Healing of Body: Spiritual Leaders Unfold the Strength & Solace
  in Psalms *Edited by Rabbi Simkha Y. Weintraub, CSW*
  6 x 9, 128 pp, 2-color illus. text, Quality PB, 978-1-879045-31-6 **$14.99**
Mourning & Mitzvah, 2nd Edition: A Guided Journal for Walking the Mourner's
  Path through Grief to Healing *By Anne Brener, LCSW*
  7½ x 9, 304 pp, Quality PB, 978-1-58023-113-8 **$19.99**

Tears of Sorrow, Seeds of Hope, 2nd Edition: A Jewish Spiritual Companion for
  Infertility and Pregnancy Loss *By Rabbi Nina Beth Cardin*
  6 x 9, 208 pp, Quality PB, 978-1-58023-233-3 **$18.99**
A Time to Mourn, a Time to Comfort, 2nd Edition: A Guide to Jewish
  Bereavement *By Dr. Ron Wolfson*
  7 x 9, 384 pp, Quality PB, 978-1-58023-253-1 **$19.99**

When a Grandparent Dies: A Kid's Own Remembering Workbook for Dealing
  with Shiva and the Year Beyond *By Nechama Liss-Levinson, PhD*
  8 x 10, 48 pp, 2-color text, HC, 978-1-879045-44-6 **$15.95** *For ages 7–13*

Holidays/Holy Days

Rosh Hashanah Readings: Inspiration, Information and Contemplation
Yom Kippur Readings: Inspiration, Information and Contemplation
Edited by Rabbi Dov Peretz Elkins with Section Introductions from Arthur Green's These Are the Words
An extraordinary collection of readings, prayers and insights that enable the modern worshiper to enter into the spirit of the High Holy Days in a personal and powerful way, permitting the meaning of the Jewish New Year to enter the heart.
RHR: 6 x 9, 400 pp, HC, 978-1-58023-239-5 **$24.99**
YKR: 6 x 9, 368 pp, HC, 978-1-58023-271-5 **$24.99**

Jewish Holidays: A Brief Introduction for Christians
By Rabbi Kerry M. Olitzky and Rabbi Daniel Judson
5½ x 8½, 144 pp, Quality PB, 978-1-58023-302-6 **$16.99**

Reclaiming Judaism as a Spiritual Practice: Holy Days and Shabbat
By Rabbi Goldie Milgram
7 x 9, 272 pp, Quality PB, 978-1-58023-205-0 **$19.99**

7th Heaven: Celebrating Shabbat with Rebbe Nachman of Breslov
By Moshe Mykoff with the Breslov Research Institute
5⅛ x 8¼, 224 pp, Deluxe PB w/flaps, 978-1-58023-175-6 **$18.95**

Shabbat, 2nd Edition: The Family Guide to Preparing for and Celebrating the Sabbath
By Dr. Ron Wolfson 7 x 9, 320 pp, illus., Quality PB, 978-1-58023-164-0 **$19.99**

Hanukkah, 2nd Edition: The Family Guide to Spiritual Celebration
By Dr. Ron Wolfson. Edited by Joel Lurie Grishaver.
7 x 9, 240 pp, illus., Quality PB, 978-1-58023-122-0 **$18.95**

The Jewish Family Fun Book: Holiday Projects, Everyday Activities, and Travel Ideas
with Jewish Themes *By Danielle Dardashti and Roni Sarig. Illus. by Avi Katz.*
6 x 9, 288 pp, 70+ b/w illus. & diagrams, Quality PB, 978-1-58023-171-8 **$18.95**

The Jewish Lights Book of Fun Classroom Activities: Simple and Seasonal
Projects for Teachers and Students *By Danielle Dardashti and Roni Sarig*
6 x 9, 240 pp, Quality PB, 978-1-58023-206-7 **$19.99**

Passover

My People's Passover Haggadah
Traditional Texts, Modern Commentaries
Edited by Rabbi Lawrence A. Hoffman and David Arnow, PhD
A diverse and exciting collection of commentaries on the traditional Passover Haggadah—in two volumes!
Vol. 1: 7 x 10, 250 pp (est), HC, 978-1-58023-354-5 **$24.99;**
Vol. 2: 7 x 10, 250 pp (est), 978-1-58023-346-0 **$24.99**

Leading the Passover Journey
The Seder's Meaning Revealed, the Haggadah's Story Retold
By Rabbi Nathan Laufer
Uncovers the hidden meaning of the Seder's rituals and customs.
6 x 9, 224 pp, HC, 978-1-58023-211-1 **$24.99**

The Women's Passover Companion: Women's Reflections on the Festival of Freedom
Edited by Rabbi Sharon Cohen Anisfeld, Tara Mohr, and Catherine Spector
6 x 9, 352 pp, Quality PB, 978-1-58023-231-9 **$19.99**

The Women's Seder Sourcebook: Rituals & Readings for Use at the Passover Seder
Edited by Rabbi Sharon Cohen Anisfeld, Tara Mohr, and Catherine Spector
6 x 9, 384 pp, Quality PB, 978-1-58023-232-6 **$19.99**

Creating Lively Passover Seders: A Sourcebook of Engaging Tales, Texts & Activities
By David Arnow, PhD 7 x 9, 416 pp, Quality PB, 978-1-58023-184-8 **$24.99**

Passover, 2nd Edition: The Family Guide to Spiritual Celebration
By Dr. Ron Wolfson with Joel Lurie Grishaver 7 x 9, 352 pp, Quality PB, 978-1-58023-174-9 **$19.95**

Inspiration

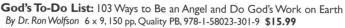

Happiness and the Human Spirit: The Spirituality of Becoming the Best You Can Be *By Abraham J. Twerski, MD*
Shows you that true happiness is attainable once you stop looking outside yourself for the source. 6 x 9, 176 pp, HC, 978-1-58023-343-9 **$19.99**

The Bridge to Forgiveness: Stories and Prayers for Finding God and Restoring Wholeness *By Rabbi Karyn D. Kedar*
Examines how forgiveness can be the bridge that connects us to wholeness and peace. 6 x 9, 176 pp, HC, 978-1-58023-324-8 **$19.99**

God's To-Do List: 103 Ways to Be an Angel and Do God's Work on Earth
By Dr. Ron Wolfson 6 x 9, 150 pp, Quality PB, 978-1-58023-301-9 **$15.99**

God in All Moments: Mystical & Practical Spiritual Wisdom from Hasidic Masters
Edited and translated by Or N. Rose with Ebn D. Leader
5½ x 8½, 192 pp, Quality PB, 978-1-58023-186-2 **$16.95**

Our Dance with God: Finding Prayer, Perspective and Meaning in the Stories of Our Lives *By Karyn D. Kedar* 6 x 9, 176 pp, Quality PB, 978-1-58023-202-9 **$16.99**
Also Available: **The Dance of the Dolphin** (HC edition of *Our Dance with God*)
6 x 9, 176 pp, HC, 978-1-58023-154-1 **$19.95**

The Empty Chair: Finding Hope and Joy—Timeless Wisdom from a Hasidic Master, Rebbe Nachman of Breslov *Adapted by Moshe Mykoff and the Breslov Research Institute*
4 x 6, 128 pp, 2-color text, Deluxe PB w/flaps, 978-1-879045-67-5 **$9.99**

The Gentle Weapon: Prayers for Everyday and Not-So-Everyday Moments—
Timeless Wisdom from the Teachings of the Hasidic Master, Rebbe Nachman of Breslov
Adapted by Moshe Mykoff and S. C. Mizrahi, together with the Breslov Research Institute
4 x 6, 144 pp, 2-color text, Deluxe PB w/flaps, 978-1-58023-022-3 **$9.99**

God Whispers: Stories of the Soul, Lessons of the Heart *By Karyn D. Kedar*
6 x 9, 176 pp, Quality PB, 978-1-58023-088-9 **$15.95**

Restful Reflections: Nighttime Inspiration to Calm the Soul, Based on Jewish Wisdom
By Rabbi Kerry M. Olitzky & Rabbi Lori Forman 4½ x 6½, 448 pp, Quality PB, 978-1-58023-091-9 **$15.95**

Sacred Intentions: Daily Inspiration to Strengthen the Spirit, Based on Jewish Wisdom
By Rabbi Kerry M. Olitzky and Rabbi Lori Forman 4½ x 6½, 448 pp, Quality PB, 978-1-58023-061-2 **$15.95**

Kabbalah/Mysticism/Enneagram

Awakening to Kabbalah: The Guiding Light of Spiritual Fulfillment
By Rav Michael Laitman, PhD 6 x 9, 192 pp, HC, 978-1-58023-264-7 **$21.99**

Seek My Face: A Jewish Mystical Theology *By Arthur Green*
6 x 9, 304 pp, Quality PB, 978-1-58023-130-5 **$19.95**

Zohar: Annotated & Explained
Translation and annotation by Daniel C. Matt; Foreword by Andrew Harvey
5½ x 8½, 176 pp, Quality PB, 978-1-893361-51-5 **$15.99** *(A SkyLight Paths book)*

Ehyeh: A Kabbalah for Tomorrow
By Arthur Green 6 x 9, 224 pp, Quality PB, 978-1-58023-213-5 **$16.99**

The Flame of the Heart: Prayers of a Chasidic Mystic *By Reb Noson of Breslov. Translated by David Sears with the Breslov Research Institute* 5 x 7¼, 160 pp, Quality PB, 978-1-58023-246-3 **$15.99**

The Gift of Kabbalah: Discovering the Secrets of Heaven, Renewing Your Life on Earth
By Tamar Frankiel, PhD 6 x 9, 256 pp, Quality PB, 978-1-58023-141-1 **$16.95;**
HC, 978-1-58023-108-4 **$21.95**

Kabbalah: A Brief Introduction for Christians
By Tamar Frankiel, PhD 5½ x 8½, 208 pp, Quality PB, 978-1-58023-303-3 **$16.99**

The Lost Princess and Other Kabbalistic Tales of Rebbe Nachman of Breslov
The Seven Beggars and Other Kabbalistic Tales of Rebbe Nachman of Breslov
Translated by Rabbi Aryeh Kaplan; Preface by Rabbi Chaim Kramer
Lost Princess: 6 x 9, 400 pp, Quality PB, 978-1-58023-217-3 **$18.99**
Seven Beggars: 6 x 9, 192 pp, Quality PB, 978-1-58023-250-0 **$16.99**

See also *The Way Into Jewish Mystical Tradition* in Spirituality / The Way Into... Series

Life Cycle
Marriage / Parenting / Family / Aging

The New Jewish Baby Album: Creating and Celebrating the Beginning of a Spiritual Life—A Jewish Lights Companion
By the Editors at Jewish Lights. Foreword by Anita Diamant. Preface by Rabbi Sandy Eisenberg Sasso.
A spiritual keepsake that will be treasured for generations. More than just a memory book, *shows you how—and why it's important*—to create a Jewish home and a Jewish life. 8 x 10, 64 pp, Deluxe Padded HC, Full-color illus., 978-1-58023-138-1 **$19.95**

The Jewish Pregnancy Book: A Resource for the Soul, Body & Mind during Pregnancy, Birth & the First Three Months
By Sandy Falk, MD, and Rabbi Daniel Judson, with Steven A. Rapp
Includes medical information, prayers and rituals for each stage of pregnancy, from a liberal Jewish perspective. 7 x 10, 208 pp, Quality PB, b/w photos, 978-1-58023-178-7 **$16.95**

Celebrating Your New Jewish Daughter: Creating Jewish Ways to Welcome Baby Girls into the Covenant—New and Traditional Ceremonies *By Debra Nussbaum Cohen; Foreword by Rabbi Sandy Eisenberg Sasso* 6 x 9, 272 pp, Quality PB, 978-1-58023-090-2 **$18.95**

The New Jewish Baby Book, 2nd Edition: Names, Ceremonies & Customs—A Guide for Today's Families *By Anita Diamant* 6 x 9, 336 pp, Quality PB, 978-1-58023-251-7 **$19.99**

Parenting As a Spiritual Journey: Deepening Ordinary and Extraordinary Events into Sacred Occasions *By Rabbi Nancy Fuchs-Kreimer* 6 x 9, 224 pp, Quality PB, 978-1-58023-016-2 **$16.95**

Parenting Jewish Teens: A Guide for the Perplexed
By Joanne Doades
Explores the questions and issues that shape the world in which today's Jewish teenagers live.
6 x 9, 200 pp, Quality PB, 978-1-58023-305-7 **$16.99**

Judaism for Two: A Spiritual Guide for Strengthening and Celebrating Your Loving Relationship *By Rabbi Nancy Fuchs-Kreimer and Rabbi Nancy H. Wiener; Foreword by Rabbi Elliot N. Dorff* Addresses the ways Jewish teachings can enhance and strengthen committed relationships. 6 x 9, 224 pp, Quality PB, 978-1-58023-254-8 **$16.99**

Embracing the Covenant: Converts to Judaism Talk About Why & How
By Rabbi Allan Berkowitz and Patti Moskovitz 6 x 9, 192 pp, Quality PB, 978-1-879045-50-7 **$16.95**

The Guide to Jewish Interfaith Family Life: An InterfaithFamily.com Handbook
Edited by Ronnie Friedland and Edmund Case 6 x 9, 384 pp, Quality PB, 978-1-58023-153-4 **$18.95**

Introducing My Faith and My Community
The Jewish Outreach Institute Guide for the Christian in a Jewish Interfaith Relationship
By Rabbi Kerry M. Olitzky 6 x 9, 176 pp, Quality PB, 978-1-58023-192-3 **$16.99**

Making a Successful Jewish Interfaith Marriage: The Jewish Outreach Institute Guide to Opportunities, Challenges and Resources *By Rabbi Kerry M. Olitzky with Joan Peterson Littman*
6 x 9, 176 pp, Quality PB, 978-1-58023-170-1 **$16.95**

The Creative Jewish Wedding Book: A Hands-On Guide to New & Old Traditions, Ceremonies & Celebrations *By Gabrielle Kaplan-Mayer*
9 x 9, 288 pp, b/w photos, Quality PB, 978-1-58023-194-7 **$19.99**

Divorce Is a Mitzvah: A Practical Guide to Finding Wholeness and Holiness When Your Marriage Dies *By Rabbi Perry Netter; Afterword by Rabbi Laura Geller.*
6 x 9, 224 pp, Quality PB, 978-1-58023-172-5 **$16.95**

A Heart of Wisdom: Making the Jewish Journey from Midlife through the Elder Years
Edited by Susan Berrin; Foreword by Harold Kushner
6 x 9, 384 pp, Quality PB, 978-1-58023-051-3 **$18.95**

So That Your Values Live On: Ethical Wills and How to Prepare Them
Edited by Jack Riemer and Nathaniel Stampfer
6 x 9, 272 pp, Quality PB, 978-1-879045-34-7 **$18.99**

Meditation

The Handbook of Jewish Meditation Practices
A Guide for Enriching the Sabbath and Other Days of Your Life
By Rabbi David A. Cooper Easy-to-learn meditation techniques.
6 x 9, 208 pp, Quality PB, 978-1-58023-102-2 **$16.95**

Discovering Jewish Meditation: Instruction & Guidance for Learning an Ancient
Spiritual Practice *By Nan Fink Gefen*
6 x 9, 208 pp, Quality PB, 978-1-58023-067-4 **$16.95**

A Heart of Stillness: A Complete Guide to Learning the Art of Meditation
By David A. Cooper 5½ x 8½, 272 pp, Quality PB, 978-1-893361-03-4 **$16.95** *(A SkyLight Paths book)*

Meditation from the Heart of Judaism: Today's Teachers Share Their Practices,
Techniques, and Faith *Edited by Avram Davis*
6 x 9, 256 pp, Quality PB, 978-1-58023-049-0 **$16.95**

Silence, Simplicity & Solitude: A Complete Guide to Spiritual Retreat at Home
By David A. Cooper 5½ x 8½, 336 pp, Quality PB, 978-1-893361-04-1 **$16.95**
(A SkyLight Paths book)

Ritual/Sacred Practice

The Jewish Dream Book: The Key to Opening the Inner Meaning of
Your Dreams *By Vanessa L. Ochs with Elizabeth Ochs; Full-color illus. by Kristina Swarner*
Instructions for how modern people can perform ancient Jewish dream practices
and dream interpretations drawn from the Jewish wisdom tradition.
8 x 8, 128 pp, Full-color illus., Deluxe PB w/flaps, 978-1-58023-132-9 **$16.95**

God in Your Body: Kabbalah, Mindfulness and Embodied Spiritual Practice
By Jay Michaelson
The first comprehensive treatment of the body in Jewish spiritual practice and an
essential guide to the sacred.
6 x 9, 288 pp, Quality PB, 978-1-58023-304-0 **$18.99**

The Book of Jewish Sacred Practices: CLAL's Guide to Everyday & Holiday
Rituals & Blessings *Edited by Rabbi Irwin Kula and Vanessa L. Ochs, PhD*
6 x 9, 368 pp, Quality PB, 978-1-58023-152-7 **$18.95**

Jewish Ritual: A Brief Introduction for Christians
By Rabbi Kerry M. Olitzky and Rabbi Daniel Judson
5½ x 8½, 144 pp, Quality PB, 978-1-58023-210-4 **$14.99**

The Rituals & Practices of a Jewish Life: A Handbook for Personal Spiritual
Renewal *Edited by Rabbi Kerry M. Olitzky and Rabbi Daniel Judson*
6 x 9, 272 pp, illus., Quality PB, 978-1-58023-169-5 **$18.95**

The Sacred Art of Lovingkindness: Preparing to Practice
By Rabbi Rami Shapiro 5½ x 8½, 176 pp, Quality PB, 978-1-59473-151-8 **$16.99**
(A SkyLight Paths book)

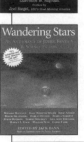

Science Fiction/Mystery & Detective Fiction

Mystery Midrash: An Anthology of Jewish Mystery & Detective Fiction
Edited by Lawrence W. Raphael; Preface by Joel Siegel
6 x 9, 304 pp, Quality PB, 978-1-58023-055-1 **$16.95**

Criminal Kabbalah: An Intriguing Anthology of Jewish Mystery & Detective Fiction
Edited by Lawrence W. Raphael; Foreword by Laurie R. King
6 x 9, 256 pp, Quality PB, 978-1-58023-109-1 **$16.95**

Wandering Stars: An Anthology of Jewish Fantasy & Science Fiction
Edited by Jack Dann; Introduction by Isaac Asimov
6 x 9, 272 pp, Quality PB, 978-1-58023-005-6 **$16.95**

More Wandering Stars: An Anthology of Outstanding Stories of Jewish Fantasy and
Science Fiction *Edited by Jack Dann; Introduction by Isaac Asimov*
6 x 9, 192 pp, Quality PB, 978-1-58023-063-6 **$16.95**

Spirituality

Journeys to a Jewish Life: Inspiring Stories from the Spiritual Journeys of American Jews *By Paula Amann*
Examines the soul treks of Jews lost and found. 6 x 9, 208 pp, HC, 978-1-58023-317-0 **$19.99**

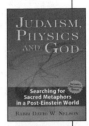

The Adventures of Rabbi Harvey: A Graphic Novel of Jewish Wisdom and Wit in the Wild West *By Steve Sheinkin*
Jewish and American folktales combine in this witty and original graphic novel collection. Creatively retold and set on the western frontier of the 1870s.
6 x 9, 144 pp, Full-color illus., Quality PB, 978-1-58023-310-1 **$16.99**
Also Available: **The Adventures of Rabbi Harvey Teacher's Guide**
8½ x 11, 32 pp, PB, 978-1-58023-326-2 **$8.99**

Ethics of the Sages: *Pirke Avot*—Annotated & Explained
Translation and Annotation by Rabbi Rami Shapiro
5½ x 8½, 192 pp, Quality PB, 978-1-59473-207-2 **$16.99** *(A SkyLight Paths book)*

A Book of Life: Embracing Judaism as a Spiritual Practice
By Michael Strassfeld 6 x 9, 528 pp, Quality PB, 978-1-58023-247-0 **$19.99**

Meaning and Mitzvah: Daily Practices for Reclaiming Judaism through Prayer, God, Torah, Hebrew, Mitzvot and Peoplehood *By Rabbi Goldie Milgram*
7 x 9, 336 pp, Quality PB, 978-1-58023-256-2 **$19.99**

The Soul of the Story: Meetings with Remarkable People
By Rabbi David Zeller 6 x 9, 288 pp, HC, 978-1-58023-272-2 **$21.99**

Aleph-Bet Yoga: Embodying the Hebrew Letters for Physical and Spiritual Well-Being
By Steven A. Rapp. Foreword by Tamar Frankiel, PhD and Judy Greenfeld. Preface by Hart Lazer.
7 x 10, 128 pp, b/w photos, Quality PB, Layflat binding, 978-1-58023-162-6 **$16.95**

Does the Soul Survive? A Jewish Journey to Belief in Afterlife, Past Lives & Living with Purpose *By Rabbi Elie Kaplan Spitz; Foreword by Brian L Weiss, MD*
6 x 9, 288 pp, Quality PB, 978-1-58023-165-7 **$16.99**

First Steps to a New Jewish Spirit: Reb Zalman's Guide to Recapturing the Intimacy & Ecstasy in Your Relationship with God *By Rabbi Zalman M. Schachter-Shalomi with Donald Gropman* 6 x 9, 144 pp, Quality PB, 978-1-58023-182-4 **$16.95**

God in Our Relationships: Spirituality between People from the Teachings of Martin Buber *By Rabbi Dennis S. Ross* 5½ x 8½, 160 pp, Quality PB, 978-1-58023-147-3 **$16.95**

Judaism, Physics and God: Searching for Sacred Metaphors in a Post-Einstein World
By Rabbi David W. Nelson 6 x 9, 368 pp, Quality PB, inc. reader's discussion guide, 978-1-58023-306-4 **$18.99**;
HC, 352 pp, 978-1-58023-252-4 **$24.99**

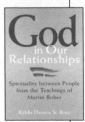

The Jewish Lights Spirituality Handbook: A Guide to Understanding, Exploring & Living a Spiritual Life *Edited by Stuart M. Matlins*
What exactly is "Jewish" about spirituality? How do I make it a part of my life? Fifty of today's foremost spiritual leaders share their ideas and experience with us.
6 x 9, 456 pp, Quality PB, 978-1-58023-093-3 **$19.99**

Bringing the Psalms to Life: How to Understand and Use the Book of Psalms
By Daniel F. Polish 6 x 9, 208 pp, Quality PB, 978-1-58023-157-2 **$16.95**;
HC, 978-1-58023-077-3 **$21.95**

God & the Big Bang: Discovering Harmony between Science & Spirituality
By Daniel C. Matt 6 x 9, 216 pp, Quality PB, 978-1-879045-89-7 **$16.99**

Minding the Temple of the Soul: Balancing Body, Mind, and Spirit through Traditional Jewish Prayer, Movement, and Meditation *By Tamar Frankiel, PhD, and Judy Greenfeld*
7 x 10, 184 pp, illus., Quality PB, 978-1-879045-64-4 **$16.95**
Audiotape of the Blessings and Meditations: 60 min. **$9.95**
Videotape of the Movements and Meditations: 46 min. **$20.00**

One God Clapping: The Spiritual Path of a Zen Rabbi *By Alan Lew with Sherril Jaffe*
5½ x 8½, 336 pp, Quality PB, 978-1-58023-115-2 **$16.95**

There Is No Messiah ... and You're It: The Stunning Transformation of Judaism's Most Provocative Idea *By Rabbi Robert N. Levine, DD*
6 x 9, 192 pp, Quality PB, 978-1-58023-255-5 **$16.99**

These Are the Words: A Vocabulary of Jewish Spiritual Life
By Arthur Green 6 x 9, 304 pp, Quality PB, 978-1-58023-107-7 **$18.95**

Spirituality/Lawrence Kushner

Filling Words with Light: Hasidic and Mystical Reflections on Jewish Prayer
By Lawrence Kushner and Nehemia Polen
5½ x 8½, 176 pp, Quality PB, 978-1-58023-238-8 **$16.99**; HC, 978-1-58023-216-6 **$21.99**

The Book of Letters: A Mystical Hebrew Alphabet
Popular HC Edition, 6 x 9, 80 pp, 2-color text, 978-1-879045-00-2 **$24.95**
Collector's Limited Edition, 9 x 12, 80 pp, gold foil embossed pages, w/limited edition silkscreened print, 978-1-879045-04-0 **$349.00**

The Book of Miracles: A Young Person's Guide to Jewish Spiritual Awareness
6 x 9, 96 pp, 2-color illus., HC, 978-1-879045-78-1 **$16.95** *For ages 9 and up*

The Book of Words: Talking Spiritual Life, Living Spiritual Talk
6 x 9, 160 pp, Quality PB, 978-1-58023-020-9 **$16.95**

Eyes Remade for Wonder: A Lawrence Kushner Reader *Introduction by Thomas Moore*
6 x 9, 240 pp, Quality PB, 978-1-58023-042-1 **$18.95**

God Was in This Place & I, i Did Not Know: Finding Self, Spirituality and Ultimate Meaning 6 x 9, 192 pp, Quality PB, 978-1-879045-33-0 **$16.95**

Honey from the Rock: An Introduction to Jewish Mysticism
6 x 9, 176 pp, Quality PB, 978-1-58023-073-5 **$16.95**

Invisible Lines of Connection: Sacred Stories of the Ordinary
5½ x 8½, 160 pp, Quality PB, 978-1-879045-98-9 **$15.95**

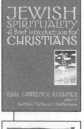

Jewish Spirituality—A Brief Introduction for Christians
5½ x 8½, 112 pp, Quality PB, 978-1-58023-150-3 **$12.95**

The River of Light: Jewish Mystical Awareness
6 x 9, 192 pp, Quality PB, 978-1-58023-096-4 **$16.95**

The Way Into Jewish Mystical Tradition
6 x 9, 224 pp, Quality PB, 978-1-58023-200-5 **$18.99**; HC, 978-1-58023-029-2 **$21.95**

Spirituality/Prayer

Pray Tell: A Hadassah Guide to Jewish Prayer
By Rabbi Jules Harlow, with contributions from many others
8½ x 11, 400 pp, Quality PB, 978-1-58023-163-3 **$29.95**

Witnesses to the One: The Spiritual History of the *Sh'ma* *By Rabbi Joseph B. Meszler; Foreword by Rabbi Elyse Goldstein* 6 x 9, 176 pp, HC, 978-1-58023-309-5 **$19.99**

My People's Prayer Book Series

Traditional Prayers, Modern Commentaries *Edited by Rabbi Lawrence A. Hoffman*
Provides diverse and exciting commentary to the traditional liturgy, helping modern men and women find new wisdom in Jewish prayer, and bring liturgy into their lives. Each book includes Hebrew text, modern translation, and commentaries from all perspectives of the Jewish world.

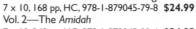

Vol. 1—The *Sh'ma* and Its Blessings
7 x 10, 168 pp, HC, 978-1-879045-79-8 **$24.99**
Vol. 2—The *Amidah*
7 x 10, 240 pp, HC, 978-1-879045-80-4 **$24.95**
Vol. 3—*P'sukei D'zimrah* (Morning Psalms)
7 x 10, 240 pp, HC, 978-1-879045-81-1 **$24.95**
Vol. 4—*Seder K'riat Hatorah* (The Torah Service)
7 x 10, 264 pp, HC, 978-1-879045-82-8 **$23.95**
Vol. 5—*Birkhot Hashachar* (Morning Blessings)
7 x 10, 240 pp, HC, 978-1-879045-83-5 **$24.95**
Vol. 6—*Tachanun* and Concluding Prayers
7 x 10, 240 pp, HC, 978-1-879045-84-2 **$24.95**
Vol. 7—Shabbat at Home
7 x 10, 240 pp, HC, 978-1-879045-85-9 **$24.95**
Vol. 8—*Kabbalat Shabbat* (Welcoming Shabbat in the Synagogue)
7 x 10, 240 pp, HC, 978-1-58023-121-3 **$24.99**
Vol. 9—Welcoming the Night: *Minchah* and *Ma'ariv* (Afternoon and Evening Prayer) 7 x 10, 272 pp, HC, 978-1-58023-262-3 **$24.99**
Vol. 10—Shabbat Morning: *Shacharit* and *Musaf* (Morning and Additional Services) 7 x 10, 240 pp, HC, 978-1-58023-240-1 **$24.99**

Spirituality/Women's Interest

The Quotable Jewish Woman: Wisdom, Inspiration & Humor from the Mind & Heart
Edited and compiled by Elaine Bernstein Partnow
6 x 9, 496 pp, Quality PB, 978-1-58023-236-4 **$19.99**; HC, 978-1-58023-193-0 **$29.99**

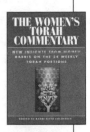

The Divine Feminine in Biblical Wisdom Literature: Selections Annotated &
Explained *Translated and Annotated by Rabbi Rami Shapiro*
5½ x 8½, 240 pp, Quality PB, 978-1-59473-109-9 **$16.99** *(A SkyLight Paths book)*

The Women's Haftarah Commentary: New Insights from Women Rabbis on the
54 Weekly Haftarah Portions, the 5 Megillot & Special Shabbatot
Edited by Rabbi Elyse Goldstein 6 x 9, 560 pp, HC, 978-1-58023-133-6 **$39.99**

The Women's Torah Commentary: New Insights from Women Rabbis on the
54 Weekly Torah Portions *Edited by Rabbi Elyse Goldstein*
6 x 9, 496 pp, HC, 978-1-58023-076-6 **$34.95**

The Year Mom Got Religion: One Woman's Midlife Journey into Judaism
By Lee Meyerhoff Hendler 6 x 9, 208 pp, Quality PB, 978-1-58023-070-4 **$15.95**

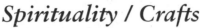

See Holidays for *The Women's Passover Companion: Women's Reflections
on the Festival of Freedom* and *The Women's Seder Sourcebook: Rituals &
Readings for Use at the Passover Seder.* Also see Bar/Bat Mitzvah for *The
JGirl's Guide: The Young Jewish Woman's Handbook for Coming of Age.*

Spirituality / Crafts
(from SkyLight Paths, our sister imprint)

The Knitting Way: A Guide to Spiritual Self-Discovery
By Linda Skolnick and Janice MacDaniels
Shows how to use the practice of knitting to strengthen our spiritual selves.
7 x 9, 240 pp, Quality PB, 978-1-59473-079-5 **$16.99**

The Quilting Path: A Guide to Spiritual Self-Discovery through Fabric,
Thread and Kabbalah *By Louise Silk*
Explores how to cultivate personal growth through quilt making.
7 x 9, 192 pp, Quality PB, 978-1-59473-206-5 **$16.99**

The Painting Path: Embodying Spiritual Discovery through Yoga, Brush
and Color *By Linda Novick; Foreword by Richard Segalman*
Explores the divine connection you can experience through art.
7 x 9, 208 pp, 8-page full-color insert, Quality PB, 978-1-59473-226-3 **$18.99**

The Scrapbooking Journey: A Hands-On Guide to Spiritual Discovery
By Cory Richardson-Lauve; Foreword by Stacy Julian
Reveals how this craft can become a practice used to deepen and shape your life.
7 x 9, 176 pp, 8-page full-color insert, b/w photos, Quality PB, 978-1-59473-216-4 **$18.99**

Travel

Israel—A Spiritual Travel Guide, 2nd Edition
A Companion for the Modern Jewish Pilgrim
By Rabbi Lawrence A. Hoffman 4¾ x 10, 256 pp, Quality PB, illus., 978-1-58023-261-6 **$18.99**
Also Available: **The Israel Mission Leader's Guide** 978-1-58023-085-8 **$4.95**

12-Step

100 Blessings Every Day: Daily Twelve Step Recovery Affirmations, Exercises for
Personal Growth & Renewal Reflecting Seasons of the Jewish Year
By Rabbi Kerry M. Olitzky; Foreword by Rabbi Neil Gillman
4½ x 6¼, 432 pp, Quality PB, 978-1-879045-30-9 **$16.99**

Recovery from Codependence: A Jewish Twelve Steps Guide to Healing Your Soul
By Rabbi Kerry M. Olitzky 6 x 9, 160 pp, Quality PB, 978-1-879045-32-3 **$13.95**

Twelve Jewish Steps to Recovery: A Personal Guide to Turning from Alcoholism &
Other Addictions—Drugs, Food, Gambling, Sex ...
By Rabbi Kerry M. Olitzky and Stuart A. Copans, MD; Preface by Abraham J. Twerski, MD
6 x 9, 144 pp, Quality PB, 978-1-879045-09-5 **$14.95**

Theology/Philosophy/The Way Into... Series

The Way Into... series offers an accessible and highly usable "guided tour" of the Jewish faith, people, history and beliefs—in total, an introduction to Judaism that will enable you to understand and interact with the sacred texts of the Jewish tradition. Each volume is written by a leading contemporary scholar and teacher, and explores one key aspect of Judaism. The Way Into... series enables all readers to achieve a real sense of Jewish cultural literacy through guided study.

The Way Into Encountering God in Judaism
By Neil Gillman
For everyone who wants to understand how Jews have encountered God throughout history and today.
6 x 9, 240 pp, Quality PB, 978-1-58023-199-2 **$18.99**; HC, 978-1-58023-025-4 **$21.95**

Also Available: **The Jewish Approach to God:** A Brief Introduction for Christians
By Neil Gillman
5½ x 8½, 192 pp, Quality PB, 978-1-58023-190-9 **$16.95**

The Way Into Jewish Mystical Tradition
By Lawrence Kushner
Allows readers to interact directly with the sacred mystical text of the Jewish tradition. An accessible introduction to the concepts of Jewish mysticism, their religious and spiritual significance and how they relate to life today.
6 x 9, 224 pp, Quality PB, 978-1-58023-200-5 **$18.99**; HC, 978-1-58023-029-2 **$21.95**

The Way Into Jewish Prayer
By Lawrence A. Hoffman
Opens the door to 3,000 years of Jewish prayer, making available all anyone needs to feel at home in the Jewish way of communicating with God.
6 x 9, 208 pp, Quality PB, 978-1-58023-201-2 **$18.99**

Also Available: **The Way Into Jewish Prayer Teacher's Guide**
By Rabbi Jennifer Ossakow Goldsmith
8½ x 11, 42 pp, PB, 978-1-58023-345-3 **$8.99**
Visit our website to download a free copy.

The Way Into Judaism and the Environment
By Jeremy Benstein
Explores the ways in which Judaism contributes to contemporary social-environmental issues, the extent to which Judaism is part of the problem and how it can be part of the solution.
6 x 9, 288 pp, HC, 978-1-58023-268-5 **$24.99**

The Way Into Tikkun Olam (Repairing the World)
By Elliot N. Dorff
An accessible introduction to the Jewish concept of the individual's responsibility to care for others and repair the world.
6 x 9, 320 pp, HC, 978-1-58023-269-2 **$24.99**; 304 pp, Quality PB, 978-1-58023-328-6 **$18.99**

The Way Into Torah
By Norman J. Cohen
Helps guide in the exploration of the origins and development of Torah, explains why it should be studied and how to do it.
6 x 9, 176 pp, Quality PB, 978-1-58023-198-5 **$16.99**

The Way Into the Varieties of Jewishness
By Sylvia Barack Fishman, PhD
Explores the religious and historical understanding of what it has meant to be Jewish from ancient times to the present controversy over "Who is a Jew?"
6 x 9, 288 pp, HC, 978-1-58023-030-8 **$24.99**

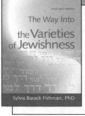

Theology/Philosophy

A Touch of the Sacred: A Theologian's Informal Guide to Jewish Belief
By Dr. Eugene B. Borowitz and Frances W. Schwartz Explores the musings from the
leading theologian of liberal Judaism. 6 x 9, 256 pp, HC, 978-1-58023-337-8 **$21.99**

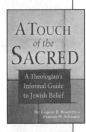

Talking about God: Exploring the Meaning of Religious Life with
Kierkegaard, Buber, Tillich and Heschel *By Daniel F. Polish, PhD*
Examines the meaning of the human religious experience with the greatest theolo-
gians of modern times. 6 x 9, 160 pp, HC, 978-1-59473-230-0 **$21.99** *(A SkyLight Paths book)*

Jews & Judaism in the 21st Century: Human Responsibility, the
Presence of God, and the Future of the Covenant
Edited by Rabbi Edward Feinstein; Foreword by Paula E. Hyman
Five celebrated leaders in Judaism examine contemporary Jewish life.
6 x 9, 192 pp, HC, 978-1-58023-315-6 **$24.99**

Christians and Jews in Dialogue: Learning in the Presence of the Other
By Mary C. Boys and Sara S. Lee; Foreword by Dr. Dorothy Bass
6 x 9, 240 pp, HC, 978-1-59473-144-0 **$21.99** *(A SkyLight Paths book)*

The Death of Death: Resurrection and Immortality in Jewish Thought
By Neil Gillman 6 x 9, 336 pp, Quality PB, 978-1-58023-081-0 **$18.95**

Ethics of the Sages: Pirke Avot—Annotated & Explained
Translation & Annotation by Rabbi Rami Shapiro
5½ x 8½, 208 pp, Quality PB, 978-1-59473-207-2 **$16.99** *(A SkyLight Paths book)*

Hasidic Tales: Annotated & Explained
By Rabbi Rami Shapiro; Foreword by Andrew Harvey
5½ x 8½, 240 pp, Quality PB, 978-1-893361-86-7 **$16.95** *(A SkyLight Paths Book)*

A Heart of Many Rooms: Celebrating the Many Voices within Judaism
By David Hartman 6 x 9, 352 pp, Quality PB, 978-1-58023-156-5 **$19.95**

The Hebrew Prophets: Selections Annotated & Explained
Translation & Annotation by Rabbi Rami Shapiro; Foreword by Zalman M. Schachter-Shalomi
5½ x 8½, 224 pp, Quality PB, 978-1-59473-037-5 **$16.99** *(A SkyLight Paths book)*

A Jewish Understanding of the New Testament
By Rabbi Samuel Sandmel; Preface by Rabbi David Sandmel
5½ x 8½, 368 pp, Quality PB, 978-1-59473-048-1 **$19.99** *(A SkyLight Paths book)*

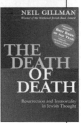

Keeping Faith with the Psalms: Deepen Your Relationship with God Using the Book
of Psalms *By Daniel F. Polish* 6 x 9, 320 pp, Quality PB, 978-1-58023-300-2 **$18.99**

A Living Covenant: The Innovative Spirit in Traditional Judaism
By David Hartman 6 x 9, 368 pp, Quality PB, 978-1-58023-011-7 **$20.00**

Love and Terror in the God Encounter
The Theological Legacy of Rabbi Joseph B. Soloveitchik
By David Hartman 6 x 9, 240 pp, Quality PB, 978-1-58023-176-3 **$19.95**

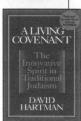

The Personhood of God: Biblical Theology, Human Faith and the Divine Image
By Dr. Yochanan Muffs; Foreword by Dr. David Hartman 6 x 9, 240 pp, HC, 978-1-58023-265-4 **$24.99**

Traces of God: Seeing God in Torah, History and Everyday Life
By Neil Gillman 6 x 9, 240 pp, HC, 978-1-58023-249-4 **$21.99**

We Jews and Jesus: Exploring Theological Differences for Mutual Understanding
By Rabbi Samuel Sandmel; Preface by Rabbi David Sandmel
6 x 9, 176 pp, Quality PB, 978-1-59473-208-9 **$16.99** *(A SkyLight Paths book)*

Your Word Is Fire: The Hasidic Masters on Contemplative Prayer
Edited and translated by Arthur Green and Barry W. Holtz
6 x 9, 160 pp, Quality PB, 978-1-879045-25-5 **$15.95**

I Am Jewish
Personal Reflections Inspired by the Last Words of Daniel Pearl
Almost 150 Jews—both famous and not—from all walks of life, from all around
the world, write about many aspects of their Judaism.
Edited by Judea and Ruth Pearl
6 x 9, 304 pp, Deluxe PB w/flaps, 978-1-58023-259-3 **$18.99**
Download a free copy of the *I Am Jewish Teacher's Guide* at our website:
www.jewishlights.com

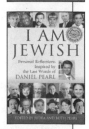

About Jewish Lights

People of all faiths and backgrounds yearn for books that attract, engage, educate, and spiritually inspire.

Our principal goal is to stimulate thought and help all people learn about who the Jewish People are, where they come from, and what the future can be made to hold. While people of our diverse Jewish heritage are the primary audience, our books speak to people in the Christian world as well and will broaden their understanding of Judaism and the roots of their own faith.

We bring to you authors who are at the forefront of spiritual thought and experience. While each has something different to say, they all say it in a voice that you can hear.

Our books are designed to welcome you and then to engage, stimulate, and inspire. We judge our success not only by whether or not our books are beautiful and commercially successful, but by whether or not they make a difference in your life.

For your information and convenience, at the back of this book we have provided a list of other Jewish Lights books you might find interesting and useful. They cover all the categories of your life:

Bar/Bat Mitzvah	Life Cycle
Bible Study / Midrash	Meditation
Children's Books	Parenting
Congregation Resources	Prayer
Current Events / History	Ritual / Sacred Practice
Ecology/ Environment	Spirituality
Fiction: Mystery, Science Fiction	Theology / Philosophy
Grief / Healing	Travel
Holidays / Holy Days	12-Step
Inspiration	Women's Interest
Kabbalah / Mysticism / Enneagram	

Stuart M. Matlins, Publisher

Or phone, fax, mail or e-mail to: **JEWISH LIGHTS** Publishing
Sunset Farm Offices, Route 4 • P.O. Box 237 • Woodstock, Vermont 05091
Tel: (802) 457-4000 • Fax: (802) 457-4004 • www.jewishlights.com
Credit card orders: (800) 962-4544 (8:30AM–5:30PM ET Monday–Friday)
Generous discounts on quantity orders. SATISFACTION GUARANTEED. Prices subject to change.

For more information about each book, visit our website at www.jewishlights.com